Anthropology of Law in Muslim Sudan

Leiden Studies in Islam and Society

VOLUME 7

The titles published in this series are listed at *brill.com/lsis*

Anthropology of Law in Muslim Sudan

Land, Courts and the Plurality of Practices

Edited by

Barbara Casciarri
Mohamed A. Babiker

BRILL

LEIDEN | BOSTON

Published with the support of French ANR (Agence Nationale de la Recherche).

Cover illustration: Old Dongola 1984. Photo by Jean-Pierre Ribière.

The Library of Congress Cataloging-in-Publication Data is available online at http://catalog.loc.gov

Typeface for the Latin, Greek, and Cyrillic scripts: "Brill". See and download: brill.com/brill-typeface.

ISSN 2210-8920
ISBN 978-90-04-35911-6 (paperback)
ISBN 978-90-04-36218-5 (e-book)

This book is printed on acid-free paper and produced in a sustainable manner.

Contents

Foreword: Law in Sudan: An Anthropological Perspective IX
Baudoin Dupret
Acknowledgements XIV
Transliteration of Arabic Terms XVII
List of Illustrations XIX
Abbreviations XX
Notes on Contributors XXII
General Map of Sudan and Greater Khartoum XXVII

Introduction: The Anthropology of Law in Muslim Sudan 1
Barbara Casciarri

PART 1
Land Issues: Dynamics of Appropriation and Legal Frameworks

1 Land Alienation as a Legal, Political, Economic and Moral Issue in the Nile Valley of North Sudan 23
Enrico Ille

2 Claiming Tribal Land Rights in a Global Context. Institutional Bricolage and Definitions of *ʿurf* among Pastoralists in Khartoum State 53
Barbara Casciarri

3 Ambiguous Land Ownership in al-Ṣalḥa, Omdurman: Land Grabbing or "Business as Usual"? 76
Munzoul M.A. Assal

4 Access to Land for Non-Muslims in Greater Khartoum: Disclosing Divergent Minority Models in International and Sudanese Laws 94
Philippe Gout

5 Communal Customary Land Rights in Sudan: The Need for a Comprehensive Reform of Statutory Land Laws 125
Mohamed A. Babiker

PART 2
Statutory and Non-Statutory Courts: Principles and Practices for Dispute Settlement

6 **Dynamics of Dispute Management in South Gedaref State, Eastern Sudan: An Anthropological Approach** 147
Zahir M. Abdal-Kareem

7 **Voluntary Dispute Resolution Forums in al-Ḥilla al-Jadīda Squatter Settlement, Omdurman** 171
Musa A. Abdul-Jalil

8 **Conflict, Property, Mortgage and State Courts in Khartoum** 187
Yazid Ben Hounet

9 **Customary Courts: Between Accommodating and Countering the Hegemony of the Laws of the State: The Case of Mayo** 203
Azza A. Abdel Aziz

10 **Customary Law and Courts in the Context of Sudan's Legal Pluralism: Marginalized or Empowered under English Common Law and Islamic Law?** 236
Mohamed A. Babiker

Annexes

Fieldwork Legal Documents 263

1.1 Map of the 42 registered *sagiyya* land plots of Kerma Balad in 1929 (photographed in the land office in Argo, 15 November 2016) 263

2.1 Land possession certificate (*shihādat ḥiyāza*) for a rain-fed agricultural plot issued by the village Popular Committee, Timaim, 20 March 2005 264

3.1 Land property certificate (*shihādat milkiyya*) issued by the Sudan Judiciary, Abu Seʿid, 2 May 2012 265

4.1 Initial application for land registration and building licence, Sudan Church of Christ, Medinat al-Bashir Gharib, July 1992 266

4.2 Cadastral plan of Medinat al-Bashir Gharib, Local Planning Office, 1992 267

4.3 Complaint to Haj Yusif Locality (*Maḥalliyya*), Sudan Church of Christ, Medinat al-Bashir Gharib, 22 April 1996 & hand-written reply from the Director of the Mahalliya 268
4.4 Application for land registration and building licence before the Head of the Popular Committee for Medinat al-Bashir Gharib, Sudan Church of Christ, Medinat al-Bashir Gharib, 27 May 2007 269
4.5 Initial approval from the State Ministry of Guidance and Endowments & decision of non-objection from the Council of Appeals of the State Ministry of Social and Cultural Affairs, Khartoum, 31 August 2010 270–271
8.1 Road traffic accident complaint form, General Administration of Traffic, Khartoum, 28 June 2004 272
8.2 Withdrawal of mortgage on land, Khartoum Penal Court of the Circulation Administration, 19 July 2010 273

Excerpts from Sudan's Statutory Land Laws 1900–2015 274

Index 312

FOREWORD

Law in Sudan: An Anthropological Perspective

Baudoin Dupret

This volume is part of a broad comparative programme dealing with the anthropology of law in Muslim contexts. Various countries were surveyed, among them Indonesia, Algeria and Morocco. Although the theme of property was initially central, the programme turned out to focus on two additional issues: legal pluralism, and law in Islam. In this short preface, I shall concentrate on these three themes.

•••

Faced with the problems arising from attempts at defining law and from the static approach to the norm, some authors have promoted a method founded on practical case studies and the processes of conflict resolution (courtroom studies). The study of problematic cases has been the focus of American legal realism: how law is practised, informed by a certain mode of behaviour (behaviourism). Another trend has attempted to show how the parties to a litigation conceive the norms and negotiate them during the conflict, how the norms are stated and applied and also neglected or violated, making the conflict itself the focus of attention. These perspectives are fruitful, but do not necessarily constitute the dominant paradigm today, as theories of legal pluralism currently prevail. Here, the centrality of state law is perceived as an ideology. In its most radical formulation, the plurality of laws is considered as the result of the ever-increasing gulf between legal practices and textual legal provisions.

In our view, however, the plurality of practices is not an expression of legal pluralism.[1] We contend that we must adopt a much more praxeological approach to legal phenomena. If we closely examine the fine details of cases, and especially the ways in which people respond to the supposedly many laws and norms, we arrive at a much better picture of what law is and is not for these people. We also form a much better understanding of its plural sources and the non-pluralistic ways of its implementation, and of the many places where laws interfere with each other and the very few places where they remain totally

1 For an introductory reading on legal pluralism, see Dupret, Berger and al-Zwaini 1999.

autonomous. Last but not least, norms, laws and legal practices cease to be confounded. No set of norms is necessarily law, and law is no longer diluted in the all-encompassing and little-analysed category of "social control". Many practices can be characterized as legal practices rather than as parallel social, normative or legal fields. Legal practices are those practices that develop around an object of reference identified by the people as law (which may be state law or any other law recognized as such). In other words, a legal practice is everything that is done in a way in which it would not be done if the law of reference did not exist.

With regard to the legal practices of Muslims, very few studies have followed this praxeological path. Our intention was to look "into the *comprehensibility of society*, into the ways in which social life can be understood and described when seen from within by members" (Sharrock and Watson 1988, p. 59). This praxeological approach requires using the "criteria that participants have for determining the salient features of interactional episodes" (Maynard 1984, p. 19), which does not provide an interpretation of people's conduct. Rather, analysis is "based on, and made valid by, the participants' own orientations, characterizations, and exhibited understandings" (*ibid.*).

•••

The programme was interested in legal practices related to the questions of land ownership, commercial transactions and family relationships, originating from various places functionally devoted to the resolution of the legal cases that may arise in these matters, or to the formulation and registration of documents related to property. These places may or may not be linked to a state, and the laws of reference may also be official or unofficial. Thus, it is advisable to give an account of plural situations. However, instead of a dichotomic analysis of the legal fact that opposes the monism of state law to the pluralism of unofficial bodies, it would surely be necessary to propose a double shift of one's point of view. First, it means carrying out an analysis of normative systems connected with official law, in the sense that they are based on written or oral rules that a group of people are supposed to know and interpret; that they are equipped with bodies (this same group of people) charged with enforcing them; and that people refer to them as an alternative legal system to official law. Second, it means considering the ways by which the actors perceive, understand and act in their legal environment, permanently opposing the plurality of the social norms of reference to the "unique" character of the prevailing law.

Durkheim (1950, p. 144) made the protection of "personal property" the second rule of human morality. Contractual law is related to the issue of property since it concerns its acquisition and transfer, e.g. through inheritance.

The programme set out to conduct research to identify – in the context of societies wholly or partly Muslim – those systems that objectify property relations between a person and an asset (contract, inheritance, gift), create a legal norm in this respect, and offer support to those who are charged with ensuring its observance. The study of legal practices concerning these relationships began from a locus: that of the institutions in charge of property management.

Our intention was thus to explore property phenomena and to offer an ethnographic description of the practices linked to them. It included the identification of the modes by which an asset can be acquired, the means of establishing rights of ownership, the channels available for asserting such rights, the ways of reasoning in such instances, the part played by oral or written language, and the conceptions of property as they operate "in action". What is often characteristic of the anthropology of contracts is its propensity to model transactions and to set them within a deterministic sequence. In that sense, the contract is not studied in and for itself, as an instrument of transaction formalization, documentary support, evidence, reference, etc. Our aim was thus to look for what was left aside and to carefully describe it.

All in all, the management of property rights is the focal point of norms and the methods of using and referencing them. For instance, the analysis of a conflict about a property and its resolution can make explicit the laws on property that are in force in a certain context: the various ways in which the people concerned refer to it; the form that a disagreement may take as soon as it is taken up by an authority entrusted to deal with it; but also the relations between law or other types of normativities and the structure, even the nature, of these relations, such as they are perceived from the legal places.

•••

The anthropology of Islam and of Muslim countries is deeply influenced by culturalism, where Islam becomes the central and dominant code of meaning. This is also true of anthropological investigations on Muslim minorities in Europe. Islamic law is thus, as Clifford Geertz has it, perceived as a cultural code of meaning making it possible to interpret the world: "The 'law' side of things is not a bounded set of norms, rules, principles, values, or whatever from which jural responses to destilled events can be drawn, but part of a distinctive manner of imagining the real" (Geertz 1983, p. 173). In this hermeneutic project, "the words are keys to understanding the social institutions and cultural formulations that surround them and give them meaning" (Merry 1988, p. 886).

Our aim was also to break away from the postulate of the cultural exceptionality of legal interpretations in totally or partially "Muslim" societies. The works on law in these societies seem to focus on looking for the Islamic portion of law and stopping there: the multiplication of the works on property, *waqf*, *ḥabūs*, on Islamic finance and more broadly on 'Islamic law' is a perfect example. Analyses to determine to what extent such or such a portion of law is Islamic, and to what extent such or such a portion of law should be explained or not by any historical development of Islamic law, continue to tend to impose their structure on legal phenomena and activities, instead of seeking to discover how the latter operate. In so doing, research fails to describe both the phenomena it should nevertheless document and, in particular, the ways people understand and express their understanding of any given situation, take into account the context and its constraints, and behave and act in a more or less orderly fashion in spatially and temporarily similar contexts. Still, even in situations where an Islamic genealogy can be identified (as with family law in numerous countries), an *a priori* characterisation of "Islamic law" fails to give a true depiction of what people do in a particular legal context when they address issues related to family, acts that can only be addressed by describing people's practices outside any pre-established interpretative framework. What can we then say of these domains where the relation to Islam cannot even be established genealogically?

It should be clear by now that the purpose of this programme was not to present willy-nilly the secret of an "exotic" legal universe. On the contrary, it attempts to describe such activity without any prejudice as to what, from a legal viewpoint, differentiated these societies, *a priori*, from other contexts. It does not even postulate the existence of such differences. In other words, this programme is related to legal practices in an overwhelmingly Muslim environment, not to the depiction of an "Islamic" culture observed through the prism of law. To tell the truth, Islamic culture is but one of the multiple components of the context, always unique and never uniform, in which the legal practices are deployed. In the assumption that this cultural component is preeminent lies the risk of not paying sufficient attention to the other possible components, as is the case in many matters on which the members of the judiciary and legal environment of these societies conveniently focus during their actions. This also runs the risk of overestimating the impact of culture. The corollary of culturalism is non-translatability – a concept formulated in Arabic cannot be adequately conveyed in English because its essence can only be accessible in the language in which it was originally formulated. In contrast, we consider that any phenomenon, regardless of the language in which it is expressed, remains translatable into another language and accessible to observation and to description. This implies, however, "rather than supposedly reading over the shoulder of an imaginary native a text completed in a culturally standardised form [to read] line after line the continuous production of a real autochthonous speech" (Moerman 1987, p. 5).

•••

This volume on Sudan is an excellent example of what can be achieved in the anthropological study of law, in general, and of property, particularly in a Muslim environment. Its chapters, which are all empirically documented, detail the ways in which some conflicts, such as on land issues, are dealt with, how the law is produced, managed, used and dodged, and how conflicting norms are practically attuned. It will certainly break the ground for further studies in the praxeological spirit of the programme in which it was partly advocated.

References

Dupret, B, Berger, M, and al-Zwaini, L (eds) 1999, *Legal Pluralism in the Arab World*, Kluwer Law International, The Hague.

Durkheim, E 1950, *Leçon de sociologie*, PUF, Paris.

Geertz, C 1983, *Local Knowledge: Further Essays in Interpretive Anthropology*, Basic Books, New York.

Maynard, DW 1984, *Inside Plea Bargaining: The Language of Negotiation*, Plenum Press, New York.

Merry, SE 1988, 'Legal Pluralism', *Law & Society Review*, vol. 22, no. 5, pp. 869–896.

Moerman, M 1987, *Talking Culture*, Cambridge University Press, Cambridge.

Sharrock, W & Watson, R 1988, 'Autonomy among Social Theories. The Incarnation of Social Structures', in G Fielding (ed.), *Actions and Structures*, Sage Publications, London.

Acknowledgements

This volume is the outcome of a long-term collective project for which more people than its editors and contributors deserve our acknowledgements. We first thank the French ANR (Agence Nationale de la Recherche) for funding this three-year research project and making it possible to carry out most of the fieldwork inquiries whose results are presented in the following chapters.[1] More particularly, our gratitude goes to Baudoin Dupret, who efficiently and energetically took care of the general scientific coordination of the ANDROMAQUE Programme (Anthropologie du Droit dans les Mondes Musulmans Africains et Asiatiques), while he was the director of the Centre Jacques Berque in Rabat (Morocco): through his competence and enthusiasm, we were able to be enrolled as a "Sudanese team" within this passionate and ambitious comparative project. The stimulating debates he solicited during the meetings of a huge interdisciplinary and international team have marked us all, along with the informal talks we had with him during our trips to discover elements of ordinary daily life in Rabat and Istanbul at the time of our workshops. Among the *équipe* working with him for the project, special thanks are due to Khadija Chabraoui, general secretary of the Centre Jacques Berque, for her kindness and indispensable support in responding to all the ANDROMAQUE researchers' requests. We also thank François Ireton, who in the initial preparatory phase made the first proposal to include Sudan as a country where the programme's envisaged research activities could be expanded.

In Sudan, the feasibility of the project has vitally depended on the support of several persons and institutions. Here, we first thank the University of Khartoum, and especially the researchers in the Department of Sociology and Social Anthropology, who through their involvement in this new programme contributed to the consolidation of an earlier French-Sudanese scientific collaboration. Without the patient support of Musa A. Abdul-Jalil (former Head of Department) and Hassan al-Haj Ali (former Dean of the Faculty of Social and Economic Studies), it would have been impossible to fulfil our mission in Sudan. We also need to thank the CEDEJ Khartoum (Centre d'Etudes et

1 This volume was published with the support of the French National Agency for Research (ANR), as an outcome of the research project "Anthropologie du droit dans les mondes musulmans africains et asiatiques" (ANDROMAQUE) that was conducted within the frame of the program SUDS II and associated teams affiliated to the Centre Jacques Berque (CJB) in Morocco and the Institut français de Pondichéry (IFP) in India.

de Documentation Economiques et Juridiques) and particularly its former coordinator, Alice Franck, who, despite her busy agenda and numerous responsibilities, constantly gave us unconditional help, both by allowing our research team to access her institution's facilities and by sharing with us her knowledge of Sudan during the workshops held in Khartoum. Finally, we also want to express our gratitude to others who more occasionally shared with us interesting discussions about customary law in Sudan: at the Judiciary in Khartoum, Judge Al-Amin Musa and his efficient and welcoming collaborators Salah ad-Din A. Abdel-Gadir and Ismail M. Adam; at Jeily Rural Court, Fadul Yas and Tayb; and at the Department of Law of the University of Khartoum, Professor Abudhar. Warmest thanks also go to the young lawyer Narmin Maher Saad, who in March 2013 accompanied us for all the (short yet complementary) part of work among official legal institutions. We would also like to thank Abrar Isam for collecting and scanning a set of official legal texts on land which, although they could not be included in this book entirely because of their sheer size, have been an important source and will possibly constitute the basis for a future book, complementary to the present volume.

The production of the book was also a long process for which we wish to thank several people. Thanks to Léon Buskens, whom we were able to meet during the final ANDROMAQUE workshop in Rabat, for presenting our initial book proposal to Brill Publishers. We also thank the anonymous reader of the manuscript for his/her enthusiastic review and interesting comments on the first draft of the volume. Others who deserve special acknowledgement for the book's final version include: Peter Miller, for the English editing, Alice Franck, for the general map of Sudan and of Greater Khartoum, Francesco Staro for compiling the Index, and Jean-Pierre Ribière for the cover illustration.

Too often forgotten in similar academic works, are the "subjects" of this volume's chapters: all the rural and urban dwellers in the various parts of Sudan where we carried out our inquiries, deserve our most sincere acknowledgements. In a particularly harsh period of Sudan's recent history – the conjunction of economic and political crises catalysed by the separation of South Sudan after 2011 – we were astonished and moved by their kindness and accessibility, welcoming us into their houses, discussing and answering questions about sensitive issues affecting them and their groups. Besides these crucial "fieldwork actors", who are too many to name, there are others who supported us and made our daily life more pleasant during our stay in Sudan, among whom we want to thank particularly Khalid, Abusufian, Elmas "Bargikko" and her son Amanil. A last special thank you goes to our families and particularly to Idir, for his enduring patience and curiosity about the work of his sometimes too busy mother.

During the process of research and preparation for this volume, two outstanding anthropologists of the Arab and Muslim world (and of its pastoral people), with whom we had an opportunity to share an intellectual debate about some of our work's crucial themes, sadly passed away. First, Pierre Bonte, distinguished specialist on Tuareg and Arab pastoralists of Niger and Mauritania, founder and coordinator of the *Equipe d'anthropologie comparative des sociétés musulmanes* (Laboratoire d'Anthropologie Sociale, Paris), who allowed us to benefit from his deep understanding of Muslim societies at the opening ANDROMAQUE workshop in Rabat (January 2011), died suddenly in November 2013. Second, Ugo Fabietti, another eminent anthropologist of pastoral societies in Saudi Arabia and Baluchistan, who had recently focused his analysis on the sacred dimension of cultures, also left us all too soon in May 2017. This volume is dedicated to the memory of these two major scholars: they will remain a reference for anthropological studies on Muslim societies, and some among us will always remember them as passionate teachers and wonderful human beings.

The moment of this volume's publication is a crucial one both for Sudan and the world as a whole, as far as one of the main focuses of our research is concerned. Recent international conjuncture has made "Islam" one of the most debated and abused topics within academic, political and public opinion discourses. Today, political instrumentalization makes various actors in the North as well as in the South – or should we say here the "West" and the "East"? – jump cynically at the opportunity to fuel military interventions against global terror, erecting stronger (both physical and symbolic) walls between citizens and refugees, imposing oppressive emergency legislation and hiding old inequalities and exploitations behind alleged clashes of civilisations, either in the name of Islam or against the danger it poses. This volume's editors' wish is to make a modest contribution towards enabling a better understanding of Muslim societies – their configuration and their relationship with non-Muslims – far from mainstream ideologies, in order to unfold dynamics of social injustice, dispossession and conflict that religious labels have too often concealed and threaten to go on doing so even further in the coming years.

Barbara Casciarri
July 2017

Transliteration of Arabic Terms

In this volume, the transliteration of Arabic terms (which are generally written in italics, except for the proper names of places and persons) uses the following:

ا	*ā* (*a, i* or *u* at the beginning of the word)	ر	*r*	ق	*g* (dialect); *q* (classical)
ب	*b*	ز	*z*	ك	*k*
ت	*t*	س	*s*	ل	*l*
ث	*th*	ش	*sh*	م	*m*
ج	*j*	ص	*ṣ*	ن	*n*
ح	*ḥ*	ض	*ḍ*	ه	*h*
خ	*kh*	ط	*ṭ*	و	*w, u, ū* or *ō*
د	*d*	ظ	*ẓ*	ي	*y, ī* or *ē*
ذ	*dh*	ع	ʿ	--ة	-- *a*
		غ	*gh*	ء	ʾ
		ف	*f*		

We normally use the singular form of Arabic words, adding the suffix 's' for the plural (e.g., *farīg*s, 'camps', rather than *furgān*), unless the plural form expressly refers to a particular phenomenon (e.g., *awlād*, plural of *walad*, 'son', which means a kinship group in the Sudanese context). On the other hand, for the names of ethnic or tribal groups, the plural form is used (without italics) for the singular (e.g., 'the Aḥāmda' and 'an Aḥāmda leader' rather than 'a ḥāmmedi leader', as it would strictly be in the singular Arabic form of this ethnonym). In transliterating local terms, we opted to follow the pronunciation of the Sudanese standard dialect. Accordingly, the letter ق is transcribed as 'g' (which is close to the vernacular phonetic pronunciation) rather than 'q' (as used in classical Arabic). The same rule applies to the sounds of standard Arabic consonants that are not used in the dialect (the letters ث, 'th', and ذ, 'dh', simplified as 't' and 'd') and for vowels (such as 'o' or 'e') that exist only in dialectal usage. However, we use the standard classical Arabic transliteration for terms mentioned with reference to written sources or official discourse, which are not given in dialect. For cases in which an accepted transliteration is widely used in written texts, we use such forms even though they may differ from the local vernacular (e.g., 'sheikh', without italics, instead of *shaykh*). We apply the same rationale to personal names (e.g., 'Mahdi', 'Ingaz', instead of

Mahdī, Inqādh) and toponyms (e.g., 'Khartoum', 'Darfur', instead of Kharṭūm, Dārfūr). The same principle is also adopted for ethnic names that are generally known by a simplified transcription in the literature on Sudan (e.g., 'Baggara', 'Nuba', instead of Baggāra, Nūba). A translation is given (in parentheses) at the first use of a term in vernacular Arabic in each of the articles. This may be further elaborated with a footnote if the term requires detailed explanation.

List of Illustrations

Figures

2.1 Rain-fed plot (*taras*) for sorghum (*dhura*) cultivation in Wadi at-Tumām. Photograph by the author 58
4.1 Process of circular applications by the Sudanese Church of Christ in Ḥāj Yūsif 101
4.2 Translation of the international religious minority model in the context of discrimination over land rights in Greater Khartoum 112
6.1 Fieldwork assistant Ḥassan Abū Ṣiddīg sitting in front of the rural court (*al-maḥākam ar-rifiyya*) of Basunda area. Photograph by the author 160
6.2 The gathering of the courts – civil, criminal and *sharīʿa* – in Gedaref town. Photograph by the author 165
7.1 Abdalla Kafi presiding over his "court". Photograph by the author 179
7.2 Noon prayers in the *rakūba*. Photograph by the author 180

Maps

4.1 Khartoum IDPs areas in 2004. Source: Khartoum State Interagency Rapid Assessment Report, 2004 99
6.1 Basunda locality council in Gedaref State. © Max Planck Institute for Social Anthropology 152

Abbreviations

AACC	All Africa Conference of Churches
ANDROMAQUE	Anthropologie du Droit dans les Mondes Musulmans Asiatiques et Africains
ANR	Agence Nationale de la Recherche
CBS	Central Bureau of Statistics
CEDEJ	Centre d'Etudes et de Documentation Economiques et Juridiques
CPA	Comprehensive Peace Agreement
CTA	Civil Transaction Act
DIU	Dams Implementation Unit
ECS	Episcopal Church of Sudan
EPLF	Eritrean People's Liberation Front
EU	European Union
FAR	Fellowship for African Relief
GOS	Government of Sudan
HAC	Humanitarian Aid Commission
ICCPR	International Covenant on Civil and Political Rights
IDP	Internally Displaced Person/People
INC	Interim National Constitution
KPCTA	Khartoum Penal Court of Traffic Administration
LSRO	Land Settlement and Registration Ordinance
MHPU	Ministry of Housing and Public Utilities
MSF	Médecins Sans Frontières
NCP	National Congress Party
NGO	Non-Governmental Organization
NIF	National Islamic Front
OCHA	Office for the Coordination of Humanitarian Affairs
PLACE	People Legal Aid Center
PLO	Prescription and Limitation Ordinance
PCP	Popular Congress Party
SCC	Sudan Church of Christ
SDG	Sudanese dinar/Sudanese pound
SIL	Summer Institute of Linguistics
SLJR	Sudan Law Journal and Reports
SLR	Sudan Law Reports
SNCS	Sudan National Comprehensive Strategy
SPLA/M	Sudan People's Liberation Army/Movement

ULA	Unregistered Land Act
UN	United Nations
UNEP	United Nations Environment Programme
UNHRC	United Nations Human Rights Committee
UOK	University of Khartoum
USCIRF	United States Commission on International Religious Freedom
USD	United States Dollar
WAMAKHAIR	Water Management in Khartoum International Research
WCC	World Council of Churches

Notes on Contributors

Azza Ahmed Abdel Aziz
holds a PhD in Social Anthropology, with a special focus on Medical Anthropology, School of Oriental and African Studies, University of London. Her research focuses on cultural understandings of health and well-being, which largely feature an exploration of the interface between such understandings and biomedical configurations of health. She has in-depth experience of working on these issues among individuals and groups whose lives have been subject to experiences of movement or migration in different forms. In 2006, she worked as a research fellow on a project related to the reproductive health of Bedouin women in Syria in conjunction with the Centre for Migration Studies, Queen Elizabeth House, University of Oxford. In London, she has worked closely with migrants in situations of cultural and psychosocial dislocation, and refugees who have been subjected to torture. She is currently conducting field research among diverse Southern populations residing in Khartoum in light of their altered legal status after the creation of the state of South Sudan in July 2011.

Zahir Musa Abdal-Kareem
holds a PhD from the Martin Luther University of Halle-Wittenberg (Germany). He is currently a research fellow in the Department of Integration and Conflict at Max Planck Institute for Social Anthropology (Germany) and a lecturer in the Department of Sociology and Social Anthropology, University of Khartoum (Sudan). His PhD thesis title is 'Group Identification and Resource Conflicts in Gedaref State, Eastern Sudan: Who allies with whom? Why? And how?' (2016) and his current postdoctoral project goes under the title 'The Challenges of Migration and Integration of Muslim Arab and African Refugees in Germany and Western Europe'. His recently published works include: 'Contested Land Rights and Ethnic Conflict in Mornei, West Darfur: Scarcity of Resources or Crises of Governance?', in B. Casciarri, M. Assal & F. Ireton (eds), *Multidimensional Change in Sudan 1989–2011: Reshaping Livelihoods, Conflicts, and Identities* (2015) (with Musa Adam Abdul-Jalil) and 'Small-scale Farming in Southern Gedaref State, Eastern Sudan', in S. Calkins, E. Ille & R. Rottenburg (eds), *Emerging Orders in the Sudans* (2015).

Musa Adam Abdul-Jalil
is Associate Professor and previous head (2007–2013) of the Department of Sociology and Social Anthropology, University of Khartoum. He was also

Deputy Dean for Academic Affairs (2013–2015) of the Faculty of Economic and Social Studies at the same university. His research and publications have focused largely on the topics of ethnicity, migration, customary land tenure and law and traditional mechanisms for conflict management. His recently published works include an edited book (with Munzoul Assal) *Past, Present and Future: Fifty Years of Anthropology in Sudan* (2015). He has also recently published a co-authored book chapter with Zahir Abdal-Kareem: 'Contested Land Rights and Conflicts in Mornei (West Darfur): Scarcity of Resources or Crises of Governance?', in B. Casciarri et al. (eds), *Multidimensional Change in Sudan 1989–2011: Reshaping Livelihoods, Conflicts and Identities* (2015).

Munzoul M. Abdallah Assal
is Professor of Social Anthropology and Deputy Director of the Peace Research Institute at the University of Khartoum. Prior to his current position he was the Director of Graduates Affairs Administration (2009–2012) at the same university. His research focuses on refugees, IDPs, humanitarianism and citizenship. His major publications include *Sticky Labels or Rich Ambiguities? Diaspora and Challenges of Homemaking for Somalis and Sudanese in Norway* (2004); *Diaspora within and without Africa: Homogeneity, Heterogeneity, Variation* (2006; co-edited with Leif Manger); *An Annotated Bibliography of Social Research on Darfur* (2006); *Multidimensional Change in Sudan 1989–2011: Reshaping Livelihoods, Conflicts and Identities* (2015 co-edited with Barbara Casciarri and François Ireton).

Mohamed Abdelsalam Babiker
is Associate Professor of Public International Law, Lawyer, Founding Director of the Human Rights Centre and Head of International and Comparative Law Department at the Faculty of Law, University of Khartoum. He was also a Visiting Fellow at Grey College, University of Durham, UK (2014). His field of research is international criminal law, refugee law, humanitarian law and human rights. He is the author of *Application of International Humanitarian Law and Human Rights Law to the Armed Conflicts of the Sudan: Complementary or Mutually Exclusive Regimes?* (Oxford, 2007). He is also co-editor of *Enfants soldats et droits des enfants en situation de conflit et post-conflit* (Paris, 2013) and *Constitution Making and Human Rights Protection in South Sudan* (London, 2018). He has published chapters in books and in peer reviewed international journals in the the UK, France, Italy, USA and South Africa. He has also contributed to research projects with academic and research institutions in European and American Universities. M.A. Babiker also worked as a Legal Advisor and a Human Rights Officer with several UN and AU peacekeeping operations in

Sudan such as AMIS, UNMIS, UNMAID and as a consultant with a number of UN agencies, IOM, ILO and international NGOs, with particular focus on Darfur. In September 2016, he was nominated by the Consultative Committee of the UNHCR for the position of Special Rapporteur for the Islamic Republic of Iran, Session 33.

Yazid Ben Hounet

is a social anthropologist, research fellow at the Centre National de Recherche Scientifique, member of the Laboratoire d'Anthropologie Sociale (CNRS – Collège de France – EHESS). He holds a PhD from the Ecole des Hautes Etudes en Sciences Sociales (Paris). His dissertation was published in 2009 and discussed tribal issues in contemporary Algeria. His past and current research lays at the intersection of legal and political anthropology in Muslim contexts. He has also carried out research in the field of kinship studies. After he completed his PhD thesis, he studied the local processes of reconciliation in Algeria and Sudan, but also legal practises in matters of property. Recent publications include: *Truth, Intentionality and Evidence: Anthropological Approaches to Crime* (edited with Deborah Puccio-Den;2017); 'Heritage Process amongst Pastoralist Groups in Muslim Contexts', special issue of *Nomadic Peoples* (edited with Anne-Marie Brisebarre & Sandra Guinand; 2016).

Barbara Casciarri

holds a PhD in Ethnology and Social Anthropology from the Ecole des Hautes Etudes en Sciences Sociales in Paris (France). She did fieldwork on economic and political anthropology in Sudan (1989–2016), among Arabic-speaking pastoralists and then in a working-class neighbourhood of Khartoum (Deim), and in Morocco (2000–2006), on the relationship between Berber-speaking nomads and Arabic-speaking farmers. She was coordinator of the CEDEJ in Khartoum between 2006 and 2009. Since 2004, she has been Associate Professor at the Department of Sociology, University Paris 8 (France) and researcher at the LAVUE-UMR 7218. She co-edited a special issue of *Nomadic Peoples* 13(1), 2009 'Pastoralists under Pressure in Present-day Sudan' (with A.M. Ahmed); a special issue of *Journal des Anthropologues* 132–133, 2013 'Anthropology and Water(s)' (with M. van Aken) and the volume *Multidimensional Change in Sudan 1989–2011: Reshaping Livelihoods, Conflicts and Identities* (2015) (with M. Assal & F. Ireton). She has been scientific coordinator of two ANR Projects in Sudan: WAMAKHAIR (2008–2012) and ANDROMAQUE (2011–2014). Since 2009, she has been responsible for the scientific agreement between the Faculty of Economic and Social Studies, University of Khartoum, and Paris 8 University.

Baudoin Dupret
is educated in Law, Islamic Sciences and Political Sciences. He is Director of Research at the French National Centre for Scientific Research and a guest lecturer at the University of Louvain (Belgium) and at the University of Leiden (Netherlands). He has published extensively in the field of the sociology and anthropology of law, legislation and media, especially in the Middle East. He has (co-)edited numerous volumes, the latest being *Law At Work: Studies in Legal Ethnomethods* (with M. Lynch and T. Berard, 2015), and authored several books: *Practices of Truth: An Ethnomethodological Inquiry into Arab Settings* (2011), *Adjudication in Action: An Ethnomethodology of Law, Moral and Justice* (2011), and *La Charia: Des sources à la pratique, un concept pluriel* (2014; English translation forthcoming with Hurst).

Philippe Gout
is a PhD candidate in international law at the Institute of Higher International Studies (Paris 2 Panthéon-Assas University). After obtaining his master's degree at Paris I Panthéon-Sorbonne University and completing professional experiences within two international criminal tribunals, he started his PhD research on 'Legal Orders in motion: Sudanese Customary Laws in International Peacebuilding'. He conducted long-term field research with a PhD-scholarship from the CEDEJ-Khartoum and was a guest researcher at the Legal Anthropology Department, Max Planck Institute for Social Anthropology (Halle-Saale). He is a member of the scientific network L.O.S.T (Law, Organization, Science & Technology) of the Department of Philosophy & Anthropology, Halle-Wittenberg University. His PhD research deconstructs the model of peacebuilding from a legal perspective and addresses its neoliberal roots at the end of the Cold War. The peacebuilding model reconfigures the international law system away from its original subjects. Building on legal systemic and translation theories, he tries to determine how Sudanese tribal actors negotiate or resist these changes. He investigates the ways in which these actors rely on – or escape from – internationally defined legal status to build their legal capacity and protect their interests. He finally examines processes of normative swapping between tribal and other legal orders to emphasize the static model of liberal and individualistic human rights.

Enrico Ille
has a PhD in Social and Cultural Anthropology from the University of Halle, Germany, and is a member of the Law, Organization, Science and Technology Research Network. After holding positions as Assistant Professor at the

Martin Luther University of Halle and at Ahfad University for Women, Sudan, he is currently Urgent Anthropology Fellow (The British Museum / Royal Anthropological Institute, London) with research on supply chains involving date production along the Nile in northern Sudan. He co-edited the volume *Emerging Orders in the Sudans* (with Sandra Calkins and Richard Rottenburg, 2014) and published an annotated bibliography and a number of journal and book articles on the Nuba Mountains, discussing history, land issues and political economy, as well as development initiatives for agricultural production and water supply. His general research interest is the relations between state institutions, companies and communities in mineral resource extraction and food supply chains throughout Sudan.

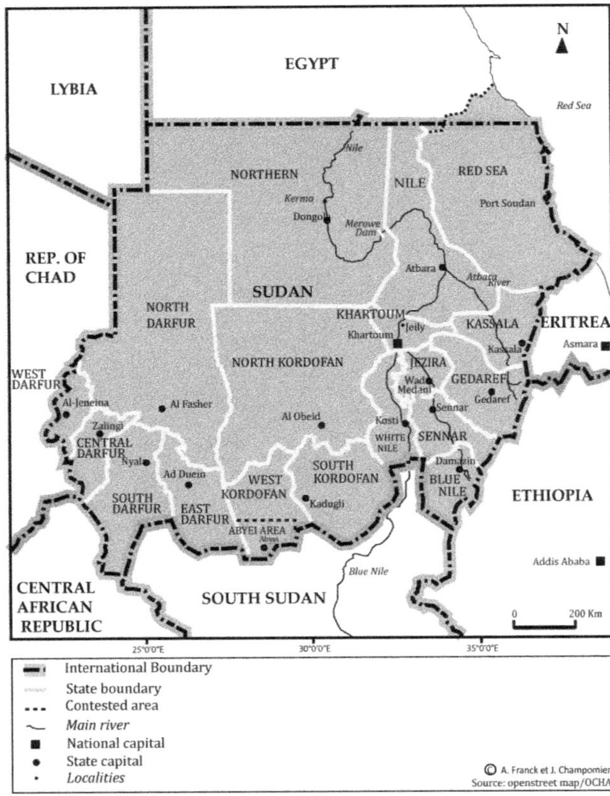

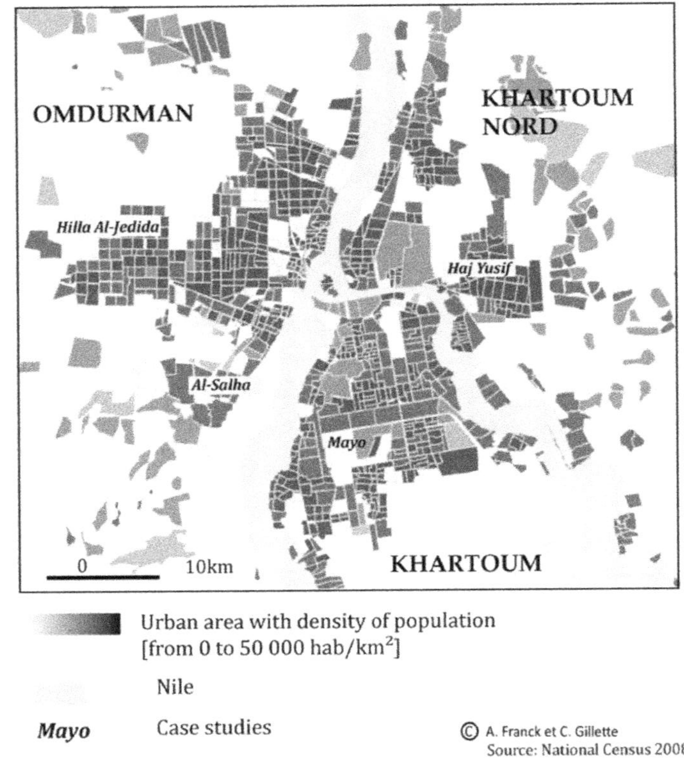

General Map of Sudan and Greater Khartoum.

INTRODUCTION

The Anthropology of Law in Muslim Sudan

Barbara Casciarri

The Genesis of the Book and the ANDROMAQUE Programme

This volume is the outcome of a research programme bringing together several international scholars with the common aim of questioning the status of law systems in countries whose populations and legal frameworks are inspired, to varying degrees, by their being "Muslim". The ANDROMAQUE (*Anthropologie du Droit dans les Mondes Musulmans Africains et Asiatiques*) programme, led by Baudoin Dupret and funded by the French ANR (*Agence Nationale de la Recherche*), was a challenging and stimulating project for various reasons. First, it had an interdisciplinary and comparative dimension in terms of academic disciplines (Sociology, Anthropology and Law) as well as covering a diversity of countries (Morocco, Algeria, India, Indonesia, Mauritania, Lebanon, Germany). Second, the project had an original approach, as it mainly aimed to focus on "legal practices" more than "normative legal systems" in comparable jurisdictions. For this reason, the proposal to include a Sudanese research team in the programme was received with great enthusiasm by the group of researchers who started to work on forming an "ANDROMAQUE Sudan Team" in 2011. The possibility of relying on a small coherent group of Sudanese and European researchers (mainly anthropologists), who had collaborated closely for several years in joint academic research programmes[1] and partnerships for university training, was an advantage for the practical organization of the working *équipe*. Moreover, inclusion in the ANDROMAQUE programme gave us a real opportunity to revisit previous fieldwork – or to open new fields – by sharing a common perspective, the focus on a crucial (and rather new for most of us) analytical category, Islam, within a fascinating interdisciplinary cross-cultural framework able to go beyond comparing countries allegedly linked

1 This collaboration started in 1994 with the Kassala-Gedaref Programme (CEDEJ, DSRC) on Eastern Sudan. It was followed by a triennial programme (2006–2009) on "Transformation Processes among Rural and Urban Communities: Resource Access and Management in the Context of Globalization" (CEDEJ, UoK), then by the ANR WAMAKHAIR (2008–2012) (CEDEJ, Paris 8, Paris 10, Bayreuth and Ahfad Universities) on "Water Management in Khartoum". For more details see the introduction to Casciarri, Assal and Ireton, 2015, pp. ix–xii.

 | DOI 10.1163/9789004362185_002

by their regional inclusion in the same continent. Furthermore, we thought that Sudan could be an emblematic context in which we could test the programme's wider approach and hypotheses. Being among the few African countries that have officially been ruled by *sharīʿa* (Islamic Law) for more than three decades – after the Islamization of laws in 1983 and the coup d'état of June 1989 – and due to its particular history, Sudan also represents an ambiguous transitional area between Muslim Africa and Sub-Saharan Africa, whose sociocultural and political dynamics feed academic debates about the pertinence or weakness of clear-cut definitions of "regional" or "cultural areas" and their borders. Finally, the historical context in which the programme started (2011) added a further element of interest: Sudan was experiencing at that time a watershed in its history because of the separation between Sudan and South Sudan and the revival of a crucial (and often dramatic) debate about the issues of defining *who* is an Arab and/or a Muslim, and *what* is the place of Islam in society (Woodward 2012). Although our fieldwork was expected to be based solely in Sudan (formerly North Sudan), the aftermath of the 2011 separation of the "two Sudans" allowed us to adopt a dynamic approach, inasmuch that redefinitions of "Arab" and "Islamic" identities could be the entry point from which to consider social processes *in fieri*.

The initial core of the research team was made up of six scholars (three Sudanese and three Europeans), all with a socio-anthropological background.[2] This combination was particularly fitting for the programme's main approach, with its decision to focus on "socio-legal practices" in order to avoid the *a priori* emphasis given to the "Islamic reference" in the approaches most commonly adopted by law scholars or Oriental Islamic studies (Buskens and Dupret 2012). We started by following a double objective: first, to provide fresh original fieldwork data on a variety of case studies from different contexts in Sudan, and, second, to test in each context the validity of the deductive idea that Muslims are predominantly governed by Islamic laws and norms. Although the notion of "legal pluralism" obviously provided an underlying framework for the academic debate and interpretation, we wished nonetheless to go beyond this general paradigm in order to question the actual legal practices of targeted

2 The researchers were, on the French side, Barbara Casciarri (Team Coordinator), François Ireton and Yazid Ben Hounet, and, on the Sudanese side, Munzoul M.A. Assal, Musa A. Abdul-Jalil and Zahir M. Abdal-Kareem. In a final phase, two other anthropologists, Azza A. Abdel Aziz and Enrico Ille, joined the programme. We thank François Ireton, who was forced to stop his collaboration in the last part of the programme and was not able to write a chapter for this volume, for his contribution to the team work during general theoretical discussions and in sharing the results of his fieldwork in Kurguz, Northern Nile Valley.

peoples, together with their related representations, through the creative practical configurations of their behaviours in relation to the law. Being aware of the impossibility of covering an exhaustively representative sample of local Sudanese groups, we aimed to maximize the variety of contexts, by working on case studies in rural, pastoral or agricultural, areas, and in urban and peripheral quarters of Greater Khartoum. Whilst the researchers were given freedom to emphasize the most pertinent aspects that their shared methods of ethnographic qualitative inquiry allowed to emerge from each case, after the first year of fieldwork (2011–2012) the nexus between land and property appeared as a crucial and pervasive topic throughout the case studies. Consequently, this was made the core of our transversal reflection, followed by another significant topic: the presence of multiple courts or institutions invested with legal authority, and their operational dimensions as mediums of conflict resolution.

When we entered the second phase of the programme (2012–2013), whilst continuing to pursue data collection and analysis on our respective fieldwork activities, we felt the need to be joined by legal researchers whose approaches would enrich our anthropological data analysis. The inclusion of two scholars specialized in law issues[3] was a decisive step for the evolution of the programme, giving us all the opportunity to extend our disciplinary perspectives and to approach more critically our initial categories and theoretical hypotheses. The various discussions held in Khartoum during the bi-annual meetings of the Sudan team have been some of the most interesting and decisive moments in this collective work. This intellectual experience has been further enriched by discussions with colleagues working on similar topics in other countries during the ANDROMAQUE general meetings held in Istanbul (2012) and Rabat (2011 and 2015). After four years since the programme's launch, and of intensive field inquiries by the Sudanese team (2014), this volume started to emerge and take its final shape. Today, we present it to readers with the aim of both filling a gap in the Sudanese Studies tradition and enriching academic debate about relations between Islam and societies, a debate that has been dramatically resurrected by recent international events.

3 They were Mohamed Abdelsalam Babiker, professor at the Department of Law, University of Khartoum (and member of a previous project "Islam Research Program" led by the CEDEJ), and Philippe Gout, PhD candidate from University Paris 2 and then the Max Planck Institute.

The Tricky Issues of "Arabization" and "Islamization" in Sudan

The central approach followed by the research programme that created this volume aimed to focus on the analysis of "legal practices". This meant that, despite the importance of having general knowledge about official normative law systems[4] that have either succeeded one another or coexisted, our investigation needed to go beyond a purely juridical perspective, and focus on questioning further certain domains more particular to a wider anthropological and historical academic debate. The importance of this essentially anthropological approach is underlined by two observations. First, at the level of "data production", the microscale approach suggested by the methodological principles of an "*ethnography* of legal practices" was conceived as a heuristic device, enabling us to grasp the contextual configurations of law-related behaviours and identify a potential degree of variation even *within* alleged coherent "communities" (quarters, villages, tribes, ethnic or sociocultural groups). Second, at the level of theoretical categories and interpretation, we needed to come back to longstanding reflections that take into account some persisting ambiguities with reference to the crucial issues of "Arabization" and "Islamization" processes among Sudanese populations, with both political and academic debate often suggesting an implicit link between the two dimensions, despite the absence of a clear and legitimate intrinsic association. In order to better situate the specific case studies presented in this volume, we need to sketch a general background to these complex issues, their historical configurations and the debate that they may raise.

The Alleged Arab vs *African Dichotomy and the Inappropriate Merging of Arabization and Islamization*

A broad description of the historical constitution of Sudan as a coherent geographical and social entity may be summarized as follows: although some sporadic pre-Islamic migrations of Arab groups from the Red Sea are mentioned, it is conventionally said that increasing waves of (mainly Bedouin) Arab *and* Muslim tribes came from Egypt between the seventh-century spread of Islam into North Africa and the Middle-Ages, bringing about the progressive Arabization *and* Islamization of the country. In this process, a crucial

4 Two chapters in this volume (Chapter 5 and Chapter 10) provide a detailed presentation and analysis of Sudanese law systems, with an historical overview and a special focus on present-day legislation and jurisprudence. An annex to the volume also reports extracts of law texts (in English) issued in colonial and post-colonial periods concerning the main domains (land and courts) dealt with by the case studies examined here.

benchmark is said to have been the establishment of the first larger central state formation, the Sultanate of Sennar (1504–1821), which started claiming an Arab and Muslim identity for Sudan (former Northern Sudan).[5] Accepted both by colonial (MacMichael 1922; Trimingham 1949) and post-colonial historians (Fadl Hasan 1967), most local groups' narratives still contain the basic elements of the same vulgate, without major discordance with the discourse shared by modern scholars. Even if it would be difficult to condemn the core statement of this succinct presentation of Sudan's Arabization and Islamization as "false", some intellectual malaises emerge and the need for a more nuanced vision is felt, especially as the categories "Arab" and "Muslim" are an intrinsic concern of our research approach. In this sense, some scholars admit being struck by "… the extent to which the processes of Arabization and Islamization have been taken for granted in the history of that country" and by the political Sudanese elites assumption of the "natural feature" of this wave of socio-cultural change (Manger 1994, p. 11), alongside scholarly discussions about ethnicity, identity and nationalism concepts "… in ways that have confused rather than clarified [such] issues" (Manger 2012, p. 328).

The tendency to implicitly take for granted the close association between the two elements, "Arabness" and Islam, leads us to comment here on the importance of taking into account more complex, nuanced and flexible situations when we focus on Sudanese groups and their social practices. The definition of *who* is an Arab (and *what* an Arab is supposed to be and to do) in Sudan is the first issue that is underlined by a plural reality that goes beyond comforting ideologies of unequivocal biological descent. As a prior observation, we should remember that the term *ʿarab* itself is used in Sudan to refer both to "pastoral nomads" (Grandin 1980; Casciarri 2015) and to "ethnically" Arab groups (with contrasting hierarchical connotations). Moreover, the latter sense only started gradually to be used in the country relatively recently, coinciding with Turco-Egyptian rule in the second half of the 19th century (Vezzadini 2015). On this subject, it is also important to recall some seminal anthropological and historical works that have either proven the flexibility of

5 In this regard, a colonial historian reports as follows the emblematic event, at the beginning of the Sennar Kingdom, when its first king, Amara Dunqas, aimed to prevent the invasion from Egypt in 1520 by Salim, Sultan of Turkey: "'Amara took alarm at this as a threat against its own kingdom and sent a message stating that if Salim was thinking of taking the *jihad* against him, he should know that he and his people were Arabs and true believers. As proof of this he sent genealogical tables drawn up by one as-Samarkandi, who is responsible for most of the fictitious genealogies in the Sudan, to prove that the Funj [Sennar kings' ethnic group] belonged to the Bani Umayya" (Trimingham 1949, p. 85).

ethnic borders through the cases of Fur "becoming" Baggara (Arabs) mainly on the basis of economic strategies in Darfur (Haaland 1969), or evoked the softening of dividing lines between Nuba and Arabs thanks to the construction of a shared identity as a colonial working-class in the cotton industry in South Kordofan (Saavedra 1998).[6] Other significant remarks could be added to such insights on the shifting and problematic identification of the Arab components in Sudan. This applies to the early linguistic Arabicization of non-Arab groups, which makes the lack of an overlap between linguistic markers and ethnicity claims a particularity of the Sudanese context as far as Arabic-speaking groups are concerned (Miller 2009). Although Arabicization (in the linguistic sense) does not automatically bring people to claim an Arab identity, their often parallel Islamization may lead them to adopt the material culture and secular practices of Sudanese Muslim Arabs, legitimating their doing "… as Arabs do" (Baumann 1987, p. 130), a statement which should push scholars to analyse the historical processes of social change in the specificities and complexity of their long-term dynamics. In previous conjunctures of the country's history, both Sudanese people and scholars have been keener to take into account the ideas of flexible borders between "Africanism" and "Arabism" on the road to building a national identity (Abd al-Rahim 1971), or the legitimate claim of an "Afro-Arab" identity (with religious affiliation playing a secondary role) in response to the "multiple marginality" of Sudan (Mazrui 1971). Today, after decades of civil wars in the former Sudan (1956–1972; 1983–2005), and particularly after the renewed emphasis placed by the elites on the essential Sudan's clear-cut homogeneous identity as an Arab Muslim nation after the split with South Sudan in 2011 (Woodward 2012), such flexibility is no longer on the agenda. Nonetheless, we still need to examine thoroughly all uses of the practical as well as analytical categorizations implying Arab and Islamic labels (and their alleged natural overlap), in order to avoid their ambiguous assumption as simply matters of fact. As a longstanding ambivalence remains in the implicit identification between (Sudanese) Arabs and Muslims, which contemporary political processes strive to reinforce, an approach that aims to focus on Islam as a source of socio-legal practices should not avoid the interrogation of the questionable definition of the other element of this pair, the categorization of "Arab" in this African country.

6 A similar approach is persuasively developed by an anthropologist through the reconstruction of historical dynamics of ethnicity (mainly of West African migrants in Sudan), with reference to processes of labour force formation within the context of peripheral capitalist development in Sudan (O'Brien 1986).

The Historical Manipulation by Political Elites of "Arab" and "Muslim" Sociocultural Borders

A second element to stress is the long history of manipulation, led by political elites (colonial and post-colonial, local, national and international), of the complex and multifarious definitions of local ascriptions to ethnic, religious and cultural categories covered by labels such as Arab and Muslim, or both. As far as the colonial period is concerned, historians have made clear the efforts made by the British in defining clear-cut administrative units coherent with ethno-tribal homogeneous entities, to which the Native Administration policy attached a pyramidal apparatus of tribal chiefs (Grandin 1982; Abu Shouk 1998). The attitude of the Sudanese Political Service oscillated between, on the one hand, a sort of orientalism-driven "fascination" for the groups conceived as "pure" Arab (mainly nomadic) and Muslim (Grandin 1982), seen as more civilized, and hence deserving higher levels of autonomy in self-administration through traditional chiefs and customs, and, on the other, a strong involvement in opposing Islam as a potential enemy and a source of joint insubordination to their power. The policies of the so-called "Closed District", together with other interventions – such as the emblematic prohibition of the use of Arabic even in contexts (such as the Nuba Mountains) where it had already replaced some vernacular languages among non-Arab groups (Baumann 1987; Manfredi 2015) – bear witness to two interesting dynamics: first, the impulse given by the British colonial administration to dichotomize Sudanese people as Northern/Arab/Muslim *vs* Southerners/African/pagan or Christian; and second, the implicit assimilation of being Arab with being Muslim.[7] Even if this may seem a contradiction, it is important to note that, following a classical divide-and-rule policy, the British nevertheless continued to pursue political alliances with the Northern Arab-Muslim Sudanese "tribal elites": faced with the new dangers of national movements striving for independence (Bleuchot 1989), colonial powers stigmatized as "detribalized" individuals or communities – mainly urban groups of mixed ethno-tribal mostly non-Arab origins (Boddy

7 In his historical analysis of the Nuba Mountains Miri groups, Baumann shows how British interventions to prevent the use of Arabic in schools were linked to the idea that linguistic Arabicization might foster the Islamization of the Nuba people (1987, pp. 46–58). The so-called "Nuba Policy" (following the lines of the better known "Southern Policy") significantly accentuated inter-ethnic divisions (and the polarization between Arab-Muslims and non-Arab/non-Muslims) during colonial times (Salih 1990). We can find similar trends far later, during the post-conflict period (2005–2011), when US Christian NGOs or research institutes, such as the SIL, fostered the rediscovery and protection of Nuba "endangered languages" with an analogous wish to contrast Arab and Islamic influences on alleged Christian and African groups (Manfredi 2015).

2009; Vezzadini 2015) – that did not fit into their ideal category of homogenous Arab-Muslim tribes. The same ambiguity and political contradictions were visible in the treatment of Islam and its role in the government of local societies. If the introduction of "Mohameddan Courts" as a way of administering justice through *sharīʿa* soon after the establishment of colonial domination (1902) was mainly thought of as a tool for preventing the resurgence of an Islamic-based resistance (Grandin 1982), their actual authority was limited by a certain flexibility (Bleuchot 1994), and the following decades showed that most Sudanese – even Northern groups who were dominantly Muslim – preferred to address the Native Courts and customary legal systems.[8] It is therefore interesting to look to some recent works stressing the persisting legacy of colonial political and legal ideologies, like those found in the Sudanese context. In their analysis, the "dualist nature" of the judiciary established by the British is conceived as the crucial aspect of a "colonial geography" marked by Manicheism (Ibrahim 2008), whose compartmentalization of "citizens" and "subjects", reinforced by the "decentralized despotism" of Native Administration (Mamdani 1996), is seen as a form of governance whose long-term influence has proved most dramatic in its hindrance of local people's efforts towards an actual decolonization, and can be linked to the emergence of an authoritarian Islamism to replace other forms of religiosity among Muslim people of Sudan (Ibrahim 2008).

If we can thus identify the colonial moment as a crucial period both of polarization and of dichotomization of Sudanese groups as far as the categories of Islam and Arabness are concerned, it is possible to state that the situation was not further clarified after Sudanese Independence. Despite various emphases placed by the governments in power after 1956 on issues of secularism and ethnicity within the process of defining a national identity and consequent policies, it is possible to note, first, that the prickly issue of the role of Islam in Sudanese society (and its law systems) has never been clearly settled and, second, that the nexus between identification as Muslim and Arab referred to above has also remained an ambiguous background issue. After the June 1989 coup d'état, when a military government backed by the Muslim Brothers took

8 Although it is still possible today to note among Sudanese law practitioners and academics the implicit assumption that Sudanese Muslims should all be subject to Islamic law (thus considering "customary law" as the specific almost exclusive domain of non-Muslim "African" tribes), a few law scholars have remarked that a fair part of Muslim people in the country do not follow principles of Islamic law, even in some personal law matters (marriage, inheritance) (Akolawin 1971).

power in Khartoum, the reintroduction of *sharīʿa* took place in the framework of an ambitious "Civilizational Project", in which Islamic universalism was conceived as a tool for co-opting peripheral non-Arab groups (Musso 2015). The idea of investing Islam with a supra-tribal unifying role, able to achieve a mission in which decades of post-colonial efforts for nation building had not succeeded, could sound quite coherent with some of the foundational principles of the Qur'an. Nonetheless, against this background, the 1994 campaign to revitalize Native Administration systems and tribal leaderships (Casciarri 2009; Delmet 2005) again raised doubts about the dilemma surrounding the categorizations associated with the definition of Islamic, Arab and, we might add, tribal identities in Sudan. The politization of these categories, often disguised by treating them as if they were almost natural, traditional and clear-cut parameters for delimiting social units, can be found, alongside the strategies of Sudanese governments, in the equally misleading uses of the terms that have been spread by the "international community", Western powers and humanitarian aid actors during recent decades, and gains particular strength in the context of civil wars and conflicts (de Waal 2005, p. 203). Besides this more politically driven sphere, we must note that, despite several crucial works, to which we owe the unveiling of the political (instrumental) weight of Sudanese ethnic categorization into inflexible patterns (Grandin 1982), the overlapping of demographic, ecological and economic factors in reshaping ethnicity (Prunier 1991; O'Brien 1986; Assal 2006), and the complex melding of Sudanese, Islamic and tribal identities (Baumann 1987; de Waal 2005), scholars still somewhat run the risk of being caught in essentialist primordialist traps, as witnessed by the persisting ambiguities and short-cuts in the use of notions such as "Arabization" or "Islamization" (Delmet 1991; Fluehr-Lobban 1987), "Sudanization" or "Arab Muslim way of life" (Doornbos 1988), which reveal underlying assumptions of the reified existence of autochthonous, original and authentic cultures.[9]

9 We find the same ambiguity in some seminal works about Islamic law in Sudan, such as that by Fluehr-Lobban (1987), who says: "...Arabization and Islamization followed relatively quickly after the fall of Dongola [Christian Kingdom], but a distinctly Sudanese culture and character *remained intact*, and indeed certain ethnic groups, notably the Nuba and Beja peoples, retained their languages and *specific pre-Islamic cultural configurations*" (Fluehr-Lobban 1987, p. 23 [our italics]).

The Contributions to the Volume

As the contributions to this volume will show, the issues of being (or not being) Arab and/or Muslim – and, we should add, of belonging to one "tribe"[10] – emerge in their interplay as recurrent meaningful paradigms of the conceptualizations and practical behaviours among both the groups we describe here, and the formal or informal organizational instances that constitute the framework for their actions. For this reason, far from proposing a definitive, clear-cut and stable definition of this tricky issue, we decided as a theoretical precondition, to forewarn our readers of the complexity and plurality of these labels, by showing their multiple and shifting configurations in their historical contexts. In fact, it would be an over-hasty reduction of this complexity to simply summon up the blanket cover of "legal pluralism" or the alleged opposition between "Islamic law" and "customary laws" as a background to our analysis. Instead, we based our approach on the other option – focusing on local groups' legal practices and arenas, and possibly showing the pragmatic and contextual embeddedness of Islamic law and other law paradigms, and in this lies the work's potential contribution to enriching, through a consideration of the Sudanese case, the wider problematic of the relation between Islam and dominantly Muslim societies. Such has been the common thread that inspired the individual researches carried out for the ANDROMAQUE programme, and the idea of maximizing the variety of our fieldwork, though far from an intention to establish high-level generalizations, was also intrinsically linked to our approach. The contributors found it interesting to diversify the spaces of their investigations by focusing on rural (pastoral or agricultural) and urban (central or peripheral) groups, in the capital city or in other regions of the country. This approach was conceived from the beginning as a device that would allow the emergence of the interplay of a multitude of factors (such as geographical, productive, ethno-tribal, class and cultural situations), whose influence and interaction on "socio-legal practices" we are able to suggest. There follows

10 The brevity of this introduction prevents us from entering into the huge debate about "tribal structures". However, as most of the chapters show, the issue of the "tribe" (*gabīla* in vernacular Arabic) stands as a meaningful paradigm, both of conceptualization and of the multidimensional behaviour of Sudanese local groups, whose influence is also visible at the level of legal practice, which is the focus of this volume. The pertinence of the reference to tribal institutions has been underlined elsewhere for the Sudanese context (Casciarri and Ahmed 2009), as has the need to take it into account in the wider anthropological debate on expressions of tribalism in the "Arab Muslim" worlds (Bonte et al. 1991; Bonte, Conte and Dresch 2001; Abdul Jabbar and Dawod 2003).

an overview of the topics covered by the ten chapters and of the structure of the book.

The First Part of the volume comprises five contributions with a common focus on legal practices and normative systems concerning land appropriation and its uses in Sudan. The fact that the "land issue" has emerged as a prominent element is linked to the particular context in which the fieldwork was conducted. As observed in other recent works (Gertel, Rottenburg and Calkins 2014; Casciarri, Assal and Ireton 2015), during the past decade (2005–15), and more particularly after the oil boom linked to the end of the civil war, neoliberal policies that gradually began to be implemented in the mid-1990s reached their apex as Sudan became increasingly integrated into the global capitalist economy. One of the main effects of this trend has been the rush for land ownership by a myriad of national and international investors, and the generalization of "land grabbing" dynamics, in both rural and urban areas, followed by the weakening of local livelihoods and the growing insecurity of peoples' access to land and its resources. Most of the chapters in the first part have this situation as a general background and deal with the common association between land access and ethno-tribal identity claims.

Chapter 1 (E. Ille) focuses on the status of land access among riverine groups of the northern Nile Valley, notably in Dār Manāṣīr and Kerma. By thoroughly reconstructing historical agricultural practices and their codification, the author stresses the multiplicity of social dimensions embedded in land usage. The case study is particularly interesting, as far as it goes beyond the illustration of "traditional" sedentary tribal groups' access to land, by following the sensitive issue of the conflict between the Manāṣīr and the Sudanese state, fueled by the construction of the Merowe Dam in the mid-2000s, and the consequent eviction of local farmers from their land. While Islam (and Islamic law) are not a prominent reading-key for understanding the legal aspects of this context (apart from the mere fact that the Manāṣīr are an archetypal Sudanese Arab-Muslim tribe and their counterpart is an Islamic government), the case study confirms the need to embed legal practices concerning land into wider economic, political and moral configurations.

Chapter 2 (B. Casciarri) moves the focus to another category of Sudanese people, pastoral nomadic groups, which, notwithstanding persistent marginalization and "invisibilization", are a relevant component in the historical and contemporary socio-economic configuration of the country. The Aḥāmda pastoralists of rural Khartoum State experienced during the last decade an increasing fragmentation of their territory and dispossession, whose main consequence has been the multiplication of inter-tribal micro-conflicts. Here, through the concept of "institutional bricolage", the author examines their legal strategies for claiming land rights. Despite the constant reference by the Aḥāmda to the *gabīla* (tribe) and to a flexible notion of *ʿurf* (customary law), their actual practices defy the alleged dichotomies between customary/state laws, tribe/state, oral/written, collective/individual, while also revealing the "weakness" of an Islamic legal reference (at least that of *sharīʿa*) in the social life and legal behaviour of another archetypal Arab-Muslim tribe.

Chapter 3 (M. ASSAL) deals with land issues in an urban (more precisely peripheral) context, the locality of al-Ṣalḥa, in the western part of Greater Khartoum, where processes of land alienation have become relevant during recent years. The history of the accelerated urbanization of this former village is depicted, together with the development of strategies used by the "autochthonous" old-timers, the Jamūʿiya, to play on two different – apparently contradictory – levels: the claiming of tribal rights for appropriating (then selling) land, and the transformation of land transfer into a profitable business as land prices and demand rose due to the booming expansion of Khartoum. An example of another configuration of legal practices mobilizing contextually different institutions and norms for claiming land, this case study also sheds light on two elements: the strategic role of the *lajna shaʿbiyya* (popular committees introduced by the Islamic government since 1989) in micro-level land alienation processes, and the pertinence in the urban context of the tribal paradigm, which is conventionally thought of as a feature of rural areas.

Unlike previous case studies, where groups are delimited by territorial or tribal parameters of belonging, the group focused on in Chapter 4 (P. GOUT) concerns another significant category in the Sudanese context: the Christian communities living in Khartoum, whose presence increased as a result of displacements during civil wars. Based on rich fieldwork on recent cases of church destruction or confiscation in the peripheral quarters of Gereif and Haj Yusif, this case study puts religious (Islamic) reference at the core of the analysis. Empirical data allow the author to question both the contradictions of the "dualist nature" of the Sudanese legal order (in which *sharīʿa* is supposed to grant legal rights to non-Muslim as *dhimmīs*), and the weakness of international legislation on "minority rights". The attention paid to Christian Sudanese IDPs, more frequently evoked in the framework of "human rights" discourses, is here however centred on their land rights' dispossession, a threat increased by the political context after the separation of South Sudan in 2011 and the strengthening of a dominant discourse on Sudan's Muslim identity.

Finally, Chapter 5 (M. BABIKER) draws a detailed historical overview of various legislative systems which, since colonial times, have framed access to the ownership and transfer of land. The author highlights some milestones in Sudanese land legislation with a particular focus on "customary land law", which by reason of the demographic, socio-economic and territorial configuration of the country, concerns historically huge groups of people. Far from adopting a purely descriptive approach, the author aims to underline the "hybrid nature" of both colonial and post-colonial law orders, and also to stress that such legislation has seriously encroached upon traditional and communal ownership of land. The persisting neglect of "collective land" rights, one of the main drivers of Sudanese military and political conflicts, is confirmed by the illustration of the neo-liberal trend that has increasingly inspired Sudanese land legislation since the coming to power of the Islamic government, which has favoured major private investors' interests rather than the legal rights of the country's citizens and communities. Focusing more strictly on the juridical domain, this final chapter of this first part stands as a significant synthesis of and macro-level insight into the topics dealt with through the micro-scale fieldwork cases in previous chapters.

The chapters in the Second Part of the volume share a common focus on customary courts and concrete cases of conflict negotiation. This constitutes an issue that needs to be better grasped in the context of contemporary Sudan: as tensions have progressively increased in recent decades as a consequence of the major factors of livelihood pauperization, land grabbing and territorial dispossession, violent urbanization and forced mobility, the issue of justice administration has become crucial. This general trend has led politicians, development actors and scholars to discover a renewed interest in "grassroots" or "informal" justice (Pankhurst and Assefa 2008), in Sudan as well as the post-conflict conjuncture of the CPA (2005–2011), which has given rise to a new consideration of local native mechanisms of conflict resolution (Rahama and Elhussein 2005; Parmar 2007). Thus, an intrinsic link may be found between the "tribal issue", which permeates most of the chapters in the first part, and the "customary" or "native courts" issue, the focus of most of the chapters in the second. Like the cases of the first part, where we wanted to go beyond the notion of "legal pluralism" by claiming a more nuanced vision of legal practice interactions and hybridization, the contributions to this second part also defy the binary simplistic opposition between "formal" and "informal" justice, by basing their analysis on a wide range of complex and hybrid configurations, also in both urban and rural contexts.

Chapter 6 (Z. ABDAL-KAREEM) is centreed on the study of a conflict between cattle herders and agricultural wage labourers in Basinga locality, Gedaref State (Eastern Sudan). Starting from the idea that processes of conflict negotiation are a more significant entry point than normative orders for understanding legal configurations, the author carries out a detailed ethnography of the dynamics of conflict mediation triggered by this case. The analysis illustrates a strategy of "forum shopping behaviour", where multiple legal authorities of different orders (customary council of mediation, Native Administration leaders, "official" rural courts) are involved, and notes the simultaneous appeal to some *sharīʿa* principles – such as the Islamic moral duty of forgiveness. Nonetheless, the wider social environment of the parties involved and their belonging have to be taken into account, as proved by the refusal to apply this equity principle in the case of non-Muslim Ethiopian wage labourers.

Chapter 7 (M. ABDUL-JALIL) shifts again into the urban context with the case of al-Ḥilla al-Jadīda, a former "squatter neighbourhood" in the Western part of Omdurman, Greater Khartoum, where an influential personality from the Nuba Mountains, Sultan Abdallah Kafi, fostered the establishment of a local court for dispute resolution. Beyond the reach of both Native Administration and newly created Town Courts, the predominantly IDP inhabitants of this peripheral quarter succeeded in creating an adapted institution for their local justice administration. This case is not only an outstanding example of the creative ways in which local groups shape their voluntary forums of legal authority, but it also challenges the idea that "tribal homogeneity" is a necessary condition for the existence of customary courts, as the inhabitants of the quarter belong to different Arab and non-Arab tribal groups, mainly from western Sudan. It is clear that their shared Muslim identity is perceived as a base of this moral and legal cohesion, yet it remains far from the framework of official *sharīʿa* urban courts.

The case study in Chapter 8 (Y. BEN HOUNET) shares the methodological approach of an ethnography carried out *inside* the courts (and during procedures), but its originality lies in the decision to study cases in the Khartoum Penal Court of the Traffic Administration. The focus on a case of homicide due to a car accident allows the author to establish an interesting bridge with classical anthropological studies on blood-money (*diya*) compensation among rural groups in Sudan and in other Muslim countries. The analysis of court negotiations and debates about *diya* (which in Sudan is both a customary legal practice and an official device of the *sharīʿa* penal code) raises interesting questions about the adaptation of this juridical form of compensation in the framework of an urban context and through a case highly emblematic of the recent Khartoum landscape, where booming urbanization has led to a rapid increase in fatal car accidents.

Chapter 9 (A. ABDEL AZIZ) focuses on another significant category of Sudanese citizens, the IDPs living at the periphery of Greater Khartoum. After making an in-depth presentation of IDP camps and their place in the marginalization policies and the social control apparatus of the Sudanese state, which are linked to relegation ideologies backed by the "Civilizational Project" of the

Islamic government, the author leads us into an analysis of the Native Courts in Mayo, a camp mainly inhabited by Southern IDPs. By showing the contradictory attitudes by governmental authorities, which officialised the institution of native leaders and courts among Southern IDPs (which is quite atypical in the Khartoum urban context) as a means of both controlling potentially dangerous groups and delegating the difficult task of local justice administration, the author argues that the Mayo Native Courts may act as a tool for countering state law hegemony. Furthermore, in the present context, the potential reactivation of these customary courts (whose function was rather limited to camps and to the interim CPA period) could be an interesting tool of aggregation and support for the numerous Southerners who are fleeing back to Khartoum after the outbreak of civil war in South Sudan (2013).

Like the first part, this second part concludes with an overview of Sudanese legislation on "customary courts". Chapter 10 (M. BABIKER) provides a historical review of customary institutions since colonial times and also explores their relationship to statutory and Islamic legal systems. The author argues that traditional justice institutions should remain an integral part of Sudan's pluralistic justice system and not be marginalized, as has often been the case under both colonial and postcolonial rule. While insisting on the critical role of customary courts and norms in ensuring peaceful settlements of disputes, the chapter also raises the question of their compatibility with international legislation on human rights. The volume ends with a final section whose annexes include ten original documents collected by the contributors in the context of their fieldwork research and an annexe with extracts from land laws issued in Sudan between 1900 and 2015.

In conclusion, we would like to note some elements that mark the originality of the contributions to this volume. First, even though anthropological studies have a rich and solid tradition in Sudan, and the same could be said – although to a lesser degree – concerning law studies, the merging of the two disciplinary approaches (and the common questions and debates this raises), are something of a novelty in the panorama of Sudanese Studies. Second, we underline the unique approach (in this case, suggested by the wider ANDROMAQUE program) of an "anthropology of law", which aims to shift the focus from normative legal systems to contextual socio-legal practices appreciated through the micro-scale of qualitative original fieldwork on contemporary cases. Finally, the historical conjuncture of the post-2011 period, in which all the fieldwork is based, makes our reflections particularly stimulating: the separation of South Sudan has reactivated and invested with new dimensions earlier debates and processes about the definition of the role of Islam in Sudanese society, in its simultaneous reconfigurations in line with other parameters, such as tribal or ethnic (mainly Arab) affiliations, and within the wider (though underestimated) long-term economic dynamics of globalized neoliberal Sudan. All this seems to provide other interesting and more unusual reading-keys, besides the macro-political, historical or juridical ones. In this framework, we may say that the title of this volume itself points, in a "provocative" way, to the association of the label "Muslim" with "Sudan". In fact, all the chapters in the book seem to agree that Sudan continues to be labelled (particularly after 2011), without major nuances, as a Muslim country both by its governing elites and by the international political community, but also that our main scientific interest lies in detecting and unveiling the multidimensional processes this simplified categorization conceals. Our case studies show that Sudanese Muslims are embedded in much more complex dynamics related to their self-ascription as such, and that they can both resort to a contextual hybrid reference to Islam(s) in their socio-legal practices, but also even ignore such reference without contesting their religious affiliation. We hope that these ethnographical insights into the actual ways urban and rural groups in a Muslim country behave and think will not only make a contribution to the knowledge of Sudanese social processes, but also enrich a wider sensitive debate about the socio-cultural and historical dimensions of contemporary Islam, which is at risk of being misunderstood and instrumentalized by the current international political conjuncture.

References

Abd al-Rahim, M 1971, 'Arabism, Africanism and Self-identification in Sudan', in Y Fadl Hasan (ed.), *Sudan in Africa*, Khartoum University Press, Khartoum, pp. 228–239.

Abdul Jabbar F & Dawod H (eds) 2003, *Tribes and Power. Nationalism and Ethnicity in the Middle East*, Saqi, London.

Abu Shouk, AI 1998, 'From Tribes to Nazirates', in E Stiansen & M Kevane (eds), *Kordofan Invaded. Peripheral Incorporation and Social Transformation in Islamic Africa*, Brill, Leiden, pp. 120–144.

Akolawin, NO 1971, 'Islamic and Customary Law in the Sudan. Problems of Today and Tomorrow', in Y Fadl Hasan (ed.), *Sudan in Africa*, Khartoum University Press, Khartoum, pp. 279–301.

Assal, MAM 2006, 'Sudan. Identity and Conflict over Natural Resources', *Development*, vol. 49, no. 3, pp. 101–105.

Baumann, G 1987, *National Integration and Local Integrity. The Miri of the Nuba Mountains in the Sudan*, Clarendon Press, Oxford.

Bleuchot, H 1989, 'Le Soudan anglo-égyptien', in M Lavergne (ed.), *Le Soudan contemporain*, Karthala, Paris, pp. 171–226.

Bleuchot, H 1994, 'La formation du droit soudanais', *Egypte/Monde arabe*, vol. 17, pp. 133–141.

Boddy, J 2009, 'Endogamy and Alliance in Northern Sudan', in G Schlee & E Watson (eds), *Changing Identifications and Alliances in North-East Africa*, Vol. 3 (Sudan, Uganda and the Ethiopia-Sudan Borderlands), Berghahn Books, New York/Oxford, pp. 103–115.

Bonte P, Conte E, Hamès C & Ould Cheikh AW 1991, *Al-Ansâb. La quête des origines. Anthropologie historique de la société tribale arabe*, Editions de la MSH, Paris.

Bonte P, Conte E & Dresch P (eds) 2001, *Emirs et présidents. Figures de la parenté et du politique dans le monde arabe*, Editions CNRS, Paris.

Buskens, L & Dupret, B 2012, 'Qui a inventé le droit musulman? Une histoire des études occidentales de la normativité islamique et leur diffusion en Orient', *Maghreb et sciences sociales*, vol. 1, pp. 51–61.

Casciarri, B 2009, 'Hommes, troupeaux et capitaux. Le phénomène tribal au Soudan à l'heure de la globalisation', *Etudes rurales*, no. 184, pp. 47–64.

Casciarri, B 2015, 'De l'altérité et de l'invisibilité des groups pastoraux au Soudan. Repenser les études soudanaises en partant de leurs marges mobiles', *Canadian Journal of African Studies*, vol. 49, no. 1, pp. 147–174.

Casciarri, B & Ahmed, AA 2009, 'Pastoralists under pressure in present-day Sudan. An Introduction', *Nomadic Peoples*, vol. 19, no. 1, pp. 10–22.

Casciarri, B, Assal, MA & Ireton, F (eds) 2015, *Multidimensional Change in Sudan 1989–2011. Reshaping Livelihoods, Conflicts and Identities*, Berghahn Books, New York/Oxford.

Delmet, C 1991, 'Société dominante et cultures locales. Violence et intégration au Dar Funj', in H Bleuchot, C Delmet & D Hopwood (eds), *Sudan. History, Identity, Ideology*, Ithaca Press, Oxford, pp. 121–142.

Delmet, C 2005, 'The Native Administration System in Eastern Sudan. From Its Liquidation to Its Revival', in C Miller (ed.), *Land, Ethnicity and Political Legitimacy in Eastern Sudan*, CEDEJ/DSRC, Cairo/Khartoum, pp. 145–172.

de Waal, A 2005, 'Who are the Darfurians? Arab and African Identities, Violence and External Engagement', *African Affairs*, vol. 104, no. 415, pp. 181–205.

Doornbos, P 1988. 'On Becoming Sudanese', in T Barnett & A Abdelkarim (eds), *Sudan. State, Capital and Transformation*, Croom Helm, London, pp. 99–120.

Fadl Hasan, Y 1967, *The Arabs and the Sudan*, Khartoum University Press, Khartoum.

Fluehr-Lobban, C 1987, *Islamic Law and Society in Sudan*, Franck Cass, London.

Gertel, J, Rottenburg, R & Calkins, S (eds) 2014, *Disrupted Territories. Land, Commodification and Conflict in Sudan*, James Currey, London.

Grandin, N 1980, 'Note bibliographique sur les pasteurs nomades au Nord Soudan', *Production Pastorale et Société*, no. 7, pp. 98–118.

Grandin, N 1982, *Le Soudan nilotique et l'administration britannique (1898–1956). Eléments d'une interprétation socio-historique d'une expérience coloniale*, Brill, Leiden.

Haaland, G 1969, 'Economic Determinants in Ethnic Processes', in F Barth (ed.), *Ethnic Groups and Boundaries. The Social Organization of Culture Difference*, Universitetforlaget, Oslo, pp. 58–73.

Ibrahim, AA 2008, *Manichaen Delirium. Decolonizing the Judiciary and Islamic Renewal in the Sudan, 1898–1985*, Brill, Leiden.

MacMichael, HA 1922, *A History of the Arabs in the Sudan*, Oxford University Press, Oxford.

Mamdani, M 1996, *Citizen and Subject. Contemporary Africa and the Legacy of Late Colonialism*, Princeton University Press, Princeton, NJ

Manfredi, S 2015, 'One tribe, One Language. Ethnolinguistic Identity and Language Revitalization among the Laggori in the Nuba Mountains', in B Casciarri et al. (eds), *Multidimensional Change in Sudan 1989–2011*, Berghahn Books, New York/Oxford, pp. 281–301.

Manger, LO 1994, *From the Mountains to the Plains. The Integration of the Lalofa Nuba into Sudanese Society*, Scandinavian Institute of African Studies, Uppsala.

Manger, LO 2012, 'Anthropological Reflections on the Break-up of Sudan', *International Journal of Middle Eastern Studies*, vol. 44, no. 2, pp. 327–329.

Mazrui, AA 1971, 'The Multiple Marginality of Sudan', in Y Fadl Hasan (ed.), *Sudan in Africa*, Khartoum University Press, Khartoum, pp. 240–255.

Miller, C 2009, 'La situation linguistique au Soudan. Evolution et enjeux', in B Casciarri (ed.), *Cycle de Conférences du CEDEJ Khartoum au Centre Culturel Français 2007–2008*, Azza Publishing House, Khartoum, pp. 15–36.

Musso, G 2015, 'The Islamic Movement and Power in Sudan. From Revolution to Absorption into the State', in B Casciarri et al. (eds), *Multidimensional Change in Sudan 1989–2011*, Berghahn Books, New York/Oxford, pp. 245–262.

O'Brien, J 1986, 'Toward a Reconstitution of Ethnicity. Capitalist Expansion and Cultural Dynamics in Sudan', *American Anthropologist*, vol. 88, no. 4, pp. 898–907.

Pankhurst, A & Assefa, G (eds) 2008, *Grass-root Justice in Ethiopia. The Contribution of Customary Dispute Resolution*, Centre Français d'Etudes Ethiopiennes, Addis Ababa.

Parmar, S 2007, *An Overview of the Sudanese Legal System and Legal Research*, Globalex, New York, accessed 20 November 2016 http://www.nyulawglobal.org/globalex/Sudan.html.

Prunier, G 1991, 'Ecologie, structures ethniques et conflits politiques au Dar Fur', in H Bleuchot, C Delmet & D Hopwood (eds), *Sudan. History, Ideology, Identity*, Ithaca Press, London, pp. 85–103.

Rahama, AA & Elhussein, DM 2005, *A Case Study of Conflict in the Nuba Mountains*, Intercommunal Conflict in Sudan. Causes, Resolution Mechanisms and Transformation series, vol. 5, Ahfad University for Women, Omdurman.

Saavedra, M 1998, 'Ethnicity, Resources and the Central State. Politics in the Nuba Mountains, 1950s to the 1990s', in E Stiansen & M Kevane (eds), *Kordofan Invaded. Peripheral Incorporation and Social Transformation in Islamic Africa*, Brill, Leiden, pp. 223–253.

Salih, KO 1990, 'British Policy and the Accentuation of Inter-Ethnic Divisions. The Case of the Nuba Mountains Region of Sudan 1920–1940', *African Affairs*, vol. 88, no. 356, pp. 417–436.

Trimingham, JS 1949, *Islam in the Sudan*, Oxford University Press, London.

Vezzadini, E 2015, 'Setting the Scene of the Crime. The Colonial Archive, History, and Racialization of the 1924 Revolution in Anglo-Egyptian Sudan', *Canadian Journal of African Studies*, vol. 49, no. 1, pp. 67–93.

Woodward, P 2012, 'Sudan after the South Secession. Issues of Idendity', in GM Sorbo & AM Ahmed (eds), *Sudan Divided. Continuing Conflict in a Contested State*, Palgrave Macmillan, New York, pp. 89–102.

PART 1

Land Issues: Dynamics of Appropriation and Legal Frameworks

CHAPTER 1

Land Alienation as a Legal, Political, Economic and Moral Issue in the Nile Valley of North Sudan

Enrico Ille

Introduction

A broad spectrum of issues in the relation between the moral and market principles of economics are raised when looking at the tension between commodification and the social value of inalienability. The "great transformation" that occurs during the extension of alienability to a wide range of previously non-marketable goods and services has therefore become a central field of inquiry for the evaluation of the social consequences of economic exchange in contemporary societies (Polanyi 1944). Land, with its potential for the concentration of social value as "homeland", is an important part of such an inquiry.

In Sudan, land alienation is often a complex process, not least because of political tensions connected to past and present appropriation of customary land, in some cases fuelling or even causing violent conflicts. Land disputes often go beyond the question of how to find immediate or institutionalized solutions to them, and bring cases into the realm of political economy and sociocultural development. Among the issues involved in such cases are contested notions of land as an identity marker or commodity, fertile or resource-rich land as communal, private or state property, and competition over land usage, e.g., for urban settlement, agriculture, mineral extraction or dam construction.

In the Nile Valley north of Khartoum, this last matter of land usage has been an issue throughout most of the second half of the 20th century and continues up to today. The construction of dams has had significant impacts on land structure both in the 1960s (Aswan) and in the 2000s (Merowe, Upper Atbara); further dams are under consideration. The resultant creation of flooded areas has had and will have an impact on settlements, agriculture, archaeological sites and the recently increasing activity of gold mining. However, even within each of these claims on land use there are competing approaches and actors, such as between extending urban areas and rural structures, between small-scale family-owned and large-scale industrial farming, between foreign-funded archaeological projects and protectionist or predatory approaches to

 | DOI 10.1163/9789004362185_003

sites, between state-sponsored industrial mining and artisanal mining at odds with state regulation.

In present discourses, the treatment of land as invariably alienable is an issue both for the transformation of customary (communal) into private (commercial) or state property, and for the consequences of this treatment for environmental health and protection. The former is central for discussions of colonial and post-colonial land policies and is still fiercely debated in areas with significant claims to indigenous land rights, including several regions in Sudan. Accordingly, land alienation as a process of coerced commercialization or outright violent expropriation has been repeatedly identified as a key problem for social peace in Sudan (Pantulliano 2007), affecting most of its areas (e.g. Babiker 2008 for North Kordofan, Mohamed Salih 1998, Suliman 1999 and Komey 2010 for Nuba Mountains, Miller 2005 on eastern Sudan) and arguably increasing in the frame of recent land grabbing (El Hadary and Obeng-Odoom 2012, Gertel, Rottenburg and Calkins 2014).

On a conceptual level, land alienation can thus be understood both as "the transferral of ownership of rights in the land/property, and the loss of rights which effectively makes one an alien, or foreigner, in the land" (Olwig 2005, pp. 30–31). This also implies the differentiation between a legalistic concept of consensual transfer of land property and a political critique of coercive expropriation that may be legalized in the process. This process may furthermore be actively challenged and may lead to de facto prevention of actual use of legally owned land, which necessitates not only distinguishing between property, ownership, access and usage, but also between legality and (situational) legitimacy.[1] The latter has also to do with the economic circumstances of land use, i.e., the physical, organizational and distributional characteristics of resource exploitation, as well as the social values surrounding land, which are termed here as the moral aspect of land alienation in the sense of a "state of being separated or cut off" (Hailwood 2015, p. 16).[2]

On this basis, this chapter illustrates the interconnections emerging from a multifaceted discussion of social practices of land alienation. The overall argument is that land alienation in Sudan is not only a normalized and institutionalized process concerning the body of land-related laws in the national legal system, but also a politically charged and highly situational process concerning

1 A similar argument has been made in Ille and Calkins (2013) concerning gold mining and in Calkins et al. (2015) concerning general land rights issues.

2 The contingent effects of the commodification of land on law, political economy and social values as one of the bases of "primitive accumulation" also form an important part of the Marxist concepts of *Entäußerung / Entfremdung* (alienation / estrangement).

social practices, reflecting the overall political economy in the country. While this is all but surprising, the illustration of this difference highlights the need for a practice-oriented approach that goes beyond the impression of legal regularity suggested by written laws and public reference to them. Such an approach is not just a matter of analytical accuracy, since nearly all major conflicts in present Sudan are centrally or even causally related to land disputes.

Apart from long-term studied regions such as Darfur and the Nuba Mountains, this concerns the Nile-adjacent areas in northern Sudan to a high degree. While the former two regions deal with existential threats to physical and socio-cultural survival, northern Sudan experiences, in the form of flooding due to dam construction, an existential threat to surface land itself. In a situation where scarcity already produces tense competition for fertile land, this results in the confrontation of deeply rooted notions of homeland with imminent threats to land property. These different layers of meaning, following a not exclusively legal approach to land alienation, can thus be very well illustrated with case studies from this region. At the same time, such studies contribute to the unceasingly relevant debates on land transfers in and beyond Africa, specifically "disputes over the (in)alienability of land" (Lentz 2010, p. 57).

This chapter will present a case study of the agricultural lands between the Third and Fourth Nile Cataract, with focus on Dār al-Manāṣīr and Kerma, about 60 km north of Dongola.[3] In general, anthropological research has been rare in northern Sudan, and only the advent of major displacement prompted significant resources to be made available for ethnographic research, mostly adjacent to archaeological excavations. Dār al-Manāṣīr has been comparatively well-documented due to the existential threat it recently faced, as a significant part of it has been submerged since 2008 under an artificial reservoir fronted by the Merowe Dam. This research led to the 2012 volume *We Are the People of the River*, edited by Cornelia Kleinitz and Claudia Näser, which forms the basis of the Manāṣīr case study, together with preceding and parallel studies on the area, particularly Abdelrahim Mohammed Salih's *The Manasir of Northern Sudan* (1999), Kurt Beck's research in the 1990s and the recent PhD research of Valerie Hänsch (2016). Kerma was the subject of the present author's own fieldwork between September 2016 and March 2017, funded by the Urgent Anthropology Fellowship under the administration of the British Museum and the Royal Anthropological Institute; the material presented here comes from preliminary analysis and serves as supplementary data.

3 Given this focus on agricultural land, there will be no discussion of the nomadic population.

The analysis is based on the codification of primary data and text passages in the secondary literature, according to four pre-defined categories, namely legal, political, economic and moral aspects. The codification was followed by organization by scale (e.g. local, regional, national legal context). The analytical focus was then on contingent effects across different scales with the aim of reconstructing a seemingly legislative and juridical problem (alienation as transfer of land property) on a broader, sociologically informed basis. The four categories are thus intended to provide complementary perspectives, which allow a more comprehensive look at social legal practices.

Land Alienation as a Legal Issue

Legality, as defined in this article, means a judgement on lawfulness of a social action based on a pre-existing self-referencing legal code. It is, accordingly, the question of how far and in which way the alienation of land is defined as lawful in a specific legal code, in this case the legal code used in the national legal system of Sudan, which will be addressed here. However, it is not intended to provide a general discussion of land laws and specifically land alienation in Sudan, but rather to refer to existing laws as they pertain to practices of land property and ownership transfer in the study area.

The general legal pluralism existing in Sudan's court system is a complication in jurisdiction that adds to the discretion within one legal reference system the discretion of choice between different reference systems. Concerning the transfer of land property, there is on the one hand a clear historical line from the early colonial ordinances concerning land titles and registration to present legislation, and, on the other, the wide existence and relevance of locally specific juridical authorities and rules, which often preclude the activation of the state court mechanism, making this seemingly clear point of reference an elusive one when it comes to legal practices and actual disputes.

The cornerstones of the transfer of land property are demarcation and exchange, meaning the existence of a concrete, demarcated land plot and an agreement to transfer ownership of this plot in exchange for some specified equivalent. Land registration is the dominant process to make land property accessible to codified jurisdiction, as it is intended to take land out of an unspecified natural or communal context and relate it clearly to an individual owner or group of owners. As a second step, the owner or owners have to have unrestricted rights to transfer their land property to somebody else, and follow a prescribed process for this transfer. The following discussion therefore focuses on procedures of demarcation, ownership structure and restriction on land alienation.

Leaving earlier strains of state-supported individual land ownership aside (Spaulding and Kapteijns 2002), the foundational state regulation of land registration in Sudan originates in no less than sixteen ordinances issued between 1899 and 1930. The pillars of present jurisdiction on land alienation, privately or state-wise, are the Land Settlement and Registration Ordinance of 1925 (LSRO), the Unregistered Land Act of 1970 (ULA) and the Civil Transaction Act of 1984 (CTA, amendments 1991 and 1993); the last currently guides the private acquisition of land. These pillars established a strong position for registration as proof of claim, but also opened a wide range of opportunities for governments to confiscate land with reference to national priorities (El Mahdi 1977; Gordon 1986).

In the study area, the Land Survey and Demarcation Ordinance (1905) and the Land Settlement Ordinance (1905) had arguably the most lasting effects on legal disputes. They gave the general direction for the work of a land settlement committee in then Dongola and Berber Provinces, supported by a land survey and demarcation team under C.F. Ryder. In 1904, "those who sold their land during the famine years in the pre-colonial time were given the choice to have their land titles back" (Mohammed Salih 1999, p. 93); in the following year, the survey started "at the lower border on the right side of the river and ended in 1909 at the upper border on the left side of the river" (Mohammed Salih 1999, p. 93).

It has to be noted that British colonial rule followed periods of oppressive taxation, famine and war, which had instigated significant migration in northern Sudan: this historical dynamic was mostly obliterated by the status-quo character of the survey. Omer (1985, p. 32) wrote about Ottoman rule in the Dongola area, for instance, that

> Turkish authorities used to sell the land of those who were not able to pay. What made the situation worse was the inability of some returnees [...] to retrieve their lands, and they had either to stay landless or migrate to other parts of the Sudan [...].

In any case, the result of the land survey and the land registers based on it remained the only cadastre-like documentation of land property in the area.[4]

4 A visit to the land office in Argo on 15 November 2016 showed that the original maps from the beginning of the 20th century, on which the writing is very faded, were still used as reference

Mohammed Salih (1999, pp. 92–102) has put together a far-reaching analysis of complications arising from this process in Dār al-Manāṣīr. Since the legal practices to be looked at here are strongly connected to the legal arrangements built into the land registration that took place, it is relevant to repeat some details.

The aim of the survey had been the creation of a reference map and of a land register to be used for taxation and in future land disputes. The general map that was produced showed five sheikhdoms, and the sheikhs were asked to provide a list of land holders and boundaries of plots, which were numbered opposite to the direction of the Nile, following the Title of Arable Lands Ordinance 1899 and the Land Tax Ordinance 1899. On the basis of a standardized land measurement, land marks were produced as final demarcation of the plots. While only official measurements would be allowed in future court cases, the village maps, unlike the general map, made use of local measurement conventions as well (Mohammed Salih 1999, pp. 92–93).

The complex existing ownership structure, to be discussed further below, was adjusted to the requirements of registration and noted in two different registers, the aboriginal title (*sijil al-aṣl*)[5] and the title of cultivation (*sijil al-miswaq*), corresponding to two kinds of registration cards given to the title holders and to the official land ownership forms (Legal Form No. E4). The so-called Form 13 noted, among other information, the shares (*ḥiṣa*) in such titles; these were customarily called bones (*ʿaḍum*), which divided the ownership, not the physical land plot, into twelve shares. Any permanent changes to ownership, e.g., through inheritance or sale, were to be noted on all these registers, and an overseer for each plot (*sammad*) was named to manage the system (Mohammed Salih 1999, pp. 94–98).

For several reasons, this clear system of land registration and ownership transfer rules did not easily fit the reality of land use. For one, the limited availability of arable land in the area had given rise to a very detailed system of soil classification, which was locally considered when defining shares; this meant that each area with a different soil quality within a plot was treated separately and harvested crops were distributed according to these shares. Apart from that, four main types of land were defined, namely *jarf*, good soils at the riverside; *khawī*, seasonally flooded channels between islands, also very fertile;

in land disputes (see Annexe 1.1. *sāqiyya* map of Kerma Balad, 1929); attempts to reproduce and digitalize were limited to areas with agricultural investment schemes.

5 The terms in Arabic reflect the locally used terms as documented by the respective authors; transliteration rather than transcription has been used and therefore spelling may differ from the original source.

ashuw, next to the riverside lands and planted with date trees; and *sāqiyya*, the irrigated plots further inland, the main land for cultivation.[6]

Land registration designed to create a reliable and durable point of reference tended to deal with the seasonally unchanging land types, namely *ashuw* and *sāqiyya*, while the seasonally disappearing and constantly changing types were often disregarded, although registered *jarf* land can be found as well. However, the distribution of crop shares rather than physically demarcated land plots contradicted the territorial logic of land registration, and the actual complexity of land use removed local land rights even further from national legislation. In addition, local measurements were either proportional, as only relative shares were significant, or insufficiently standardized. Insufficient updates on different forms, errors in documentation and unequal access to registered information further reduced the clarity of the introduced system, and opened the way to manipulation for the sake of distributional advantages, especially among the political elites (Mohammed Salih 1999, pp. 98–102, example pp. 113–115).

Later legislative changes increased rather than reduced the uncertainties arising when specific land disputes were brought into the national court system. The general acquisition of unregistered land by the government through the land legislation of 1970 and 1984 turned the previous disregard for seasonally arable land into expropriation, and cemented the legal differentiation between uplands and riverside land, as well as between freehold private property (*masajala*), leasehold government property (*matara*) and government-owned property (*mīrī*).[7] The survey mission and the legislative thresholds of the LSRO (1925), the ULA (1970) and the CTA (1984) gave this differentiation its historical reference points: *masajala* were those upland land plots that were demarcated in the survey mission, distinguished into *ashuw* and *sāqiyya*, as well as into *ḥaqq al-aṣl* and *ḥaqq al-miswaq*; *matara masajala* were those upland land plots that were registered before April 1970 according to the LSRO and the Prescription and Limitation Ordinance (PLO) of 1928; *matara mīrī* were registered after April 1970. Most riverside lands would fall under the last category, but were not only mostly below the legal threshold for registration, but

6 Around Dongola, the differentiation of land in reference to the Nile included *jarf* and *satūka*, which are accessible and used during the low Nile level, *sāqiyya* as agricultural area on higher ground and *karū* beyond that (Omer 1985, p. 31).

7 A similar division into fully and individually owned land (*milk*) and collective leasehold of government land (*mīrī*) can be found along the agricultural lands adjacent to the Nile (e.g. Omer 1985, pp. 31–35 on Dongola).

also too unstable for the lengthy bureaucratic process (Mohammed Salih 1999, pp. 112–120).

Legislation thus drew a historical line for land claims, namely registration before 6 April 1970. From a practice-oriented point of view, the primary question is the relevance of those categories for social practices, and it is perceptible that this relevance coincides with the activation of the national court system in the frame of land disputes. Mohammed Salih (1999, pp. 191–196) gives an overview of state institutions potentially involved in local land disputes, and identified village committees and native courts as those institutions where codified and non-codified customary laws can be found to overlap, once disputes are brought beyond quarrels between neighbours and kindred.

"Customary law" does not necessarily denote more or less durability, as its application may be rather conservative or innovative, rather consistent or situational as well; it is the involvement of socially more closely related circles on all sides of the dispute that gives the development and outcome of the process deeper social consequences, and thus a stronger orientation towards immediate social consequences on the part of the judge or mediator. In consequence, a court case beyond such a level will have to fit the legally codified categories, which may include consideration of customary law, while the dispute itself will develop according to socially institutionalized rules and values. The extent to which a specific case involves such rules and values may be limited by how much a legal actor is personally or politically invested in the specific dispute, rather than merely by the institutional level within the court hierarchy.

Beyond the legal land categories outlined above, there are thus numerous additional categories that play a role in how land property is perceived by those laying a claim to it. In the study area, land rights were mostly related to arrangements for land use. Arguably a historical survival from the feudal system under Funj rule (1504–1821), a more or less abstract differentiation of *ḥaqq al-aṣl* and *ḥaqq al-miswaq* has remained in use, where a former feudal land donor (*sīd al-aṣl*) turned into a land owner with all rights, while the designation *sīd al-miswaq* for the land cultivator did not change. In any case, both land titles have been included in the land registration process, with the same rules of transfer and inheritance within one title system, but without a clear definition of the relation between them, as it cannot be captured in terms of rent or lease or tenure. In social practice, the only stable rule seemed to be that the cultivator is the full beneficiary of the crops he or she cultivated, but that a third of the harvest from dates and other wild trees belonged to the owner, who also retained full property rights to the trees. But in fact, the specific sets of rights and duties apportioned to each had many variations, and were combined with further arrangements to form a complex network of rules guiding who benefits how from a piece of land. This includes the right of irrigation (*ḥaqq al-jadwāl*), allowing the extension of an irrigation canal across a plot owned by somebody else; the right over newly formed land (*ḥaqq al-quṣād*), which regulates how reappearing or newly formed land in the river is distributed between owners of adjacent land on the same island or on the riverbanks; *ḥaqq al-mirin*, which divides land expected to temporarily disappear between left bank and right bank land owners; and *mudāyara*, the already mentioned distribution of shares in land according to strips of equal soil quality (Mohammed Salih 1999, pp. 197–206; compare similar arrangements along the Nile in El Mahdi 1976). In many instances, the temporary nature of disappearing or changing riverside lands gave a natural necessity to the flexible application of land rights, but also invited a wide range of land disputes.

On this basis, several restrictions on land alienation can be identified and will be discussed in the following sections.[8] It has to be noted, however, that land sales were almost non-existent in the study area and most transfers of land property took place along the lines of inheritance rules, which were invariably informed by *sharīʿa*. Through Marriage Clerks, District Sharia Courts and the State Sharia Court of Appeal, related disputes were also treated separately in the court system.

The specific rules of inheritance are complicated and have been discussed by Mohammed Salih (1999, pp. 207–220) in detail, also with a specific focus on their role in the widespread problem of land fragmentation (Mohammed Salih 1999, pp. 167–190; Omer 1985, p. 32), which was aggravated by the general scarcity of land. What is relevant at this point is the way exclusion from inheritance already implied the socially practised alienation from land that contradicted nationally and religiously codified inheritance laws.

Inheritance rules explicitly state the right of descendants to parts of the property of a deceased, which implicitly excludes other descendants from such a right. The most obvious example is the preference given to sons and father's brothers over daughters. This legally codified disconnection of daughters from equal shares of their father's land may be bridged through a pre-mortem donation (*hiba*) or a post-mortem will (*waṣiyya*). Among Manāṣīr, such an individual decision was of specific importance, as female heirs and their descendants, in contradiction to Islamic inheritance laws, were customarily disinherited and a legal counter-claim was considered dishonourable (Mohammed Salih

8 One of the restrictions on the possibility of land property transfers is the rule of pre-emption, already codified as national law in the Pre-Emption Ordinance of 1928 and following "a general Islamic principle which aims to prevent involvement of strangers in sales and deals between members of families and co-owners" (Mohammed Salih 1999, p. 82).

1999, pp. 219–220).[9] At the same time, the conscious, even long-term planned integration of inheritance and marriage practices played an important role in the land property regime of the strongly endogamous social groups of the region (Kurt Beck, personal communication 28 August 2016).

In a related present case observed in Kerma, a long-term court case around the largest *sāqiyya* of the area involved, among other claims, the open demand for harvest shares by female descendants against the contention of some male relatives that the former's lack of active involvement in cultivation as well as their economic dependence on their husbands disqualified such a demand (present author's fieldwork in November 2016). This is one of the more subtle notions of alienation from land that may still be significant for an individuals' social situation. In any case, the strong focus on patrilineal preservation of land property added a social value to the legal regulations in this matter.

The complex inheritance laws, which created small land plots with many owners, were in practice complicating or even preventing a consensual sale of land. But even without these complications, the people of the area were not prone to selling land, even in situations of economic hardship, and land registration did not change this; rather the contrary, as Mohammed Salih argues:

> There is no evidence that land sale transactions have increased due to registration or land reforms, even land registration is one of the main obstacles for land sale in the area under study. Selling land requires the presence of all heirs in front of a court to be allotted their land shares according to inheritance law. Any agreement for a sale deal should be formally concluded in front of a court. The system of sharing products of plots rather than the plots themselves is one of the basic challenges to land sales.
>
> MOHAMMED SALIH 1999, P. 104

In a different way, perceiving land property as an individual legal claim on natural resources became a crucial issue regarding compensation for land and other real property that was to be flooded due to dam construction on the Nile. In Dār al-Manāṣīr, the negotiation of such compensation was a very complicated and lengthy process that ultimately gave way to unilateral political

9 The inheritance case analysed by Mohammed Salih (1999, pp. 214–220) showed this to be one of the means by which fragmentation as a result of full compliance with Islamic inheritance laws was circumvented. In the case at hand, a land plot of about 7 feddan would have to be divided among 394 persons, which was brought down to 24 actual land users through a number of "antifragmentation mechanisms".

decision-making by the government (see below); the following passage thus serves here to show that land surveys in the area that may seem organized by legal principles still cannot be adequately grasped without a deeper understanding of their political, economic and social context:

> In 1999, the dam administration conducted a survey of properties and population numbers in the three affected areas. Many peasants perceived this census as a means to raise further taxes. Afraid of raised tax rates, many understated the extent of their properties. Other Manâsîr considered the census as another preliminary study. The peasants were not told the exact purpose of the survey, but the dam administration later declared it to be the basis for compensation payments. But since the survey does not report the true property status among the Manâsîr, and since changes in that regard occurred throughout the following years, all three local groups were to demand a new census later, so as to register the current status of properties, such as land, date palms, houses and further belongings.
>
> HÄNSCH 2012, PP. 210–211

This observation draws attention to the close link between political rule and control over land in different concepts of property, and the importance of this link for the question what constitutes "one's own land" in a wider than a legal sense.

Land Alienation as a Political Issue

The stabilization of power through the regulation of land property is a common feature of nearly all political entities, but there are differences in the intensity and exclusivity of such regulations. The foundational registration process described in the previous section had much to do with the consolidation of early colonial rule through an attempt to appease local elites by way of their economic interests (Serels 2007, p. 59). The areas between the Third and Fourth Cataract were never a focal area of such regulation, due to the absence of large-scale arable land, but they have experienced political intervention through the distribution of land titles in relation to the formation of political alliances (see Mohammed Salih 1999, pp. 59–78, pp. 85–91 for more details).[10] Widespread

10 The owners of waterwheel (*sāqiyya*) land around Kerma experienced the colonial politics of land distribution when the members of the royal family in Argo were given registered

private ownership based on waterwheel irrigation systems had developed out of the land given to politically important religious leaders during Funj rule, and grew under Turkish-Egyptian rule to such an extent that land sales, rent and mortgage were widely known. The Mahdiyya brought some restrictions on rent as an un-Islamic practice, but not on sale, which seems to have been normally practised until the end of the 19th century (Mohammed Salih 1999, p. 90). Up to that point, "[i]ntermarriage between members of the different clans, land sale and mortgage, state intervention, and the introduction of new land allotment systems based on individual ownership of land, have influenced the residence of individual families" (Mohammed Salih 1999, p. 85).

In general, the intensity with which local, regional or larger political processes influenced claims to and control of specific pieces of land has had a significant importance for social practices in this regard. A court case documented by Mohammed Salih (1999, pp. 233–242) shows the intermingling of such political processes with issues of legal pluralism and social conflicts between individuals. The case originates from the 1870s, when Manāṣīr headman Niʿmān wad Qamr married the daughter of the head of the Jaʿal clan, Aḥmad al-Malik Faḍul, Fāṭima. Apart from being married against the will of other Jaʿal members, who feared an increase in Manāṣīr influence on the island of Shirrī, Fāṭima also remained disconnected from Niʿmān's other wives by living with her servants on a separate piece of *sāqiyya* land, granted by her father. After her husband's death, she married his brother, who also died after a few years.

During the land survey, Fāṭima registered *ḥaqq al-aṣl* for herself, nine shares (*ʿaḍum*) of *ḥaqq al-miswaq* as a donation to Niʿmān, the son of her first husband, and three shares for one of her servants; all other descendants and relatives were excluded. After her death in 1933, usage of the house, waterwheel, land and date trees remained in the hands of the son and the servants, but Fāṭima's other legal heirs, demanded their shares in *ḥaqq al-aṣl*, which was refused by the Manāṣīr Native Administration leader on the basis of the fact that no trees were productive at that point. Over the coming decades, the conflict remained on the level of social distance between Fātima's son and his relatives, but in 1972 it broke out between ʿAbullāhi, one of Fāṭima's legal

land plots on unregistered family land to consolidate their rule over this area, which weakens court cases against past expropriation up to today. This was observed during my own fieldwork in Kerma in September and November 2016, where several long-term court cases involving descendants of the royal family were encountered. Supporting evidence was a comparison of the *sāqiyya* map of 1912, which does not show Argo-related property in Kerma, and the *sāqiyya* map of 1929, which does.

heirs, and Niʿmān, following the felling of a tree on the border between the *jarf* land of the former and the *sāqiyya* land of the latter. During local arbitration, the unresolved issue of *ḥaqq al-aṣl* came up again and finally the legal heir activated the Sharia Court and the civil court to claim his inheritance. It took about two years to gather all the required documents and information on legal heirs, many of whom had migrated, followed by another year to organize shares smaller than a quarter *ʿaḍum* into registrable shares. After this update of the land register, ʿAbdullahi continued as representative of the heirs to the civil court, and "asked for one third of the produce of the planted date trees, half of the produce of the wild grown date trees, half of the produce of other fruit trees, and all wood trees" (Mohammed Salih 1999, p. 235), referring to all harvests since 1972. The counter-claim referred to limitations, as 95 years had passed without the claimants asking for their rights.

While the court accepted *ḥaqq al-aṣl* as a legal principle, the cadastre only reproduced what was already known about the state of affairs in 1909, so additional witnesses were requested. This highlighted the limits imposed by an inflexible registration system, aggravated by the practical difficulties in updating and obtaining information from the distant provincial capital, and so the case developed into an anticipated precedent for numerous similar claims. Mohammed Salih reflects the various levels of social involvement of the legal actors in the court:

> The claimant [...] raised a plea of jurisdiction to the court against the defense witnesses as both of them were outmigrants a great deal of their life, describing them as adverse hostile witnesses. Moreover, one of the defense witnesses was a close kin of the defendant. The civil court then asked for fairer defense witnesses. The defendant nominated other two peasants, one of them a Imam of the mosque and the other the head of the native court, who later on refused to give witness. The Imam of the mosque, who was supposed to be a defense witness, gave witness in favor of the claimant [...]. Meanwhile, the defendant appointed a lawyer to follow up the case with the civil court on his behalf. The appointed lawyer was a neighbor of both disputed parties. His involvement in the dispute could be attributed to local politics, while the members of the *Jaʿal* clan were opponents of his brother in the last election of the members of the rural council.
>
> MOHAMMED SALIH 1999, P. 237

At this point, the court started to read the case in the frame of another customary law and re-interpreted *ḥaqq al-aṣl* as a contract of partnership for date tree cultivation (*ʿaqad al-mughārasa* or *al-mushātala*). The relevant difference between them is that the latter, widely used throughout northern Sudan, refers only to the sharing of the produce of the tree between tree owner and land cultivator, with a varying distribution of costs and accordingly of shares in the harvest. In other words, the court removed all basic and registered property rights on the land itself from the *ḥaqq al-aṣl* holder, probably due to the lack of economic consequences of such rights, and reduced it to an argument over harvested crops and the distinction between original and newly planted trees.

In both cases, though, the claimants had no further right to enter the contested land property. When both the Appeal Court and the Supreme Court confirmed the verdict in 1994 and in 1995, respectively, what remained was over twenty years of embittered legal dispute that had not ended the social dispute. The defendant pointed out in an interview that the restriction on the claimants' physical entry onto his land was preventing them from verifying what production actually occurred on it, and the inimical way the case went would certainly not incline him to be honest about it. In the end, "[t]here is no customary law nor statutory rule that regulates ways and times of harvesting date trees" (Mohammed Salih 1999, p. 240).

As Mohammed Salih also notes, the political aspect of this dispute lay in the selective way claims were made, as no party to it took issue with the servant's piece of land. Moreover, for most of those involved there was no question of economic interest, but rather "a kind of moral obligation to support a kin in conflict with a rival group" (Mohammed Salih 1999, p. 241). In other words, what was interpreted by the court as a conflict over tree produce and subsequently legally reduced to that, had much more to do with status group formation and the role land titles play in it, which makes land alienation by the *de iure* loss of title a *de facto* loss of status.[11]

If such a demarcation of group boundaries through land titles remained of significant importance up to the 1990s, the complete loss of land, even if compensated according to some definition of equivalence, can thus not be regarded as insignificant for group existence. What set Jaʿal against Manāṣīr in the cited case, confronted the whole population of the area with the national government when the dam construction at the Fourth Nile Cataract was initiated.

By now, resistance to stark transformations of landscapes through dam construction has become one of the most urgent political issues in the Nile Valley north of Khartoum (e.g. Hashim 2010; Abd Elkreem 2016). Accordingly, the empowerment of the government agency implementing such transformations,

11 A further case detailed by Mohammed Salih (1999, pp. 242–256) illustrates an even wider involvement of competition for political status in a land dispute.

the Dam Implementation Unit (DIU), has been a priority of the present regime, and the militant security apparatus built into the unit is a clear expression of how resistance was planned to be met if other means fail (see e.g. Verhoeven 2015, pp. 143, 192–194). The political struggles and the human rights violations that occurred during and after the construction of the dam have been well-documented (e.g. Hildyard 2008; Hänsch 2012, Dirar et al. 2015), so it is even more important here to highlight the intertwining of legal and political processes that took place.

The general legal basis of expropriation for the purpose of state projects had been built into previous land legislation and was strengthened by a number of investment laws and regulations (e.g., Investment Encouragement Act 1999, amended 2000, 2003, 2007; Investment Encouragement Act 2013). One of the central tools for avoiding lengthy processes around such expropriations was the presidential decree. In the case of the dam at the Fourth Nile Cataract, the legal basis was provided early on through a law on resettlement and compensation passed by the National Assembly on 27 November 2002, legitimized by Presidential Decree No. 353 of 27 September 2002. An earlier decree, No. 78 of 2001, had appointed the head of the Merowe Dam Project Implementation Unit (later the DIU) as Minister of State at the Ministry of Irrigation, followed by Presidential Decree No. 363 of 2001, which put the President at the head of the High Political Committee formed in 1993 to initiate the dam construction and administration. The final say on compensation was set out in By-Law No. 2 in February 2003. In a final step, Presidential Decree No. 277 of 2003 gave the land property rights of all resettlement areas, defined in By-Law No. 1, to the dam administration, which would thus become the landlord to the resettled tenants (Hänsch 2012, pp. 211–212).

This legalization by presidential authority went parallel to and devaluated negotiations with residents' representatives. It is important to point out that the main focus of Manāṣīr resistance was initially not the fact of expropriation, compensation and resettlement, but the way a consensual agreement was prevented from being made before construction and the violent suppression of resistance started (see also Dirar et al. 2015, p. 86). Technical committees established to formulate the basis of compensation were dominated by government representatives, and residents' disagreement was thus rendered indecisive. Final rates, such as 500 SDG per date palm, were insignificant compared with the value of even one year's harvest (Hänsch 2012, p. 212), and flooding started well before an agreement had been reached, hitting an unprepared population (Hänsch 2012, pp. 182–193). This process also alienated many previous NCP supporters among the Manāṣīr, who "were no longer willing to accept the ongoing abuse of their legal rights", but nevertheless "rejected the option of alliances with political parties to gain extra support, as they wanted to prevent the politicisation of the negotiation for their rights" (Hänsch 2012, p. 214). The sudden full force of coercive state power experienced during the flooding was an unprecedented event and "profoundly shattered the Manâsîr self-image as loyal Sudanese citizens pursuing a rightful claim" (Hänsch 2012, p. 211).[12]

This is not an isolated case of a specific negotiation between governmental organs and citizens, but reflects the entrenched entanglement of political economy and the legal system, which feeds mistrust in the independence of the latter.[13] The economic context of land alienation is thus strongly interconnected with its legal and political conditions.

Land Alienation as an Economic Issue

The obstacles to selling land and the political processes outlined in the previous two sections hint at the importance of usage rights, which far outrank a notion of original ownership when it comes to economic practices, i.e., the way land use is socially and politically organized.

It has been noted that the early registration process created a class of land that "has been, not only economically valuable, but a prestigious asset, and hence protected from any intrusion by strangers or relatives who were dispossessed" (Omer 1985, p. 32); as of 2007, 54% of cultivated land in the Dongola area still fell in this category (Fragaszy and Closas 2016, p. 145). At the same time, the notion that land should be made available to those who were willing and able to cultivate was important to the colonial capitalist projects, and has

12 Apart from the legal pathways created by presidential decrees, existing legislation, such as, for example, the legal procedures stipulated in the Environmental Protection Act of 2001 for the review of Environmental Impact Assessments, was also simply by-passed (Ahmed 2012, pp. 260–261; Dirar et al. 2015, pp. 95–96). One successful legal action against the National Information and Security Service in 2007 had only a limited impact on the overall struggle, as it merely achieved the release of seven members of the Manāṣīr Executive Committee, who had been detained for more than two months without charge. A new agreement between the Nile State and the committee that followed the court's decision was simply ignored and flooding commenced regardless (Dirar et al. 2015, p. 42; Hänsch 2012, pp. 220–221).

13 This is also reflected in the reaction to a perceived increase in date palm fires throughout northern Sudan after 2006, which have been frequently identified by local inhabitants and anti-dam activists as a deliberate attempt by the Sudanese government to reduce the presence of people to be resettled and of real property for which compensation would be required.

remained so after Independence. The requirement to use land is not an exclusively capitalist concept, however, and can be argued to represent the consensus in Islamic scholarship as well, connected to the state's "powers to alienate use of the land to deserving grantees" (Sait and Lim 2006, p. 62). According to the CTA, land belongs fundamentally to God, while the state acts as God's representative, and this understanding informs several laws based on Islamic principles, arguably making land both a general social responsibility and open to individual ownership (Sait and Lim 2006, pp. 61–62).

As has been noted, the land rights system among Manāṣīr allowed both for a general land title and a separate title for land users, without imposing on the latter the status of tenant or leaseholder. The latter category was introduced by national legislation, and with the laws of 1925, 1970 and 1984, all driven by a similar intention to empower state-supported development projects. The possibility of general expropriation was constantly in view and became a reality at the beginning of the 21st century.

Between land registration and resettlement, the area had experienced a development of economic practices by which individual or group control over relatively small pieces of land as a means of production was of changing, but unceasing importance. The basic conditions dominating these practices were land scarcity and land fragmentation, which are both a consequence of and a reaction to close-knit communities of land users. Such communities were, however, far from clear-cut economic units, and close observation was necessary to distinguish the relationship between family as nuclear kin, *usra* as an extended kin group, *bayt* (house) as a group sharing a residence, and household as a group sharing property, production and consumption. Polygamy and a high level of individual mobility, especially of young men, increased this complexity further (Mohammed Salih 1999, pp. 15–19; on patterns of outmigration see Beck 1999).

The approximately 50,000 Manāṣīr reported as displaced by the dam had shared a challenging physical setting, "a rocky cataract zone with narrow strips of arable land along the river banks" (Mohammed Salih 1999, p. 23, see maps pp. 25–30),[14] and Mohammed Salih (1999, p. 37) makes the observation that "the importance of land, kinship ties and kinship networks in the village is that these things together make the community".

While land distribution, together with the registration of alms receivers, was one of the indicators of the general socio-economic status of a household,

14 Several visualizations of the structure of agriculture in this area have been produced in recent years, among them in Ritter 2012 and at http://www2.hu-berlin.de/aknoa/hune/hune.htm.

income was much more affected by remittances, off-farm activities, trade and livestock production (Mohammed Salih 1999, p. 43). This made land a communal rather than an individual matter of survival. In fact, like the adjustment of inheritance rules, the economic imperative to keep land of usable size close to the community can be seen in the practical circumvention of the Islamic-informed rule of prescription (*waḍʿ al-yad*). The rule was acknowledged and codified in the 1928 Prescription and Limitation Ordinance, which specified that ten years of peaceable, public and uninterrupted possession would result in an undisputed right of ownership. However, nominal land rents (*al-rasan*) were used to prevent the application of this rule (Mohammed Salih 1999, p. 204). At the same time, as a lengthy process documented by Mohammed Salih (1999, pp. 242–251) shows, the constant requirement to make new land arable rendered entrepreneurial initiatives to extend land ownership by clearing land, building a house or planting trees a regular application of the prescription rule, and this application was supported by state government law, state officials and civil courts.

In contrast to the presumption that a strong status of communal land rights prevents initiative and entrepreneurship, a look at the social history of irrigation systems in the area shows the importance of flexible cultivation methods and technological adjustment. Apart from land scarcity and fragmentation resulting from inheritance being the only way of ownership transmission, the Nile Valley economy north of Khartoum is based on the essential irrigation of all uplands. Prior to the introduction of diesel-powered water pumps, waterwheel irrigation (*sāqiyya*), as generally used along the Nile, led to land users being organized into a complex system of interrelated functions, which has been thoroughly analysed by Kurt Beck (2012).

The most relevant implication of this system is that the *sāqiyya* was connected to a specific relation of production to sharecropping (*taddān*), and "[e]very participant in the production process was entitled to a certain proportion of the harvest" (Beck 2012, p. 18). This is part of a relational economy with "two or more partners combining their resources for some productive purpose and sharing the gains in prearranged mutually agreed proportions" (Beck 2003, p. 154). This specific partnership, in spite of inevitable power asymmetries, is much more the result of a negotiation of an arrangement that relates interdependent parties to each other, in contrast, for instance, to simple contract farming or land-rent. This interdependence is also implemented through the proportional distribution of harvests, which reduces the problem of supervision and thus the need for subordination, since any success or failure in cultivation will be shouldered by all the parties involved (Beck 2003, pp. 158–159).

In Manāṣīr agriculture, there were, apart from the land title holder: the person driving the animals (*awrattī*); the owner of the animals (*sīd al-baqqar*); and the workers (*tarābla*, sing. *turbāl*), "whose tasks were hacking, sowing, planting and directing water into the planting beds" (Beck 2012, p. 18). In the rather unusual case that the owner of the waterwheel (*sīd al-dawlāb*) was not the land title holder, a lease was to be paid as well, but the main channel (*al-jadwal al-dakar*) and possibly the waterwheel construction were a communal effort, if not delegated to a skilled master (*uṣṭa* or *baṣīr*).

The economic crisis that occurred in the 1940s and 1950s, to a high degree attributed to the limitations of the waterwheel technology, paved the way for the slow acceptance of diesel-powered pumps as a feasible alternative (Beck 2012, pp. 25–32). While Elfeil (1988) continued to argue that the animal drawn *sāqiyya* as still used in Egypt at that time would be a more appropriate technology, partly because of the shortage of fuel and electricity in the 1970s, the diesel-powered water pump had prevailed by the 1990s. The existence and extension of *sāqiyya* land usage had always been subject to the means available for irrigation. The decision to return from migration, for instance, depended very much on a man's access to enough land to irrigate and cultivate, in order to compensate for his loss of income as labourer in the towns; at the same time, a wife and children might still be living in the rural area, as part of a multi-sited household (Beck 1999, p. 206). Therefore, the significant increase in the amount of water drawn by the new technology also extended the land that could be activated for cultivation.

The organizational principle of waterwheel irrigation seemed to be reproduced – *sīd al-baqqar* became pump owner (*sīd al-bābūr*); the *baṣīr* became mechanic or engineer (*muhandis*); the *awrattī* became driver (*sawwāq*) but the early investment in pumps by some land title holders and not others created an economic disparity, which caused disputes over harvest distribution (Beck 2012, pp. 33–35). Instead of leading to capitalist class formation, however, the collective ownership in the means of production was also applied to the diesel-powered pumps, and social stratification was actively prevented by keeping irrigation below the levels technically possible in favour of participatory production (Beck 2012, pp. 35–37).

On this basis, land alienation during resettlement could be read as an issue of control over means of production, which, especially concerning the control over water, was passed from individual farmers to the distant administration in new irrigation schemes. In fact, there were two different lines of resettlement, which represent different responses to this prospect of reduced autonomy in production. The first was compliance with the by-laws by moving to the designated resettlement schemes (see Dirar et al. 2015, pp. 31–38, pp. 65–70 for a review of the compensation and resettlement process).[15] The al-Mukābrāb Agricultural Project (*mashrūʿ al-mukābrāb al-zirāʿī*) was set up as part of the ed-Damer Food Security Pump Scheme, well beyond the Fifth Nile Cataract, which also includes several domestic and foreign investment projects (Calkins 2012, pp. 233–238); the irrigation system was based on a main channel 24 km from the Nile and two sub-channels for plots of six acres each (Sayed 2007, p. 49; see also Hänsch 2012, pp. 221–222 fn 96). The scheme led not only to a far-reaching reorganization of agricultural production, but also to the cessation of a wide range of off-farm activities, among them gold washing, herding at the river bank and various handicrafts connected to the manifold use of the date palm (Mohammed Salih 1999, p. 49). The resettlement can thus also be interpreted as a multi-faceted transformation process that involves "expanding mechanisation along with controlling wage-labour relations" (Hoffmann 2013, p. 178).[16]

The second line was a successive reluctant retreat from the approaching flood, supported by an initial interpretation that it was an extreme form of the annual Nile flood (*damīra*), owing to a lack of official information about the real situation (Hänsch 2012, p. 184). This interpretation was "in stark contrast to the rational resettlement economy of recent years" (Hänsch 2012, p. 187), but related to on-going negotiations with the Nile State for resettlement close to the new reservoir and disbelief at the "total and deliberate destruction of the taken for granted, the home" (Hänsch 2012, p. 187). After the experience of being made refugees by their own government, this disbelief shifted to active self-organization, but the organizational principles guiding economic activities before had given way to a life of uncertainty (*ḥayya mujahjaha*), settlements became camps, and self-reliant food production became food aid or sharecropping (Hänsch 2012, p. 187, p. 194).

Concrete developments in the various areas have still to be followed up,[17] especially concerning changes to the intricate arrangements of land ownership

15 This compliance did not save from mistreatment however, as the houses of those agreeing to go to the resettlement schemes were flooded before they could move their belongings as well (Hänsch 2012, p. 186).

16 Calkins (2012, p. 237) points out that the Manāṣīr scheme itself created land alienation, which was unequally recompensed by the government, which acknowledged Jaʿaliyyīn farmers, but disregarded groups like the Rashaida of Tukna, who had no land titles, but potential prescription rights from long-term usage by cultivation.

17 UNEP (2007, p. 230) points out, for instance, that food production in many previous schemes was well below expectation, as they often involved low fertility soils, and that the net gain in food production has to be closely followed. A significant effort in this direction has been made by Valerie Hänsch in her PhD thesis (2016).

and sharecropping in Dār al-Manāṣīr, but it is in any case important to note that these arrangements represented what can arguably be described as "contractual solidarity" (Beck 2003, p. 168). This does not only point to the important question of how to organize labour in a situation of land and workforce scarcity, i.e., an economic imperative of practicality rather than a mere legal and socio-economic distinction of land-ownership status. It also implies that the social relations established for and confirmed by arrangements of land usage can become an important, if not intrinsic part of the value of land. In this and other cases, land usage becomes an expression and functional part of a social status quo.

This extends the concept of alienation from a legalized commercial exchange and divisive tool of political economy to a process of social change. The actual or threatened resettlement in the study area is once again a good example, though, to show that even such an extension fails to grasp significant elements of social practice, especially the complexity of individual actions and standpoints. Aspects such as the tendency to self-organization, the reluctance to sell land and resistance to resettlement also relate to values that imply a notion of moral alienation, which is the issue discussed in the final section, below.

Land Alienation as a Moral Issue

> All people in the area are extremely keen to retain their land even if they reside in towns. Consideration of the social value of land in the area dominates all other aspects of land. Sale of land is shameful and rare. There is not one single case of land sale reported in the last 20 years.
>
> MOHAMMED SALIH 1999, P. 104

An explanation for this antipathy towards selling land may follow from the observation that "land is not a simple commodity, but rather a complex material asset embedded in the society and interwoven with non-economic aspects of life" (Mohammed Salih 1999, p. 120). Attachment to land can then be interpreted as an anthropogeographic constant that glues a specific group of humans to a specific territory, and accordingly "the links between territory and identity are deeply entrenched and the loss of the former poses clear symbolic threats to the latter" (Dirar et al. 2015, p. 105). It has been pointed out by Kurt Beck, though, that this attachment, while not exclusively rational, i.e., void of emotional content, was a matter of choice in a society where migration is common, "a deliberate choice in favour of the riverside lifestyle within a stable community [...] that is certainly also marked by the absence of major class distinctions and thus promises a dignified life according to their own ideals, at arm's length from the impositions of state authority and urbanism" (Beck 2012, p. 7). In other words, it carries the ideals of close relationships and relative autonomy embedded in the term "homeland".[18]

Accordingly, an exclusively economic assessment of the advantages and disadvantages of land alienation lacks a basic feeling for the social values at play here. Those values can also be found to extend to other assets. The existence of date palms on the narrow patches of land, for instance, made them both a marker and essential part of communal ownership, as their inter-generational presence and their inclusion in the property system and inheritance closely connected them to land and people (Mohammed Salih 1999, pp. 47–49), in addition to their essential importance in Manāṣīr's material and nonmaterial culture (Haberlah 2012). This made their 'compensation' a basically flawed search for monetary equivalents, and a breach of the previous "inconceivability of selling palm trees" (Haberlah 2012, p. 54).[19]

At the same time, the relation to the land was an ambiguous one, ranging from glorification as a seat of one's honour, to a questioning of its real economic value, to the attribution of all major conflicts in Manāṣīr society to disputes over it (Mohammed Salih 1999, pp. 106–107). Accordingly, Mohammed Salih (1999, pp. 229–232) also highlights what was called *kujjār*, harmful methods used during disputes simply for the sake of damaging to the opponent. This ambiguousness was clearly intensified when different parts of the population, sometimes within families, took different routes after being confronted with the offer – or threat – of resettlement away from their home areas. The whole process did not only produce alienation from the national legal and political system, as well as an ultimate alienation from land that had been the basis of economic existence and self-identification for many generations. It also created a deep fracture in Manāṣīr society.

18 Among the verbal expressions of such values noted by David Haberlah are "exceptional safety and honesty (*fī 'amān*), tranquility (*al-jaww hādi' wa naẓīf*), untainted beauty of their country (*al-balad simiḥ*)" (see https://en.wikipedia.org/wiki/Dar_al-Manasir). The description of the area as hard to cultivate and poverty-stricken, but of visual beauty can already be found in a travel report by H.C. Jackson, who noted that "the natives still have a very real affection for their ancestral homes" (Jackson 1926, p. 9). Similar expressions have been noted by Innes (1931, p. 184); Kurt Beck (1999, p. 202) adds further examples.

19 A further example is food, as "[t]he production of their own food is given top priority among the settled people. Selling from one's own food stock for any reason is considered to be dishonorable" (Mohammed Salih 1999, p. 52).

Positioning with regard to resettlement was a complicated process, because its clear advantages were also identified.[20] Many Manāṣīr women of Kirbekān, for instance, were found to expect better access to educational services, especially for their daughters, much better health services and easier access to water for the household. At the same time, the loss of riverside land also meant the loss of a range of economic activities, such as gold washing and small livestock herding, which would remove a source of income and thus economic influence. This loss of status was also seen in the stronger control by the Islamic government in the new areas, with a reduction of public roles that had already set in before the resettlement. However, the same state control also increased the chance of full implementation of Islamic inheritance rules, which had been reduced to their disadvantage before (Weschenfelder 2012, pp. 84–86).

Accordingly, it has been highlighted repeatedly that the point of contention was not resettlement itself, but the modalities of resettlement. Those rejecting the modalities that the dam administration tried to enforce stressed partnership and participation as a value of self-organized inclusion in the modernization process (Beck 2012, pp. 41–44). Fractures appeared when some accepted conditions that others found inadequate or blatantly insulting, and these fractures led to significant social alienation.

It has been pointed out that the development of alliances and hostilities between Manāṣīr in these matters was complex and not reduced to the issue of compensation; the interests of the political elite and other socio-political and socio-economic aspects played an essential role as well (Hänsch 2012, p. 213). It was, however, when the first compensation payments were accepted that social conflicts and mistrust escalated and, amidst a radicalization of stances, those who agreed to be resettled on the dam administration's conditions, even if they belonged to one's own nuclear family, were called "traitors" and ostracized (Hänsch 2012, p. 220). The fight for survival and many acts of solidarity during the flooding strengthened this differentiation of those who stayed from those who left.

The intensity of this split was stronger among those going for the "local option", remaining close to the flooded areas of the homeland, and they used the term *karazayāt* (those of / like Karsai) in reference to the US-dominated president of Afghanistan, expressing the sense of being betrayed by those who allowed government incentives to weaken their resistance. This developed into

20 Beck (1997) had already argued in the 1990s that support for resettlement "was particularly common among the landless and among young men who wanted to escape the land shortage and reckoned that resettlement would entail the distribution of land" (Hänsch 2012, pp. 207–208 fn 55).

a militant group, the Fallujah, who demolished the houses left by the resettled people (Dirar et al. 2015, pp. 82–83). This break in relations was also followed by exclusion from customary entitlements to land, and although a recent improvement in relations has been observed, it shows that land rights continued to be used in drawing social boundaries (Dirar et al. 2015, pp. 71–73).

Finally, tensions could also be felt by researchers visiting the area. For instance, a research team in Kirbekān was confronted with concerns that their questions about the economic activities of women were an attempt to "get census dates [sic] to evaluate the compensations claims of the villagers" (Weschenfelder 2012, p. 77). A much more sustained problem was faced by archaeological teams. Coming with a government concession to do rescue archaeology, their activities were perceived as closely linked to the "wrapping-up" of settlement in the area, and they were eventually expelled by the Manāṣīr Executive Committee (Näser and Kleinitz 2012; see Ahmed 2012 for the general developments around rescue archaeology in Sudan).[21]

In spite of a strong "cultural tradition" of male migration among Manāṣīr, the fear of alienation from home had already been a constant issue (Beck 1999, p. 207). This fear had substantial reasons, as "[f]or a country boy the good things in life – money, meat, sweetness, cinema, sex, the excitement of urban life, the permissiveness of anonymity and the dream of personal success – are all situated outside their home *saqiya*" (Beck 1999, p. 208) – only later migration turns into a narrative of economic necessity, in the course of "generation-specific worldviews" (Beck 1999, p. 209). But in contrast to this cyclical dynamic of migration and return, resettlement threatened irreversible changes:

> Having lost their established agricultural lifestyle, the Manâsîr are increasingly questioning their identity as irrigation peasants. Their unsettled lifestyle is compared with that of nomads who own no land and lead an impoverished existence in the desert. The lifestyle of riverside agriculture, desirable in Manâsîr eyes, is losing its situational frame of

---

21 A reflection by one of the involved archaeologists afterwards was the recognition how "alien" the main target of the "rescue", namely pre-Islamic sites, were to the contemporary sense of heritage among Manāṣīr, who could only relate to local sites of *baniyyāt*, manifestations of Muslim saints (Näser and Kleinitz 2012, pp. 282–284). Another aspect is that archaeological concessions as centralized state tools to temporarily remove control over specific and large-scale tracts of land is not too different from other instances of temporary or permanent expropriation for investment and development purposes (Calkins and Ille 2014).

> action and consequently the frame of reference for identity construction is being challenged.
>
> HÄNSCH 2012, P. 198

The forced migration (*hijra qasriyya*) brought about by the government's oppressive approach was thus seen as an act of injustice and immorality,[22] as it used the alienation of land and people to break resistance to its own political agenda, notwithstanding its consequences for the former residents' social life.

These processes are, however, not limited to Dār al-Manāṣīr and the adjacent areas affected by the Merowe Dam resettlement. Apart from the extensive ecological effects of the dam, plans for additional dams at the Third (Kajbar) and the Second (Dal) Nile Cataract have made the complex threat of "being drowned" (*al-gharīg*) a ubiquitous issue in the north-Sudanese Nile Valley, part of which has at the same time recently acquired significant economic importance as the site of gold mines and large-scale irrigation schemes. Resistance to the dams and resettlement in these areas appears to be much unidirectional, consolidated and well-organized, but it also forms part of several dynamics of social change affected, for instance, by migration, agricultural mechanization, urbanization and, increasingly, environmental pollution, all of which are inscribed in different ways into land and the values it holds.

Conclusion

This chapter has argued that land alienation in Sudan, as the process by which someone's land ceases to be someone's land, cannot be adequately understood through purely legalistic approaches, but also needs to grasp the political, economic and moral aspects that shape it. While this can also be shown, for instance, through a focus on current urban land grabs or large-scale expropriation for agricultural investment schemes, this article has illustrated the

22 Notions of justice used during the resistance have been analysed in Dirar et al. (2015, pp. 100–105). A further aspect is the importance of international notions of justice, although they had limited direct impact on local political action. However, the whole process involved a significant number of international actors (see overview in Dirar et al. 2015, pp. 88, 91, 94–95) and a number of international responses and legal actions have been initiated (Dirar et al. 2015, pp. 43–47), with very limited results. A court case against the consultant firm Lahmeyer International was brought by flood victims at a German court in May 2010. In April 2016, the prosecutors finished investigations with the conclusion of no intent; further legal action is in preparation (https://www.ecchr.eu/en/our_work/business-and-human-rights/lahmeyer-case.html).

argument through a case study from northern Sudan, where land sales – the conventional focus of the legal concept "land alienation" – were rare, but politically enforced, economically damaging and morally appalling. Land alienation took and potentially will take place in the form of forceful displacement by flooding for hydroelectric power dams.

The article started with a review of land legislation, where land alienation was clearly defined in terms of authority and procedure. Its insufficient recognition of social, political and economic history, however, was shown through the short-comings of land surveys at the beginning of the 20th century that attempted to demarcate a status quo for land registration. Although categories used for land registration incorporated some social legal practices, the technical implementation overrode much of its actual complexity, and political favouritism influenced this "technical" process and thereby legalized contested claims to control over land, as highlighted through a specific court case. A look at survey activities before the implementation of the Merowe Dam at the end of the 20th century indicated that political strategies still had a strong influence on how they were conducted and used.

This latter aspect came to the fore during a review of the resettlement process, which was accompanied by situational legalization through presidential decrees, which in effect disenfranchised ongoing negotiations with the citizens of the areas to be flooded. In addition to this authoritarian nature of government-citizen relations, a more intensive look at the social relations at play in previous land use clarified that the negotiation was not just about equivalence of compensation, in the form of land plots elsewhere, but touched issues of communality and social change at large. Social friction between individuals and groups taking different decisions in face of the given options confirmed that basic questions of belonging and moral judgements were at stake.

In consequence, a practice-oriented approach to social legal practices was proposed to provide a complementary reading of the strong interconnections between the legal, political, economic and moral aspects of land alienation in the study area and beyond. The lack of clear explanatory models emerging from the given ethnographic account indicates that such an approach will not result in the clear-cut conclusions of factor analysis or other variable-based approaches. However, contingent effects resulting from these interconnections seem not to be so easily "tamed" as more unambiguous approaches suggest.

Not least, such an approach resists the lure of official accounts that attempt to depict land alienation as a regular legal process, to which only backward enemies of development will object. The construction of "the peasant communities near the Fourth Nile Cataract as primitive, traditionalist and opposed to innovation" (Beck 2012, p. 5) had been at the basis of the public campaign for the dam; the resettlement areas represented, accordingly, "the whole array of civilised achievements that distinguish barbarism from modernity" (Beck 2012, p. 6, see also Hänsch 2012, pp. 179–180).[23] Critical ethnographic inquiries very clearly support a strong and well-founded refutation of such accounts.

References

Abd Elkreem, T 2016, 'Power Relations of Development. The Case of Dam Construction in the Nubian Homeland, Sudan', Unpublished doctoral thesis in Anthropology, University of Bayreuth, Bayreuth.

Ahmed, KA 2012, 'From Dam to Dam. Encounter at the Cataracts', in C Kleinitz & C Näser (eds), "Nihna nâs al-bahar – *We Are the People of the River." Ethnographic Research in the Fourth Nile Cataract Region, Sudan*, Harrassowitz Verlag, Wiesbaden, pp. 253–268.

Babiker, M 2008, *Communal Land Rights and Peace-building in North Kordofan. Policy and Legislative Challenges*, Sudan Working Paper no. 3, Chr. Michelsen Institute, Bergen.

Beck, K 1997, 'Die Verbäuerlichung der Bank – Oder. Von den Niltalbauern lernen', in M Schulz (ed.), *Entwicklung. Theorie – Empirie – Strategie*, Lit, Hamburg, pp. 81–98.

Beck, K 1999, 'Escaping from Narrow Confines – Returning to Tight Communities. Manasir Labour Migration from the Area of the Fourth Cataract', in P Hahn & G Spittler (eds), *Afrika und die Globalisierung*, Lit, Hamburg, pp. 201–211.

Beck, K 2003, '"Livelihood Is Agreement". Sharecropping among the Manasir of the Nile Valley', in H d'Almeida-Topor, M Lakroum & G Spittler (eds), *Le travail en Afrique noire. Représentations et pratiques à l'époque contemporaine*, Karthala, Paris, pp. 153–169.

Beck, K 2012, 'Crisis, Innovation and the Social Domestication of the New: One Century of Manâsîr Social History', in C Kleinitz & C Näser (eds), "Nihna nâs al-bahar – *We Are the People of the River." Ethnographic Research in the Fourth Nile Cataract Region, Sudan*, Harrassowitz Verlag, Wiesbaden, pp. 5–48.

Calkins, S 2012, 'Agricultural Encroachment in Wadi Mukabrab Area. Policies of Recompense, Differentiation and "Tribal" Belonging', in C Kleinitz & C Näser (eds), "Nihna nâs al-bahar – *We Are the People of the River." Ethnographic Research in the Fourth Nile Cataract Region, Sudan*, Harrassowitz Verlag, Wiesbaden, pp. 229–252.

23 In fact, the areas had been neglected by "modern" public services, and requests for government support had long been ignored (Mohammed Salih 1999, p. 35), making these derisive statements the more cynical.

Calkins, S & Ille, E 2014, 'Territorities of Gold Mining. International Investment and Artisanal Extraction in Sudan', in J Gertel, R Rottenburg & S Calkins (eds), *Disrupting Territories. Land, Commodification and Conflict in Sudan*, James Currey, Woodbridge, pp. 52–76.

Calkins, S, Ille, E, Lamoureaux, S & Rottenburg, R 2015, 'Rethinking Institutional Orders in Sudan Studies. The Case of Land Access in Kordofan, Blue Nile and Darfur', *Canadian Journal of African Studies*, vol. 49, no. 1, pp. 175–195.

Dirar, A, El Moghraby, A, Jalal Hashim, M & Zeitoun, M 2015, *Displacement and Resistance Induced by the Merowe Dam. The Influence of International Norms and Justice.* (DEV Report and Policy Paper 12), School of International Development, University of East Anglia, Norwich.

Elfeil, Mohamed AAR 1988, 'Transfer and Adoption of the Egyptian Improved "Sagiya" in the Northern and Khartoum Provinces of Sudan', MSc thesis, Department of Agricultural Economics, Michigan State University.

El Hadary, YAE, & Obeng-Odoom, F 2012, 'Conventions, Changes, and Contradictions in Land Governance in Africa: The Story of Land Grabbing in North Sudan and Ghana', *Africa Today*, vol. 52, no. 2, pp. 58–78.

El Mahdi, SMA El 1976, 'Some General Principles of Acquisition of Ownership of and Rights over Land by Customary Prescription in the Sudan', *Journal of African Law*, vol. 20, no. 2, pp. 79–99.

El Mahdi, SMA 1977, 'Limitations on the Ownership of Land in the Sudan', *Sudan Notes and Records* vol. 58, pp. 152–158.

Fragaszy, S & Closas, A 2016, 'Cultivating the Desert: Irrigation Expansion and Groundwater Abstraction in Northern State, Sudan', *Water Alternatives*, vol. 9, no. 1, pp. 139–161.

Gertel, J, Rottenburg, R & Calkins, S (eds) 2014, *Disrupting Territories. Land, Commodification and Conflict in Sudan*, James Currey, Woodbridge.

Gordon, CN 1986, 'Recent Developments in the Land Law of the Sudan. A Legislative Analysis', *Journal of African Law*, vol. 30, no. 2, pp. 143–174.

Haberlah, D 2012, 'Cultural Landscape of Dar al-Manasir', in C Kleinitz & C Näser (eds), "Nihna nâs al-bahar – *We Are the People of the River." Ethnographic Research in the Fourth Nile Cataract Region, Sudan*, Harrassowitz Verlag, Wiesbaden, pp 49–74.

Hailwood, SA 2015, *Alienation and Nature in Environmental Philosophy*, Cambridge University Press, Cambridge.

Hänsch, V 2012, 'Chronology of a Displacement. The Drowning of the Manâsîr People', in C Kleinitz & C Näser (eds), "Nihna nâs al-bahar – *We Are the People of the River." Ethnographic Research in the Fourth Nile Cataract Region, Sudan*, Harrassowitz Verlag, Wiesbaden, pp. 179–228.

Hänsch, V 2016, 'Der Versuch zu bleiben. Dammbau und Krise im sudanesischen Niltal', Unpublished doctoral thesis in Anthropology, University of Bayreuth, Bayreuth.

Hashim, MJ 2010, 'The Dams of Northern Sudan and the Policy of Demographic Engineering', *International Journal of African Renaissance Studies*, vol. 5, no. 1, pp. 148–160.

Hildyard, N 2008, 'Neutral? Against What? Bystanders and Human Rights Abuses. The Case of Merowe Dam', *Sudan Studies*, vol. 37, pp. 19–38.

Hoffmann, C 2013, 'The Contradictions of Development. Primitive Accumulation and Geopolitics in the Two Sudans', in T Allan, M Keulertz, S Sojamo & J Warner (eds), *Handbook of Land and Water Grabs in Africa. Foreign Direct Investment aFood and Water Security*, Routledge, London/New York, pp. 167–201.

Ille, E & Calkins, S 2013, 'Gold Mining Concessions in Sudan's Written Laws, and Practices of Gold Extraction in the Nuba Mountains', in E Grawert (ed.), *Forging Two Nations. Insights on Sudan and South Sudan*, OSSREA / BICC, Addis Ababa / Bonn, pp. 112–126.

Innes, N McL 1931, 'The Monasir Country', *Sudan Notes and Records*, vol. 14, no. 2, pp. 185–190.

Jackson, HC 1926, 'A Trek in Abu Hamed District', *Sudan Notes and Records*, vol. 9, no. 2, pp. 1–35.

Komey, GK 2010, *Land, Governance, Conflict and the Nuba of Sudan*, James Currey, Woodbridge and Rochester.

Lentz, C 2010, 'Is Land Alienable? Historical and Current Debates on Land Transfers in Northern Ghana', *Africa*, vol. 80, no. 1, pp. 56–80.

Miller, C (ed.) 2005, *Land, Ethnicity and Political Legitimacy in Eastern Sudan*, CEDEJ/DSRC, Cairo/Khartoum.

Mohamed Salih, MA 1998, 'Land Alienation and Genocide in the Nuba Mountains, Sudan', *Cultural Survival Quarterly*, vol. 22, no. 4, pp. 36–38.

Mohammed Salih, MA 1999, *The Manasir of Northern Sudan. Land and People*, Rüdiger Köppe Verlag, Köln.

Näser, C & Kleinitz, C 2012 'The Good, the Bad and the Ugly. A Case Study on the Policisation of Archaeology and Its Consequences from Northern Sudan', in C Kleinitz & C Näser (eds.), "Nihna nâs al-bahar – *We Are the People of the River." Ethnographic Research in the Fourth Nile Cataract Region, Sudan*, Harrassowitz Verlag, Wiesbaden, pp. 269–304.

Olwig, KR 2005, 'Representation and Alienation in the Political Land-scape', *Cultural Geographies*, vol. 12, pp. 19–40.

Omer, El Haj Bilal O 1985, *The DanaglaTtraders of Northern Sudan. Rural Capitalism and Agricultural Development*, Ithaca Press, London.

Pantulliano, S 2007, *The Land Question. Sudan's Peace Nemesis.* (HPG Working Paper), Humanitarian Policy Group, Overseas Development Institute, London.

Polanyi, K 1944, *The Great Transformation. The Political and Economic Origins of Our Time*, Farrar and Rinehart, New York.

Ritter, M 2012, 'Boni Island – Holozäne Landschaftsdynamik und Mensch-Umwelt-Beziehung am Vierten Nil-Katarakt (Nord-Sudan)', Doctoral dissertation, Faculty of Mathematics and Natural Sciences, University of Köln, Köln.

Sait, S & Lim, H 2006, *Land, Law and Islam: Property and Human Rights in the Muslim World*, Zed Books, London and New York.

Sayed, O 2007, 'The Impact of Merowe Dam on Real Estate Activities in Nile and Northern States of Sudan', MSc thesis, Department of Real Estate and Construction Management, Division of Building and Real Estate Economics, KTH Architecture and the Built Environment, Stockholm.

Serels, S 2007, 'Political Landscaping. Land Registration, the Definition of Ownership and the Evolution of Colonial Objectives in the Anglo-Egyptian Sudan, 1899–1924', *African Economic History*, vol. 35, pp. 59–75.

Spaulding, J & Kapteijns, L 2002, Land Tenure and the State in Precolonial Sudan, *Northeast African Studies*, vol. 9, no. 1, pp. 33–66.

Suliman, M 1999, 'The Nuba Mountains of Sudan: Resource Access, Violent Conflict, and Identity', in D Buckles (ed), *Cultivating Peace: Conflict and Collaboration in Natural Resource Management*, IDRC/World Bank, Ottowa/Washington, pp. 205–220.

UNEP 2007, *Sudan. Post-Conflict Environmental Assessment*. Nairobi: UNEP.

Verhoeven, H 2015, *Water, Civilisation and Power in Sudan. The Political Economy of Military-Islamist State Building*, Cambridge University Press, New York.

Weschenfelder, P 2012, 'Manâsîr Women's Contributions to Economic and Social Life. A Case Study from Kirbekân', in C Kleinitz & C Näser (eds), "Nihna nâs al-bahar – *We Are the People of the River." Ethnographic Research in the Fourth Nile Cataract Region, Sudan*, Harrassowitz Verlag, Wiesbaden, pp. 75–88.

CHAPTER 2

Claiming Tribal Land Rights in a Global Context. Institutional Bricolage and Definitions of *ʿurf* among Pastoralists in Khartoum State

Barbara Casciarri

Introduction

In the Sudanese context, land issues among pastoral groups are a significant perspective from which to grasp the interplay of alliance, competition and conflict dynamics *within* and *between* local small-scale groups or between these groups and both the state and private actors. The persistence of pastoralists using particular forms of land exploitation, despite relevant transformations affecting their systems (Casciarri and Ahmed 2009; Krätli, El-Dirani and Young 2013), and the ambiguous status of collective tribal lands (Shazali and Ahmed 1999; Babiker 2009), have made these groups a main target of territorial dispossession during recent decades of deep socio-economic and political transformation (Casciarri, Assal and Ireton 2015), which has been marked by increasing liberalization, privatization and land grabbing processes supported by national/international investors and favoured by the Sudanese government (Gertel, Rottenbourg and Calkins 2014). In this framework, the plurality of pastoralists' strategies in claiming and accessing land can be properly appreciated through an in-depth qualitative ethnography. By following social actors' practices and narratives, the case study in this chapter aims to shed light on legal practices around land appropriation and related conflicts, and to question the role of Islamic law in the juridical universe of Muslim Sudanese peoples.

Our focus is on legal practices observed among a group of pastoralists of nomad origin, the Aḥāmda of the rural area of Khartoum State.[1] Processes of sedentarization and a growing inner stratification of the *gabīla* (tribe), the recent expansion of Khartoum and the impact of urbanization on this region (Denis 2005), and the violent encroachment of new forms of land exploitation

1 This chapter is mainly based on data collected among the Aḥāmda between 2011 and 2014 during eight missions for the ANDROMAQUE programme. Previous fieldwork among the same group for our PhD thesis (1989–1995) (Casciarri 1997) provided us with a deeper knowledge of the socio-historical configuration of the group.

 | DOI 10.1163/9789004362185_004

by private actors and the state, have all made claims on "tribal collective land" a crucial issue for this group in its struggle to safeguard access to land and water resources. After drawing the framework of historical land appropriation and cases of territorial dispossession that took place in the last decade (2005–2015), we analyse the strategies elaborated by the Aḥāmda to face inter-tribal conflict on a micro-scale by means of an "institutional *bricolage*" (Cleaver 2002), bringing together, in new creative configurations, elements of both state-written laws and courts, and so-called "customary law". We then focus on the notion of customary law (*ʿurf*) as conceived in the narratives of the Aḥāmda in this context. Finally, we open a discussion on the marginal relevance of Islam as a "legal reference" in the practices of Muslim Aḥāmda. This will brings us, on the one hand, to present the need to embed "law issues" within a wider socio-economic, political and cultural background in order to understand legal behaviours in a global context marked by forms of "legal insecurity" (von Benda-Beckmann and von Benda-Beckmann 2006), typical of capitalist "accumulation by dispossession" (Harvey 2006) and, on the other, to link this perspective with the recent debate on the prominence and ambiguity of the "tribal paradigm" in contemporary African and Middle East Muslim contexts (Bonte and Ben Hounet 2009).

Towards a Political Ethnography of Pastoral Land Dispossession

An insight into the historical dynamics of territorial appropriation will help to grasp the actual practices followed by the Aḥāmda for claiming land rights. In fact, in most contemporary territorial entitlement claims, social actors state as unavoidable the idea of historical legitimacy linked to their ancient local presence. In order to incorporate our data into a wider socio-historical context, we try to identify distinct periods and to stress continuities and breaking points within this trajectory.

Historical Forms of Tribal Land Appropriation and Recent Conflicts

Land appropriation among Khartoum State's Aḥāmda has been marked by alternation between high conflict moments, fluid phases of negotiation and periods of stability and normative codification. We summarise this process in three phases between the beginning of colonization and today. A first phase (1899–1950) was marked by intense conflict with other local nomad groups in this area, considered as "detribalized".[2] The Aḥāmda, here a product of

2 Proximity to the capital and the impact of the military and political events of Mahdism (1885–1898) often made pastoral peoples in this area lose tribal homogeneity and association

territorial and tribal recomposition elsewhere than their original homeland (Casciarri 1997), faced opposition from groups claiming prior rights to the region since the beginning of the 20th century. Later, colonial intervention through the Native Administration system – providing the delimitation of "tribal territories" and the appointment of "tribal chiefs" – strengthened and institutionalized the presence of the *gabīla* Aḥāmda in this territory. Around the 1940s, their collective land rights were thus confirmed. A second phase, from the last stages of colonial rule and into a long post-colonial period (1950–1995), was marked by relative stability. Despite the abolition in 1970 of Native Administration (support of tribal/collective lands) and the legal status of "state land" for all unregistered land, the remoteness and low profitability – beyond pastoral use – of lands occupied by the Aḥāmda allowed them to exploit their land quite freely and autonomously, following the principles of an implicit customary law strictly linked to *gabīla* institutions. These rights (orally defined) were accepted without major problems and used to support inter-tribal conflicts, which were quite rare during this phase. A third phase (1995–2015) started in a period when national transformation and the capital region's expansion (Denis 2005) favoured high competition over land. In this contemporary framework, the Aḥāmda's land has suddenly become attractive to new actors and for new usages, unknown in the first phase of conflict and negotiation between pastoral tribes.

During the last fifteen years (2000–2015), land access and use for the Aḥāmda have been shaken by the impact of several attacks to their territory: the construction of a refinery and the creation of a Free Trade Zone (with a residential area for the Chinese oil company's technical staff) on their northern grazing area (2001); the creation of a middle-scale dam on Khor Al-Kanjar, the main water course in the Aḥāmda territory (2003–2004); the building of a huge asphalt road to link Khartoum North to Jeily (refinery site), crossing the territory used by the Aḥāmda for dwellings and herds (2006–2009); and the arrival of small private investors quarrying for the urban building industry or developing small-scale commercial agriculture projects (since 2005). This progressive land grabbing by "outsiders" for uses competing with the Aḥāmda's agro-pastoral exploitation, has fuelled conflicts with neighbouring tribal groups. By discovering the interest in and potential profitability of former "desert lands", these groups, with whom a long historical process of negotiation had produced a

with a defined territory (Delmet 1989; Casciarri 1997). Drought and starvation, human and animal decimation, displacements, and increased mixing between peoples weakened tribe/territory relations. The new colonial administration defined the area as "detribalized" (Penn 1933; Sarsfield-Hall 1936) and brought about here more than elsewhere the reshaping of tribal chiefs and territories.

settled *status quo* through the recognition of reciprocal tribal territorial rights, entered a new phase of conflict with the Aḥāmda. Since 2007, this conjuncture has led to the development of several intertribal micro-conflicts: one with their pastoral neighbours the Kababish over ancient rain-fed plots (ending with an Aḥāmda "victory" after a long trial at state courts) (2007–2010); a second with their pastoral neighbours the Batahin, who laid claim to part of the Aḥāmda's "empty" land close to the new asphalt road (2011); and a third with the Sororab, a section of the Jaʿalyin farmers from a Nile village, who claimed Aḥāmda lands on the basis of the latter's late and illegitimate arrival as nomads in the region (2012).[3] This third phase of high conflict between local groups over collective tribal lands is different from the first phase of conflict between nomads which the Aḥāmda experienced a century ago. The first difference lies in the plurality of actors involved in land competition: besides former historical enemies (pastoral tribes), we find settled riverine villagers, urban small- and middle-scale entrepreneurs, major foreign investors, and the state. The second is the diversity of land uses, which before the 1990s were unconceivable in this remote desert land, negatively and unanimously stigmatized as a space only suited to nomads (*ʿarab*):[4] formerly limited to agro-pastoralism beyond direct or exclusive market valorisation, land exploitation is now led by the logic of profit within a dominant market economy and takes a number of forms (residential projects, commercial activities, extraction of building materials, the oil and electricity industries, modern transportation). This twofold novelty of the nature of recent land grabbing may explain the plurality of the Aḥāmda responses, which we shall examine in the next part of this chapter.

The Multifarious Role of the Gabīla *in New Strategies to Cope with Land Grabbing*

All the above-mentioned territorial intrusions – beyond variations in extent, status of promoters and land use – share two features. First, they are considered by the Aḥāmda as the actions of "outsiders" (to the *gabīla* as well as to the territory), and, second, dispossession is conceived as an illegitimate action on land that is seen as an ancient inalienable tribal property. We find it interesting to note that, in this context, the Aḥāmda response, far from being

3 For more detail about these territorial intrusions, following conflicts and the Aḥāmda reaction, see Casciarri 2015c.

4 In this sense, the term *khala*, formerly used for all land east of the Nile villages (notably east of the British railroad track), stigmatized a desert, socio-cultural as well as geographical, space inhabited by nomads (*ʿarab*), conceived by sedentary people as outside civilization and modernity (Casciarri 2015a).

homogeneous, varied according to the status and identity of the actors, which led to the identification of three scenarios. A first scenario is the situation in which the counterpart is the state or a major (foreign) investor. In this case there is no explicit organized opposition by the Aḥāmda, because of their awareness that the unfavourable balance of power makes successful resistance impossible. A second scenario concerns the diffuse micro-scale dispossession led by the building industry or small-scale commercial agriculture investors. The modest dimensions and the scattered nature of such intrusions provokes two alternative reactions: either the Aḥāmda tolerate these activities (if the area encroached upon is not crucial) or they attempt to negotiate with the investor in order to obtain modest amounts of money, contributions to the implementation of local infrastructures (such as wells and school classrooms), or the recruitment of their tribesmen as workers, the deal being guaranteed by precarious oral agreements. Finally, a third scenario is the situation in which the competitor is perceived as an actor of the same status and identity as the Aḥāmda – i.e., another tribal group presumed to share the same socio-cultural values (and the same legal assumptions in the sense of a "tribal customary law"). Thus the three above-mentioned cases of conflict over land with other local *gabīlas* have been the only ones to trigger open conflict both in a physical encounter and in resort to mediation through informal justice institutions or state courts. Our ethnography focuses on the third of these scenarios, in which theoretical and practical reconfigurations of rights and norms are more visible. The dynamics we are going to examine illustrate how the Aḥāmda try to cope with this new context by playing simultaneously on different legal levels, by producing a *bricolage* of normative and institutional elements aimed at integrating several instances of an "extra-tribal" universe whilst pursuing the embedding of legal practices within an overarching "tribal paradigm", which is strongly claimed (Casciarri 2009a).

Matching Tribal Possession and Modernist Discourses: The Case of Rain-fed Agricultural Lands

Rain-fed cultivation of sorghum (a staple cereal for human consumption and animal fodder) has always been an important complement to Aḥāmda pastoralism. Plots were accessed without purchase or registration, their use rights relying on the *gabīla* appropriation of a larger territory open to the solidarity group of *awlād ʿamm*.[5] Because of inadequate rainfall and socio-economic changes (decline in mobile herding, increase in wage labour, schooling for

5 In kinship vocabulary, the literal meaning of this term is "paternal uncle's children", i.e., parallel paternal cousins but in a wider sense it refers to every member of the *gabīla* Aḥāmda,

FIGURE 2.1 *Rain-fed plot* (taras) *for sorghum* (dhura) *cultivation in Wadi at-Tumām.* PHOTOGRAPH BY THE AUTHOR.

children) these plots have been neglected over recent decades. In the recent conjuncture of economic crisis (rising prices of cereals and food, labour insecurity) and growing competition for land, now targeted by new investments as a result of urban expansion and new infrastructure projects (roads, electricity, water), the status of these lands and their historical belonging to the Aḥāmda have been contested. This fuelled conflict between the Aḥāmda and two neighbouring tribal groups.

There were several plots of this category – called generally *arḍ zirāʿiyya* or *turūs* – on Aḥāmda territory, and those near to the western area (more affected by the mentioned intrusions) became a site of conflict. Despite their location north of Timaim village (which might have led to their being dealt with as a "local problem"), the discourse of tribal unity in defence of every little piece of the territory has worked to bring about a broader mobilization of the *gabīla*, beyond the defence of individual cultivators. Unlike grazing lands, which are appropriated and exploited collectively by all the tribesmen, rain-fed plots

---

stressing the basis of a political and territorial solidarity shared by those conceived as descendants of the same eponymous ancestor.

are individual or family property. Sometimes classed under the *waḍʿ al-yad* regime – by which repeated cultivation results in *de facto* ownership[6] – these lands are accessible only because they are located within a territory whose "abstract appropriation" (Bonte 1981) is exclusively granted by the *gabīla* to all its members.

This conceptualization supported the Aḥāmda's claims to contested land during the first phase of the conflict, when only tribal institutions were involved, and also in the second phase, when the case was brought to the official courts. However, fearing a renewal of the conflict after their first "legal victory", the Aḥāmda pursued two strategies to strengthen their entitlement. The first was the production of documents aimed at "securing" each owner's parcel of land (and hence the wider territorial rights of their *gabīla*): the *lajna shaʿbiyya* (popular committee)[7] in Timaim took charge of the creation of "certificates of title" (*shihādat ḥiyāza*) in order to attest farmers rights by dating appropriation to the colonial period (Annexe 2.1). The second was the creation of a farmers' cooperative (*jamaʿiyya zirāʿiyya*), following patterns spread in Sudan during the 1970s: written certification of the land's shared uses was matched with objectives of adopting mechanized agriculture and a market orientation (quite new by comparison with the previous working of the land by family manpower for subsistence farming). Thus, on the one hand, the Aḥāmda strove to establish a tribal, collective and inalienable status for these lands, but, on the other, they were open to "extra-tribal" elements: the titles' written codification, their official recognition by a state institution such as the *lajna shaʿbiyya*, and the resort to cooperative patterns and notions of modernization through mechanized market-oriented agriculture. Their discourse thus fell in between the customary legacy, rooting land rights in the institutions and values of the *gabīla*, and including elements of official state law and state-based institutional structures.

6 Plots are barely visible outside the period of their cultivation in the rainy season; even if stones or trees are sometimes used to mark borders, more often their borders are simply "known" (*maʿrūf*) thanks to an "oral cadastre" mentioning the names of the cultivators of adjacent parcels of land. Most of these plots have never been registered or purchased: transferred by inheritance (keeping the name of the ancestor who first started to work them), they actually remain inalienable according to the *gabīla*'s founding principles of land appropriation.

7 Whereas the law, which after the 1989 coup d'état created popular committees as local representatives of minor administrative units (quarters, villages, camps), never mentions its prerogatives on land issues, in most rural and peri-urban contexts the *lajna shaʿabiyya* performs the official recognition of land titles and also produces certificates of purchase.

The Redistributing *Gabīla*: The Case of Building Land as a New Category Managed by a New Local Institution

The building of a huge asphalt road across Aḥāmda territory led to speculation about the potential for profitable commercial activity in the surrounding areas. Some neighbouring groups therefore tried to occupy parts of this area, which was formerly a place where Aḥāmda people and herds passed through, and which they considered as their own according to *gabīla* principles of land appropriation. In this framework, conflict arose, first, as a violent encounter between men from the two *gabīla*s (with material support from tribesmen, including those far from the disputed area), and, second, after the failure of mediation by traditional leaders, as a legal process in state courts. Through this encounter, the Aḥāmda became aware of the stakes linked to such land, while some of them, living in the most crowded areas such as Timaim,[8] discovered an interest in coping with the recent phenomenon of demographic growth and the changes in life patterns that were taking place in parallel to pastoralism's decline and the sedentarization of pastoralists.

Because of their scepticism of the court process, the Aḥāmda deployed parallel strategies to guarantee the defence of contested lands. The experience of dispossession fostered the creation of a new category of land and a new local institution. Some educated young men from Timaim created a *lajnat al-arḍ* (land committee) – which did not exist at the official level – under the umbrella of the *lajna shaʿbiyya*. The land committee took charge of drawing up an artisanal land cadastre, and then went on to organize plot distribution among tribesmen: mainly young couples and new families.[9] This operation needed formal criteria for allocating plots as well as the invention of a new category of land. The notion of *arḍ sakaniyya*, "residential land", took shape as a new category that was meaningless in the previous pastoral context, where "habitable" land was not codified as such, because, first, availability was higher than demand and, second, underlying solidarity made it possible to find suitable arrangements for new homes among *awlād ʿamm*. In establishing the principles for assigning land, the committee referred to various registers. On the

8 Thanks to earlier sedentarization, Timaim, an ancient dry-season camp, is today the biggest Aḥāmda village. It has a population of about 1500 individuals, far more than the average in the *farīg*s (desert camps), which have 50–100 persons, and even other settled villages, which do not normally have more than 500 inhabitants.

9 Because of demographic growth, young couples cannot follow traditional residential patterns according to which married sons build their dwelling close to their father's. Those who wish to remain in the village after marriage (as is usual) have thus to look for other residential solutions.

one hand, allocation was influenced by urban patterns: the plots were created with the same dimensions, their numbering and registration were linked to individual names, and title validation was supervised by a recognized state institution, thanks to the inclusion of the *lajna shaʿbiyya* president as a member of the land committee. But, on the other hand, the committee's practices were far from official forms of property ownership and stressed the priority of norms linked to the *gabīla* ethos: the document granted to the beneficiary is not worded as a "certificate of title" but as a simple receipt (*rusūm*) for payment of a symbolic amount (0.50 SDG), transfer through inheritance was considered legitimate but plot alienation was forbidden, and it was decided that the basic eligibility criterion for accessing land would be evidence of patrilineal filiation within the Aḥāmda.[10] The discourse and practices concerning this case, led by a new committee and introducing a new category of land, show that the dynamics of legal practice are a creative in-between space where customary law, grounded in the tribal paradigm as a historical basis for land legitimacy, meets the adaptation to other legal forms, stemming from state authority, where land entitlement integrates elements previously ignored by the *gabīla* (written and registration, payment for certificates, official recognition by a non-tribal institution).

Reshaping Customary Laws and Adapting the *Gabīla* in Contemporary Land Conflicts

Whereas the codes of an official (written) law enforced by state institutions (Islamic or other) become more widely known, the legal universe that is vaguely categorized by the observer as "customary law" – usually labelled as *ʿurf* in the Muslim context – needs to be better illustrated through ethnography. In this section, we focus on the main elements of the conceptualization of customary law as defined in the Aḥāmda discourse.

The Status and Features of ʿurf *in Local Actors' Narratives*

As an introduction, we need to make some observations about the empirical aspect of data collection, notably the difficulty in identifying a terminological

10 Members of the land committee explained that these norms (agnatic descent, inalienability, symbolic payment) were set up in order to avoid the shrinkage of land witnessed in other periurban zones, as in Idd Babiker's ancient nomad territory. Here, the corruption of *gabīla* leaders coupled with urbanization pressures, meant that some collective land concessions opened the way for tribal land commodification.

and conceptual category proper to local actors' discourses and able to cover accurately categories such as "law" (in general) and "customary law" or *ʿurf* (in particular) as they are conceived by jurists and researchers. In fact, although these domains are undeniably present in the experience and accounts of the Aḥāmda (notably during recent conflicts), the notion and term itself (*ʿurf*) did not come up spontaneously in our discussions. We therefore decided to introduce explicit questions about *ʿurf* in our interviews. Far from nullifying the results here described about the way the Aḥāmda define the nature of their "customary law", this is interesting inasmuch as it questions the pertinence of an abstract vision (that of researchers or law experts) of legal spaces and categories to the practical vision of social actors. Also, as we did not come across references to *ʿurf* during our previous long study among the Aḥāmda, we argue that "customary law" is something that emerges as a topic of discussion, redefinition and collective memory re-construction, in particular situations where an ongoing conflict "reactivates" it in the search for practical tools and strategies for claiming contested rights.

The first and commonest element underlined by the Aḥāmda definition of *ʿurf* focuses on its embeddedness within the wider universe of social and symbolic relations of the *gabīla*, as a group that recognizes itself as "governed" at multiple levels by the tribal reference. Statements from fieldwork interviews[11] prove that actual local definitions of *ʿurf* are meaningless outside the interaction of the legal framework with a sociocultural complex of practices and values shared by members of the *gabīla*, whose unity is symbolized in common agnatic descent and materialized in modes of territorial appropriation and autonomous political management. Frequently arising elements in the interviews made it possible for us to describe *ʿurf* as a set of norms followed by a group of tribesmen, whose main features are related to: territorial appropriation, tribal leadership, inalienability and an ethos contrary to commoditization, orality, "inter-knowledge", and historical status. Let us see in detail how this set of principles is evidenced in Aḥāmda narratives.

11 While general social dynamics analysis is based on data collected throughout our fieldwork among the Aḥāmda (1989–1995; 2006–2012), in this section we rely on 48 interviews carried out between 2011 and 2014 for the ANDROMAQUE project, questioning our respondents on issues of territorial conflict, legal practice and customary law. Our intention was to increase variation by choosing informants according to various parameters: age, socio-economic status, education, lineage affiliation, role in local political institutions (tribal leadership, popular committees, land committee). Despite the variety of the sample, we have no women informants, which confirms the weight of sexual division (and women's exclusion) in this domain.

First and foremost, *ʿurf* is said to deal (almost exclusively) with issues of territorial rights. Land appropriation is a collective process, implying available resources (grazing land, water, cultivation plots, dwelling spaces) on which people accepted as *awlād ʿamm* (a polysemous term shifting from kinship to political solidarity) can establish their rights through favourable power relations, and hence define physical and socio-cultural borders that distinguish them from "others". Discourses about *ʿurf* frequently refer to *ḥidūd* (borders), be it in foundation stories – telling histories of the first ancestors who proved the exclusivity of collective possession mainly in the colonial period when the British administration ratified tribal groups rights and their native leaderships – or in discourses about recent land conflicts, defending the territory against people outside the *gabīla* (but who sometimes share the same tribal paradigm).

In addition, *ʿurf* is intrinsically linked to "tribal chiefs", who, by representing all tribesmen, are also privileged witnesses of collective land appropriation and the main referents in cases of conflict (with the state or with other tribes, but also within the *gabīla*). These persons, whose authority is recognized by their own group, may, depending on the context, be leaders (sheikhs or *ʿomda*s) formally appointed by Native Administration (during the colonial period but also more recently in the case of the revival of this system by the Islamic government since 1994; see Casciarri 2001, 2009b), or individuals whose status as mediators is more occasional, linked to specific situations without being either permanent or hereditary (a difference from tribal leaderships as reshaped by the British Native Administration; see Grandin 1982).

At another level, *ʿurf* draws on an ethos of core *gabīla* values (which underlies the social interactions of its members) that is in line with the concept of common land and disapproval of its commoditization (Casciarri 2009a) as a resource whose usage rights are only acquired by means of patrilineal descent from the eponymous ancestor Hammed, the alleged source of the tribe's unity as *awlād ʿamm*. Inalienability (implying the refusal of access to "foreigners" – i.e., those not belonging to the *gabīla*) is an essential condition for access both to the goods (the territory as a whole), which guarantees abstract appropriation (Bonte 1981), and to territorial resources where actual appropriation takes place (wells, *ḥafīr*s rain-water reservoirs and rain-fed plots). These tribal goods are linked to a name, either that of the *gabīla* or that of the lineage's ancestor, and people state that "one cannot sell the name" (*al-isim mā tebiʿhu*).[12]

12 This may be seen as emblematic of divergences between customary and written laws, despite their superficial convergences: in written official laws, the apposition of the name or the nominal link of a good, is the condition *sine qua non* for stating individual private

Another feature of *ʿurf* is that it falls almost exclusively under the domain of orality: its norms are known, passed on, lived, without the intervention of writing as a seal, and this does not obstruct their force and legitimacy. Far from being a mere consequence of illiteracy, the absence of written codification stands as an ethical requirement, because the "inter-knowledge" (arising from kinship networks) between individuals linked by the same customary law is the guarantee of respect for such rights, inspired by a sound morality and a spirit of equal sharing, whereas resorting to writing assumes distrust. This means that the use of writing is limited to serious cases of conflict or to situations where more powerful actors (such as the state) require it.[13] The privilege granted to orality also give potential operational margins for negotiation and adjustment, to which written law is an impediment. The notion of (inter)knowledge, linked to the tribal paradigm of the *gabīla*, shows connections with the semantic field of the root *ʿ-r-f*, "to know", inasmuch the term *maʿrūf* ("known" and, by extension, "depending on oral collective norms of *ʿurf*") is applied to certain goods (wells, *ḥafīrs*) that their founders wished to keep outside the possibility of division by inheritance (hence possible alienation), termed *waritha*.[14]

Finally, far from being a stereotyped vision, *ʿurf* is not conceived by its practitioners as a "tradition" existing since immemorial times and always the same. While being rooted in temporality – i.e., proving ancestry and longevity of association between the *gabīla* and its land – is a crucial factor in customary land claims, people seem to admit the historical nature of *ʿurf*. For the Aḥāmda, the existence of *ʿurf* does not simply coincide with their presence as a group showing unity on a territory; it is said to be "constructed" during a process in which

full property rights; in the tribal context, "the name" seems rather to evoke a complex of honour and ethical values that constitute the symbolic capital of the group and its members and does not automatically result in "private property" (*milk*) entitlement.

13 Resorting to government (*ḥakūma*) written laws and courts is usually avoided as they symbolize a legal universe alien to local practices, but also because it is conceived as proof of weakness, subordination and loss of autonomy in managing tribal political affairs. In a few cases resorting to state laws has been strategically pursued by the Aḥāmda for "getting rid" of other groups' claims – as in the matter of the Idd ad-Dalaja well, a hydric structure crucial for their territorial affirmation in the colonial period (Casciarri 2015b). In general, resorting to written state law remains rare and contextual, and keeping "outside" the state written legal space is generally valued and considered as more appropriate to the *gabīla* ethos.

14 Even if translation uses the term "inheritance" both for goods' division following *sharīʿa* laws and for the sharing of collective goods through agnatic descent from the *gabīla* as a "collective owner", in the local use only the first case is properly defined as *waritha*, which refers to Islamic law (and private property).

the group strengthened its status as well as its military and political solidarity, and became able to face neighbours and to establish favourable power relations for the appropriation of a common territory. Thus, starting from such a moment, continuous land use led to the *gabīla* confirming its borders and the exclusivity of collective rights to the territory (on which they rely today when opposing attempts at dispossession), but witnesses admit that this *ʿurf*, its rights and practices, were only confirmed during the first decades of British colonization,[15] which corresponds to the phase in which various sections of the Aḥāmda reunited at the territorial, political and identity level (Casciarri 1997). The historicity of collective tribal customary law , along with the rejection of writing, provides potential for openness and flexibility. In principle it opens the possibility for the borders of a common space to continue to adapt to the contingency of local groups' mobility and negotiations. If the Aḥāmda today appear to resist acknowledging the flexibility of their customary appropriation, this is due more to the extent and brutality of territorial dispossession of their land in periods of globalization (and the absence of viable alternatives), than to the incompatibility of the idea of an *ʿurf* with moving negotiable physical and social borders. Moreover, the two cases focused on in the first part of this chapter show that, in the context of actual legal practice (in which conflict situations make the practice of *ʿurf* more visible by activating collective discussions and memories about it), the Aḥāmda do not hesitate to merge customary norms with principles stemming from other sources of law and legal institutions.

The ʿarrifiyyīn, *from Historical Tribal Institution to State "Invented Tradition"?*

In order to confirm the idea of a historical and contextual configuration of *ʿurf* – as well as the "double movement" of state laws shifting towards customary laws and vice versa – it is interesting to examine the recent revival of the legal role of *ʿarrifiyyīn*, seen as "customary law experts" who represent the *gabīla*, mainly in

15 Linking *ʿurf* both to the *gabīla* and its territory (*ʿurf baladi*) and to the phase between the end of Mahdism and British colonization, a respondent says that, before this period, people occupied and exploited land *sakit*, "simply, like this", which means "without rights, norms", i.e., not only without a written legal framework but also without recognizing the framework of *ʿurf* orally agreed by a tribal group. The vision of a sort of "tribal anarchy" may also be found in discourse about tribal chiefs (sheikhs), whose functions are said to be occasional and fluid at that time, often based on self-appointment by force and against tribal consensus.

situations of land conflict.[16] The *ʿarrifiyyīn* are considered as the experts both on the borders of the *gabīla* collective lands and on their usage history, and their knowledge leads people to consult them in major cases of conflict over land (particularly with foreigners). At the time of our fieldwork, there were two *ʿarrifiyyīn* among the Aḥāmda. They belonged to different lineages (*fariʿ*) of the *gabīla* and had various points in common: aged about 70 and illiterate, they were among the Aḥāmda who had only recently abandoned nomadic pastoralism and, despite progressive sedentarization since the 1990s, they still kept herds using domestic manpower and accessed common resources (grazing land and water) during seasonal transhumance. As is suggested by the root of the term *ʿarrifiyyīn* (the same as *ʿurf*), their longstanding integration with a pastoral way of life makes them the repository of detailed practical knowledge, coupled with rich information about the features of the tribal territory in ancient times and the memory of wider inter-tribal relations and of local groups who had access to it.

Although the Aḥāmda agreed to grant both tribesmen the authority required for this role and the legitimacy to represent the *gabīla*'s territorial rights in conflict situations,[17] inquiry revealed that these appointments were quite recent and were eoncouraged by the state rather than by the *gabīla* itself. The state court system faced difficulties due to the unavailability of written documents to certify rights to contested land and the inability to solve the first of the three intertribal conflicts. In order to help the judges in charge of the affair to reach a decision, each *gabīla* was asked to name two *ʿarrifiyyīn* who would give oral testimony to the land rights and practices of their tribe. At this stage, the Aḥāmda *gabīla* proposed the two men, whose new function was duly recorded by the judicial instances. They were taken round the territory by car together with the *qāḍī* and the *ʿarrifiyyīn* of the disputant tribe, and provided the information they were asked for (features, borders and historical possession of the territory), which constituted evidence to be taken into account for the final verdict in the absence of written certificates.[18]

---

16 No such persons appeared in data collection during all our earlier fieldwork, and we first witnessed them in 2011 when we started our interviews on land issues and conflicts.

17 Other tribesmen, who could fulfil this role on the basis of their deep knowledge of the territory and customary practices, were too old and had failing mental fitness: everybody agreed that the two appointed *ʿarrifiyyīn* were old enough to have the knowledge but still mentally alert and with excellent rhetoric capacities.

18 The story of this trip made by the four *ʿarrifiyyīn* of the opposing *gabīla*s, the judge and other government officials has many narrative elements in common with a similar story that is part of the collective memory of the Aḥāmda, in which the ancestor and sheikh Ahmed Abu Shora is said to have been brought by the British commissioner, riding camels, with Ahmed Abu Harira, sheikh of the Batahîn *gabīla*, to decide on the borders of tribal

After discovering this recent episode, which led to the appointment of the two *ʿarrifiyyīn*, we pursued our inquiry to better understand the status and genesis of this crucial figure in the implementation of "customary law". When asked whether the *ʿarrifyyīn* existed before the recent state intervention, the Aḥāmda answered in various ways, which led us to argue for a more fluid and contextual conception of local laws and institutions of their collective representation. Those who are today called *ʿarrifiyyīn* (formerly referred to as *ʿurfān*) do not exactly correspond to an institutionalized tribal function, durably allocated to specific individuals. On the one hand, it was in specific circumstances of conflict (mostly over land) that the *gabīla* members gathered to designate one or more of those who "better knew" the circumstances of territorial appropriation and related historical rights. If the conflict took place with another nomad *gabīla* (as was almost always the case in previous times), both parties shared similar ethos and forms of tribal organization and conceptualization, which guaranteed that both would address the appointed *ʿurfān* and would tend to agree on similar negotiation principles. On the other hand, all our respondents stressed that more often there was no need to appoint *ad hoc ʿurfān*, as existing tribal leaders, sheikhs or *ʿomda*s already had authority to represent their group's claims – thus they were *ʿurfān de facto* – as historical knowledge of territorial borders and negotiation practices was the basis of their status as "tribal leaders".

We can make two main observations from this history of revival (if not invention) of a "traditional" legal figure. The first concerns the recurring dynamics of the relation between the Sudanese state (colonial as well as independent) and nomadic tribes. Through the establishment of Native Administration from the 1920s, the colonial state erased the intrinsic flexibility of former native tribal leaders (and the same can be said of borderlines between tribes as both physical and identity markers), thus making the functions of sheikh, *ʿomda* and *nāẓir* more rigid, strictly codified and hereditary (Asad 1970; Grandin 1982; Abu Shouk 1998). Similarly, the contemporary Sudanese state, facing the increase in inter-tribal micro-conflicts and fearing their development into harsher armed conflicts, intervenes, relying on so-called local traditions and customary laws, but also in a certain sense noticeably altering their features. A clear example may be seen in the fixed and institutionalized role imposed on new *ʿarrifiyyīn*, who had most probably not existed as such for a long period – at least during the second phase of "relative stability" of the Aḥāmda's appropriation of their territory. The second observation is that the local-level category – which we may describe as the "tribal framework" – is not alone in straying beyond its

territories where conflict had arisen between the two tribes. According to the Aḥāmda, in both cases state representatives adjudicated in favour (*ḥakamu le*) of the Aḥāmda claims.

specific normative domain: just as tribesmen may integrate into their practices the use of "state law" norms and institutions, so the opposite movement is also possible, when the state mitigates the inefficiency of its legal apparatus by resorting to tribal networks. The contemporary crisis-ridden Sudanese state may also set aside its image of modernity – based on a written law, favouring private property and its registration, stressing the relevance of Islamic law – and look for support in the domain of oral, tribal and collective "customary laws" and institutions. This strategy, which may be found in land conflict situations other than the Aḥāmda's, can be read more as a manifestation of pragmatism than as an indicator of so-called "legal pluralism", and, in our view, is to be interpreted as evidence of a powerful instrumental intelligence on the part of the state, rather than as a simple affirmation of its weakness and lack of control over its "tribal citizens".

Pastoral Legal Practices between and beyond *ʿurf* and *sharīʿa*

At the end of this chapter on the practical dimensions of legal behaviour in conflict contexts and notions of customary laws among a pastoral tribal group, we would like to focus the discussion on a more general interpretation of our data. The Aḥāmda case does not allow us to make generalizations about either "Muslim" or "Sudanese" people's legal practices. Nonetheless, it acts as an interesting point from which to raise wider questions about research approaches to these analytical categories. On the one hand, the undeniable pertinence of the religious marker as a shared parameter of the group's identity (together with its inclusion in a society in which *sharīʿa* is the official ruling principle), coupled with the quasi-invisibility of Islamic law, and, on the other, the strong and shared representations of local configurations of *ʿurf*, with their bricolage of customary norms and other legal references in land claims strategies, stand not as mere contradictions, but as an entry point for redefining perspectives and analytical tools to grasp the legal processes in play among small-scale groups in a contemporary Muslim milieu.

The Place of Islam in the Legal Universe of Muslim Sudanese: A Pastoral Perspective

Our ethnography on issues of land law leads us to note the weakness of Islamic law among a group for which Islam is a historical identity marker.[19] In the

19 This statement particularly concerns land issues, which are the focus of our chapter. The presence of an Islamic legal reference is much more evident among the Aḥāmda as far as personal and family issues are concerned.

management and conceptualization of territorial rights, despite some ambivalences, customary law or *ʿurf* constitutes the main operational framework for land appropriation and conflict mediation. Neither *sharīʿa* and religious texts nor courts and judicial institutions controlling their implementation stand as major pertinent references for our group, except as a vague reference to piety values that should support the provision of goods essential to life (such as water) and the need to protect them from strictly private appropriation.[20] Rather, in local narratives and practices, the clash is more often between a flexible local customary right and the fuzzy legal universe of written laws, applied by state courts: here the distinction between *ganūn*[21] and *sharīʿa* fades, allowing us to argue that the real contrast is not between "Islamic" and "non-Islamic", but between the practices of rural and pastoral groups that favour the collective dimension and orality, and settled and urban law systems, based on written juridical cultures and the centrality of private property.

Nonetheless, if we separate Islamic reference from *sharīʿa*, we may ask whether Islam enters into the arena of law by means of other trajectories. From this perspective, two different elements seem relevant. The first concerns the role of Sufi brotherhoods and their sheikhs, which are very strongly rooted among this pastoral group. Among the Aḥāmda, a lineage of the *gabīla*, called Sheikhāb, holds such religious prerogatives and the homogeneous affiliation of the tribal group (Casciarri 1997). These representatives of a local Sufi Islam are not prior legal actors, but they participate in three ways in the realm of law. First, they are the holders of the only written version of the *nisba*

20 Talking about access to *ḥafīr*s (rain-water reservoirs) built by *farīg* (camp) members, an informant stressed that the original builder, though considering his family and descendants as priority users, would never turn them into *waritha*, alienable individualised inheritance bequests, which could prevent access to other *gabīla* members or occasional outsiders. He added that this attitude is *ajur*, an act of piety, which God will reward in the hereafter. He also mentioned a local saying that even if only a desert bird (*gumriyya*) drank this water, God would reward its builder. However, the notion of "Islamic piety" seems to be an *a posteriori* interpretation of the prior value put on "common assets" by the tribal ethos and the principles of equity and solidarity. In addition, this equity and piety is not applied universally to human kind or to the whole Muslim community, and it often does not go beyond *gabīla* borders. While foreigners may be granted access to grazing and water when there is no high pressure on resources (an act which could in the future start a process of "transformation" of foreigners into agnatic kin), this openness fades during high conflict situations, when tribal border flexibility stops and the identity of the *gabīla* as an exclusive political and territorial body emerges again.

21 Though *ganūn* can be considered as the most general term for "law" in standard as well in vernaculair Arabic, the Ahâmda use it with the meaning of every law system which is neither *shar'ia* nor *'urf*.

(genealogy), proving the Arab origin of the Aḥāmda *gabīla* by connecting the ancestor Hammed with ʿAbbas (the Prophet's uncle), a role that, beyond its identity function, makes it a sort of "customary tribal certificate", establishing the legitimacy of territorial appropriation by the Aḥāmda thanks to the evidence of their "noble" Arab ancestry. Second, even if more occasionally compared to the political sheikhs, the function of these religious sheikhs as mediators in some intertribal conflicts, thanks to the seal of their holiness, is another instance of their entry in the legal space. Third, in a few cases some members of the *gabīla* resort to the Sheikhāb for writing documents (simply defined as *waraga* or *kitāba*, "a paper" or "writing") intended to support claims to ownership of herds, *ḥafīrs* or rain-fed plots. Therefore, we may argue that these patterns constitute an element that introduces Islamic references into the domain of Aḥāmda law, even if we need to stress that we are not dealing here with Islam of *fiqh* or a *qaḍī* of the *sharīʿa* court, but with Sufi Islam, deeply rooted in the values of this pastoral group and filled with meaning by the association between holiness and the control of writing techniques.[22]

The second element concerns the role of the *lajna shaʿbiyya*. As we saw in the first part, by means of the institutional and normative bricolage pursued by the Aḥāmda to adapt their strategies during inter-tribal conflict, the group tries to seal its territorial claims by involving the local *lajna shaʿbiyya* to write certificates of titles or by establishing links with local informal committees for land distribution. These popular committees, which have recently increased in rural areas since their creation after the 1989 coup d'état, reveal other dimensions of the potential reference to Islam in legal spaces. One of the primary functions granted by the state to the popular committees is that of guaranteeing respect for *sharīʿa* morality among their people. In Aḥāmda villages, one of the first demonstrations of the *lajna shaʿbiyya* tasks has been the prohibition of activities at marriage celebrations that are contrary to Islamic norms (music, dancing and mixing between the sexes). At another level, even if it would not be correct to state that every member of every *lajna shaʿbiyya* is a fervent promoter of the governing political party (NCP)[23] – which for almost

22 Before the expansion of primary schools in the territory (which is recent and still partial) the Sheikhāb were the only Aḥāmda who, thanks to their religious function, had access to writing and reading. This was part of their privileged role among tribesmen and explains why they were consulted in specific situations when the production of written documents was considered unavoidable.

23 Fieldwork analysis of micro-political dynamics in rural and periurban contexts indicates that the situation of political alliances and conflicts is more complex than the monolithic

30 years has led to the Sudanese government being categorized as "Islamist" – it is true that, in tense situations, some local elites who are involved in the popular committees and more connected to national political arenas, have functioned as the local enforcers of "social control" and repression by demanding the loyalty and support of tribesmen in the face of unpopular state policies.[24] This is a religious sphere far from the context of Sufi brotherhoods referred to above, but we may raise the same question of whether this role of the *lajna shaʿbiyya* in the legal universe of the Aḥāmda could be interpreted as representing a more general role of Islam. Whatever the answer, both elements (Sufi sheikhs and the presence of the popular committee) are quite far from common notions of "Islamic law" as a legal reference. Be that as it may, both contextual configurations of Islam invite a more general questioning of the nature and expressions of Islam (or Islams) within the actual juridical universe of local Muslim groups. This could take our reflection beyond some of the current simplifications, by which researchers often support a stereotypical vision of so-called "African customary laws", depicted as manifestations of ancestral harmony with animist and collectivist conceptions of land (le Bris, le Roy and Mathieu 1991), hence supporting another stereotypical and dichotomized vision of legal practitioners working in Islam-ruled African countries, who take it as a matter of fact that their Muslim populations follow *sharīʿa* codes, and relegate "customs" and/or *ʿurf*[25] to the (implicitly inferior) legal universe of their non-Muslim minorities.

The Persistence of ʿurf *as a Tool against "Legal Insecurity": Pleading for the Embeddedness of Legal Practices within Ethnographies of Global Dispossession*

In the second part of this chapter we tried to summarise a definition of the status and prerogatives of *ʿurf* among the Aḥāmda, persuaded that this aspect constitutes the most valuable contribution we can expect from qualitative

image (also fostered by researchers and international agencies) that stresses an absolute coincidence between popular committees and government strategies.

24 For example, in the case of state territorial intrusion, as in the case of dam building, mentioned above, some Aḥāmda were complaining that their *lajna shaʿbiyya* impeded the organization of action against it that was wanted by some of the tribesmen, who were against this intervention in their territory.

25 This seems to be the case in Sudan, where writings and discourses by Muslim legal experts consider "customary law" issues as relevant only to non-Muslim (often Southern) Sudanese groups.

ethnographical inquiry. The fact that, when explicitly questioned about their customary laws, most respondents of a varied (except for the gender parameter) and quite large sample share a relatively similar vision of this legal complex, should not allow us to overlook two points. First, actual practices may partially diverge from the uniform connotation of abstract constructions about "tribal customary rights", and such divergence may also indicate paths of inner stratification and controversy among tribesmen. Second, although emotional and symbolic stress brings the Aḥāmda to identify their proper "law universe" as one of *ʿurf*, on one hand, they remain open to a conception of the latter as a historical set of norms, subject to constant negotiation and reshaping, and, on the other, they do not feel this contradicts the possibility of "mixing" *ʿurf* settings in contextual strategies for claiming rights by constructing hybrid combinations, where dichotomies such as written/oral, state/tribe, rural/urban are no longer absolute. Nonetheless, the analysis of their legal practices and narratives leads us to point out two general elements – about which comparison with other cases could be drawn – namely, the embeddedness of legal issues, and the historical use of customary rights as a bulwark against land dispossession.

Legal micro-scale ethnography, such as that is pursued here for the Aḥāmda case, stresses the need to grasp local "legal spaces" through an approach grounded in an extra-legal social complex. The researcher's attempt to embed legal issues within wider social configurations – for which qualitative anthropological methods are essential – may be a fruitful approach in the attempt to reflect accurate meanings and strategies of these dynamics. The forms of economic organization and resources exploitation among a pastoral group, the paradigm of the multi-functional *gabīla* institution (Casciarri 2009a), the settings of agnatic kinship and other identity categories, the micro-scale political dynamics, the symbolic value and ethical dimension of such processes, all are elements without which the effort to understand this complex legal universe can be frustrated. It is interesting here to go back to the notion of *embeddedness* that Karl Polanyi (1944) introduced to plead the rooting of economics within its socio-institutional configurations. This notion, transferred to other domains of analysis such as water social management (Casciarri 2008 and forthcoming), could provide a basic approach to the study of legal practices. Although we need to use the "embeddedness paradigm" while avoiding "… the threat of a culturalist and homogenising shift" (Olivier de Sardan 2013, p. 283), this analytical tool may allow us to grasp these practices through an inevitable exit from the juridical sphere *stricto sensu*, and by questioning the rigid definition of the normative law universe, often imposed by the hyperbolic hold of jurists, reinforced, in our context, by the weight of a powerful erudite tradition on Islamic law.

The perspective of the social embeddedness of the legal domain also sheds new light on the actual arrangements followed by local social actors (independently from their specific nature) in their material implementation of laws. In the Aḥāmda case, reactions to recent attacks on their territorial rights and conflicts with other groups make visible a trend that we can define as "institutional bricolage" (Cleaver 2002). Far from both an alleged dichotomy between "customary law" or "state law" (Islamic or other) and a simplified notion of "legal pluralism", the normative, ethical and practical references of distinct juridical systems are thus reshaped in a creative, pragmatic and contextual way, by the social actors concerned. These actors put in place behaviours inspired by a certain coherence and efficiency, but whose durability (and the shared ethical investment) are only provided by a set of factors historically determined, far away from notions of "rational choice" – another frequent risk for "anti-utilitarian" and institutionalist approaches (Olivier de Sardan 2013). The resort to narratives on "traditions" and customs, the appeal to cooperative patterns sealed by previous experiences, the creation of *ad hoc* local land committees, the patronage by state institutions such as the *lajna shaʿbiyya*, and the state-driven revival of customary right figures, all these phenomena can be read as means to construct tools for the securitization of the (collective) rights of the group. Another perspective thus arises from these processes, strictly linked to a global context (not specific to the Aḥāmda or to Sudanese/ Muslim pastoralists) and open to the quest for understanding legal practices of land appropriation. From this perspective, the notion of "legal insecurity" (von Benda-Beckmann and von Benda-Beckmann 2006) becomes crucial to the analysis of dynamics that are having an increasingly drastic effect on rural populations in African contexts, where processes of land grabbing progressively take away the life and production spaces of such groups. Such land grabbing is favoured by the alliance between states and markets, in which reference to Islam becomes marginal when compared to the idea of "might is right". In this regard, a political ethnography of dispossession, called by some scholars an indispensable reading-key of contemporary global capitalism (Harvey 2006), provides a meaningful hint to researchers whose starting point is the social analysis of legal phenomena. Contemporary Sudan, marked by the spreading and dramatic crushing of local peoples' rights to land (felt by themselves as the essential problem of injustice more than the lack of "freedom rights" in a liberal individual acception), may stand as an interesting test ground in which to address such crucial questions.

References

Abu Shouk, AI 1998, 'From Tribes to Nazirates', in E Stiansen & M Kevane (eds), *Kordofan Invaded. Peripheral Incorporation and Social Transformation in Islamic Africa*, Brill, Leiden, pp. 120–144.

Asad, T 1970, *The Kababish Arabs. Power, Authority and Consent in a Nomadic Tribe*, Hurst, London.

Babiker, M 2009, 'Pastoral Land Rights and Peace-building in North Kordofan. Policy and Legislative Challenges', *Nomadic Peoples*, vol., no. 1, pp. 134–153.

Bonte, P 1981, 'Marxist Theory and Anthropological Analysis. The Study of Nomadic Pastoralist Societies', in JS Kahn & JR Llobera (eds), *The Anthropology of Precapitalist Societies*, MacMillan Press, London, pp. 22–57.

Bonte, P & Ben Hounet, Y 2009, *La tribu à l'heure de la globalization*, special issue *Etudes Rurales*, vol. 184.

Casciarri, B 1997, 'Les pasteurs Ahāmda du Soudan central. Histoire d'une recomposition territoriale, politique et identitaire', PhD Thesis in Social Anthropology and Ethnology, EHESS, Paris.

Casciarri, B 2001, '"La *gabîla* est devenue plus grande". Permanences et évolutions du modèle tribal chez les pasteurs Ahāmda du Soudan arabe', in P Bonte, E Conte & P Dresch (eds), *Emirs et présidents. Figures de la parenté et du politique dans le monde arabe*, CNRS, Paris, pp. 273–299.

Casciarri, B 2008, 'Du partage au clivage. Marchandisation de l'eau et des rapports sociaux dans un village du Maroc présaharien (Tiraf, Vallée du Dra)', in E Baumann *et al.* (eds), *Anthropologues et économistes face à la globalisation*, L'Harmattan, Paris, pp. 87–127

Casciarri, B 2009a, 'Between Market Logics and Communal Practices. Pastoral Nomad Groups and Globalization in Contemporary Sudan', *Nomadic Peoples*, vol. 13, no. 1, pp. 69–91.

Casciarri, B 2009b, 'Hommes, troupeaux et capitaux. Le phénomène tribal au Soudan à l'heure de la globalization', *Etudes Rurales*, vol. 184, pp. 47–64.

Casciarri, B 2015a, 'De l'altérité et invisibilité des groupes pastoraux au Soudan. Repenser les études soudanaises en partant de leurs marges mobiles', *Revue Canadienne des Études Africaines/Canadian Journal of African Studies*, vol. 49, no. 1, pp. 147–173.

Casciarri, B 2015b, 'Water Management among Sudanese Pastoralists. End of the Commons or "Silent Resistance" to Commoditization?', in B Casciarri, M Assal & F Ireton (eds), *Multidimensional Change in Sudan (1989–2011). Reshaping Livelihoods, Conflicts and Identities*, Berghahn, Oxford/New York, pp. 140–160.

Casciarri, B 2015c, 'Ethnographie des pratiques légales autour de la revendication des droits fonciers chez les groups pastoraux de l'Etat de Khartoum', *L'année du Maghreb*, Dossier XIII: "Pratiques du droit et propriété au Maghreb", pp. 39–60.

Casciarri, B (forthcoming), 'Tribal Networks under the Water Network. The Case of Former Nomad Batahin in Periurban Khartoum (Idd Babiker)', in D Blanchon, B Casciarri, O Graefe & D Mueller-Mahnn (eds), *Khartoum Waterscapes. The Hydro-political Ecology of Urban Transformation.*

Casciarri, B & Ahmed, AM (eds) 2009, *Pastoralists under Pressure in Present-day Sudan*, special issue *Nomadic Peoples*, vol. 13, no. 1.

Casciarri, B, Assal, M & Ireton, F (eds) 2015, *Multidimensional Change in Sudan (1989–2011). Reshaping Livelihoods, Conflicts and Identities*, Berghahn, Oxford/New York.

Cleaver, F 2002 'Reinventing Institutions: Bricolage and the Social Embeddedness of Natural Resource Management', *The European Journal of Development Research*, vol. 14, no. 2, pp. 11–30.

Delmet, C 1989, 'Sociétés rurales et structures sociales au Soudan central', in M Lavergne (ed.), *Le Soudan contemporain*, Karthala, Paris, pp. 57–83.

Denis, E 2005, 'De quelques dimensions de Khartoum et de l'urbanisation au Soudan', *Lettre de l'OUCC*, no. 6–7, pp. 19–29.

Gertel, J, Rottenbourg, R & Calkins, S (eds) 2014, *Disrupted Territories. Land, Commodification and Conflict in Sudan*, James Currey, London.

Grandin, N 1982, *Le Soudan nilotique et l'administration britannique (1898–1956)*, Brill, Leiden.

Harvey, D 2006, *Spaces of Global Capitalism. Towards a Theory of Uneven Geographical Development*, Verso, London.

Krätli, S, El-Dirani, OH & Young, H 2013, *Standing Wealth. Pastoralist Livestock Production and Local Livelihoods in Sudan*, UNEP, Nairobi.

le Bris, E, le Roy, E & Mathieu, P (eds) 1991, *L'appropriation de la terre en Afrique noire. Manuel d'analyse, de décision et de gestion foncières*, Karthala, Paris.

Olivier de Sardan, JP 2013, 'Embeddedness and Informal Norms: Institutionalisms and Anthropology', *Critique of Anthropology*, vol. 33, no. 3, pp. 280–299.

Penn, AED 1933, *Handing Over Notes on Khartoum North and Rural District*, Civil Secretary, Khartoum, National Record Office.

Polanyi, K 1944, *The Great Transformation. The Political and Economic Origins of Our Time*, New York.

Sarsfield-Hall, EG 1936, *Progress in Khartoum Province between 1928 and 1935*, Civil Secretary, Khartoum, National Record Office.

Shazali, S & Ahmed, MA 1999, *Pastoral Land Tenure and Agricultural Expansion. Sudan and the Horn of Africa*, International Institute for Environment and Development, London.

von Benda-Beckmann, F & von Benda-Beckmann, K 2006, 'Social Insecurity, Natural Resources and Legal Complexity', in C Eberhard & G Vernicos (eds), *La quête anthropologique du droit. Autour de la démarche d'Etienne Le Roy*, Karthala, Paris, pp. 221–248.

CHAPTER 3

Ambiguous Land Ownership in al-Ṣalḥa, Omdurman: Land Grabbing or "Business as Usual"?

Munzoul M.A. Assal

Introduction

As the title of this chapter indicates, acquisition and ownership of land in Sudan's capital, Khartoum, are surrounded by ambiguity. Systems and ways of land allocation are problematic and encourage malpractice in land transactions. The situation in Khartoum can be described as a form of urban land grabbing, as this chapter endeavours to illustrate.[1] Land is a central issue for both rural and urban communities in Sudan. It is not just a means of livelihood and of basic survival, but also has profound cultural and socio-political dimensions (Pantulliano 2007). The ambiguity surrounding matters related to urban land is the result of the lack of a unified legal framework for land tenure across the country, for both rural and urban areas. A mixture of formal and informal processes governs the allocation of land and its ownership regimes, and this situation is a major contributing factor to many of the malpractices in transactions over land described in this chapter.

Several factors make the commercialization of land in Sudan conspicuous. The oil boom (2000–2010) contributed to this commercialization and also to real estate development, leading to increases in land prices. Land grabbing is part of this phenomenon since in unregistered lands, senior government officials, private investors, land speculators and urban residents (migrants from the countryside to urban areas) simply grab land. Moreover, in recent years, as shown by de Wit (2004, p. 30), the government has been issuing long-term land leases for community lands to privileged citizens and foreigners, without due local consultation and the genuine consent of the customary land owners.

1 The primary data on which this chapter is based was gathered during various periods of time. The first fieldwork was done in 2008 and was meant to focus on the relationship between old-timers and newcomers (Assal 2015). The second round of fieldwork was done in October-November 2012 and was meant to analyse the processes involved in transactions over land. I am indebted to the ANDROMAQUE Project for supporting the latter. Thanks also go to my research assistant, Wala Nogdalla, who conducted interviews in October and November 2012.

 | DOI 10.1163/9789004362185_005

In the past few years, there have been several disputes involving local communities and the government over the appropriation of land for investment purposes. Elsewhere (Assal 2015), I have tackled the communal nature of land ownership in al-Ṣalḥa, and shown that the government had to compensate an ethnic group whose land was appropriated for the purpose of establishing a new international airport the government is intending to build with a Chinese loan. In 2015, another conflict between a community and the government occurred. This was in al-Giraif East, on the eastern bank of the Blue Nile, where inhabitants organized themselves to resist government plans to appropriate land for residential and investment purposes. The conflict is not yet resolved, but it is likely that a deal will be reached in which the locals will get some form of compensation.

In Khartoum, there is, so to speak, a scramble for land. This is obvious in the processes of buying and selling land, which are registered and unregistered without due diligence. Buying unregistered land, selling the same plot to multiple buyers, and grabbing land that belongs to the government and/or private owners occurs, especially in peripheral or peri-urban areas of the city. These processes are described at length later in the chapter. Here, however, the following cases are illustrative of the issues and problems to be tackled, and serve as a prelude to the analysis in the article:

> Buying and selling land here takes place informally, without papers. Greedy people sell the same plot again when the prices go up. This has created a lot of problems. Previously, people had more than one plot and when the owner sells a plot more than once, he can compensate one of the buyers by giving them another land plot. All this happens informally. But things are getting complicated and people have started to go to court. There are certain names that are known as bad people and buyers are warned not to buy land from them. I bought a piece of land close to the Nile three years ago. I paid SDG 3000 plus a car. The size of the land is 400 square metres. After three months, I brought building materials as I was intending to build a house. It appeared that this land belongs to another family; it was an inherited land. The seller gave me land in another place but it happened that this plot has problems too. The seller was unable to give my money back, and I had to report the case to the police and the case was taken to court. The judge decided that this is a civil case. I hired a lawyer and so far, I have paid SDG 8000. I pay rent for the house I am living in now.[2]

2 Interview, Mohamed Abdalla, al-Ṣalḥa, November 2012.

> I am the head of the Popular Committee in al-Ṣalḥa East. The population of the area is 13,000 persons. I was born and grew up here and I inherited this plot. In the old days, we used to give land for free but since 1980 people started to sell land. In 1980, land was sold for 10 to 20 pounds. Today some plots fetch SDG 150,000. Most problems here relate to the multiple selling of land plots. One problem is that people do not get in touch with the *lajna shaʿbiyya* (popular committee). People try to get registration certificates but the fee is high. Fortunately, al-Ṣalḥa East is part of the 1983 aerial map and hence the registration fee is reasonable compared to areas outside the map. For areas outside the 1983 map, registration fees range between SDG 10,000 and SDG 20,000. For me, land is not only money. It is heritage.[3]
>
> In 1994, a steering committee was formed to register people and their land plots as a prelude to the organization of al-Ṣalḥa. In 1996, the committee approached the Village Organization Administration to acknowledge peoples' possessions that are known as *ḥiyāza*.[4] The *ḥiyāza* were acknowledged and registered, and owners were verified. These activities preceded the reorganization process that started in 2007. A registry was opened in the area in February 2008, and since then many people have gotten registration certificates.[5]

The above three cases are telling regarding how land is acquired and how transactions over it, legally or otherwise, are carried out. They also show a process that can be described as land grabbing. As stated, far from having only symbolic value, urban land is becoming economically valuable because of population increase and a lack of trust in other investment avenues. There is a sort of scramble for land in urban areas and al-Ṣalḥa is an example of this, although other similar areas in the national capital are also amenable to this.

Land acquisition in Khartoum is challenging for people with limited income as the simmering demand for it has increased its price. The demand for land grew because of several factors, prominent among which are speculative investment in real estate and migration from the countryside and conflict-ridden areas to the national capital. Long years of protracted conflicts resulted in

3 Interview, Awad al-Sid Mohamed Fadlalmawla, Head of Popular Committee, al-Ṣalḥa East, October 2012.

4 *Ḥiyāza* is any unregistered piece of land. It does not matter who uses it, or who claims it: whether a community, a leader or an individual. If it is unregistered, it is *ḥiyāza*.

5 Interview, Hassan Mohamed Hussien, al-Ṣalḥa, October 2012. Hassan is an old-timer and, like his compatriots, he blames newcomers for the fraudulent transactions in the area.

population drifts from the countryside to major urban areas in Sudan (Assal 2011). The movement of people from the countryside to the city increased the demand for residential land and hence land prices, for the various categories or classes of land, which have risen substantially over the first decade of the 21st century (Pantulliano *et al.* 2011). As a result of the population increase in Khartoum, the value of land has increased substantially, making it less affordable for urban residents.

The deterioration of the economy and the weakness of the Sudanese pound have boosted the value of land. As a result of this, land is seen not only as a symbol of identity but also as a "store of value", which has led to speculative practices that contribute in turn to increasing the prices of urban land and land grabbing. Acquisition is quite a complicated process, with social and legal aspects that require closer scrutiny. In recent years, communal ownership or claims to land acquisition have led to confrontations between communities and the government (Assal 2015).

It is argued that the lack of functionality of land administration both at central and local levels is a key part of the problems surrounding dealings in land (Pantulliano 2007, p. 7). Ownership and access to land are regulated by a dual system: formal and customary. In the countryside, land transactions follow customary rules, whilst the formal registration system prevails in urban areas. In reality, there is a combination of both systems to varying degrees in both the countryside and urban areas. The ways of acquisition that will be described in this chapter correspond to two ownership regimes: freehold and leasehold. The former indicates permanent ownership which cannot be appropriated without fair compensation to the title holder, while the latter is a system whereby the government leases land for a specific period of time, after which the authorities may appropriate such land for other purposes, without having to compensate the leaseholder (El Mahdi 1979). These different types of title have implications for the value of land, its price and transactions. For instance, a freehold plot is more valuable financially than a leasehold plot.

A parcel of land can be acquired through the following three ways: (1) Applying to the relevant authorities, such as the MHPU. For the application to be successful there must be supporting documents that include: certificate of citizenship,[6] marriage certificate, birth certificates of children, affidavit from the popular committee confirming the candidate's residence in the area, and any other documentation that can be provided to support the

6 A citizenship certificate or *jinsiyya* is obligatory. Without it, the application will be rejected, since foreigners are not allowed to own property in Sudan, especially land, although investment firms have been allowed to obtain land leases in Sudan in recent years.

application (Banaga 2010). This option is tedious and can take a long time to take effect, sometimes decades. For this reason, people tend to resort to the other two options. (2) Buying. This is a straightforward process but presents many problems, which are described below. Anyone who can afford the price may buy land, either from an individual owner or from the government. The latter sometimes organizes land auctions, but prices at such auctions are high and only rich people or land speculators can afford to buy auctioned land. The price of land depends on several factors: whether the land is first, second or third class; whether it is freehold or leasehold; whether it is registered or not (Pantulliano *et al.* 2011). Unregistered land is far cheaper and therefore more affordable for low-income buyers, but it has problems as will be adumbrated later. (3) Grabbing by buying and asserting *ḥiyāza* (occupancy). This is a situation in which a person grabs a piece of land and, over time, claims its ownership. This usually happens in peripheral areas, where land is unregistered. *Ḥiyāza* also makes it possible for people to buy and sell unregistered land and hope to register it in due course. In most cases, the authorities regulate the process and legalize ownership, especially if the *ḥiyāza* holders have been residing on the land for a long time. In cases where the squatting or *ḥiyāza* is on registered land or land that belongs either to the government or to private owners, *ḥiyāza* owners will simply be kicked out, without any obligation for the authorities to compensate them.[7]

But *ḥiyāza* should not be perceived as a simple case of land grabbing. Since land in Sudan belongs to communities, there is no such thing as "no man's land". Those who grab land can only do so by obtaining the consent of the communities in question, or traditional authorities in these communities. In al-Ṣalḥa, traditional authorities or those who claim to own the land used to give land for free to people who wanted to reside in the area. This was many decades ago, when the demand for residential land was not as high as it is today. At present, people sell and buy land that is occupied by *ḥiyāza*, although this is risky since the government banned *ḥiyāza* in 2012.

7 In some cases, however, the authorities compensate people by allotting them residential plots in designated areas. Such was the case with squatters in Soba area, which was owned by the military and the University of Khartoum. People who were expelled from Soba were compensated by being allocated land in the al-Fatih area north of Omdurman (Assal 2011). This type of compensation is approved by the government in a bid to avoid political repercussions from not doing so.

Apart from these three main ways to acquire residential land in urban areas, there are other ways, but they are relatively unimportant.[8] In this chapter, we shall attempt to describe and analyse the social and legal aspects of land transactions in the al-Ṣalḥa area of Omdurman. The description and analysis of this article will focus on two ways of acquiring land, buying *ḥiyāza* land and grabbing or squatting, since the first method listed above (applying to the authorities) does not apply in the case of al-Ṣalḥa. The chapter is based on fieldwork carried out in October-November 2012 and also benefits from earlier fieldwork in the area (Assal 2015), especially for background information. In addition to the above introduction, two sections follow, including a brief background about the area and then the dynamics of *ḥiyāza* and the processes involved in acquiring land. Finally, some conclusions are offered based on the material analysed.

Al-Ṣalḥa: A Brief Background[9]

Located about 13 km south-west of Khartoum on the western bank of the White Nile, al-Ṣalḥa emerged during the late 1990s as an attractive residential area affordable to public sector salaried employees and low-income people. Residential areas in Khartoum emerge either because of urban planning or as natural extensions to older residential areas as a result of the increase in the urban population. Al-Ṣalḥa, however, does not represent either case, but is an amalgam of scattered villages that are far away from each other geographically but closer ethnically. Even so, al-Ṣalḥa is much more than an amalgam of old villages; it is more a case of some old villages being connected and joined together by the arrival of newcomers whose ethnic and socioeconomic backgrounds are different, but who managed to penetrate the area and become integrated into its present-day social system.

As old-timers describe it,[10] the life of the older population groups in the area seemed simple as it represented a typical village way of life, in which people practised rain-fed and irrigated agriculture and animal husbandry. Old-timers in al-Ṣalḥa belong to the Jamūʿiyya group, a branch of the Jaʿālīn in north central Sudan. The Jamūʿiya are scattered across the western bank of the White Nile;

8 One way is the so-called *hiba* (gift), when an owner gives a piece of land for free; usually to a close relative or friend.

9 This section is based on earlier fieldwork. See Assal (2015).

10 The term "old-timers" refers here to inhabitants of the old villages in the area, i.e., those who lived in the area before the influx of newcomers to al-Ṣalḥa.

extending from Abu Si'id to Jebel Awlia. The Zanarkha clan of the Jamūʿiyya are the key group in al-Ṣalḥa, even though, following the expansion of the area, many groups from different parts of the country live there. Traditional authority in al-Ṣalḥa is still present and relevant, and is combined with the modern system of popular committees (*lajna shaʿbiyya*). Traditional authority rests with the Jamūʿiyya: each of the old villages used to have a sheikh and the area has an *ʿomda* who is currently the head of the popular committee of Jadain area.[11]

According to the *ʿomda*, the Jamūʿiyya moved from northern Omdurman to this area 175 years ago in search for fertile grazing lands for their sheep, camels and cattle. They combined animal husbandry with sorghum and millet cultivation and also grew vegetables on the White Nile bank. The Jamūʿiyya continued to cultivate and rear animals until the 1980s, when the tree cover was lost as a result of tree felling for the charcoal making practised by local inhabitants. The area became a desert that could not support animals. The Jamūʿiya still practise gardening along the Nile banks, and they depend on land for agriculture.

Administratively, al-Ṣalḥa is part of Omdurman Southern Rural Council or what was historically called *nitāg al-rīf al-janūbi*.[12] Today, al-Ṣalḥa is part of Abu Si'id Locality (*maḥalliyya*). To the north-west of al-Ṣalḥa is Umbadda Locality. The villages comprising al-Ṣalḥa are located close to the White Nile and extend from north to south. They include Sirew, al-Ushara, al-Geeia, Jadain, Higleiga and al-Ṣalḥa. Of all these villages, al-Ṣalḥa is the most famous, owning to its history and this chapter is mainly concerned with al-Ṣalḥa.

Geographically, the area is a plain that slopes towards the White Nile, and is permeated by a few small streams. The soil is sandy in the western parts but rocky and muddy towards the White Nile bank in the eastern part. The area was a dense forest dominated by acacia until the early 1980s, but is now part of the semi-desert climate that is characteristic of North Kordofan.

According to old-timers, the area was given the name (al-Ṣalḥa) by a religious sheikh and a Sufi leader named Sheikh Abdelmajid al-Jamūʿi who was a resident of Abu Siʿid. The sheikh used to come to the area when it was forest. Al-Ṣalḥa itself lies in the middle of the area, but for simplicity and because of

11 The area has three popular committees: Jadain, al-Ṣalḥa and Higeleiga.

12 This translates as "southern rural area", which is in a way an amalgamation of villages south of Omdurman. There is also the so-called *nitāg al-rīf al-shimālī* (northern rural area). These names do not have any administrative connotations and they do not represent administrative bodies, especially at present, when the formally recognized administrative bodies are the localities and local administrative units.

the positive implications of the name,[13] Al-Ṣalḥa is used to refer to the whole area that originally contained sixty-four scattered villages.

Some of the original villages in the area have retained their traditional structures in terms of ethnic composition and social interaction, but al-Ṣalḥa and a few adjacent ones have been affected by an influx of newcomers from different parts of Khartoum, and have thus been part of the new situation, in which there are more newcomers than old-timers. The newcomers are ethnically and socially heterogeneous. They are also heterogeneous in terms of livelihood strategies and opportunities – some are government employees, while others are not – and in terms of life-style and residential patterns. Some inhabitants already have houses built with permanent materials while some others still live in mud houses. There are also many empty residential plots whose owners are either unable to build or would like to keep them as a future investment.

Due to the rapid population influx, many old villages have disappeared.[14] Most of al-Ṣalḥa's inhabitants are young, especially the newcomers. These newcomers bought residential land plots from the old-timers, the Jamūʿiyya, who are becoming a homogeneous minority amidst an ethnically and socially heterogeneous community. Social relationships and interactions between old-timers and newcomers are, at best, ambiguous, since the newcomers are perceived by the old-timers as "foreigners" or *aghrāb*.

Ḥiyāza Dynamics: Grabbing or "Business as Usual"?

What is happening in areas like al-Ṣalḥa needs to be seen within the wider dynamics of the rapid growth of Khartoum, whose population is in the 6–8 million range. This has led to pressure on land for housing developments and other purposes, including the building of schools, hospitals and shops. With the increase in land prices, everyone seems to be looking for land. Newspapers in Khartoum abound with stories of fraudulent land deals, which sometimes involve senior government officials. There are situations where, with the power of influence, individuals, mainly senior government officials,

---

13 Literally, al-Ṣalḥa means "the pious woman".

14 People spoke about 1998 as the beginning of the conspicuous influx of newcomers to al-Ṣalḥa. Since then, the influx of people continued as al-Ṣalḥa is valued as a residential area for its proximity to the centre of Khartoum, and because land prices are somewhat affordable when compared with other areas in Omdurman and other parts of the national capital.

can allocate many plots of land to themselves.[15] These fraudulent practices may be facilitated a variety of factors, including the ineffective land registration system and the existence of large undeveloped tracts of land in urban peripheries. Ideally, urban land should be measured, titled and registered. This means that every parcel of land should be referenced to its cadastral points, and there should be a land register with information freely accessible, so that anyone can check before embarking on any transaction. But apparently, this is too good to be true in the case of Sudan.

Since the Jamūʿiya are *ḥiyāza* landholders, they sell land to newcomers. Al-Sadiq Ziyyada was a former secretary of the popular committee in al-Ṣalḥa West. He says:

> I have one plot of land which I bought from the Jamūʿiya in 2003. I registered the land with a lawyer and got a *ḥiyāza* card from the popular committee. When the government started the planning process I wanted to get a registration certificate. My plot is 500 square metres and to register it I must pay SDG 20 per square metre. This is a lot of money and I cannot afford it.[16]

Al-Sadiq mentions a frequent problem: "conflict takes place because the Arabs [the Jamūʿiyya] sell the same plot of land to many people. In most cases, the buyers divide the land, but if one refuses this solution they resort to the court." Al-Sadiq is a newcomer to the area and his story contrasts with that of an old-timer:

> We do not have problems in al-Ṣalḥa east because we are relatives. We avoid selling our land to *aghrāb* [foreigners] and we also avoid having them amongst us. When we get into problems, we solve them through *jūdiya* (arbitration). The *aghrāb* go to the court. We do not.[17]

15 In 2014, the dailies in Khartoum published material to the effect that the incumbent Undersecretary of the Ministry of Justice had appropriated many land plots to his personal benefit while he was Registrar of Land. The charges were never investigated, although he was removed from office.

16 Interview, al-Sadiq Ziyyada, al-Ṣalḥa, November 2012.

17 Interview, an old-timer, al-Ṣalḥa, October 2012. The terms *aghrāb*, *ajānib* and *wāfidīn* are frequently used by the old-timers when referring to the newcomers. There are tensions between these two groups, with each accusing the other of contributing to problems in the area.

Al-Ṣalḥa is a peripheral urban area and huge tracts of land are undeveloped – typical of areas that attract land grabbing. According to the 1970 Land Act, such undeveloped land belongs to the government. But as noted above, the land actually belongs to the community, the Jamū'iya in this case. Be that as it may, the fact is that undeveloped land attracts land grabbers, who are usually recent migrants from the countryside or people who move from one part of the city to another in search of land on which to construct houses. In the recent history of Khartoum, and in some cases, IDPs have occupied certain areas and forced the government to recognize their right to plots of land (Assal 2011). If the occupied land belongs to the government, there is a possibility that the authorities may simply reorganize it, allowing people to stay legally. Komo (2014, p. 4) cites a similar example from the city of Dar es Salam, Tanzania, where a group of people invaded land that belonged to a factory, although they were eventually evicted as the factory won a court case against them.

The practice of *ḥiyāza* is much more complex than it appears. The occupation of land by groups such as IDPs or other politically motivated groups is one form. Buying and selling unregistered land is another, and this article deals basically with buying and selling unregistered land, land that is claimed by default. Without going into detail, it should also be noted that the notion of *ḥiyāza* has a religious foundation. In Islamic jurisprudence, there is a saying: "Land is for whoever is living on it", *al-arḍ li-ghatiniha*. This means that someone who occupies a piece of land has a good chance of acquiring ownership, even if it belongs to someone else.

Transactions over land in al-Ṣalḥa require two witnesses in addition to the buyer and the seller. For land that has a registration certificate (*shihādat baḥth*), the transaction is straightforward and is verified by a lawyer in the presence of two witnesses who possess valid identity cards and the lawyer authenticates the transaction. Without such authentication, the buyer cannot transfer the ownership to his/her name. The process is described below in an interview with a buyer who recounts his experience of getting the registration certificate. Here, however, it should be noted that transactions over unregistered land are less formal and have loopholes that get buyers into problems. One woman argues:

> The main problem here is multiple selling. You buy land and after a while someone appears and tells you that this is their land. You see that piece of land [denoting to a neighbouring piece of land], its owner had a serious problem for many years. It was only three months ago that he was able to reclaim it. People get fake witnesses and corrupt lawyers. The registration certificate is important because it guards against these problems. I do not

> have a registration certificate, although I want one. It is too expensive. I have done all the steps except this one and I do not understand why they are making it so expensive. I am waiting for a discount.[18]

Indeed, the fee for a registration certificate is high and not commensurate with the level of the owner's income. Informants said that the fee for land registration could be as high as SDG 20000 (USD 4000 in 2012). Abdel Rafi' Mustafa argues:

> I am keen to register. I have a paper showing that this is my land; unfortunately, I cannot afford to pay the registration fee. My plot is 1000 square metres and I must pay SDG 20000, which I do not have.[19]

Abdelmoneim Abdelrahman is an old-timer and has three plots: "I am an old-timer and I have three plots. I have a registration certificate for one plot and a *ḥiyāza* card for the other two. I do not have enough money to get certificates for the remaining two."[20]

According to locals, empty land plots attract brokers. Owners who leave their land unattended for a long time risk having such plots sold or grabbed by those in need for a place to live. Muna Ahmed traveled to Libya before building her house in al-Ṣalḥa. When she got back, someone was living on her land:

> When I came back from Libya, I found someone I do not know living on my land. He had a room. I brought my luggage and built a room. The man brought a court order to evict us and he destroyed the room I built. I filed a court case asking for compensation and the case is under consideration by the court. I got a registration certificate and as you can see I am living in my place now.[21]

Ḥiyāza (in the sense of grabbing someone's land and squatting on it, or buying unregistered land) is the main way in which people in al-Ṣalḥa acquire land. But since many people either have registration certificates or are staying on their land, and since the government outlawed *ḥiyāza* in 2012, buying is becoming the only way to acquire land,. The government declares that those who acquire land through *ḥiyāza* are committing a felony. Their ownership will not

18 Interview, Halima Ibrahim, al-Ṣalḥa, November 2012.

19 Interview, Abdel Rafi' Mustafa, al-Ṣalḥa, November 2012.

20 Interview, Abdelmoneim Abdelrahman, al-Ṣalḥa, November 2012.

21 Interview, Muna Ahmed, al-Ṣalḥa, November 2012.

be recognized and they may even be charged with illegal transactions over land. However, the banning of *ḥiyāza* contravenes communal land rights and it is not clear how the government will deal with communal land claims. For instance, the government recognizes the communal rights of the Jamūʿiyya and in fact the newcomers mostly buy land from the old timers: the Jamūʿiyya. This was the case during the first few years of al-Ṣalḥa's development. At present, however, land is changing hands between different categories of people, between buyers and sellers, between brokers and buyers, and between brokers and sellers.[22] One of the old-timers argues that disputes are concentrated in the older parts of the area:

> Old Ṣalḥa is where most problems occur because it was the first part where people started selling land. And the prices were so low. My neighbour sold his land for a gas cylinder [he laughs while telling this story]. In the early days, disputes were solved locally through arbitration because at the time prices were not high. Today if a person is asked to return the money based on current prices then no one can do that. That is why people go to court.[23]

Apart from the problem of multiple selling, other less problematic disputes include the encroachment onto a neighbour's plot: "Disputes over plot borders occur. Old-timers do not make a fuss out of this though because they are relatives. The *aghrāb* (newcomers) brought problems and they go to court even for minor things."[24] Another problem is encroachment onto public spaces such as playgrounds or other empty spaces reserved for public use.

In al-Ṣalḥa, as in other parts of Khartoum, brokers are also active buyers and sellers. Their position enables them to fish for the best deals as they have insider information about land. They get land maps from the survey department and know which land has problems and therefore avoid it. Brokers get commission from sellers and some invest it in land. They are involved in land transactions and know how to buy their way into the system. Generally, land brokerage is a lucrative business in Sudan.

---

22 Brokers are very active in the land market in Khartoum generally, as land is perceived as a store of value. People invest in land since they do not trust the Sudanese pound, which has lost value substantially since the secession of South Sudan.

23 Interview, Juma'a al-Tigani, al-Ṣalḥa, November 2012.

24 Interview, al-Faki Ali Mustafa, al-Ṣalḥa, November 2012. Al-Faki is an old-timer and complains about his inability to get a registration certificate.

Social networks ease the process of land acquisition. It is through such networks that people find out about land possibilities. Such networks may also help buyers to get some kind of discount or a reduced price, although in most cases the transaction is permeated with haggling between the buyer and seller, during which the broker may also intervene and facilitate the process. Brokers are authorized dealers and have a professional union in Sudan. While they are not involved in the process of land registration, buyers solicit their help since they know the area well, and they also know a lot about which land is good, where it is located, the prices and much more.

In some cases, buyers and sellers interact directly, especially if they know each other. Buyers prefer to use the services of a broker since, as said above, brokers know whether a piece of land is problematic or not.[25] If the land is not registered, the process of buying and selling is not complicated: the buyer simply pays money to the owner and that ends the deal. This is normally the case with land plots that are communally owned, where traditional leaders who claim ownership sell the land. In some cases, buyers insist on having a contract drawn up by a lawyer in the presence of two witnesses.

The problem of multiple selling arises most often with unregistered land. The case of Mukhtar, who bought a plot of land in al-Ṣalḥa West in 2007, is illustrative. It turned out that the owner sold the same plot to two other buyers and that the land was not registered. When Mukhtar brought some building material in 2011, two other owners showed up and claimed ownership. The three of them had papers showing that they were the owners, but all the papers were signed by different witnesses. "The original owner is a crook. He used different witnesses to cover up his wrongdoing. This is complicated and is going to take long time to resolve since the land is not registered," argues Mukhtar. This case is currently in court.

In the case of registered land, the process of transferring land is tedious and slightly complicated. The Land Registration Department (part of the Judiciary), where the process of registration takes place, does not accept transactions that are not verified and authenticated by a lawyer. When a person buys land, it is required that he or she completes a registration process whereby the ownership is transferred from the seller to the buyer. Osman, who recently bought land in al-Ṣalḥa describes the process as follows:

---

25 Brokers have insider information about plots of land. Because the value of land is very high, there are a lot of malpractices: some plots of land are bought and sold to more than one person at the same time.

> I started by asking the broker about land prices here. He provided me with many options that I should consider. He also introduced me to some sellers so I established a direct contact with them. I was successful in buying land. I had authenticated the process through a lawyer. When I went to get the registration certificate from Omdurman Land Office, I was asked to go to the Survey Department first, to locate the plot on the ground and describe or reference it to its cadastre points, in terms of size and class, and whether it is residential or commercial. Then I went back to the Land Office, paid the registration fee and was asked to go to the Land Registration Department to get the certificate. The process is tedious and in all the steps I was asked to show either my passport or the document I used when authenticating the purchase in front of the lawyer. Finally, I got my registration certificate. I am an owner now.[26]

Almost all disputes about land ownership are dealt with in court, as selling and buying involve large sums of money and this makes it difficult for traditional leaders to play a role even if they do play important part in dealing with other disputes. Interviews with lawyers involved in land transactions show that local authorities (popular committees) are, in some cases, also part of the problem. Their role must therefore be looked at critically. One lawyer argued:

> During the period 1996–1999 there was a registration office in al-Ṣalḥa. The office was closed, and most people did not register at this office because they did not have enough money. They size of most *ḥiyāza* plots was big and people could not afford to pay. The locality delegated its authority to issue *ḥiyāza* ownership to the *lajna shaʿbiyya*. The problem is that the members of the *lajna shaʿbiyya* with a stamp started selling land. They became land brokers.[27]

This lawyer is involved in *ḥiyāza* buying and selling transactions. She describes the transactions as follows:

> The seller [the owner of the *ḥiyāza*] agrees to forego his *ḥiyāza* to the buyer in the presence of two witnesses with valid identity cards. Four people are involved. The buyer pays the price and the parties then go to

26 Interview, Osman, al-Ṣalḥa, October 2012.
27 Interview, Sana'a Dafallah, a lawyer in al-Ṣalḥa, October 2012.

> see the plot to make sure it exists. Then the transaction is verified and authenticated by the lawyer's stamp.[28]

Like other parts of Khartoum, al-Ṣalḥa is growing rapidly. The areas where this fieldwork was carried out (al-Ṣalḥa East and West), has a population of about 13,000 based on the population census of 2008 (CBS 2009). Popular committee members estimate the total number of residential plots in al-Ṣalḥa East and West to be 3000. In terms of services, there are 16 kindergartens, one public primary school, four private primary schools, five private high schools, eleven mosques, one public health centre, five private health centres, and one police station.

However, part of the story is that land is increasingly becoming an economic commodity as brokers are there to buy and sell, and many investors are also buying land. A broker in al-Ṣalḥa West argued:

> What is happening is that the rich people are speculating over land. Land is viewed as a trustworthy asset, one that keeps the value of money. Traders who used to buy and sell foreign currency are now buying land. Investing in land is a guaranteed business.[29]

With the government banning *ḥiyāza* in 2012, acquiring land became difficult for low-income groups, but this is perhaps a necessary step towards standardizing the legal aspects of acquiring land, and may also contribute to reducing the incidence of fraudulent deals in unregistered land. However, as indicated earlier, it remains to be seen how the government will be able to enforce this decision, especially in land that is communally owned or claimed.

Conclusions

A combination of factors contributes to a process that could be dubbed ambiguous land grabbing in al-Ṣalḥa. Looking at this problem in its wider context, we can consider a typology of land grabbing practices. While inappropriate transactions may take place for registered land, most cases concern unregistered peri-urban land, as the case of al-Ṣalḥa illustrates. The stories presented in this chapter illustrate several issues related to the problems surrounding residential land in the national capital. While the story here has been about al-Ṣalḥa,

28 *Ibid.*

29 Interview, Abdalla Ibrahim, al-Ṣalha, November 2013. Abdalla is a broker in the area.

it is possible to argue that other similar places may also have similar stories to tell. Communalist and individualist tendencies compete: old-timers versus newcomers, *ḥiyāza* versus formal registration, etc. This is all happening in the context of the absence of a functioning land registration system in Sudan, and increasing rural-urban migration, which fuels the demand for urban land.

In the view of policy makers, and probably of academics too, the transactions over land in al-Ṣalḥa constitute illegal land grabbing. For people in al-Ṣalḥa, however, it is business as usual. For sellers, particularly old-timers, the land belongs to them and so they have the right to sell it. For buyers, the need for land is legitimate and so they engage with the system in play. Ironically, the land transaction business is lucrative even to the government, since it receives substantial revenues from land registration fees. In the context of a badly performing economy, land is a source of government revenue.

Multiple sales of the same land appear to be the main problem people are concerned about in al-Ṣalḥa. Those who do not have land registration certificates (Annexe 3.1) are in constant fear: someday, someone may appear and claim their land, even though the area has been reorganized since 2007 and a registry has been open there since 2008. People cannot afford to pay registration fees, as they are high, especially in areas outside of the 1983 aerial map. In as much as registration guards against fraudulent practices, the inability to register land increases the likelihood of multiple selling. And with the 2012 ban on *ḥiyāza*, inhabitants are under the threat of being evicted by the government.

The government's move to ban *ḥiyāza* is ironic, since the area sprang up through *ḥiyāza* occupancy that was later reorganized and formally registered, although most people have not registered yet. In fact, most peripheral urban areas in Khartoum began through *ḥiyāza* and were later reorganized by the authorities. Old-timers in al-Ṣalḥa are not keen to register because they know who owns what and they trust each other. They have been living in the area for a long time and are not bothered about the need to register, even though some of them have registered their land, or part of it, as seen in one of the interviews. The situation is different for newcomers, who try to get registration certificates since they do not know much about the dynamics of land in the area, and they are also wary about the possibility of having their land sold.

Tensions exist between the old-timers and newcomers. This chapter reinforces the findings of earlier work (Assal 2015) about the relationships between old-timers and newcomers to the area. It has been shown that the two groups blame each other for malpractices related to transactions over land. Lack of trust is one issue here: in the view of the newcomers, old-timers engage in multiple selling; in the view of the old-timers, newcomers are greedy and involved in faking documents and appropriating land that does not belong to them. It will take time for such divisions to disappear, but they may persist, especially if land continues to be unregistered.

Lajna sha'biyya (popular committees) play an important role in matters related to land allocation. In certain periods, the MHPU authorized popular committees in al-Ṣalḥa to issue *ḥiyāza* cards for residents, to verify and authenticate claims to ownership, and to be involved in other transactions, such as the buying and selling of land. The role of popular committees, for good or ill, is critical. From one perspective, they help to organize the area and protect the rights of the inhabitants. From another, they can be perceived as part of the problem, since they may take advantage of their position, as claimed by one of the lawyers in the area.

Jūdiya, or the traditional arbitration mechanism, is used to resolve disputes. *Jūdiya* can be resorted to for minor disputes and disputes between old-timers, as some informants claim. In cases of multiple selling, and if the seller has land, the second buyer can be compensated. But if the seller does not have land and cannot compensate the buyer, the case is taken to court, as the first interview extract shows. More people are resorting to the courts since transactions over land currently involve large sums of money. In taking cases to court, people may end up paying a lot of money to lawyers, since court cases normally take a long time to settle, with cases of land disputes taking a particularly long time to be resolved. One of the examples shown in the article illustrates this.

Finally, there is a need to codify customary practices relating to land. In the case of Sudan, reference is frequently made to the 1970 Act that made all unregistered land government property. However, in practice, land belongs to communities. While this has long been the case in the countryside, in recent years, and owing to the increasing value of land, communities in urban areas have started claiming communal ownership. In many cases, including al-Ṣalḥa, the government has acquiesced to these claims by recognizing communal rights. There is, so to speak, a de facto codification of customary practices, although the government does not want to formalize this, so that it can retain its leverage over communalist land claims in both rural and urban Sudan.

References

Assal, M 2015, 'Old-timers and Newcomers in al-Salha. Dynamics of Land Allocation in an Urban Periphery', in B Casciarri, M Assal & F Ireton (eds), *Multidimensional Change in Sudan 1989–2011*, Berghahn Books, New York/Oxford, pp. 15–32.

Assal, M 2011, 'From the Country to The town', in J Ryle, J Willis, S Baldo, & JM Jok (eds), *The Sudan Handbook*, James Currey, London, pp. 63–69.

Banaga, S 2010, 'The Development of Khartoum. Urban Structure and Agenda 21', presentation at the City Day seminar, University of Khartoum.

CBS 2009, *Preliminary Results of the 5th Population Census for Sudan*, CBS, Khartoum.

de Wit, P 2004, *Land and Poverty Study in Sudan. Scoping of Issues and Questions to Be Addressed.* Prepared under project OSRO/SUD/409/HCR, financed by UNHCR, the Norwegian Refugee Council and FAO, Khartoum.

El Mahdi, S 1979, *Introduction to the Land Law of the Sudan*, Khartoum University Press, Khartoum.

Komo, F 2014, *Urban Land Grabbing and Its Implications to Urban Development*, Conference paper, FIG Congress, Kuala Lumpur, Malaysia, 16–21 June.

Pantulliano, S 2007, *The Land Question. Sudan's Peace Nemesis*, Humanitarian Policy Group Working Paper, Overseas Development Institute, London.

Pantulliano, S *et al.* 2011, *City Limits. Urbanization and Vulnerability in Khartoum*, Overseas Development Institute, London.

CHAPTER 4

Access to Land for Non-Muslims in Greater Khartoum: Disclosing Divergent Minority Models in International and Sudanese Laws

Philippe Gout

Introduction

In this chapter, I shall focus on the issue of access to land rights for non-Muslim communities in Greater Khartoum after the secession of South Sudan in July 2011. I shall delve into the discordant legal categorization of religious minorities in international law and Sudanese Islamic law, and attempt to reveal the epistemic and normative gap existing between international and Sudanese legal orders that has led to an opposing modelling of religious minorities. This epistemic gap will be examined in land claims by non-Muslims in Greater Khartoum and will illustrate the incapacity of international law to accurately relativize its classification of religious minorities in Sudan. Though most of the argument refers to Christian communities, some specific Muslim groups – notably Shiʿas – adopt a version of Islam diverging from that of the political elite and the majority of the Sudanese population, so reference to "non-Muslims" in the Sudanese political context also means pointing to "non-Sunni" mainstream groups. In this introduction, I first present the setting, followed by the methodology and the argumentation, and finally an overview of the chapter.

Presenting the Setting

My study is based on a series of interviews with representatives of religious communities and lawyers, which also resulted in the collection of data, including administrative documents, various official reports or NGOs' briefs and statements. This work was mostly carried out between August 2013 and March 2014 as part of my doctoral fieldwork. I specifically examine an ongoing case study of a Nuba church consecrated in 1976 in the former urban slum of Haj Yusif, north-east Khartoum, that later underwent urban planning. The religious authority in charge of the church has been seeking land registration and a licence since 1993, with no success to date. The church belongs to the Sudanese Church of Christ (SCC): a Sudanese Protestant church that became autonomous in 1962 with congregations both in Khartoum and in the

 | DOI 10.1163/9789004362185_006

Nuba Mountains. Reverend Yagūb Hamōda al-Nur, a Nuba Moro, is the head of the church.[1] The Nuba is a recently constructed aggregate of "African" ethnic groups autochthonous to the Nuba Mountains. Certain Nuba groups – notably Moro – have been politically active and sided with the former southern rebels or are now involved in the rebel activities in South Kordofan. Nuba communities partly settled in Greater Khartoum as the result of successive civil wars or labour migration. In the recent history of Sudan, Nuba communities have also experienced Christianization and Islamization, even though animism is still practised.

Even though no explicit legal definition of "minority" exists in Sudan, the church's authority in Haj Yusif is increasingly formulating its claim according to religious minority discourse. This can be explained by the fact that the granting of full citizenship in Sudan depends on membership of a specific nation, consistent with the revived "Civilization Project" of the national government, also known as the Ingaz regime. Some Christian communities therefore self-ascribe a "minority" status drawn from international law, in view of their perceived lack of basic citizenship rights. By doing so, they claim a special and autonomous legal regime consisting of a set of legal rights that would protect their distinctive identity.[2]

From 1983, *sharīʿa* became the main source of law as the Sudanese state gradually became an Islamic theocracy.[3] The protection regime for non-Muslims resulting from this reform led to a supposedly differentiated treatment that

1 Reverend Yagūb Hamōda al-Nur is also the former Secretary General of the Sudan Council of Churches located in Amarat. The Council is a Sudanese association representing the various churches active in Sudan and empowered to work out a common strategy to protect their respective interests.

2 It is only when minorities are enabled to resort to their distinctive identities, and possibly to their own organized services and institutions, to participate in the political and economic life of their state, that they can eventually acquire a legal status similar to the majority.

3 Before 1983, Islamic law was one of the legal sources for personal matters and status. *Sharīʿa* Courts adjudicated matters of personal law and status law for Muslims. They were headed by the Grand Qadi, while the Civil Courts were headed by the Chief Justice. The Judgement (Basic Rule) Act 1983, section 3, reshuffled the hierarchy of legal sources in Sudan in such a way that *sharīʿa* was no longer restricted to personal matters but gradually became the common law of Sudan. Following President Nimeiry's famous "September Laws" in 1983, *sharīʿa* gradually became the most important source of law in the Sudanese legal order. Apart from the fact that the scope of the Judgement (Basic Rule) Act extends *ratione materiae* to personal, civil and criminal law, all other legal sources have to be interpreted and implemented in accordance with *sharīʿa*. Furthermore, in the absence of express provision or in the presence of ambiguous ones, judges are required to resort to the principles of Islamic law.

had neither a "reasonable" nor an "objective" basis. These two requirements of reasonableness and objectivity, established by the UNHRC, are intended to be scrutinized on a case by case basis to prevent differentiated treatments from being discriminatory and in breach of the principle of equality before the law.[4] It will become apparent that the differentiated treatment in this case – the *dhimma* regime – does not provide for "practical" equality, but precisely sneaks in a regime that discriminates against non-Muslim groups into the Sudanese legal order. Instead of offering non-Muslims a way out of Islamic law, this regime plunges them deeper into it. I shall show that this kind of special and discriminatory regime does not meet the international standards for minority status. Nevertheless, some non-Muslims communities – notably Nuba Christians in Greater Khartoum – try to resort to this fabricated *dhimma* regime to cope with discriminatory access to land rights. A deeper insight into these groups' make-up and the rational for discrimination shows that the groups at risk are not so much religious minorities according to the legal definition but rather ethnic groups.

Methodology

Given that no explicit definition of "minority" exists in Sudanese law, assessing the existence of religious minorities cannot result from a deductive approach based on already granted legal statuses.[5] An assessment can only result from an inductive approach through the observation of *de facto* legal regimes applied to specific religious groups. This inductive approach will rely on the concept of "legal pluralism" as described in Woodman's taxonomy in his contribution to the 1996 CEDEJ's Seminar held in Cairo (1999). His taxonomy distinguishes between internal legal pluralism and deep legal pluralism. The former implies that pluralism exists within a single legal order, such as: the state legal order so that the main body of laws somehow sanctions the "deviant" or "alternative" body of laws from within. The latter assumes that the "alternative" body of laws is outside the main – state – legal order and operates autonomously, although it may govern the same situations.

4 The requirements were established by the UNHCR in its General Comment No. 18 of 1989, on the principles of non-discrimination and equality before the law. The General Comment mainly focuses on article 2 paragraph 1 and article 26 of the 1966 ICCPR.

5 Only article 47 of the Sudanese Bill of Rights seems to refer, though indirectly, to the rights of minorities, as it roughly echoes the wording of article 27 of the ICCPR, which is known as the main provision on the rights of minorities. However, even article 47 does not make any explicit or implicit reference to the notion of minority.

I suggest that the law of minorities requires the establishment of special legal regimes that reflect minorities' distinctive identities. I therefore reject the traditional analytical tool of legal syllogism and instead assess the existence of religious minorities in Sudan from the factual and inductive observation of "alternative" bodies of laws specifically dedicated to certain religious groups. Given the importance of land in the exercise of religious rights and freedoms, legal pluralism depends largely on land rights and other human rights that can be exercised through access to land. As far as Greater Khartoum is concerned, these are statutory and formal rights whose access for local communities requires interaction with public institutions. My emphasis is consequently on internal legal pluralism. I shall assert in this chapter that no internal legal minority status for non-Muslims exists in Sudan. These groups are indeed granted a status equivalent to *dhimma*,[6] but, in Sudan, this status is not distinct from *sharīʿa* but an adaptation from within it, so there is no true internal legal pluralism.[7] Thus, the Sudanese legal order does not provide for a real minority status for non-Muslim groups, even though their *dhimma* status means that they may appear to be religious minorities under international law. Consequently, these merely *de facto* fabricated religious minorities do not benefit from any kind of legal pluralism under the national legal order, although international law would classify them as *de jure* religious minorities. References to translation and actor-network theories will stress the inability of the international minority model to enter unaltered into the idiosyncratic Sudanese legal order (Callon 1986; Behrends, Park and Rottenburg 2014). This situation reveals the lack of reflexivity of various international actors who support discriminated groups on the basis of the international minority model. In so doing, the model is solidified and even less able to resolve discrimination in Greater Khartoum.

Overview

I examine first the above-mentioned on-going case study to demonstrate how the dualist nature of the Sudanese legal order facilitates discrimination in accessing land rights. The group that is discriminated against tries to overplay the theocratic nature of the Sudanese state in order to present itself as a religious

6 The original *dhimmīs* were non-Muslim subjects living under Islamic rule on the basis of a treaty concluded with the Prophet and that gave them a status called *dhimma*. According to this treaty, the *dhimmīs* accepted the sovereignty of the Islamic political system and were in return granted protection of their person and property and religious freedoms.

7 This absence of legal pluralism does not, however, automatically entail discrimination by the state.

minority and bargain for minority rights guaranteed under international standards. However, religious minority status can easily be manipulated, given the weakness of the definition of "minority" in international law. In the context of the Sudanese Islamic legal order, what seems at first glance to be discrimination against religious minorities often affects other kind of identities, such as ethnic groups. As a consequence, some groups of Christians objectified as *dhimmīs* mobilize this fabricated status in the hope of a privileged interaction with public authorities, but this does not strengthen the protection of their land rights because they are not in fact discriminated against on merely religious grounds. I shall lastly present concluding considerations on the international actors' unmindfulness of the epistemic distortion affecting the *dhimma* status. Instead, these actors refer to Christian IDPs who experience discrimination as religious minorities and they therefore support the inappropriate equivalence between international religious minority status and Sudanese *dhimma*. They are unable to realize that discrimination over land rights in Greater Khartoum affects any IDP or migrant, whether Muslim or not, whose land title is not clearly established.

The Sudanese Church of Christ Seeking Land Rights in the Dualist Sudanese Legal Order

The dualist nature of the Sudanese legal order affects the constitutionally guaranteed right to property to the detriment of the SCC, which is trying to register a land title in al-Bashir West city – Haj Yusif. The 2005 Constitution stresses the dualist nature of the Sudanese legal order, cancelling the autonomous efficacy of international human rights provisions in Sudanese law. These provisions had to be transposed into the national Constitution or legislation and so were modified to fit better with the fundamental principles of the 2005 Constitution.

Case Study: The Sudanese Church of Christ Seeking Land Registration in al-Bashir City

Four camps were originally created for the settlement of IDPs in the Greater Khartoum "Three Towns": Mayo-Mandela and Jebel Awlia south of Khartoum; Wad al-Bashir and Dar as-Salam west of Omdurman. Other settlements are recorded in UN statistics for IDPs in Khartoum, such as Navaisha, Baraka and Hamas Koreib (Fluehr-Lobban 2012, p. 189). It is difficult, however, to refer to these camps as enclosed areas and they generally developed as permanent residential districts in the way of an urban slum. In addition to IDP camps, two major urban slums housing poor populations – including IDPs – can be found

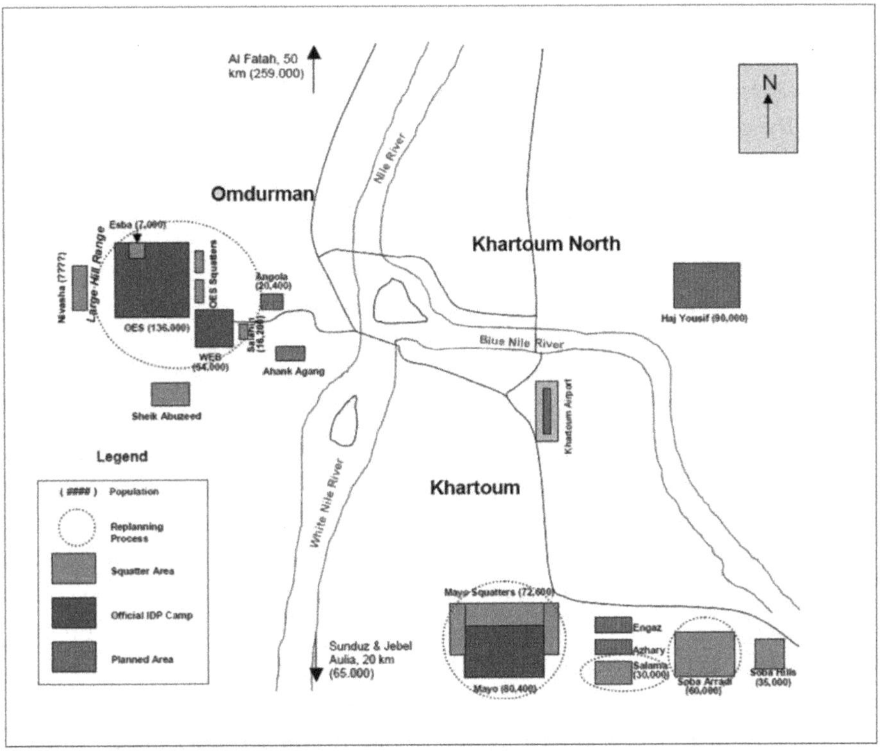

MAP 4.1 *Khartoum IDPs areas in 2004.*
SOURCE: KHARTOUM STATE INTERAGENCY RAPID ASSESSMENT REPORT, 2004.

in Soba Aradi and Haj Yusif. The latter is located in eastern Khartoum North (Bahrī) and is inhabited by a wide community of Nuba migrants who have fled the successive armed conflicts in South Kordofan (see Map 4.1). The Nuba wrestling arena, which is open every Friday, is located in this area near Suk Sitta, testifying to the significance of the local Nuba community.

The government's urban planning policy during the 1980s and 1990s aimed at relegating IDPs and migrants to the outskirts of Khartoum. Most of the migrants sent to IDP camps were from South Sudan, except in Dar as-Salam, where Darfurians were numerous. Populations able to be assimilated in line with the government policies tended to be sent into newly planned districts. Before 2003 – when the planning policies and the survey of IDP camps started – settlement in the camps was deemed temporary and no land appropriation or registration was allowed, although this was not true in urban slums or other unplanned areas where IDPs also settled. In Haj Yusif, IDPs and migrants bought unregistered land plots directly from local residents, although article 4 of the Unregistered Land Act 1970 states that unused and unregistered lands shall be the property of the government. Registration of titles to land bought by IDPs in Haj Yusif was nonetheless complicated when the State of Khartoum started the planning of this area in the early 1990s.

The case in question relates to a church built from mud and straw in 1976 in Haj Yusif, on behalf of the SCC. All the community members are Nuba. More precisely, the church is located in the sub-district known as Medinat al-Bashir Gharib (al-Bashir West city). This area is administered by a *lajna shaʿbiyya* (popular committee), which is the smallest administrative unit in the "decentralized" Sudanese administrative system.[8] Churches seek land registration with the State Ministry of Religious Affairs (Guidance and Endowments). In order to be granted a building permit, they have then to obtain a title on the land with the State Ministry of Construction and Planning and the Local Planning Office. Only after these two processes are completed may a church build a new place of worship. In the case in question, the church was built on an unregistered plot of land before the area was even surveyed by the government agencies and without completing these two required processes. The SCC started a series of applications to all the relevant administrative bodies in Khartoum State to obtain land registration and a building permit from 1993 onwards. The most edifying part of this never-ending process consists in the skill of administrative bodies in shifting the blame onto each other so that the applying church has a sense of going round in circles (Figure 4.1).

In the early 1990s Khartoum State started restructuring Medinat al-Bashir Gharib in line with its urban planning for Haj Yusif. From the start, however, the planning process took no account of the site of the church. The church community applied first in July 1993 to the Director of Endowments and Religious Affairs at the popular committee. The application was filed while the planning process was under way, to suggest that the public authorities should take due account of the church and allow for the appropriate land registration and the building permit. From this first application onwards, the church authority based its claims on religious freedoms and minority rights instead of the mere regularization of rights *in rem*. The application relies implicitly on

8 The Sudanese federal administrative system is a top-down structure: the *wilāyas* (constituent states of the federal system) are the main administrative units of federal decentralization. The constituent states oversee the *maḥalliyyas* (localities, or urban and rural councils), which replaced the former *muḥāfaẓas* (provinces) since 2006. The *lajna shaʿbiyya*, the grass-roots level of state decentralization, is a body of volunteer neighbours administering the affairs of their village or quarter. They are elected by a local constituent assembly similar to a public forum, which is notably empowered with approving the popular committee's programmes.

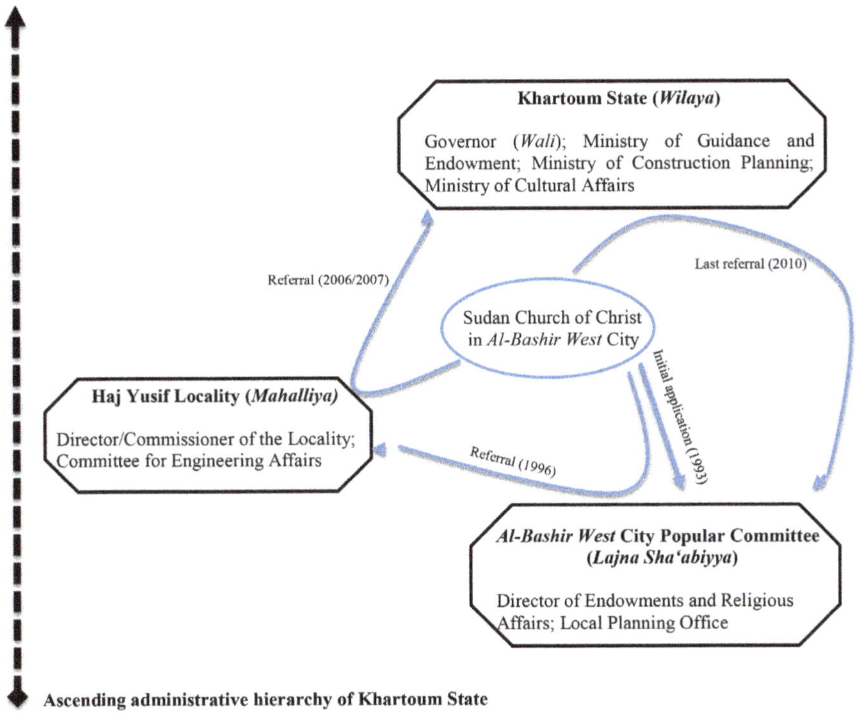

FIGURE 4.1 *Process of circular applications by the Sudanese Church of Christ in Ḥāj Yūsif.*

the right of religious minority to worship and assemble and to establish and maintain places for these purposes.[9] In its claim, the church authority notably stated: "We have no other place to practise our rituals" and "Christian believers practise their daily and weekly rituals there till now" (Annexe 4.1.). The planning process took no account of the claim and allocated the plot for public services, giving it public service number No. 353, located in Block 2 on the cadastral plan, and marking the building with the acronym GR (Governmental Registration), recalling the 1970 Unregistered Land Act (Annexe 4.2.). It is worth noting that the church is adjacent to a school that was built in the same period with the support of the Sudanese Red Crescent and was later awarded land registration and a building permit. What is obvious here is the intention

9 The application notably referred to a previous NIF conference on religions in Sudan, where the government committed itself to protect individual rights and support all religions.

of the public authorities to avoid regularization of the church by turning down the *a posteriori* awarding of land registration and a building permit.

In April 1996, the church complained to the Director of Haj Yusif Locality (*maḥalliyya*), using to the same religious rights rationale (Annexe 4.3.). The Director's hand-written reply suggests that the *maḥalliyya* did not oppose allocating land to the church "in principle", but said that such a request should be preceded by the Khartoum State processes. Similarly the Committee for Engineering Affairs of Haj Yusif Locality reported to the church on June 1996 that it should first seek the approval of the state governor (*wālī*) and several state ministers before the Committee could take any step to allocate the land. After a gap of ten years, the SCC applied in January 2006 to the Minister of Religious Affairs (Guidance and Endowments). The timing reflects the hope that the signing of the 2005 CPA would cool Sudan's hostility toward Nuba and Southerner communities living in the north. In May 2007, the church applied to the Commissioner of Haj Yusif Locality, this time referring explicitly to articles 6 and 154 of the 2005 Constitution and article 29 of the 2006 Khartoum State Constitution – all related to religious rights and freedoms and the right to have a place to worship, in a strong allusion to religious minority rights (Annexe 4.4.). In August 2010, the State Ministry of Guidance and Endowments granted its "initial approval" for the allocation of land. However, the Ministry requested final approval from the local authorities before the land could be allocated to the church. The Ministry of Social and Cultural Affairs also informed the church of its initial approval, which was here described as a "decision not to object" (Annexe 4.5.). The Minister also concluded by stating that the church should once again seek the final decision of local authorities, namely: Haj Yusif Locality's agencies, the popular committee of al-Bashir West city, and the Local Planning Office. Since this last communication, the local authorities have granted no final approval, putting the church in a very precarious position.

The Dualist Nature of the Sudanese Legal Order and the Weakened Right to Property

This case study exemplifies the tremendous effects of legal dualism on the restrictive interpretation of the provisions of the Sudanese Bill of Rights.[10] A dualist legal order underlines the distinction between national and international

10 The Bill of Rights commonly refers to the part of the Constitution related to civil, political, economic, social and cultural rights of the nationals of a given State. Constitutional Bills of Rights traditionnally stand as a landmark in the formal assessment of compliance to the Rule of Law.

legal orders and, therefore, transposition acts often have to be adopted so as to incorporate international norms within Sudanese law. As a result, the legal nature of transposed international norms shifts from international sources to national sources of law. In the case of Sudan, article 27 (3) of the 2005 Constitution testifies to the dualist nature of the national legal order by stating: "All rights and freedoms enshrined in international human rights treaties, covenants and instruments ratified by the Republic of the Sudan shall be an integral part of this Bill."

This article incorporates the provisions of ratified international human rights instruments into Sudanese law as internal legal norms. The 4th and 5th Periodic Reports on the implementation of the African Charter on Human and Peoples' Rights (2008–2012) attests to this interpretation.[11] In these reports, the government underlines that the provisions of ratified human rights conventions are now granted constitutional status and that many of them have been incorporated into the body of national legislation. (*ibid.*, p. 4). It is consequently evident that the Sudanese legal order is dualist as far as the Bill of Rights is concerned.[12] The transposed human rights provisions – notably those related to the right to property – are thereby given genuine constitutional status and, as such, should be interpreted and implemented in the light of intertwined constitutional principles. In this respect, article 27 (3) is to be linked with article 5 (1) of the 2005 Constitution, according to which Islamic *sharīʿa* remains the main constitutional source of law.

The dualist nature of the Constitution allows the government to resort to an idiosyncratic and Islamic understanding of the human rights and fundamental freedoms that are incorporated in the Bill of Rights. As for the right to property, it is worth comparing article 31 of the Sudanese Bill of Rights – on the principles of equality before the law – with its counterparts in general international law: articles 2(1) and 26 of the ICCPR. Although article 31 prohibits discrimination based on religious creed, it includes neither explicit reference to the right to property nor any mention of a positive obligation on the part of the state to take proactive steps to ensure practical equality. Article 31 of the Bill of Rights diverges from articles 2(1) and 26 of the ICCPR in all these aspects. This loose

11 Republic of Sudan, *4th and 5th Periodic Reports on the implementation of the African Charter on Human and Peoples' Rights* (2008–2012), *A.C.H.P.R.*, 51st Ordinary Session, Banjul, May 2012. The mere fact that the report is submitted 'in the name of Allah, the Gracious, the Merciful' reveals the persistent Islamic nature of the Sudanese legal order.

12 An opposite and interesting interpretation of article 27 (3) is offered by Babiker in the CEDEJ-Khartoum final report of the Islam Research Programme (Babiker 2013) and in his 2014 joint report for REDRESS (Babiker and Oette 2014).

interpretation of the right to property in Sudan has a tremendous impact on religious rights and freedoms guaranteed in article 6 of the 2005 Constitution. Although article 6 states the right to establish and maintain places of worship and acquire or possess movable and immovable property for that purpose, one might wonder whether all religious groups can actually benefit from these provisions if the right to property can be so easily subject to discrimination policies.

As for the case in question, dualism acts as a screen preventing articles 2(1) and 26 of the ICCPR to have full effect within the Sudanese legal order. The administrative bodies that received the request made no clear reference to article 6 of the Bill of Rights – or to article 43 on the right to property – although the SCC explicitly referred to it in its 2007 application. Moreover, the various replies from administrative bodies show that a restrictive interpretation of the religious rights and freedoms is used. The Ministries of Guidance and Endowments and of Social and Cultural Affairs both combined their "initial approval" decision with a statement of the need to seek the final approval of the local authorities on land registration. The local authorities have issued no final approval yet and seem unlikely to do so, given the weak wording and mandatory authority of the Ministries' replies. In the statement of the Ministry of Social and Cultural Affairs, initial approval does not amount to a proactive authorization but rather to a passive abstention from prohibiting registration. The Ministries therefore rely on the poor wording of article 6 of the Bill of Rights and avoid taking the necessary proactive steps to implement the provisions of article 2(1) and 26 of the ICCPR. The church community is consequently put in a very risky situation and is worried that the destruction or confiscation of their building for public purposes might occur at any time.[13]

It appears that the SCC is not being treated an identical way to the above-mentioned adjacent Red Crescent school. The SCC refers to this dissimilar treatment to explain the Christians' sense of being second-class citizens whose rights can only be protected through religious minority status, as translated in the Sudanese concept of *dhimma*.[14] Even so, discrimination over land rights does not make the SCC community in al-Bashir West city a religious minority. The situation of this community is related to the principles of equality before the law rather than to minority rights and status.[15] However, as will be shown

13 Comment by Rev. Yagūb Hamōda al-Nur, January and March 2014.

14 Comment by SCC representatives, January and March 2014.

15 Unlike the principles of non-discrimination and equality before the law, the differentiation of treatment for minority groups aims at protecting specific identities. When a given human right or fundamental freedom is formally guaranteed albeit in a context

below, the Sudanese dualist and theocratic legal order acts as a refractive film that distorts the international status of religious minorities. Influenced by the general advocacy policies of foreign NGOs and governments, the church community in Haj Yusif – like other Christian communities in Greater Khartoum – finds itself appealing to the distorted Sudanese religious minority model in order to bargain over land rights with Khartoum State. Interestingly, the representatives of the SCC consulted for the purpose of this research – all Nuba – despise minority statuses when it comes to their ethnic identities, but praise its utility as far as their religious rights and freedom are concerned.[16]

The Translation of the Minority Model and the Objectification of Recipient Communities

The theocratic Sudanese state emerges as the translator of a specific 'token' into its legal order (Behrends, Park and Rottenburg 2014, pp. 3–4). International religious minority status is the token extracted from international law and translated into a malleable model whose content is altered in Sudanese law. The involuntary outcome of this process is to "stabilize" the identity of some Christian actors who situate themselves as *dhimmīs* (Callon 1986). These Christian actors in Greater Khartoum hope for a privileged interaction with public authorities and isolate themselves from other non-Muslims or groups that face discrimination. However, their positioning does not strengthen the protection of their land rights, given that they are in fact not discriminated against on merely religious grounds.

The Translation of the Religious Minority Model into Sudanese Law

The assumed equivalence of the status of the Sudanese *dhimma* with international religious minority status ensues from a systemic disregard for the central role played by the Sudanese state in the arbitrary characterization of *dhimmīs*. In this highly theocratic context, the translated model covers a wider range of

---

systemically and structurally detrimental to specific identities, the aforesaid right or freedom is therefore deprived of substance. In such situations the principles of non-discrimination and equality before the law might become pointless while minority protection becomes particularly necessary. The bulk of minority protection consequently consists in permanent special measures, whereas non-discrimination and equality measures – though necessary to protect minorities – shall last until the discrimination threat disappears.

16 Comment by SCC representatives, January and March 2014.

identities than obvious religious groups. Moreover, throughout the translation process and implementation mechanisms, the *dhimma* regime is neutralized and eventually departs from a regime protecting religious minorities.

The Epistemic Confusion between International Status and the *Dhimma* Regime

Given that the main international provisions protecting minority groups are binding upon Sudan, the international legal status of minorities emerges as a model that must be transposed – or transferred – into this dualist legal order. The concept of a "travelling model" is defined by its designers as "an analytical representation of particular aspects of reality created as an apparatus or protocol for interventions in order to shape this reality for certain purposes" (Behrends, Park and Rottenburg 2014, p.1). Sudanese legal institutions have translated the minority model into Islamic legislation and jurisprudence according to their corresponding epistemic constitutional order. Because of this epistemic shift, any reflection on the minority model is "indexed" on the religious lexical field (Boltanski 2009, pp. 100–107). This gives the distorted impression of dealing with religious minorities in "practices" of discrimination against any kinds of groups or other types of minorities (*ibid.*). There is therefore an asymmetrical "representation of particular aspects of reality" between the international and the Sudanese versions of the minority model.

The main minority provision in international law is article 27 of the ICCPR, ratified by Sudan in 1986.[17] However, this provision does not define minorities, whose existence is rather a "matter of fact" – rather than a legally defined status – since a 1930 Advisory Opinion of the Permanent Court of International Justice (1930).[18] The factual assessment of minorities relies on observable criteria notably listed in 1977 by a United Nations Sub-Commission (Capotorti 1979). According to the objective criteria, minority groups shall present blatant ethnic, religious or linguistic characteristics differing from those of the rest of the population and shall be in a non-dominant situation: either numerically or in any other way.[19] The subjective criterion refer to the sense of solidarity

17 The 1992 UN Declaration on the Rights of Persons Belonging to National or Ethnic, Religious and Linguistic Minorities contains framework provisions on the protection of minorities, notably in its Preamble and article 2.

18 Permanent Court of International Justice 1930, *The Greco-Bulgarian 'Communities' Case* (Interpretation of the Convention Between Greece and Bulgaria respecting Reciprocal Emigration), PCIJ, Advisory Opinion, Series B, No. 17, The Hague.

19 In the view of the author, the numerical criterion is not to be seen as decisive in itself, but is rather part of a range of complementary indicators that can assert the factual existence

of the group and its will to preserve its distinctiveness.[20] These criteria should prevent states from deciding alone on the awarding of minority status. Despite these safeguards, a state may in fact play a crucial part in the objectification of minorities, with no international monitoring mechanism overseeing the process. The European Council has warned that this active role of the state requires distinguishing between minorities "by default" and minorities "by choice" (Pentassuglia 2004, p. 58). The former are groups willing to be integrated but prevented from doing so by the political majority. The latter are groups who emphasize their specificities in their search for differentiated treatment. The capacity of a given group to identify itself as a minority will lessen if a state has already, whether explicitly or not, "stigmatized" the group as a minority.

The distinction is particularly meaningful in Sudan, where successive regimes have unilaterally and practically characterized non-Muslims as minorities – *dhimmīs* – in a way not matching the self-identification of the targeted groups, urging them to readjust their identity discourse. To be more specific, the theocratic character of the Sudanese state implies deference to the Islamic epistemic concept of nationhood – *al-umma al-islāmiyya* – as the framework within which the Islamically defined status of minority known as *dhimma* was developed. Members of the *umma* enjoy equality before Islamic law at the expense of outsiders (el-Gailli 2004).[21] Therefore, in addition to the relationship between the state and individuals based on legal nationality – which opens the way to second-class citizenship – it is membership in the *umma* that is the gateway to full citizenship. This double threshold rules out the international citizenship standards stated in the famous *Nottebohm* international jurisprudence, according to which the making of the nationality bond should accord with the individual's "genuine connection" with the state (International Court of Justice 1955, p. 23). This genuine connection consists in "... a legal bond having as its basis a social fact of attachment, a genuine connection of existence, interests and sentiments, together with the existence of reciprocal rights and duties" (*ibid.*).

In the light of this international jurisprudence, it appears that the individual's "social fact of attachment" to the Sudanese state consists in the arbitrary

of a minority depending on their combination. That is why the "non-dominant" criterion might be seen as subsuming the numerical one. The non-dominant situation of a group may be political, economic, social, numerical, so on and so forth.

20 This general layout is widely accepted by international institutions, such as the Unrepresented Peoples and Nations Organization.

21 The Islamist reforms of the Ingaz regime have substantially weakened the legal capacity of those they qualify as outsiders to the extent that they are generally seen as *dhimmīs*.

membership to the *umma*. This relationship unveils the existence of double-standard treatment for Sudanese nationals. On the one hand, Sudan apparently grants citizenship to all the individuals fulfilling a classic range of precise criteria, presumably granting them all with equal rights. In this way, Sudan claims to take cognizance of the legal effects of the *Nottebohm* jurisprudence. But on the other hand, the state filters in from amongst its nationals those who have the appropriate "social fact of attachment" so as to provide them with a favourable degree of citizenship. This citizenship model was first asserted in the 1998 Constitution and is repeated in the current one.[22] Deceived by the apparent acknowledgement of the *Nottebohm* judgement, international actors are unable to see that the *dhimma* regime is a model translated into a theocratic context that conceals practices of discrimination targeting other groups than religious ones. A detailed examination of the translation process will confirm this assertion.

The Neutralization of the *Dhimma* Regime: A Theocratic Travel of the Minority Model

Though the 2005 Constitution seems at first glance to guarantee freedom of thought, conscience and religion, creed and worship to all Sudanese citizens, the fundamentally dualist nature of the Sudanese legal order goes against this assumption.[23] The unilateral characterization of religious minorities by the Sudanese government cannot amount to the setting up of protective differentiated regimes in line with internal legal pluralism (Woodman 1999). Rather, it shapes a societal environment detrimental to the targeted groups by objectifying them as religious groups that are structurally discriminated against, which would thus require the international religious minority status to be awarded. The asymmetrical "representation of particular aspects of reality" (Behrends, Park and Rottenburg 2014, p. 1) shows that awarding *dhimma* status in Sudan does not equate to the granting of a minority protection regime, but on the opposite results in differentiated treatments in breach of the principle of equality before the law. This would paradoxically justify a call for a religious minority's

22 The government formally declared the Islamic nature of the legal system in its 4th constitutional decree of 1991.

23 It is important to note the difference between the monist and dualist approaches to the international legal system. The distinction is not simply theoretical and it has tremendous practical consequences for the interpretation and implementation of international legal norms. The former concept – monism – assumes international and national legal orders are part of one legal system. Generally, this approach gives primacy to international law over national legislation and, in this context, the incorporation of the international legal norms does not require a national transposition act.

status consistent with the international standards. In other words, at the very most the national *dhimma* regime only establishes *de facto* and non-characterized religious minorities from an international law perspective. Furthermore, the *dhimma* regime in Sudan has been pragmatically elaborated through numbers of unrelated internal formal acts adopted within the national legal order and is, therefore, inconsistent with the two requirements of reasonableness and objectivity established by the UNHRC. As a result, this *dhimma* regime cannot be seen as exempting religious minorities from the application of *sharīʿa* for the simple reason that it is itself inserted within *sharīʿa*. In purely legalistic terms, these unrelated internal formal acts are "occurrences" (Boltanski 2009, p. 105), providing for disjointed "exceptions" within the Sudanese Islamic legal context. These occurrences however do not entail the establishment of a "dispensation" regime to *sharīʿa*, as required for any minority status based on internal legal pluralism (Woodman 1999).

These specific exceptions consist in deference to the personal law of non-Muslims in matters related to constitutions of trust, gifts, or family matters: marriage, inheritance, succession, legacies, divorce, custody, wills. If any question arises during judicial proceedings regarding the substance of specific personal laws, the judges may ask the representatives of religious communities for recommendations, which will eventually become precedents.[24] However, Sudanese jurisprudence, relying on Section 5 of the Civil Procedure Act 1974 – amended in 1983 and 2003 – includes the religious personal law of non-Muslims under the umbrella of customary law, as stated in the 1958 High Court jurisprudence Maurice Goldenburg v. Rachel Godlenburg: "The word custom in section 5 includes the personal law and the customs of the religious community concerned (…)"[25] Moreover, the Judgement (Basic Rule Act) 1983 puts custom at the penultimate level in the hierarchy of judicial interpretative sources. The religious personal law of non-Muslims can consequently be invalidated by the competent authorities or abolished by statute law. In addition, the validity of custom no longer depends on "justice, equity and good conscience", as previously stated in Section 5 of the Civil Procedure Act 1974. It now relies on its "compatibility with *sharīʿa* law and the principles of natural justice". The personal law of religious minorities is hence once again driven back into *sharīʿa* jurisprudential law by being lowered to the level of custom. It

24 Some representatives – such as the Episcopal Church's Bishop of Khartoum Ezekiel Kondo, and Melake Tsehay Abba Gebresilasie from the Ethiopian Tewahedo Church – largely ensure they regularly send indicative notes on their respective "canon law" to judges who request them (comment by Bishop Ezekiel Kondo, January 2014; comment by Bishop Melake Tsehay Abba Gebresilasie, January 2014).

25 Sudan High Court 1960, *Maurice Goldenburg v. Rachel Godlenburg* (HC.CS-441, 1958).

is a particularly resonant example of customary law's inability to function as a derogatory regime and that no internal legal pluralism exists in Sudan when it comes to the so-called minority status and rights of non-Muslims.

It therefore clearly emerges that the religious minority model lost its original materiality through the process of translation performed by the Sudanese Constitution, legislature and judicial authority. Not only does its analogy with the *dhimma* regime merely offer legal "exceptions" within the Islamic Sudanese legal order, but it also seems that these exceptions are interpreted by judicial bodies through the lens of general Islamic law. This genuine crafting of the religious minority model is the vector through which limited Christian communities bargain over land rights with public institutions in Greater Khartoum. Unfortunately, it will appear (Concluding remarks) that international and foreign NGOs – particularly Christian ones – take the so-called *dhimma* status for granted without linking it up with international standards, and refer in a general way to religious minorities in any situation where the mere religious freedoms of non-Muslims are at stake. Although anti-discrimination measures would have been sufficient from the beginning, the Sudanese Islamic legal order has extensively consolidated the evasive *dhimma* status. As this inclusive status is highly malleable, any group facing religious discrimination may be improperly defined as a religious minority by default. This *de facto* consolidation of religious minorities should be double-checked to determine whether differentiated treatment consistent with the international standards does actually exist. No such verification is undertaken, however, and, even if it were, it would reveal that the minorities in question should not in most cases be labelled religious. Taking the blank *dhimma* status for granted only blurs the definition of religious minorities by extending the scope of situations in which religious groups are treated as minorities.

The Objectification of Specific Recipient Christian Communities

Dhimma status serves as an umbrella under which specific communities try to rebalance the protection of land rights and to escape systemic discrimination. These communities are mainly Nuba – and also Southern – Christians who settled in Greater Khartoum as a result of the wars. This objectification process results in the isolation and mobilization of limited kinds of communities (Callon 1986, pp. 189–190).

The Isolation of *Dhimmīs*-IDPs from Other Non-Muslim Groups

Some non-Muslim communities either avoid or are not permitted to resort to the *dhimma* status. This is notably true of Sudanese followers of the Shi'a faith. Although Shi'as are followers of Islam, the social fact of attachment consisting in membership of the *umma* is itself highly fickle in the Sudan. This results from the theocratic nature of the state and the fact that Islamic movements therefore merge with political stances. The attractiveness of the Shiʿa faith amongst the Khartoum intellectual and social elite, and the well-structured organization of this community, arouse the Government's hostility.[26] Shiʿas in Sudan are currently facing serious discrimination, notably in Greater Khartoum where their properties and belongings are regularly seized in violation of their religious rights and freedoms and to other basic human rights. In November 2013, the National Intelligence and Security Service arrested 20 Shiʿas as they were participating in their *Mūḥarram* rituals in Khartoum, and their meeting hall– Al Hūssayniyya – was seized with no compensation given so far.[27] This apparent exclusion from the Sudanese *umma* questions the extent of the concept of *dhimma* in Sudan. The CPA and the 2005 Constitution have seemingly widened the scope of the *dhimma* status: in addition to the "People of the Book" – Christians and Jews – it now includes adherents of traditional African beliefs (art. 6 of the CPA).[28] However, questions remain as to the status of Shiʿas, who are neither part of the Sudanese *umma* nor provided with *dhimma* status (Figure 4.2). Thus, although the Sudanese *dhimma* status does not provide for a derogatory differentiated treatment, it nonetheless operates an arbitrary and distorted classification of religious minorities.

The Copts of Sudan stand at the other end of the spectrum: they are a *dhimma* community that does not experience discrimination (Figure 4.2). After

---

26 Comment by BL Ādil Ābdelghanī, April 2014.

27 The meeting hall located in Khartoum 2 was the private property of a head of the Sudanese Shiʿa community. According to one anonymous Shiʿa sheikh, this event was the result of a Salafi campaign and pressure on the government. Salafi activists published a *fatwa* on social media with a list of ten Shiʿa leading figures who should be murdered. The anonymous Shiʿa sheikh reckons political and economic relations with Saudi Arabia gag the Sudanese government. Although members of the government, such as Amin Hassan Omer, Hassan Makki and President al-Bashir himself, see Shiʿas as members of the *umma*, other political figures and *fiqh* thinkers in Sudan do not. These thinkers influence the judges and the national legislative body on the interpretation of article 125 of the Sudanese criminal code. The provisions of this article are related to the crime of blasphemy and are now structured in a way that limits the religious freedoms of the Shiʿas (comment by Shiʿa Sheikh, March 2015).

28 The 2005 Constitution similarly refers both to religions and beliefs in its article 6 on religious rights. In its General Comment 22 on article 18 of the ICCPR, the UNHRC distinguishes between "traditional religions with institutional characteristics" on the one hand, and theistic, non-theistic and atheistic beliefs on the other. This acceptation of the term "belief" would include African traditional beliefs in Sudan.

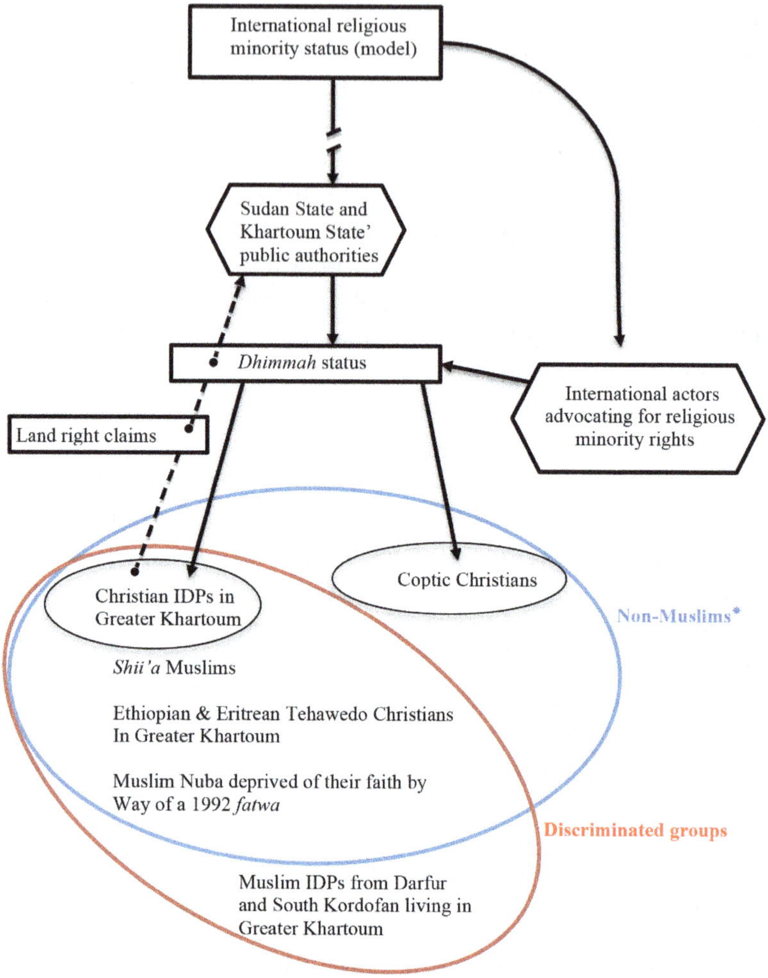

– – ➔ Mobilization

* For the purpose of this research, 'non-Muslim' is inclusive of Muslims excluded from the Sudanese *Ummah* and departing from the mainstream Sunni Islam of the Sudan

FIGURE 4.2 *Translation of the international religious minority model in the context of discrimination over land rights in Greater Khartoum.*

the military coup in 1989, relations between the Copts and the current regime started improving. As underlined by Mai Azzan, this good relationship results primarily from the Copts' unique ethnic, social and economic background (de Geoffroy 2013). Despite having Sudanese citizenship, Copts emphasize their Egyptian identity and underline their bonds with the Egyptian Coptic Orthodox Church. They consequently play the "two-tier citizenship game", relying on their own economic support and network without claiming a right to participate openly in state political and economic affairs while their Egyptian roots conversely evoke an artificial Arab identity that has proven really helpful.[29] Therefore the Government does not particularly discriminate against Coptic properties or religious assets. Although the crime of apostasy applies, the Coptic Church, unlike the Ethiopian Tewahedo Church, can nonetheless baptise non-Muslim Sudanese citizens. As for the Tewahedo Church, discrimination with regard to land rights cannot be interpreted in terms of national minority status, given that the members of that church are not deemed to be Sudanese citizens, nor the church a Sudanese institution.[30]

The gap between various Christian groups suggests that the critical issue is not so much religion as ethnicity. Without claiming that no religious discrimination is occurring in Greater Khartoum, the government's assertion that non-Muslims' right to worship is effectively guaranteed is quite correct.[31] Unobstructed religious services at All Saints Cathedral in Amarat and other churches are regularly taking place and a particularly stunning Palm Sunday celebration at the Ethiopian Tewahedo church in Khartoum 2 was organized in early 2014. The church and the whole area were crowded and no police unit was present to dissuade the worshippers from gathering.

However, as underlined above, a right that is protected in principle may nonetheless be deprived of substance. The destruction, closure and confiscation of churches' assets deprive specific ethnic or regionally labelled groups of religious freedoms and connected rights of substance. Aside from the above mentioned non-Muslims groups variously considered by the state of Sudan, Christian Nuba IDPs and South Sudanese IDPs stand in the middle of the non-Muslim spectrum (Figure 2). Like the Copts they are *dhimmīs*, but they are as discriminated against as Shi'as when it comes to access to land rights. It is hence necessary to investigate the process by which these specific Christian

29 Comment by BL Ādil Ābdelghanī, April 2014.

30 Comment by Bishop Melake Tsehay Abba Gebresilasie, January 2014; Figure 2.

31 The Minister of Guidance and Endowments formulated this assertion on April 2013, when he decided that no new licenses for building of churches would be granted.

communities mobilize a status that only objectifies them and does not solve the discrimination they face in accessing land rights.

The Mobilization of the *Dhimma* Status by Christians in Greater Khartoum

To that end, I suggest scrutinizing the process by which Nuba and Southern IDPs accept being isolated from other *dhimmīs* – that is, the Copts – and non-Muslims, to eventually mobilize their status with respect to land discrimination. This acceptance and the consequent mobilization is what Michel Callon brands the "enrolment" stage of the translation process (Callon 1986, pp. 189–193). Enrolment results from a set of actions – stratagems, *coups de force* and bilateral negotiations – stabilizing both the identity of the isolated groups and the translated model that serves as an apparatus for action (*ibid.*; Behrends, Park and Rottenburg 2014). In the aftermath of the secession fo South Sudan and in the context of land discrimination in Greater Khartoum, the enrolment mainly results from the broadcasting of political statements excluding IDP Christians from the Sudanese nation and threatening them with the drastic regularization of church's assets in Greater Khartoum. In addition to these stratagems, the consequent destruction of Christian assets in Greater Khartoum served as *coups de force*, objectifying and stabilizing the targeted groups as discriminated *dhimmīs*. In an attempt to protect their land interests, these discriminated communities sometimes actually use their objectified status to start bilateral negotiations with public authorities.

This set of actions indisputably shows that Khartoum State is rather targeting specific ethnically labelled communities when it discriminates against Christian *dhimmīs*. The government declared after the Independence of South Sudan that all individuals entitled to South Sudanese citizenship would automatically lose their Sudanese citizenship by March 2012 and would be subject to deportation (USCIRF 2013, p. 153). Following this statement and Southern independence, there has been constant destruction and confiscation of churches and Christian assets on the sole assumption that most Southerners living in Sudan are Christians (*ibid.*). This discrimination campaign also targeted Nuba Christians.

This campaign against Christian churches is now losing steam, but some of the cases that occurred are striking.[32] On 21 April 2012, some merely individual perpetrators destroyed the Sudan Evangelical Church Bible School in West Gereif and no criminal investigation cas carried out. The church facility

32 For a deeper analysis of the recent situation of Christian communities in Khartoum, see CEDEJa.

contained a clinic, a schoolhouse, student accommodation, and five worship rooms. Before the destruction, the Mayor issued a notice of acquisition of all the facility's land, together with notice of its destruction in the public interest. Church officials questioned the legality of the notices, arguing that the Mayor had no legal jurisdiction to acquire the land and that no "fair and prompt compensation" was awarded.[33] The day the troublemakers "marched on" the facility, bulldozers had already started to destroy the surrounding walls.[34] Some researchers have argued that it is likely that the government targeted this Southern church in retaliation for the Heglig incident (de Geoffroy 2013; Lamoureaux 2013). Heglig is an oil-producing area claimed by both states that was taken over by the South Sudanese military between April and May 2012.[35]

Similarly, the destruction in June 2012 of a worship centre of the St John Episcopal Church in Haj Yusif shows the same discrimination against Nuba Christians, though it also exemplifies the confusion that exists between individual and minority rights. The church was part of the Diocese of Khartoum dedicated by Bishop Ezekiel Kondo in 2009. Members and staff of the ECS are mostly from the Nuba Mountains or South Sudan. The Cathedral in Khartoum provides services in the Nuba Moro language. In addition, Bishop Ezekiel Kondo is Nuba and the church's headquarters is located in Juba. The ethnic aspect of the ECS is what makes apparent the government's intention to target ethnically labelled communities rather than mere Christians in the tense political context of Southern Independence. The ECS in Haj Yusif began in 1987, when the area was empty. Later, the government started the survey and allocated plots for housing without taking the church into account. Its representatives have been requesting official registration for 25 years with no success, thus legally proving their good faith and the government's intention to withhold regularization (de Geoffroy 2013). Eventually, the Local Authority Ministry of Planning and Housing destroyed the church for lack of valid ownership documents. The WCC stated that this destruction resulted from "... calculated attacks on Sudanese civilians who are not of the Muslim faith and their property in Khartoum, and in particular Christians" (WCC 2012).

---

33 Article 43 (2) of the INC related to the Right to Own Property.

34 Comments by SCC representatives, January and March 2014.

35 The government of Sudan accepts the Permanent Court of Arbitration's implicit identification of the area as part of its national territory by ruling it out of Abyei, which was likely to join South Sudan by referendum following the redrawing of the region by the Court. See: Permanent Court of Arbitration, Arbitration Agreement between the Government of Sudan and The SPLM/A on Delimiting Abyei Area, (*Government of Sudan v. SPLM/A*), Final Award, PCA No. GOS-SPLM/A, 22 July 2009.

In the aftermath of Southern Independence, the Sudanese government asked the churches of Sudan to clarify their assets. Minister of Guidance and Endowments Al-Fathī Taj el-Sīr further announced in April 2013 that no more land registration would be granted for the building of new churches.[36] However, church facilities are not usually registered at the Land Office for the simple reason that requests of registration have not acted upon for the last 25 years.[37] Numerous worship centres have hence been built on plots registered to individuals (Lamoureaux 2013). These properties are then devoted to collective church activities: worship, language classes and religious education, medical care, administration, and various cultural activities and events. When the government expressively seizes upon the illegal status of unplanned religious facilities, individual ownership titles are affected. The Sudan Church of Christ in Haj Yusif originally bought the land for local residents under individual property status. Public authorities object to this individual – and unregistered – land title being made available for the community and religious activities. Reverend Yagūb Hamōda al-Nur testified that his recent application to register the land was turned down with an express, though unofficial, allusion to the community's ethnic origins and religious activities.[38]

The situation Rev. Yagūb Hamōda al-Nur describes demonstrates that the nature and content of the rights in question remains vague: it seems to be all about a mere infringement of the individual right to property, although justified by the property's use for religious facilities. The question is therefore whether infringement of the individual right to property – and to other individual rights *in rem* – amounts to a discriminative practice against a single member of a religious group, in which case it would not be a question of the law of minorities but rather the principles of equality before the law. However, the above-mentioned government request for clarification of assets implies that whole religious community was being scrutinized, indicating that the debate on individual land titles is a smoke screen hiding the group's actual situation.

36 This decision was based on both the churches' lack of ownership documents and the assumption that the independence of South Sudan would cause a fall in attendance of places of worship. However, Lamoureaux (2013, p. 116) notes that a Nuba Church in Omdurman was granted a building permit in October 2012.

37 Churches have to seek registration with the Ministry of Religious Affairs (Guidance and Endowments). They have then to obtain a status on the land with the State Ministry of Construction and Planning and with the Local Planning Office before building new places of worship.

38 Comments by Rev. Yagūb Hamōda al-Nur, January and March 2014.

I also maintain that ethnic affiliations lurk behind the religious criterion, for the targeting of Christian facilities in fact ends up damaging specific ethnic or regional groups. A two-tier smoke screen thus hides the main issue, as evidenced by the parallel situation in the Nuba Mountains, where conflicts escalated again in mid-2011. In this region, Nuba Muslims – presumably siding with the rebels – are also targeted by the Sudanese Armed Forces and are referred to as "bad Muslims" and *kāfir* (infidel or pagan), as a reminder of the 1992 *fatwa* officially depriving Nuba Muslims of their faith (USCIRF 2013, p. 152). One might wonder whether these Nuba Muslims should be regarded as a religious minority, given that their religious identity is clearly denied by the government, but this denial is the result of their ethnic – and political – affiliations and a more dynamic reading of the deprivation of their rights might be helpful here (Figure 4.2). Here, the ethnic factor overrules the religious one.

This perspective supports the assertion that the destruction of Nuba and Southern Christian facilities goes beyond an infringement of their freedom to choose and manifest their religion, including their right to worship. These facilities in Haj Yusif, West Gereif and other places are not simply worship centres. They also consisted of schools, clinics or cultural centres and sometimes support the use of tribal languages.[39] The targeting of these cross-disciplinary facilities therefore also affects the rights to education and cultural rights of ethnic groups that simply happen to be Christian. Their destruction and confiscation signify that these Southerners and Nuba are deprived of their right to enjoy their own culture and to take part of their cultural life.[40] A contextual and

39 A similar instance was the search in February 2013 of the cultural centre of the Presbyterian Evangelical Church in Khartoum, whose members are mostly Nuba and Southerners (CSW 2013). Members of this church were arrested and detained without charge on the later-dropped assumption that their church received financial support from foreign countries in breach of the 1980 Awqaf and Religious Affairs Act. Non-Muslim religious organizations were previously regulated by the Missionary Societies Act 1962. This act notably regulated beforehand financial support for missionary institutions. The Humanitarian Voluntary Act 2006 now regulates social and humanitarian activities of religious organizations whereas the Ministry of Awqaf and Religious Affairs oversees proselytizing activities of organizations and churches.

40 The main international provisions protecting cultural rights are: article 18 paragraph 4 of the ICCPR (the freedom of parents and legal guardians to ensure the religious and moral education of their children in conformity with their own convictions); article 27 of the ICCPR (the right of minority members, in community with the other members of their group, to enjoy their own culture and to use their own language); article 15 of the International Covenant on Economic, Social and Cultural Rights (the right to take part to the cultural life).

dynamic reading of cultural identity would help the understanding of infringements of religious freedoms, and that the deprivation of related rights is part of a more general policy directed against targeted ethnic groups or minorities.

Rīffat Osman Makkawī, a human rights lawyer, nonetheless agrees that Christian IDPs mobilize the *dhimma* status and overplay the theocratic nature of the state to bargain over land rights in particular cases.[41] Rīffat Osman Makkawī is the head of PLACE, based in Khartoum, which comes helps IDPs and refugees with land rights issues.[42] PLACE worked on the destruction of the Sudan Evangelical Church Bible School in West Gereif and offered support to the targeted community, with a view to starting criminal proceedings against the perpetrators.[43] The leaders of the church eventually rejected the offer and decided instead to engage in informal negotiations with the government to bargain for informal compensation, unsuccessfully, as it turned out, despite the fact that the church had held a valid title since 1922 (*ibid.*). The sharp reactions from international Christian institutions criticizing the government's lack of action to protect "religious minorities" were therefore misplaced.[44]

The rejection of legal help is a strong evidence of the community leaders' acceptance of their isolation and the consequent mobilization of discrimination against them under their *dhimma* status to engage bilateral negotiations with the government (Callon 1986). In that sense, the Sudan Evangelical Church Bible School in West Gereif parallels the current situation of the Sudan Church of Christ in Haj Yusif. The latter is indeed using the same minority status strategy to secure common grounds of understanding that will make negotiation with the government possible. This strategy also triggers the support of

---

41 Rīffat Osman Makkawī, pers. comm., March 2014.

42 Rīffat Osman Makkawī is a human rights lawyer who graduated from Khartoum University and the University of Essex. He created PLACE in 1999 to help IDPs to access justice and inform them of their rights. The association has 22 lawyers in Khartoum and 70 more elsewhere in Sudan. PLACE is also active in South Sudan. The association refused registration under Sudan's HAC in order to give itself wider leeway and is therefore denied any government or international funding.

43 No criminal proceeding can be started before Sudanese criminal courts without a complaint first being filed by the presumed victim.

44 Some Christian international NGOs and private interest groups strongly condemned the conduct of the State of Khartoum and Sudanese state regarding the destruction of the Evangelical Church Bible School in West Gereif. The American Presbyterian Mission Agency, the AACC and the WCC notably took part in this campaign, issuing a joint statement on 24 April 2012 in which they specifically condemned the lack of action on the part of the government in apprehending those responsible for the destruction (AACC and WCC 2012).

international NGOs, intergovernmental organizations and foreign states, who are unable to relativize the Sudanese *dhimma* status.

Concluding Remarks: The Acceptance of the *Dhimma* Strategy by International Actors

By way of conclusion, I would like to address this last element to tie down the dynamic of domination that is affecting Christian IDPs in Greater Khartoum, that is, the advocating for Christian and religious minority rights by international actors. These actors accept the use of the Sudanese *dhimma* status to refer to discriminated Christian groups as religious minorities. This characterization enables them to start advocacy campaigns on the basis of international minority rights standards.

The most active actors are international Christian NGOs, who strongly condemned the destruction or confiscation of the above-mentioned churches in West Gereif and Haj Yusif, and of other churches in Greater Khartoum and throughout Sudan. In most of their briefings and statements, these NGOs expressively refer to the legal regime imposed on Christians – the *dhimma* regime – to wrongly characterize groups who experience discrimination as "religious minorities". Naturally, these NGOs never fail to substantiate their accusations by mentioning international human rights instruments on the protection of religious freedom and minority rights. This is true of the WCC and the AACC, who have issued individual or joint statements condemning the destruction of churches in West Gereif and Haj Yusif (WCC and AACC 2012; WCC 2012). It is also true of the Presbyterian Mission Agency (n.d.); the *Christian Post* (Zaimov 2015); the *Christian Examiner* (Tomlin 2015); and Christian Solidarity Worldwide regarding various other cases (CSW 2015).

To a lesser extent, the US State Department has also contributed to this minority discourse by referring to non-Muslims in Sudan as religious minorities in the annual reports of the USCIRF.[45] The minority characterization also features in other annual reports in the sections related to "US Policy" or the "recommendations", but never in the analysis of collected data on practices of discrimination (USCIRF 2012, 2013, 2014, 2016). Although the State Department contributes to the confusion, it by and large shows more awareness of the importance of ethnic affiliations in the dynamics of discrimination. In contrast, the Dutch Minister of Foreign Affairs showed a great inclination to confusion when it signed with the CEDEJ-Khartoum in 2008 a research programme

45 Interestingly, such references were avoided during the interim period.

called "Strengthening Knowledge of and Dialogue with Islamic/Arab World" (de Geoffroy, 2013c). The Dutch proposal notably made the prior assumption that non-Muslims in Sudan could be characterized as "minorities". However, the team of scientists – drawing conclusions from various fields of social sciences – stressed in the Synthesis of the Final Report that such an assumption was highly problematic in Sudan (CEDEJ-Khartoum 2013b, pp. 7 and 20).

Finally, practices of discrimination regarding land rights in Greater Khartoum were addressed to the Office of the United Nations High Commissioner for Human Rights, by a group of subsidiary organs, including the Independent Expert on minority issues (Special Procedures of the Human Rights Council 2013).[46] The mere existence of the latter institution does characterize straightaway these practices of discrimination according to the law of minorities.

On the whole, international actors underestimate the ethnic motive for discrimination with regard to land rights, although such motive is openly exposed in Khartoum State's town planning policy. The situation new settlers and migrants are facing in Greater Khartoum reflects the general marginalization of peripheral populations of Sudan: the planning policy in the Greater Khartoum is simply implemented at the expense of vulnerable populations from former IDP camps or slums.[47] Urban planning and surveys do not merely aim at demarcating land titles or providing inhabitants with basic public services. The main effect is rather to relocate former IDPs in remote areas or to encourage them to move back to their original region.

Practices of discrimination over land rights generally speak for themselves. After the signing of the CPA and Southern Independence, most former Southern IDPs left Greater Khartoum for South Sudan. According to official reports, there are now only 347, 000 South Sudanese living in Khartoum State, where there were previously more than 1 million formerly (OCHA 2011). Southerners were afraid the loss of their – northern – Sudanese citizenship would result in their being deprived of their property rights,[48] so they started selling their titles to the Sudanese Arab elite or Nuba IDPs in Greater Khartoum. However, Rīffat Osman Makkawī stresses these sold land titles are

46 Office of the United Nations High Commissioner for Human Rights, Special Procedures of the Human Rights Council 2013, 'Mandates of the Working group on the Arbitrary Detention; the Special Rapporteur on freedom of religion or belief; and the Independent Expert on minority issues'. spdb.ohchr.org/hrdb/24th/public_-_UA_Sudan_02.05.13_(5.2013).pdf (accessed 28 August 2017).

47 Rīffat Osman Makkawī, pers. comm. March 2014.

48 Nevertheless, new refugees continue to head straight to Khartoum following the South Sudanese internal armed conflicts that started in early 2014.

not valid, as transactions are informal and new buyers can hardly register their titles by means of bribery. Nuba IDPs are therefore vulnerable to expropriation without compensation, unlike the Khartoum Arab elite, who have efficiently registered their acquisition of a large range of Southerners' plots.[49] This situation shows that discrimination with regard to access to land is directed against any vulnerable individual or group of individuals whose land title is not clearly established. Khartoum State tries to profit from the precarious position of IDPs and migrants to help the social and political elite – those politically and ethnically close to the government – in land speculation market in Greater Khartoum. Rīffat Osman Makkawī refers to one particular case related to two Comboni Church schools in Mayo that were confiscated in June 2012 by the Commissioner of Jebel Awlia *maḥalliyya*.[50] These schools welcomed both Muslim and non-Muslim IDP students from Darfur, South Sudan and the Nuba Mountains. The confiscation was aimed at retrieving the plots in order to establish a public secondary school without paying any compensation.[51] Destruction of property also affects Muslims when titles are not registered or no building licence has been issued. This concerns unauthorized *rakūba* (shops) in markets and underground bars and clubs.[52]

Discrimination with regard to rights to access to land is indisputably more directed towards vulnerable ethnic groups settled on the outskirts of Khartoum than towards religious minorities. However, Christian IDPs in Greater Khartoum occasionally accept the *dhimma* status in order to negotiate with public authorities and gain the support of international actors. Yet, paradoxically, if one considers carefully the international requirements for the awarding of minority status, it is only Shi'as who could be categorized as a religious minority in connection with discrimination over land rights. They benefit from neither the *umma* nor the *dhimma* status and the discrimination they are facing is based directly on their religious characteristics rather than on any opportunistic strategy to speculate in land property. Because international actors turn a blind eye to the epistemic contradiction between the international

---

49 Rīffat Osman Makkawī, pers. comm. March 2014.

50 The Commissioner confiscated the schools on the basis of a letter from the Khartoum Ministry of Education stating these were two southerner schools, even though they however were registered by the Ministry of Education as being under the Khartoum Diocese authority.

51 PLACE took the case before the Court and won the case on appeal on the basis of the principles of non-discrimination and equality before the law. The case is referred to as *Ahmed Mussa and others v. The Ministry of Education in Khartoum State*. Unfortunately Rīffat Osman Makkawī was unable to provide me with the exact reference of the case.

52 Rīffat Osman Makkawī, pers. comm. March 2014.

status of religious minorities and the Sudanese *dhimma* status, an effective protection of ethnic groups in Greater Khartoum who experience discrimination cannot be offered. These ethnic groups would be better protected by the internationally agreed ethnic minority status or by the principle of equality before the law.

References

AACC and WCC 2012, 'Joint Statement'. http://www.pcusa.org/site_media/media/uploads/worldmission/pdfs/wcc_aacc_press_release_24_april_2012.pdf (accessed 28 August 2017).

Babiker, MA 2013, 'The Legal Status of Religious Minorities and the Impact of "Islamization" of Laws', in de Geoffroy, A (ed.), *Islam and Society in Sudan*, Final Report (printed version), CEDEJ, Khartoum. http://www.cedej-eg.org/spip.php?article708 (accessed 28 August 2017).

Babiker MA & Oette, L 2014, *The Constitutional Protection of Human Rights in Sudan: Challenges and Future Perspectives*, REDRESS, London. www.redress.org/downloads/publications/140127FINAL%20Sudan%20UoK%20Report.pdf (accessed May 2014).

Behrends, A, Park, SJ & Rottenburg, R 2014, 'Travelling Models: Introducing an Analytical Concept to Globalisation Studies', in A Behrends, SJ Park & R Rottenburg (eds), *Travelling Models in African Conflict Management: Translating Technologies of Social Ordering*, Brill, Leiden, pp. 1–40.

Boltanski, L 2009, *De la critique: Précis de sociologie de l'émancipation*, Gallimard, Paris.

Callon, M 1986, 'Éléments pour une sociologie de la traduction: La domestication des coquilles Saint-Jacques et des marins-pêcheurs dans la baie de Saint-Brieuc', *L'Année sociologique*, 1986, Vol. 36, pp. 169–208.

Capotorti, F 1979, *Study on the Rights of Persons Belonging to Ethnic, Religious and Linguistic Minorities*, E/CV4/Sub2/384/Rev 1, United Nations Sub-Commission on Prevention of Discrimination and Protection of Minorities, New York.

CSW (Christian Solidarity Worldwide) 2013, 'No New Church Licences To Be Issued', *Christian Solidarity Worldwide*, 18 April. http://www.csw.org.uk/2013/04/18/news/1438/article.htm (viewed 28 August 2017).

CSW 2015, 'Sudan Two Pastors Detained Incommunicado', *Christian Solidarity Worldwide*, 22 December. http://www.csw.org.uk/2015/12/22/news/2910/article.htm (accessed 28 August 2017).

de Geoffroy, A (ed.), 2013a, *Islam and Society in Sudan*, Final Report, CEDEJ, Khartoum. http://www.cedej-eg.org/spip.php?article708 (accessed October 2013).

de Geoffroy, A 2013b, 'Christian Communities in Khartoum: Facing the Independence of the South Sudan', in de Geoffroy, A (ed.) 2013a, , *Islam and Society in Sudan,* Final Report.

de Geoffroy, A 2013c, *Le Programme IRP (Islam Research Programme): Projet de publication en cours.* http://www.cedej-eg.org/spip.php?rubrique296 (accessed January 2016).

el-Gailli, AT 2004, 'Federalism and the Tyranny of Religious Majorities: Challenges to Islamic Federalism in Sudan', *Harvard International Law Journal,* vol. 45, no. 2, pp. 503–546.

Fluehr-Lobban, C 2012, *Shari'a and Islamism in Sudan: Conflict, Law and Social Transformation,* IB Tauris, London.

International Court of Justice 1955, *Nottebhohm case (Liechtenstein v. Guatemala),* Second Phase, Judgment of 6 April 1955. http://www.refworld.org/cases,ICJ,3ae6b7248.html (accessed 28 August 2017).

Lamoureaux, S 2013, 'Nuba Christianity: The Search for Security in the North', in de Geoffroy, A (ed.), 2013a, *Islam and Society in Sudan,* Final Report.

OCHA 2014, 'Sudan: Humanitarian Snapshot'. http://reliefweb.int/sites/reliefweb.int/files/resources/Sudan_Humanitarian_Snapshot_30_April_2014.pdf (accessed 28 August 2017).

Pentassuglia, G, European Council 2004, *Minorités en droit international: Une étude introductive,* Editions du Conseil de l'Europe, Strasbourg.

Presbyterian Mission Agency n.d., 'Alert: Call for Prayer from Sudanese Partners'. http://www.presbyterianmission.org/ministries/global/attack-gereif-bible-school-sudan/ (accessed May 2016).

Republic of the Sudan 2008–2012, '4th and 5th Periodic Reports of the Republic of the Sudan in Accordance with Article 62 of the African Charter on Human and Peoples Rights', African Commission on Human and Peoples' Rights, II-93. http://www.achpr.org/files/sessions/51st/state-reports/4thand5th-2008-2012/staterep4and5_sudan_2012_eng.pdf (accessed 28 August 2017).

Tomlin, G 2015, '30-year-old Sudanese Church Destroyed to Make Way for Businesses: Newer Mosque Allowed to Eemain', *Christian Examiner,* 3 November. http://www.christianexaminer.com/article/30-year-old-sudanese-church-destroyed-to-make-way-for-businesses-newer-mosque-allowed-to-remain/49731.htm (accessed 27 August 2017.

USCIRF 2012, *Annual Report,* US State Department, Washington DC. http://www.uscirf.gov/reports-briefs/annual-report/2012-annual-report (accessed 28 August 2017).

USCIRF 2013, 'Annual Report', US State Department, Washington DC. http://www.uscirf.gov/reports-briefs/annual-report/2013-annual-report (accessed 28 August 2017).

USCIRF 2014, 'Annual Report', US State Department, Washington DC. http://www.uscirf.gov/reports-briefs/annual-report/2014-annual-report (accessed 28 August 2017).

USCIRF 2016, 'Annual Report', US State Department, Washington DC http://www.uscirf.gov/reports-briefs/annual-report/2016-annual-report (accessed 28 August 2017).

Woodman, GR 1999, 'The Idea of Legal Pluralism', in B Dupret, M Berget, & L al-Zwaini, (eds), *Legal Pluralism in the Arab World*, Kluwer Law International, The Hague, pp. 3–20.

WCC 2012, 'Statement on Destruction of Church Property in Khartoum', World Council of Churches, 22 June. https://www.oikoumene.org/en/resources/documents/general-secretary/joint-declarations/statement-on-destruction-of-church-property-in-khartoum (accessed 28 August 2017).

Zaimov, S 2015, '3 Churches Destroyed in 1 Month amid Rampant Christian Persecution in Sudan', *Christian Post World*, 25 November. Viewed in March 2016 http://www.christianpost.com/news/christian-persecution-sudan-shariah-law-three-churches-destroyed-one-month-150924/ (accessed 28 August 2017).

CHAPTER 5

Communal Customary Land Rights in Sudan: The Need for a Comprehensive Reform of Statutory Land Laws

Mohamed A. Babiker

Introduction

This chapter focuses on legal norms concerning customary or communal land rights and their use in Sudan, in terms of ownership and transfer of land and as recognized and practised by local communities who apply their own customs to land. In this context, the first part sheds light on customary rights to land and usage, while the second part focuses on statutory laws governing customary ownership of land and how tribal and communal lands are affected by various statutes or enactments in the context of contemporary legal framework in Sudan. The objective of this part is to highlight some milestones in Sudanese land legislation and to give some background concerning the legal framework. In this respect, the chapter not only provides a historical overview of land legislation in Sudan as pertaining to land laws, but also looks at how such legislation (in this process) has seriously encroached upon the traditional and communal ownership of land. This has negatively impacted on the peaceful co-existence between tribal communities and affected traditional land ownership.

Accordingly, the chapter examines existing legislations dealing with land. The aim here is to highlight some milestones in Sudanese land legislation and to give some indications about Sudan's legal framework governing land ownership and use. In addition, the chapter examines the legal status of customary laws and rights governing communal and tribal ownership of land, and the extent to which such rights have been encroached upon or marginalized from the colonial era to the present day by statutory and Islamic laws. The chapter also examines the developed jurisprudence and the recognition of customary rights to land as applied by courts. It also touches on "land grabbing" and investment laws and policies, and their negative impact on traditional and communal ownership of land.

 | DOI 10.1163/9789004362185_007

The chapter also focuses on law reforms after the signing of the CPA, which calls for the establishment of land commissions mandated to adjudicate on traditional customary land rights and land polices. However, it concludes that the land reforms in the post CPA era have been a failure, as communal land ownership rights are still marginalized by statutory laws and the Constitution. Land legislation in Sudan is confused, complicated and arbitrarily used for purposes of land expropriation. Land reforms and practices to strenghten customary land rights have not taken place to date in the post CPA era, despite constant calls for reform. Hence, the chapter concludes by arguing that there is an urgency for Sudan to undertake a comprehensive review of its land laws to ensure the customary rights of local communities are respected.

Customary Land Ownership and Usage in Sudan

Historically, land in Sudan (as the most important asset of the society) is vested in the tribe as a whole, and is administered on its behalf by chiefs or tribal leaders (Macek 1993). An individual's right to land derives from his right as a community or tribe member (*ibid.*). Customary law also exclusively reserves specific areas for communal usage, which may be used by individuals but they do not have ownership rights over them nor can they exclude other members from them (*ibid.*). These areas are incapable of individual ownership and are regarded as public places for the whole tribe. These areas include: forests, livestock pastures, fishing areas, cattle camps and so on. Members of neighbouring tribes may be allowed access to these public areas, however, on a basis of reciprocity (*ibid.*). These are customary law rules which correspond with easements under English Law, such as the right of way: a footpath designated for use by members of the public who may pass across land owned by individuals. The latter are not entitled to obstruct any member of the public from using such a footpath. People may also acquire the right to pass across individual's land to go and obtain water, for example, from a well.

In eastern Sudan, for instance, each Beja tribe has its own land for farming and cultivation. They also breed cattle and dig wells. Any persons from any other tribe are allowed to pasture their cattle on their land and are not forbidden from drinking from their wells. However, it is customary that one can only have access to tribal land provided that no structural changes are made such as digging a well or farming the land without permission; these acts will be regarded as trespassing on their tribal land which may lead to fighting. Accordingly, agricultural land, wells and cattle become the main causes for fighting if tribal customs related to land are not observed by members of the host tribe. Non-Beja "guests" who dwell or settle on Beja land for a short or long time can use the land for cultivation and for pasture or access to water, provided that they do not establish permanent structures, digging wells or cutting trees (Abdel Ati 2005, p. 12). In return for using the land, guests are expected to pay to the sheikh or the *ʿomda* of the area what is traditionally known in the Beja language as *guadab*: the chest-meat of an animal. The *guadab* symbolizes "recognition" of title over land rather than rent or a tax levy, since it is not regular or defined in quantity, but depends on when guests slaughter an animal. In some areas, the *guadab* is paid in cash (*ibid.*). This small or nominal amount given may be regarded in contract law as a "consideration". In case of dispute, the legal title to the land or the right of to occupy it can be proved through a variety of ways including witnesses, signed documents (i.e., the Hadandowa and the Rashaida agreement[1]), neighbours and tribal maps. Tribal disputes over land are normally resolved by tribal maps. Such maps are recognized between tribes and easily demarcated or identified according to the *naẓāra* (extension of the tribe's geographic boundaries). However, disputes over rights to land between sub-clans and cousins, rather than between different tribes, have proved to be difficult to resolve. In this case, the *guadab* must be applied in addition to witnesses. If the dispute over the land leads to serious fighting between sub-clans, the *nāẓir* will intervene and issue what amount to an interim legal "injunction" (*ḥajz*) until the dispute is resolved. In the case of a dispute between different tribes, the *majlis* or *ajawīd* council, headed by the *nāẓir* of each tribe, will resolve the matter according to the recognized custom, to be agreed upon between the two tribes. Regarding the right of pastoralists to herd their cattle on the land of other tribes, the Hadandowa, for example, require other tribes to use certain routes. They also ask pastoralists not to travel with their families so that they can guarantee that they will return to them. The Hadandowa have signed agreements in this respect with the Rashaida and Shukriyya tribes under which they have hosted the Rashaida in their land and specified the tribal routes for the pastoralists.[2]

Courts Recognition of Customary Land Ownership and Use

Courts in Sudan historically recognized customary law (Mustafa 1971, p. 163). Unlike other areas of customary, criminal or personal law, land ownership and

1 For example, the Hadandowa signed an agreement in 1933 with the Rashaida allowing them to use the land on specific conditions.

2 In Darfur, customary ownership is also different from land ownership in eastern Sudan and other parts of Sudan such as Blue Nile, Nuba Mountains and northern Sudan. For details on this see Osman (2012).

use have been recognized and codified in statutory laws. Customary rights related to land have also been codified and land usage and customary ownership integrated into the statutory laws (El-Mahdi 1979). Section 13 (iii) of the Land Settlement and Registration Ordinance 1925 adopts the right of *amāra*.[3] Moreover, section 27 of the same law has codified customary law where the ownership of the land is distinct from the ownership of trees.

During the 1960s, Sudanese courts recognized local customs and practices, particularly customs relating to land in the northern parts of Sudan.[4] During this period, as soon as courts ascertained the existence of a custom or practice, they accepted it and enforced it on the understanding that it afforded the most equitable solution, since it had been accepted for a long time by the community in which the dispute arose. It is pertinent to note here that, outside land law, there was no development in the field of customary law with regard to other legal branches at all (i.e., criminal, personal laws) during that period (Mustafa 1971, p. 218). The courts were much more reluctant to recognize and give effect to customs and practices outside the realm of land law (*ibid.*, p. 164), and have largely failed to build up any body of law or set of legal rules with any roots in local customs and practices outside the field of land law (*ibid.*, pp. 164–165).

The courts widely applied a custom known as *karū* (rights over government land) and rights of *sīd al-amāra*.[5] Other customary rights, though not specifically provided for by legislation, are also applied as law and recognized by Sudanese courts. Most of the litigation concerned the ownership or right to cultivate islands emerging in the Nile in northern Sudan. For example, customs

3 The right of *amāra* is a customary right whereby the person who holds such a right (*sīd al-amāra*) cultivates the land owned by another (*sīd al-aṣl*) and has the right to a share of the crop.

4 These included a custom known as *idāfa* practised in the Merowe District. See *Heirs of Abdel Gabbar Mohamed v. Fatma Mohamed* (1964) SLJR 156; *mudāyara*, practised in Damer District (see *Abdall Elhussein v. Safiya Ali Abu Ali*, 1964 SLJR 62); *karū* applied Shendi District (*Heirs of Fadlalalla Oklah v. Hussein Ali Brar* (1964) SLJR 96); *ḥaqq al-arḍ* practised in various parts of Northern Province (*Osman Omar v. Mohamed Idrsi* (1958) SLJR (1958) 62); *ḥaqq al-miswaq* applied in Manasir area (*Heirs of Abdel Aziz Khamees v. Heirs of Habib Habram* (1967) SLJR 64).

5 See the cases of *Mohamed Abdel Gabbar v. Suliman Salib Tambal*, HC.-REV-28-1951; *Ahmed Abdel Hadi v. Sudan Government*, HC.-REV-6-1946; *Magboul Abdel Aal v. Zeinab Bint Mohammed*, HC-CS-138-1937.

known as *ḥaqq al-quṣād*,[6] *ḥaqq al-arḍ*,[7] *ḥaqq al-torīa*,[8] *ḥaqq al-miswaq*,[9] and *mudāyara*[10] have been recognized by the courts especially in the Northern Province. However, for these customs to be valid and applied by the courts, they must not be contrary to justice, equity and good conscience, as recognized in English law, as no Sudanese common law had emerged at the time. The policy behind this limitation was to preserve or observe the customs of the local communities while at the same time giving the courts power to scrutinize such customs, to ensure that they were in harmony with the principles of justice, equity and good conscience (Zakaria 1991, p. 70).

---

6 The *quṣād* principle was applied in the case of *Heirs of Eltoma Bint Ali v. Ali Mohammed El Sayed*, (DCCS- 472–5, 519, 805–1942 (Khat.). See also the case of *Taha El Egeil v. Suliman Dawood Mandil* (AC rev-35-8-1953, at pp. 3–4). The learned judge in this case applied the *quṣād* principle and stated: "We have no hesitation in agreeing with the learned judge of the High Court that the *quṣād* principle does in general apply to this area. It is an equitable principle governing the rights of riparian owners, which in one form or another is widely accepted in many countries and is commonly known to be similarly accepted in many areas in the Sudan, although the form in which and the extent to which the principle is applied may vary locally. The presumption therefore in … any case involving riparian rights is that some such principle applied unless a contrary local custom or practice is proved in a particular are or is so well known in that area that judicial notice has been taken of it" (Mustafa 1971, p. 163). See also *Atta El Manan Ahmed Falag v. Owners of Sagia No 6 El Damer*, HCS-401946; *Mahmoud Elnur Omer v. Ibrahim Mohamed*, HC-REV-65-1955.

7 A local custom in Merowe District, where the land owner is entitled to share any date tree planted by another on his land. For a relevant case see *Osman Omer and others* (1964) SLJR, p. 29.

8 A local custom in al-Damer District that gives the right to one-half of the produce of the date trees on the land. It does not give the ownership of an undivided share in the trees but merely a right to one-half share of the crop. See *Omer Ali Omer v. Fadl El Mula El Hussein and others*, SLJR (1962) p. 42.

9 A recognized custom in Manasir Area in the Northern Province, which gives the right to cultivate the land, besides the original right to *ḥaqq al-aṣl* (i.e., the owner of the land). Such a right is registered as an encumbrance. See *Heirs of Abdel Aziz Khames v. Heirs of Habib Habram* SLJR (1967), p. 64.

10 The system of *mudayara* is a custom applicable in Berber and Shendi whereby the shares, as numbered and shown in the register, are given no recognition by the owners, and that the one who owns a number of *'uds* (sticks), each one of them appearing in the register in different shares on land which cultivates the same number of *'uds* as one piece of land allotted somewhere in the *sāqiyya* according to *mudāyara*. See *Abdulla El Hassan Hamza v. Safiya Ali Abu Ali and another* SLJR (1962), pp. 53–54.

Town and Rural Courts

The formal judiciary has established Town and Rural Courts (both have civil and criminal jurisdiction) at the lower level of the judiciary and at the state and locality level. Such courts apply customary laws related to land disputes. The Rules of Regulations of the Town and Rural Courts 2004 create certain types of Middle Rural Courts and Rural Courts. These courts apply the predominant customs in their geographic jurisdiction in addition to other laws and regulations, provided that the custom does not contravene the law, the principles of justice and *sharīʿa* law.[11] Unlike the application of customary law during the sixties, here customary law should not contradict *sharīʿa* law or English common law. These courts are recognized as part of the formal structure of Sudan's court system and have been accorded certain powers. The jurisdiction of these courts and the appointment of their members are also defined. These courts can therefore be classified as part of the judiciary, statutorily mandated to apply customary laws, and are an integral part of the formal court structure. They are managed or supervised by judges from the Judiciary who are familiar with the customs of the area. These courts, because they are manned by prominent influential tribal figures, play important roles in most situations.

However, it is pertinent to note that such courts have limited civil and criminal jurisdiction: they are only mandated to look at a limited category of cases pertaining to land disputes and pasture. For example, the Town and Rural Courts have no criminal jurisdiction over civil claims related to land ownership or any claims against the government or any public corporation.[12] This is one of the serious gaps in the body of the law, as most disputes relate to communal land and are claims against the government or corporations or companies, particularly those allocated vast agricultural schemes under investment laws. Furthermore, such courts have civil jurisdiction over small cases only involving small sums.[13] This can also be considered as a further limitation in the law, particularly in various cases involving conflict between farmers and pastoralists in some areas where a large sum of money is involved.[14] The Middle Rural Courts and Rural Courts have specific civil jurisdiction over: (a) claims related

11 Article 22 (2) (author's translation) of the Rules of Regulations of the Town and Rural Courts 2004.

12 Article 12.

13 Article 14.

14 For example, cases involving the estimated damages to crops caused by pastoralists on agricultural land that exceed more than 20,000 USD are outside the jurisdiction of these courts. Rural and Town Courts will not have jurisdiction, as the civil case may involve large sums of money.

to pasture and farm damages or injury to cattle, without specifying the amount of damages; (b) cases related to land and boundary disputes; (c) appeal powers over decisions and orders issued by the Rural Courts related to civil cases.

Under the provisions of the Rural and Town Courts, it is apparent that customary law is relegated to a minor status. For example, customary law must not contradict statutory laws. In cases related to unregistered usufructuary land, whoever has land registration certificates over the land, will get a positive decision from the court, even if the other party proves his ownership of the land through possession (*ḥiyāza*) or occupation. This is because Sudanese laws and practices still ignore the interconnection between customary and statutory law with imported legislative blueprints such as the Civil Transaction Act 1984, which allows land grabbing by new and old elites and ignores unregistered usufructuary rights of tribes or local communities, which can be confiscated for the public good.

Currently, all states in Sudan apply the weak Rules of Regulations of the Town and Rural Courts 2004 outlined above. With the exception of North Kordofan State, states do not enact any laws to establish a powerful native judiciary to apply customary law. It is pertinent to refer here as an example to the Native Judiciary Act of North Kordofan State, 2006,[15] which can play a vital role in land disputes. The Act establishes Rural and Town Native Courts to look at cases of a customary nature. These courts consist of a head, a deputy head and a sufficient number of members, to be chosen by the Head of the Judiciary at state level after consultation with the *wālī* (Governor).[16] The candidate who presides over the Native Court must be aware of the customs and traditions of the area.[17] The court has jurisdiction over ownership in cases of land disputes and any claim against the government or a public corporation.[18] The Act also decrees that rural courts have jurisdiction over cases of damages to farms or pastures or of injured cattle.[19] Under the Act, native judges deliver justice to all people in the state in accordance with the law and customs. Rules of Procedures and Regulations were also issued under Article 29 of the Act. However, it remains to be seen whether this Act will make a difference in practice.

15 Act No 19, 12 April 2006.

16 Article 6.

17 Article 7 (2).

18 Article 10 (2).

19 Article 17.

Statutory Regulation of Land Ownership and Use

The statutory regulation of land in Sudan has been a complex product of various sources. It is a unique combination of Sudanese legislation, judge-made rules, customary laws, and *sharīʿa* law. Many of these rules are wholly of local origin, whereas others have been received from abroad with a varying degree of modification in Sudan (Thompson 1965, p. 5). Therefore, examining land legislations is an important starting point in an attempt to determine the applicable rules and procedures and their impact on customary ownership and usages.

Replacement of Diversified Indigenous Systems of Land Tenure with a Uniform State-Controlled System

One of the important legislations regulating land ownership and rights in Sudan is the Civil Transaction Act, 1984. The CTA stipulates that its provisions shall apply to all obligations and rights arising, *inter alia*, out of lease, ownership, incidents of ownership and mortgages.[20] It also governs possession, ownership and rights, including contracts with respect to land.[21] Prior to 1970, the registration and settlement of rights and interests in land had not been effected throughout Sudan. On 6 April 1970, the Unregistered Land Act 1970[22] was promulgated, stating that all land of any kind, whether waste, forest, occupied or unoccupied, which was not registered before the commencement of this Act, would on such commencement, be the property of the government and be deemed to have been registered as such.[23] The Unregistered Land Act 1970 reconfirmed in the CTA, 1984, was nothing less than a major act of land reform, which vested ownership of the greatest majority of Sudanese land in the government (Gordon 1986, p. 148). The Act has made the government the biggest landlord in Sudan and the state is declared to be in control of the land as well as the owner of all land that was not registered in the name of a private individual prior to 6 April 1970. As a consequence, no right or interest may be obtained in state-owned land unless such right or interest is registered at a government registry.[24] Thus, widely diversified indigenous systems of tenure and land management were replaced by the implementation of a uniform

20 Civil Transactions Act 1984, s. 4.

21 *Ibid.* S. 11 (12) and (13) (b).

22 See *Laws of the Sudan*, Vol. 5, pp. 226–229.

23 The Act states that "all waste, forest and unoccupied land' shall be deemed to be property of the government until the contrary is proven".

24 See CTA, 1984, s. 559 (1) (3).

and state-controlled system (de Wit 2001). Here, the state replaces the local community as the guarantor of access to land and security of tenure. This replacement could be problematic if the state does not behave as a credible and neutral grantor of land: an issue that will be critically explored in this chapter, particularly with regard to land grabbing for investment in major projects at the expense of local communities' entitlement to customary land ownership.

Although the government becomes the legal owner of all land not registered before 1970, it may, of course, permit private parties to use state-owned land. In this respect, the CTA of 1984 provides that the central, regional, and National Capital authorities shall adopt the necessary procedure for granting the usufruct of land to private persons, through the establishment of committees consisting of no less than three members.[25]

However, just as the government may grant land, Sudanese legislation similarly provides for forced acquisition by the state of land privately held when a determination has been made that such land is "required permanently or temporarily for any public purpose".[26] However, no person shall be deprived of property except through the payment of prompt consideration and in accordance with due process of law.[27] The procedure to be followed in state acquisition is that an expropriation officer is to be appointed, who gives notice to the occupiers of the land and other interested persons, identifying the land and stating its intended acquisition "for a public purpose".[28] Where the land in question has not previously been registered, it shall be registered before the acquisition is carried out.[29] The expropriation officer is to attempt to reach an agreement on compensation with the persons having rights or interests in the land.[30] In the absence of an agreement, the amount of compensation is to be determined by a board of arbitration according to a set of standards,[31] with provision made for appeal.[32] Compensation may be made either through the payment of money or the grant of other land.[33]

The registration of rights and interests in land is the process by which a government agency keeps a record of titles to land, whereby no dealing in respect

25 CTA, 1984, s. 556(1) (2).

26 Land Acquisition Act 1970, ss.4 (1), 31 2 *Laws of the Sudan* 239 (5th ed. 1976). See also The Acquisition Act, 1970 (Act no. 20).

27 CTA, 1984, s. 517 (2).

28 Land Acquisition Act, 1930, s. 10.

29 *Ibid.* s. 9.

30 *Ibid.* s. 14.

31 *Ibid.* s. 19.

32 *Ibid.* s. 23.

33 *Ibid.* s. 22.

of any parcel of land in that record is invalid unless registered. The purpose of registration is hence to facilitate proof of title and so make the transfer of land simpler, quicker and certain. The Act is still in force to date and sets out how land rights are identified and registered.

In terms of procedures, the Land Registration Act 1970 empowers the Attorney General, whenever "it appears expedient", to publish a notice in the *Gazette* stating that it is intended to affect a settlement and registration of land within a specified area.[34] Following such publication of the notice, the head of the judiciary in the governmental region in question appoints a settlement officer and demarcation officers to carry out the demarcations, settlement and registration of the settlement area. The Act specifies in detail the principles to be followed in determining outstanding rights to and interests in land, and provides dissatisfied parties with a method of appealing the decisions reached.[35] Provision is also made for the correction of information contained in land registries in the event of mistake or fraud.[36]

Limited Recognition of de facto *Customary Rights of Land Ownership* – Ḥiyāza

Tribes, clans, families and rural dwellers could consider land as *de facto* their "own" in a communal or cooperative context. This *de facto* ownership (to be called *ḥiyāza* in Arabic) is recognized by Sudan's current laws and jurisprudence as entitling communities to customary land rights. The term *ḥiyāza* is parallel to some degree with the concept of "occupation of unregistered land" in English law. Under the 1970 Land Registration Act, proof of ownership relies heavily on "occupation", i.e., highly visible land use, as in agricultural fields and residential areas.

The Civil Transaction Act, 1984 has also dealt with the customary or communal ownership of land: it specifies certain criteria to be observed by the authorities when granting land. The CTA provides for the right to use government land or land belonging to another person through the legal right of usufruct (*manfaʿa*). This right of usufruct may be acquired through deed, inheritance, will or the exercise of possession. Whoever uses rural waste land, by cultivation, building or irrigation, becomes entitled to the usufruct of the land in question. The government also has an important role to play in granting usufruct on public land. As a landlord, the central and state governments in Sudan are charged with promoting land use, and towards that end have the power to

34 Section 5 (as amended in December 1984).

35 *Ibid.* s. 84.

36 *Ibid.* s. 85.

divide, survey and register land.[37] In terms of procedural law, committees at the federal and state levels, comprised of three to five members, are to handle the grant of usufruct on public lands.[38] In granting the usufruct regarding agricultural land, the government authorities shall consider certain criteria related to pastures, agricultural enterprises and modern production techniques. The following shall be taken into consideration:

a. Preservation of villages, natural resources, animal health and natural pasture areas.
b. Preservation of small agricultural enterprises.
c. Large tracts of land should not be granted without a determination that the grantor will exploit the whole of such area in the most favourable way.
d. Protection of drainage and other services.
e. Particular land may be granted to more than one person, family or company for the purpose of agricultural production by modern techniques.[39]

At the lower administrative levels, land allocation procedures stipulate a series of important responsibilities, although it is doubtful whether these local activities are adequately implemented under the law. The local level is instrumental in resolving land disputes. A Land Conflict Resolution Committee at the *maḥalliyya* (locality) level deals with and resolves disputes over land. The customary authority must occupy a central role in these committees. In the case of an unresolved land conflict, the dispute is referred to the Civil Court. However, in terms of actual practice, it is pertinent to mention that there is a need for further investigation into how the law is applied in practice.

Land Grabbing and Encroachment on Communal Customary Land Rights under Sudan's Investment Laws

There is a dynamic relationship between customary law and rights, and land grabbing, which normally encroaches upon the customary rights and ownership of rural populations. Land grabbing is one of the main causes of conflict: it amounts to a violation of human rights including the right to food. The UN Special Rapporteur on the right to food recommends a minimum set of

---

37 CTA, 1984, s. 560 (6).
38 *Ibid.* s. 566(1) (2).
39 *Ibid.* s. 561.

principles and measures based on human rights, with regard to large scale transnational land acquisitions and leases, more commonly referred to as "land grabbing" (UN Special Rapporteur 2009). These principles and measures are intended to assist both investors and governments in the negotiation and implementation of large-scale land leases and acquisitions, to ensure that such investment works for the benefit of the population including the most vulnerable groups, and is conducive to sustainable development, with the progressive realization of the right to food (*ibid.*). The measures are grounded in the principles of international human rights law, including the right to food and the right to development (*ibid.*).

According to estimates, between 15 and 20 million hectares of farmland in developing countries have been subjected to large-scale land acquisition involving foreign investors. This already represents the size of France's farmland. Among the main target countries are sub-Saharan African countries such as Cameroon, Ethiopia, the Democratic Republic of Congo, Madagascar, Mali, Somalia, Sudan, Tanzania and Zambia.[40] As far as Sudan is concerned, from the end of the 1960s onwards there was a massive horizontal expansion of agricultural production, accompanied by an expropriation of *de facto* community land and land grabbing associated with Mechanized Farming Schemes and the Arab Breadbasket Policy. It is estimated that approximately 25–30 million feddans were placed under mechanized cultivation (de Wit 2001). The SNCS for 1992–2002 played a part in marginalizing the rural household sector in favour of large-scale commercial and mechanized farming (*ibid.*). There is the assumption that there is still plenty of land available for horizontal expansion, and that this land can be placed under production without causing social tensions (*ibid.*). Sudan's mechanized agriculture policy, which makes grants of vast areas of agricultural land for investment, sprang from a central desire to realize Sudan's agricultural potential but did not give sufficient consideration either to the viability of the policy or, most importantly, its impact on local stakeholders, particularly the rural populations who have historical customary rights to land. The result is that it has not only failed to achieve its development objectives, but has actually served to undermine existing livelihoods and local development. There is no doubt that large-scale land investments can create opportunities for development, given their potential for creating infrastructures for employment, increasing public revenue and improving farmers' access to technologies and credit. However, they may also have negative consequences. Potential impacts include: the eviction of land users who have no formal or statutory security of tenure over the land they have been cultivating

40 For details see UN Special Rapporteur (2009).

for decades; the loss of access to land for indigenous peoples and pastoral populations; competition for water resources; and decreased food security if local populations are deprived of access to productive resources (*ibid.*). Also, the policy of making large scale commercial farms available for investment is one of the main factors leading to conflict between pastoralists and farmers, as the expansion of such land has led to social tensions.

Unfortunately, Sudanese investment laws relating to the granting of land for agricultural and development schemes do not consider the negative impacts of allowing large scale commercial farms on local communities' customary rights to land. The Encouragement of Investment Acts 1999 and 2013, for instance, call for the promotion of investment, and, accordingly create favourable conditions and privileges for investors, without taking into account the customary land rights of local communities, particularly small farmers and pastoralists. The Encouragement of Investment Acts 1999, for example, encourages investment activity in areas such as agriculture and animal production.[41] Furthermore, it categorizes these investment activities as "strategic activities".[42] In order to encourage investment, the Act endows the Minister of Investment at the federal level the power to grant land for strategic projects free of charge, or for nominal or "encouraging fees" for non-strategic projects.[43] Strategic projects are exempted from paying taxation profits for ten years and the Minister can increase this period if he or she determines it appropriate to do so.[44] States or localities are not allowed to impose taxation or dues on any investment project. Similarly, at the state level, the Act gives the relevant Minister the power to grant land free of taxation and dues (when they are imposed by a state law or locality) for a period up to five years, renewable for a further five years.[45] Such projects are also exempted from any other state taxes and further land can be allocated to the project on payment of only nominal or encouraging fees.[46] Furthermore, the Minister may provide other favourable conditions for investors if projects are diverted to less developed areas: increasing the exports; realizing rural development and; creating work opportunities.[47] Most importantly, the law provides legal guarantees for the investor against nationalization or confiscation of the project or land in the public interest without payment of

41 Article 7.

42 Article 9 (Strategic Projets).

43 Article 12.

44 Article 10.

45 Article 13 (1).

46 Article 13.

47 Article 16.

just compensation.[48] Furthermore, confiscation of monies and the freezing of assets can only be implemented by judicial order.[49]

Thus, the traditional smallholder sector of traditional land owners has been marginalized by policies and legislation since the Condominium Period, through Independence and up until the present, with encouragement of the territorial expansion of commercially based agriculture at the expense of this traditional sector. Along the way, this has caused evictions from land and forced resettlements (de Wit 2001). Thus, the granting of land and land management is a sensitive issue, as land should be distributed in a transparent manner and in accordance with well-defined legal procedures that guarantee the rights of customary ownership of land and ensure that land cannot be encroached upon by large-scale mechanized farming or land grabbing. The right to allocate land by the government is therefore a subject of primary importance, particularly in the light of the large amount of land owned by the state and it is unfortunate that the state in Sudan is not perceived as a neutral agent that distributes land in a transparent manner. Furthermore, the absence of rule of law, entrenched corruption, and the capacity of state institutions to administer land are all factors that encroach upon communal customary land rights. Sudan investment law outlined above provides many guarantees to the investors while completely ignoring communities' customary rights, as well as the rights of small farmers and pastoralists. Land represents not only the main means to access and produce food for millions of stakeholders and their families, but is also an essential element in the very identity of certain peoples and communities. From a human rights perspective, any negotiations leading to investment agreements should be conducted in full transparency and with the participation of the local communities whose access to land and other productive resources may be affected by the arrival of an investor. Any shifts in land use should, as a matter of principle, be made with the free, prior and informed consent of the local communities concerned. In Sudan, it is noticeable that large-scale mechanized farming and other development projects owned by some powerful individuals have been granted huge tracts of land, which sometimes encroach upon *ḥarām al-ḥilla* (boundaries of villages and communities).

Recently, there has been increasing concern over development projects that result in forced displacement, such as the construction of the Merowe and Kajbar dams, which also prompted protests that were met with excessive force (EIPR 2013). The government of Sudan has also pursued a policy of selling off

48 Article 17 (1).

49 Article 17 (b).

land to Sudanese and foreign investors (Alden 2010). In addition to the loss of customary land rights, this practice (which is reportedly often accompanied by forced evictions), has impacted adversely on a series of rights of those affected, including the right to property and the right to housing (*ibid.*).

Thus, Sudan's legal system, far from providing adequate protection against public acquisition and expropriation of land, actually facilitates these practices, particularly the Civil Transactions Amendment Act, 1990, and the National Investment Encouragement Act, 2013 (Babiker and Oette 2015, pp. 22–25). This practice also raises concerns over its compatibility with the rights of the Sudanese people to freely dispose of their wealth and natural resources under international human rights law and the regional African human rights regime.[50]

Constitutional Guarantees of Customary Land Tenure under the Interim National Constitution 2005 and the CPA

The Interim National Constitution 2005 provides in Article 186 (3) that "all levels of government shall institute a process to progressively develop and amend the relevant laws to incorporate customary laws, practices, local heritage and international trends and practices". This important provision authorizes states to undertake a process of incorporating customary laws as part of their legal system. The Constitution also provides that the regulation of land tenure, usage and exercise of rights shall be a concurrent competence, exercised at the appropriate level of government.[51] Furthermore, rights in land owned by the government of Sudan shall be exercised through the appropriate or designated level of government.[52] The Constitution further provides for exclusive and concurrent powers to be exercised at the state level for the management of land resources. This includes state land, state natural resources and traditional and customary law.[53] State governments, too, have legislative and executive competencies related to land tenure, agriculture, water and pastures to be

---

50 Article 21 of the African Charter on Human and Peoples' Rights (to which Sudan is a party) provides that "all peoples shall freely dispose of their wealth and natural resources. This right shall be exercised in the exclusive interest of the people. In no case shall a people be deprived of it".

51 Article 186 (1).

52 Article 186 (2).

53 See Schedule (C) of the Interim Constitution of the Republic of the Sudan 2005 (Concurrent Powers 8, 13, 21, 34).

exercised concurrently with the National Federal government, including the regulation of land tenure and usage and exercise of rights in land.[54]

Although the Constitution provides for the aforementioned powers, no legislation is in place to reform existing land laws, despite the INC 2005 calling upon all levels of government to institute a process to progressively develop and amend the relevant land laws to incorporate customary laws, practices and local heritage.[55] The enactment of new laws and the incorporation of customary law, as well as the institutional mechanisms to manage land rights, shall be developed, in the new context of decentralization of state powers guaranteed by the INC 2005. In particular, customary practices related to rural land tenure systems and land rights management are to be developed to enable individual or communal rights to be registered and protected. This is a priority, as disputes over land and related resources normally ignite violent local land conflicts. Unfortunately, the state has so far often failed to establish functioning land tenure systems.

Some states' Constitutions call for the enactment of laws to regulate land ownership, land use and land rights and have the competence and powers to regulate government land as provided for in Article 186 (2) of the INC 2005.[56] For example, the Sennar State Interim Constitution provides that the state "shall initiate procedures and gradual measures to develop laws related to land to include customary practices, local heritage and international trends and practices related to land."[57] This Constitution further provides for the establishment of a Land Commission with competences to adjudicate between disputing parties willing to be finally bound by the Commission's decision, which shall be registered and enforced by courts. The Land Commission has also powers to adjudicate on land claims in the state and between parties who have interests in the disputed land but without prejudice to the competences of the judiciary. In performing its work, the Land Commission is required to take into consideration the principles of equity and justice.[58] Similarly, the White Nile State Constitution provides for the enactment of legislation to govern land ownership and usage, as well as the integration of customary practices. However, no legislation has been enacted at state level to address customary

54 See Schedule (D) of the Interim Constitution of the Republic of the Sudan 2005 (Concurrent Powers 23, 27, 31).

55 Article 183 (3).

56 See Article 88 (1) of Sennar Interim Constitution 2005.

57 Article 88 (3) of Sennar Interim Constitution 2005.

58 Article 88 of Sennar Interim Constitution 2005.

land rights. At the level of localities, legal orders can only be issued for approval by the state legislative orders.

Both the CPA and the INC 2005 provide for concurrent and exclusive powers regarding the regulation of land matters. Both documents call for the establishment of a National Land Commission and other state commissions to deal with issues pertaining to land ownership rights, land use, land tenure systems and land arbitration. The recently enacted Land Commission Act, 2009, deals with the relationship between the Commission and the ongoing rules and acts, the Commission's membership, its technical mandate on land use, its semi-judicial mandate and its arbitration powers. However, the Commission is not yet operational to tackle urgent issues related to communal customary land rights and usage.

Sudan's 2015 Constitutional Amendments and Their Impact on Land Tenure Regulations

As outlined above, questions surrounding the use of land have been at the heart of many communal conflicts. The CPA and the INC 2005 were meant to address at least some of these issues, but are largely acknowledged to have failed to bring about satisfactory solutions (Alden 2010). The INC 2005 was amended on the 4th of January 2015 and, unfortunately, article 186 was amended despite it forms a basis for developing a legal regime that considers good practice, with due regard to customary laws, practices and local heritage.[59] The revised article 186 signals a markedly different approach (Babiker and Oette 2015). It stipulates that:

(1) Acquisition and exploitation of land and enjoyment of rights over it is a common capacity exercised across the relevant level of government according to the provisions of the law.
(2) The National Assembly shall approve the National Investment Plan.

59 Article 186 stipulates: "(1) The regulation of land tenure, usage and exercise of rights thereon shall be a concurrent competence, exercised at the appropriate level of government." Article 186 (2) provides: "Rights in land owned by the Government of the Sudan shall be exercised through the appropriate or designated level of Government." Article 186 (3) provides: "All levels of government shall institute a process to progressively develop and amend the relevant laws to incorporate customary laws, practices, local heritage and international trends and practices."

(3) The President of the Republic may, from time to time, issue Presidential Decrees to define the lands to be exploited as investment, how the investment returns shall be used and the level of government concerned with running it and enjoy rights over it, observing citizen rights [sic] and the social responsibilities of investors.

The language of the amended article 186 (1) signals a shift in emphasis, moving from regulation, which ideally considers all relevant rights and interests, to "acquisition and exploitation of land", which is given textual priority over the "enjoyment of rights over it" including customary land rights (*ibid.*). The amended article 186 (2) and (3) places heavy emphasis on investment, and explicitly links land exploitation to investment. It thereby risks giving constitutional approval to a policy of selling off land that gives scant respect to local rights and interests (*ibid.*). This concern is reinforced by the provision in the amended article 186 (3), which grants the President of the Republic the power to use Presidential Decrees for the purpose of land exploitation, which, in light of recent practice, enhances the risk of executive abuse of powers. The formula "observing citizen rights and the social responsibilities of investors", which the President is to take into consideration when issuing Presidential Decrees, is insufficient to provide adequate safeguards against abuse. "Citizens' rights" are not clearly defined. "While article 43 of the Bill of Rights of the INC 2005 provides for the right to own property and to prompt and fair compensation in case of expropriation, it is widely acknowledged that the legal framework relating to land rights is seriously flawed" (*ibid.*)

Conclusion

Land laws and the legislation that regulates access to land and land use has invariably been designed to defend the interests of the state and not of the rural communities. Land legislation in Sudan is excessive, confused and complicated; "arbitrarily used"; "excessively used for purposes of expropriation of private land"; "something is wrong with our land laws and we need to address this mischief" (de Wit, Tanner and Norfolk 2009, p. 8). It is apparent that land reform and practice strengthening customary land rights have not taken place to date in Sudan post the CPA era, despite constant calls for land reform. Hence, there is a need for Sudan to undertake a comprehensive review of its land laws, including investment laws, with a view to ensuring customary rights of local communities, as well as conformity with Sudan's obligations under international human rights law.

References

Abdel Ati, H 2005, *Traditional Tribal System and Customary Law in Eastern Sudan*, Report for the Rule of Law Unit, United Nations Development Programme (UNDP), Sudan.

Alden, W 2010, 'Making Peace Impossible? Failure to Honour the Land Obligations of the Comprehensive Peace Agreement in Central Sudan', unpubished manuscript. http://mokoro.co.uk/wpcontent/uploads/making_peace_impossible_land_obligations_in_central_sudan.pdf (accessed 6 November 2016).

Babiker, MA & Oette, L 2015, 'Constitutional Reforms, Governance and Human Rights Protection: Sudan's 2015 Constitutional Amendments' (unpublished paper).

de Wit, V 2001, *Legality and Legitimacy: Access to Land, Pasture and Water*, Report of the IGAD partner Forum Working Group Planning for Peace, FAO, Rome.

de Wit, P, Tanner, C & Norfolk, S 2009, *Land Policy Development in an African Context, Lessons Learned from Selected Experiences*, Land Tenure Working Paper 14, FAO, Rome.

EIPR (Egyptian Initiative for Personal Rights) 2013, 'EIPR Launches Legal Action against Sudan for Violations Arising from the Construction of the Merowe And Kajbar Dams, press release, 7 October. http://eipr.org/en/pressrelease/2013/10/07/1842 (accessed 29 August 2017).

El-Mahdi, S 1979, *Introduction to the Land Law of the Sudan*, Khartoum University Press, Khartoum.

Gertel, J, Rottenburg, R & Calkins, S (eds) 2014, *Disrupting Territories: Land, Commodification and Conflict in Sudan*, James Currey, London.

Gordon, C 1986, 'The Land Law of the Sudan', *Journal of African Law*, vol. 30, no. 2, pp. 143–174.

Macek, J 1993, 'The Essentials for the Role of Customary Law in Southern Sudan', *Sudan Law Journal and Reports*, pp. 1–23.

Mustafa, Z 1971. *The Common Law of the Sudan: An Account of Justice, Equity, and Good Conscience Provision*, Clarendon Press, Oxford.

Osman, AM 2012, *Al-Judia: A Study on Conflict Resoultion and Reconciliation with Special Reference to the Darfur Situaiton*, Alwatania Library, Khartoum [in Arabic].

Thompson, C 1965, *The Land Law of the Sudan: Cases and Materials*, Khartoum University Press, Khartoum.

UN Special Rapporteur 2009, 'The Right to Food: Principles and Measures to Discipline "Land Grabbing"'. www.srfood.org/images/stories/pdf/press_releases/20090611_press-release_en.pdf (accessed 28 August 2017.

Zakaria, I 1991, *An Analytical Study of Some Legal Theories and Their Relevance to the Sudan*, LLM Thesis, University of Khartoum, Faculty of Law, Khartoum.

Case Law

- Heirs of Abdel Gabbar Mohamed v. Fatma Mohamed (1964) SLJR 156.
- Abdall Elhussein v. Safiya Ali Abu Ali, SLJR 62.
- Heirs of Fadlalalla Oklah v. Hussein Ali Brar (1964) SLJR 96.
- Osman Omar v. Mohamed Idrsi (1958) SLJR
- Heirs of Abdel Aziz Khamees v. Heirs of Habib Habram (1967) SLJR 64.
- Mohamed Abdel Gabbar v. Suliman Salib Tambal, HC.-REV-28-1951.
- Ahmed Abdel Hadi v. Sudan Government, H.C.-REV-6-1946.
- Magboul Abdel Aal v. Zeinab Bint Mohammed, H.C.-C.S.-138-1937.
- Atta El Manan Ahmed Falag v. Owners of Sagia No 6 El Damer, H.C.S-401946.
- Mahmoud Elnur Omer v. Ibrahim Mohamed, H.C.-REV-65-1955.
- Omer Ali Omer v. Fadl El Mula El Hussein and others, SLJR (1962), p. 42.
- Heirs of Abdel Aziz Khames v. Heirs of Habib Habram, SLJR (1967), p. 64.
- Abdulla El Hassan Hamza v. Safiya Ali Abu Ali and another, SLJR (1962), pp. 53–54.

Land Related Legislations

- Titles of Land Ordinance, 1899.
- Land Settlement Ordinance, 1905.
- Native Disposition of Lands Restriction Ordinance, 1918, 1922.
- Land Resettlement and Registration Act, 1925.
- Land Acquisition Act, 1930.
- Pre-emption Act, 1938.
- Unregistered Land Act, 1970.
- Local Government Act, 1971.
- Civil Transactions Act, 1984 (amended in 1990).
- Encouragement of Investment Act, 1999, 2013.
- Forest Act, 1989.
- Construction Planning and Land Disposition Act, 1994.
- Local Government Act, 1998.

Customary Land Agreements

- Hadandowa agreement with the Rashaida, 1933.

PART 2

Statutory and Non-Statutory Courts: Principles and Practices for Dispute Settlement

CHAPTER 6

Dynamics of Dispute Management in South Gedaref State, Eastern Sudan: An Anthropological Approach

Zahir M. Abdal-Kareem

Introduction

Social scientists have employed a variety of approaches to study negotiation as a decision-making process. One approach is that of game theorists, who deal with negotiation as a strategy. Their main assumption is that "each player decides in advance, before the game actually starts, what move he will make in any possible situation that may arise" (Harsanyi 1977, p. 94). Some scholars describe this approach as providing one of the most abstracted and tight theoretical contributions about negotiation. However, social anthropologist Philip Gulliver raises the criticism that this approach does not deal with the "particular problems that occur in the real world, but with highly generalized situations" (Gulliver 1979, p. 36). Therefore, he suggests the need to widen this approach by adding the economist's approach. According to him, the economist's approach pays more attention to the issues that tend to be ignored by game theorists, namely "the nature of changing expectations and players' tactics and the significance of uncertainties of information, perception, and evaluation" (*ibid.*, p. 37).

However, Gulliver (1979) states that the combination of the above-mentioned approaches is not enough to allow a full understanding of the real dynamics of decision-making processes, and in particular negotiation. He provides two reasons for this shortfall. First, both approaches pay little attention to cultural variations between conflicting parties and, accordingly, isolate the decision-making processes from the surrounding socioeconomic and cultural settings. Second, and more importantly, these approaches "almost universally ignore the distribution of power or, what amounts to the same thing, they assume that, like skills and knowledge, power is equally distributed to the parties" (*ibid.*, p. 51).

 | DOI 10.1163/9789004362185_008

What I seek to demonstrate in this chapter[1] is that much insight can be gained by combining game theory and bargaining with the broadened version of the extended case method, particularly that adopted by Jaap van Velsen (1967) and Keebet von Benda-Beckmann (2003). The extended case method enables us to figure out the complex association between "norms in conflict" and the strategies and choices of individuals (van Velsen 1967, p. 146). This combined theoretical perspective is what I call an anthropological approach.

There are two other issues that I shall touch upon while dealing with the question of negotiation. First, I shall examine the degree to which, and how, disputing parties practise "forum-shopping behaviour".[2] Second, I shall reflect on the question of *sharīʿa* law[3] and how some of its concepts have been interpreted and put into practice during negotiation processes in the study area.[4]

The analysis I provide in this chapter is based upon a dispute case that took place in Basingga village[5] in Basunda locality council, south Gedaref State. This dispute was settled through a local council of negotiation (*jūdiya*) held in the police centre of Basunda locality council. The disputing parties were a group of cattle herders from the Beni Amer ethnic group and an alliance of agricultural wage labourers that included people from western Sudan and Ethiopia.

The main argument I adopt in this chapter states that, while the importance of strategies and tactics used by negotiators is not denied, dispute management

1 I would like to express my sincere gratitude to both the Max Planck Institute for Social Anthropology and International Max Planck Research School on Retaliation Mediation and Punishment (IMPRS-REMEP) for their kind academic and financial support, without which this work would have not been possible. Similarly, I deeply appreciate the academic and financial support provided by the ANDROMAQUE project, through which this work has been prepared for publication in this volume. Part of this chapter together with its fieldwork are based on my PhD thesis, which is entitled *Group Identification and Resource Conflicts in Gedaref State, Eastern Sudan: Who Allies with Whom? Why? And How?* (Abdal-Kareem 2016).

2 The expression "forum shopping behaviour" indicates a situation through which "disputants have a choice between different institutions and they base their choice on what they hope the outcome of the dispute will be, however vague or ill-founded their expectations may be" (von Benda-Beckmann 1981, p. 117). Here, it is argued that in many local contexts "traditional institutions of dispute resolution have existed side by side with state courts, allowing disputants to choose between them"(von Benda-Beckmann 2003, p. 238).

3 For the purposes of this study, and as proposed by some contemporary Islamic thinkers, *sharīʿa* is identified as "a body of principles to be applied, rather than a large body of specific, timeless rules to be enforced" (Lombardi 1998, p. 96).

4 Islam has a significant influence on traditional systems of conflict resolution across almost all northern Sudan.

5 Basingga is one of the villages of Basunda locality council, in which the dispute took place.

in south Gedaref State is shaped by factors that are mostly socioeconomic and political in nature. Such factors are recognized in legal anthropology as "the environment of disputes" (von Benda-Beckmann 2003). Furthermore, I argue that the interpretation of customary legal concepts – mainly those related to *sharīʿa* law[6] – is also strongly influenced by the sociological factors mentioned above.

Focusing on Disputing Processes Rather than on Normative Orders

There are two main reasons for which I focus more on the processes of disputes than on their norms. Disputes and processes concerned with their resolution or management are among the central subjects of legal anthropology (Hoebel 1954; Pospisil 1971), and are perhaps even its "core" (von Benda-Beckmann 2003, p. 135). As legal anthropology developed between the 1960s and the 1980s, many anthropologists realized that disputes are not always taken to court or court-like institutions with the primary purpose of resolution. Rather, people may have "political motivations for going to court", while "... others may have more personal reasons; and yet others simply wish to have their day in court and be publicly heard" (*ibid.*, p. 236). Thus, I follow the trend in legal anthropology that gives more attention to processes than to the normative orders, which anticipate resolution as its goal. Such a process-centred approach has been adopted by a number of scholars (von Benda-Beckmann 2003; Bohannan 1969; Gulliver 1979; Nader and Todd 1978; Turner 1972; van Velsen 1967). The second reason for adopting this approach goes with what is argued by Peter Just, who examines the legal phenomenon from "a much broader view" that deals with conflict "as an endemic feature of social life" placing it in a "total social context" and accordingly breaks away from the effects of "judge-(and judgment-) oriented accounts" (Just 1992, p. 374).

6 In general, *sharīʿa* is "the technical term for 'Islamic law.' It is the body of rules that God revealed to man in the sacred texts of Islam. Muslims consider obedience to *sharīʿa* as a "crucial religious duty. Historically, however, "there has been no unanimity on what the *sharīʿa* consists of or on how to define it. The term Sharia has meant different things to different people in different countries, and even within one country it has meant different things over the centuries" (Lombardi 1998, p. 91).

Theoretical Clarifications about Negotiation and Adjudication

Conceptually, negotiations, including mediation, "comprise processes of interaction between conflicting parties, leading to and including joint or interdependent decision-making on the issues between them" (Gulliver 1979, p. 35). In negotiations, two individuals (or groups) usually seek to reach some settlement of a dispute or conflict between them. In such a practice, "each party is concerned to direct information, persuasion and influence to the other party with the aim of reaching an agreement which is mutually tolerable and acceptable to both"(Gulliver 1977, p. 15).

Negotiation may also involve a third-party mediator who is present during the dispute settlement process, but has no power or legitimacy to give judgements. Hypothetically, the main task of the mediator is to help the disputing parties to reach an agreement. This method is to be contrasted with adjudication, in which "each party presents his case and argument to a third party in order to obtain a decision in his favour – that third party having the power to decide on the issues in dispute and to give his judgment accordingly" (*ibid.*). However, the application of mediation and adjudication in different African communities has yielded different results from those conventionally expected. The two forms may blur in practice: "mediators can, in some extreme circumstances, virtually take control and make effective decisions, whilst adjudicators may sometimes relinquish control and seek only to improve communication and to use persuasion" (*ibid.*).

Another approach is to emphasize the conceptual and procedural distinctions between negotiation and adjudication. In this way, the two mechanisms tend to be differentiated according to their typical subjects. Thus negotiation is mostly used and required in disputes over interests, whilst adjudication is mostly appropriate and effective "when the disputes concern values, norms and the assessment of facts" (Gulliver 1979, p. 8). However, in reality this distinction is rarely clear. Many studies of disputes in both highly industrialized and traditional communities prove that it is almost impossible to distinguish interests from values.

During fieldwork, I observed that negotiations are mostly initiated when two parties are unable or unwilling to settle their dispute between themselves. In such a case, they transfer their dispute to a public or semi-public arena. Each party nominates a group of people to represent and defend its position during the dispute settlement process. These representatives or negotiators are mostly chosen from members of Native Administration coming from across Gedaref State. Each side should present its case, argument and evidence to a third party; usually a forum of members of local tribal leaders and members of Native Administration.

Declaring a negotiation successful does not necessarily require achieving a final solution or establishing an agreement that accords with society's norms or justice. But as Gulliver clarifies,

> ... as a minimum, settlement means the end of the dispute at least for the time being. It may in effect leave things pretty well as they were, or solve some but not all problems, or significantly re-establish or re-organize relations between the two parties.
>
> GULLIVER 1977, P. 20

A Synopsis of the Study Area and Its People

Basunda locality council of south Gedaref State is the geographical and social setting upon which this chapter is based. It is about 140 km south of Gedaref town, the capital of Gedaref State. It covers an area of 7,000 square km, comprises forty-two villages, and has a population that the 2008 national census estimated at 67,000. It is bordered by Ethiopia in the east and the south, Gala an-Nahal locality council in the west, Sennar State in the south-west, and al-Gurayysha locality council in the north (see Map 6.1).

As described by one of my informants, "before the 1970s the Basunda area was almost an unpopulated area of acacia forests that was mostly occupied by wild animals".[7] Hunting animals and small-scale cattle herding were the main economic activities until 1971, when the government ordered the *nāẓir* (paramount chief) of Dār Bakur, Abdullahi Bakur, to send some of his followers from villages scattered around the Rahad area to occupy sparsely populated southern Gedaref,[8] Several families, mostly of western Sudanese and West African

7 Interview with Abdulkarim Adam Hassan, *ʿomda* of East Rahad area, Gedaref town, 14 January 2012.

8 One of my informants told me that the main purpose behind this request was to stop the heavy influx of Ethiopian migrants, which was substantial during the late 1960s. However, it could be argued that the underlying cause for the settlement of western Sudanese and "West Africans" was simply the expansion of large-scale mechanized farming in south Gedaref state. These farms were controlled by the central government and some of its major merchant allies (known locally as *jallāba*). This analysis is supported by secondary literature produced at that time. For example, one author has concluded that "the major benefits of mechanized farming have been appropriated by a relatively small class of wealthy *jallāba* merchants. This has not only reinforced the existing class structure of the Sudan, but has probably assisted the process of broadening the merchant class and its economic base – a feature of the Nimeiri regime" (Shepherd 1983, p. 316).

MAP 6.1 *Basunda locality council in Gedaref State.*
© MAX PLANCK INSTITUTE FOR SOCIAL ANTHROPOLOGY.

origin responded to the *nāẓir*'s appeal and began to migrate to these areas. To attract more settlers, the authorities allowed the *nāẓir* of Dār Bakur to grant licences to new settlers to formally establish new villages.

The population of Basunda locality council, like south Gedaref State more generally, is composed of different ethnic groups. Some seventy-three tribes are recorded by the state Native Administration in Gedaref State.[9] The recorded tribes and ethnic groups originate from almost all parts of Sudan. A number of studies point out that the majority are "non-Arabs" of western Sudan and "West African" origin (Abu-Manga & Miller 2005; Assal 2005; Osman 2008). While the first group comprises the Fur, the Masalit, the Bargo, the Daju, the Zaghawa, the Berti, the Tama, the Tunjur and others, the second group includes the settled Fulbe, the Hausa, the Borno and the Zabarma. But other western Sudanese groups who identify themselves as "Arabs"[10] (e.g. the Salamat, Rashid, Taʿisha and Habbaniyya) also live in this area. This enormous presence of western Sudanese and West African groups in southern Gedaref and eastern Sudan in general is mostly attributed to the establishment of large-scale mechanized and irrigated agriculture by the British colonial authorities since the 1920s and connected to the need for agricultural labourers (Duffield 1983; Shepherd 1983; Tully 1988).

Basunda locality is considered a good dry season grazing area by several pastoral groups. Some of these herders reside locally; others migrate seasonally. For example, Shukriyya and Lahawiyyn cattle herders migrate from the Butana area in the northern region of Gedaref State to Basunda locality in the southern region. Other groups (such as the pastoral Fulbe, Beni Amer and Kenana Arabs) migrate from the neighbouring states of Kassala, Sennar and the Blue Nile. The Beni Amer, who with the pastoral Fulbe represent the majority of pastoralist groups in the area, will be foregrounded in this chapter.

The Beni Amer are defined by many scholars as part of the Beja groups. The Beja consider themselves and are widely recognized as the indigenous people of eastern Sudan (the present-day Gedaref, Kassala, and the Red Sea States). Their traditional homelands cover the areas that consist of "the Red Sea Hills and the eastern desert that extends northwards from the Eritrean and Ethiopian borders to that of Egypt; to the east the area flanks the Red Sea and to the west the Atbara and Nile Rivers" (El Amin 2004, p. 8). According to a number of researchers, the Beja are composed of four main groups, namely the Bishariyyn, the Hadandawa,

9 Interview with Abdulkarim Adam Hassan, *ʿomda* of East Rahad area, Gedaref town, 4 January 2012.

10 The terms "Africans", "Arabs" and "West Africans" used in this study have been problematized and dealt with very carefully for two reasons. The first is that these terms have been a constant subject for politicised ethnicity in the recent history of the Sudan. Second, and more importantly, it is quite noticeable that continuous processes of historical migrations have been associated with integration performances. These have constantly taken place across the various areas of Sudan, and particularly in the centre, for centuries. For more details about this issue, see O'Fahey and Spaulding (1974); Holt and Daly (2000).

the Amarar and the Beni Amer (Mohamed 2000; Paul 1954). There are other small groups such as the Artayga, the Halanga and the Ashraf, who are also identified as Beja. The Bishariyyin, the Hadandawa and the Amarar generally inhabit the north-eastern part of Sudan and speak the TuBedawiye language. TuBedawiye is identified as "the northernmost language of the Cushitic family, one of the Semito-Hamitic linguistic groups, also known as Afro-Asiatic" (Pantulliano 2014, p. 153).

In contrast, the Beni Amer basically speak the Tigre language, "a Semitic language related to Tigrinya and Amharic" (*ibid.*, p. 154), but there are a few lineages among them who are considered as native speakers of TuBedawiye. One author describes them as "less a tribe than a closely knit confederation of groups of different origins which, in addition to the small Nabtab caste and its one-time serfs, includes Aflanda, Beit Ma'ala and Agiga" (Paul 1954, p. 17). Their main settlements in eastern Sudan are located "in a wide region between South Tokar, Khor Baraka and Northern Eritrea" (Pantulliano 2014, p. 153). The bulk of the areas of the group that came under the authority of their *naẓāra* (local tribal political office) in Sudan therefore lie within the boundaries of the present-day Kassala State. In Gedaref State, the Beni Amer groups have a tribal leader who is the representative of their *naẓāra* in Kassala State. This leader, who is recognized as the deputy (*wakīl*) of the paramount chief of the Beni Amer in Gedaref State, together with other tribal assistants under his authority (sheikhs), is responsible for representing the tribe and settling its disputes across Gedaref State. With regard to their livelihood activities, the Beni Amer are known for practising trade and commerce in Gedaref town and cattle herding in the southern parts of Gedaref State.

In addition to all the above-mentioned groups, south Gedaref State includes several groups whose origins are from neighbouring countries in the Horn of Africa, particularly Ethiopians, Eritreans and Somalis. Ethiopians represent the majority among these groups. Historically, the period between the 1960s and 1990s witnessed a massive immigration of Ethiopians and Eritreans to the Gedaref area. As one researcher says, "Eritrean-Ethiopian refugees flowed into the country from the late 1960s onward, following the conflicts – and famines – that occurred in their respective countries" (Miller 2005, p. 78). My informants told me that the establishment of large-scale mechanized farming in the Gedaref area in the end of the 1960s was another factor that attracted Ethiopian wage labourers to the area. Most migrants were Tigray, Amhara or Oromo.[11]

11 Interview with Abdullatif Muhammad Hassan, *ʿomda* of Basunda area, Basunda locality council 22 June 2011.

The System of Native Administration in Gedaref State

Since its establishment under Anglo-Egyptian rule in the early 1920s, the system of Native Administration – called locally *niẓām al-idāra al-ahaliyya* – has become a major component of the administrative structure in Sudan.[12] However, this system has been subject to recurrent interventions by successive national governments. The effort to maintain the vested political interests of the ruling political elite at the central level, as argued by Delmet (2005), has been the main driving factor behind changes made to the system. The government of Ja'afar Nimeiri (1969–1985) considered the system an obstacle and weakened it, but the current government has strengthened Native Administration as a tool to consolidate political domination across the country.

In eastern Sudan, the *naẓāra* institution constitutes the main structure of Native Administration. The term *naẓāra* denotes

> a tribal political office originally instituted by the British administration. It is the highest tribal political office, heading a tribal hierarchy of junior political offices. *Naẓāra* is also a symbol of the recognition of the tribe as political entity and in most cases it corresponds to a real but vague territorial entity for the tribe.
>
> EL AMIN 2004, P. 21

According to this type of political structure, the *nāẓir* represents the paramount chief or head of the tribe. Below the level of the tribe are territorial sub-divisions called locally *khuṭūṭ* (sing. *khaṭṭ*). Each *khaṭṭ* is headed by a local leader called *sheikh al-khaṭṭ*. Below the *khaṭṭ* level is another territorial subdivision (*'omodiyya*). Each *'omodiyya* is led and controlled by an *'omda* (pl. *'omad*). The *'omodiyya* is divided into further sub-divisions called *mashaykhāt* (sing. *mashaykha*). Normally, the *mashaykha* sets up one village or a few villages to be headed by a local leader called the sheikh.

In Gedaref State, there are four *naẓāras*: the *naẓāra* of the Shukriya, the *naẓāra* of the Ḍabaniyya, the *naẓāra* of Amir Ya'gub (or Gala an-Nahal), and the *naẓāra* of Dār Bakur. These *naẓāras* embody the local tribal political office of the so-called old-timer groups, a term that denotes all the groups that were

12 Historians and social scientists highlight that the dependence of the state on local political structures to direct parts of its areas has been a constant feature of governance and administration in Sudan, even before Anglo-Egyptian rule. This phenomenon has been documented since the era of the Funj Sultanate (Delmet 2005; Schlee 2013; Spaulding 1973).

granted local tribal administrative authorities under Anglo-Egyptian rule.[13] The *naẓāra* of the Shukriya covers a massive area which extends through the north-eastern parts of Gedaref State. This area is called the Butana, and constitutes the traditional homeland of the Shukriyya ethnic group. The Shukriyya have acquired recognition of their communal land ownership and leadership of this area since the era of King Badi wad Dakin, the former *ṣulṭān* (paramount chief) of the Sennar sultanate in the late eighteenth century (Holt and Daly 2000; Holt 1961). At the beginning of the twentieth century, the British colonial authorities issued a law that opened up the western parts of the *naẓāra* as a general grazing area, making it accessible to several pastoralist groups that are found in present-day Gezira, Sennar and Blue Nile States. The groups included the Fadniya, the Baṭahīn, the Mesallamiya, Rufaʿa ash-Shariq, Kenana and the Rukābiyya. Nonetheless, it is said that the Shukriyya "remained the sole users of pasture and agricultural lands in the valleys of seasonal rivers in the Butana, specially the best provided with water; no one could enter these areas without their permission" (Delmet 2005, p. 154). The *naẓāra* of the Ḍabaniya is in the eastern parts of Gedaref State across a belt that extends from the south to the north. The main areas contained within this *naẓāra* are al-Tomāt, al-Guraysha, Doka Sharig, aṣ-Ṣufi al-Bashīr and Shashiyna. The *naẓāra* of Amir Yaʿgub joins all the areas that extend from the south of the railway lines in Gedaref town north to the areas that are located in the Dinder area to the south. This *naẓāra* together with the *naẓāra* of Dār Bakur, set up the system of Native Administration in south Gedaref State.

Other ethnic groups also live in the area without enjoying their own local political tribal office (*naẓāra*). This is due to the fact that these groups are considered "newcomers", hosted in the homelands of "old-timer" groups. Each group among "newcomers" is represented by a local leader who is called *wakīl* (lit. deputy). These deputies symbolize the authority of the paramount chiefs of their tribes and represent them in Gedaref State. Their key responsibilities are to solve the major problems of their tribesmen and to represent them in the forums of dispute settlement, which are commonly held under the authority of the "old-timers". Among the main tribal deputies in Gedaref State are the deputy of the *nāẓir* of the Beni Amer group, the deputy of the *ṣulṭān* of Fulbe groups, and the deputy of the *ṣulṭān* of the Masalit group.

---

13 I prefer to use the term "old-timer" groups rather than "indigenous" or "local" groups. Though these other terms are used in most other Sudanese areas, they produce inaccuracy: in Gedaref area "... a large spectrum of ethnic groups which came to settle at different times [had] led to major population renewal [which makes] the concept of 'local group' [...] here quite problematic" (Miller 2005, p. 33).

The Structure of the *Naẓāra* of Dār Bakur in Gedaref State

The areas that lie under the authority of the *naẓāra* of Dār Bakur[14] extend from the north-western and central parts of Gedaref town southward to the Ethiopian border. The bigger neighbourhoods under its administration in Gedaref town include Ḥay an-Naẓir, Ḥay al-Borno, Ḥay at-Taḍāmun and Farīg[15] Abakar Jibril. It encompasses Doka, Basunda and al-Gallabat ash-Shargiyya locality councils in southern Gedaref State. According to my informants,[16] the structure of the *naẓāra* of Dār Bakur comprises the *nāẓir* Naṣr ad-Din Osman Bakur, five *sheikh al-khaṭṭ*, thirty-six *ʿomda*s, and tens of sheikhs at the village level. In 1995, the Ingaz government established a new "local" administrative institution called *al-majlis al-aʿla lil-ʿomad wa ash-shuyūkh aj-jugrafiyīn* (lit. the higher council of geographical *ʿomda*s and sheikhs). Members of this institution (the geographical *ʿomda*s and sheikhs) have been granted judicial authorities and allowed to act as officials in dispute settlements across Gedaref State. Since then, this new institution has been combined with the already existing institution of Native Administration to create *al-majlis al-aʿala lil-idāra al-ahaliyya* (lit. the higher council of Native Administration). At the time of the fieldwork, Native Administration in Gedaref State was composed of the former four *naẓāra*s and the higher council of geographical *ʿomda*s and sheikhs. From now on, when we refer to Native Administration in Gedaref State we mean the higher council of Native Administration.

14 Bakur Mustafa, after whom the *naẓāra* is named, was the first *nāẓir* of Dār Bakur in the beginning of the twentieth century. Before that time, he was among the close followers of Mohamed Ahmed al-Mahdi (the founder of the Mahdist Revolution in Sudan) and one of the tribal leaders of the Fur group who were living in the Kordofan region of Western Sudan. However, his relation to the Mahdist movement caused him problems during the era of Khalifa ʿAbdullahi at-Taʿaayshi (the Mahdi's successor). At-Taʿaayshi expelled him to the Old Halfa area in the northernmost part of Sudan. When the British colonial forces defeated the Mahdist movement and conquered Sudan, Bakur Mustafa and other tribal leaders who had had troubled relations with Khalifa ʿAbdullahi at-Taʿaayshi were among their first supporters. The British colonial administration appointed Bakur Mustafa as the *nāẓir* of the areas that extend in the present-day southern and western parts of Gedaref State.

15 The term *farīg* here has the same meaning as the term *ḥay* (i.e. neighbourhood).

16 An interview with Abdulkarim Adam Hassan, *ʿomda* of the east Rahad area, Gedaref town, 4 January 2012.

Institutions of Local Dispute Management of the *Naẓāra* of Dār Bakur

In general, there is no agreed terminology to describe the institutions of the local justice system. A variety of concepts are used to describe it, including "customary law, non-state justice systems, non-state legal fields, dispute resolution systems, folk law, informal justice, popular justice and vigilantism" (Forsyth 2009, p. 29). It is recognized across Sudan that members of Native Administration enjoy judicial authorities over local justice, reconciliations and the maintenance of social relations.[17] In Basunda locality, the local justice system includes the institutions we describe in the following sections.

The Damage Assessment Committee (lajnat at-talāf)

The damage assessment committee (*lajnat at-talāf*) is one of the key institutions of dispute management that exists at the village level. According to my informants, this institution was created through an agreement between the farming and herding groups in the area in the early 1970s. The committee is normally composed of four members that include two local sheikhs from the farmers and two sheikhs from the herders. Their main task is to assess the damage caused to crops by trespassing herders and their animals.

As I observed during my fieldwork, when a small or large farm sustains damage from animal trespassing, the farm's owner or agent should first register the case in the village police centre. Then the popular committee,[18] which is the key administrative authority at the village level, intervenes through one of its members to nominate the members of the damage assessment committee and give them the order to start their proceedings. After estimating the damages, the committee makes a report to the popular committee. The popular committee should transfer this information to the head of the village police centre,

17 The Native Administration first acquired its authority and judicial powers in 1922; these have been further outlined through four laws: the Powers of the Nomad Sheikhs Ordinance (1922), Village Courts Ordinance (1925), Powers of the Sheikhs Ordinance (1927) and Native Courts Ordinances (1931, 1932). As for its judicial powers, the 1927 Sheikhs Ordinance stated that "the chief could not sentence to more than LE 100 and two years' imprisonment penalties; he was not allowed to deal with homicide, kidnapping, robbery and, in all cases, the Province Governor could veto his decisions" (Delmet 2005, p. 146).

18 The popular committee (*lajna sha'biyya*) is a formal administrative institution whose members are appointed every two years. It was introduced at the beginning of the 1990s to be implemented at the locality levels (e.g. the villages, towns and districts).

whose task is to order the wrongdoer to pay the assessed amount of compensation to the claimant in the presence of the damage assessment committee. Finally, disputants and members of the damage assessment committee should meet to negotiate and settle the dispute completely. If the committee fails to settle the dispute at the village level, the disputants can then transfer it to the local councils of mediation at the level of Basunda locality. Alternatively, disputing parties have the right to take their case to one of the rural courts of Basunda locality or to the civil court in Gedaref town.

Local Councils of Mediation (jūdiya)

The *jūdiya* is a customary institution for negotiations, particularly mediation, practised in both rural and urban settlements in Sudan. The name comes from the Arabic word *ajawīd* (sing. *ajwadi*), "the generous person". In south Gedaref State, the term mostly refers to members of local institutions of conflict management. The history of the *jūdiya* in Sudan goes back to time immemorial. In the Darfur and eastern Sudan region, the *jūdiya* has played an important role in preventing limited disputes from developing into large-scale warfare (Mutisi and Sansculotte-Greenidge 2012; Mohamed and Badri 2005; El Amin 2004). The *jūdiya* found in south Gedaref State is similar to that of the Darfur region in terms of its structure and functions. Recently, many changes have affected this institution in Gedaref State. As mentioned above in the section about the Native Administration system, the central government has created a new institution called the Higher Council of Native Administration since the mid-1990s. This institution allows all its members to act as local officials in dispute management across Gedaref State. These changes to the system were made across Sudan, but the present study is limited to Gedaref State.

Rural Courts

Three rural courts, those of Kassaab, Basunda and Doka, are found in Basunda locality council and are considered part of the *naẓāra* of Dār Bakur. They became part of the formal Sudanese Judiciary system in the early 1970s. Each court is headed by an *ʿomda* affiliated to the *naẓāra* of Dār Bakur. The Basunda rural court was established in 1947. It is composed of the head of the court (normally the *ʿomda* of Basunda area; *ʿomda* Abdullatiif Muhammad Hassan at the time of research) and two assistants from the Native Administration of Dār Bakur in Basunda area. Most of the cases dealt with in these courts concern minor disputes over animal trespassing and crop damage. Complicated criminal cases that involve homicide are mostly transferred to the court of the *nāẓir* or the criminal court in Gedaref town.

FIGURE 6.1 *Fieldwork assistant Ḥassan Abū Ṣiddīg sitting in front of the rural court* (al-maḥākam ar-rifiyya) *of Basunda area.*
PHOTOGRAPH BY THE AUTHOR.

A Case of Dispute from Basingga Village, and Its Management Process

On Saturday, 23 July 2011, two herders from the Beni Amer group were moving with their cattle out of their dry season grazing areas in south Gedaref State. They were heading north to their rainy season grazing area in the Butana area.[19] While these herders were passing by large-scale agricultural schemes on the margins of Basingga village, they were attacked by a group of wage labourers. As one of the herders related the attack:

19 For the bulk of Beni Amer herder groups in Gedaref State, while their main dry season grazing areas are located on the margins of Basunda locality in south Gedaref State, the main areas in which they spend the rainy season – normally from January to June – are in the Butana area in the northern part of the state.

> We were moving close to a large cotton project, which belongs to the merchant Makin Silihabi.[20] Suddenly, a group of wage labourers who were working on the project attacked us, and began to beat us with sticks.[21] Later, we came to know that this group consisted of four western Sudanese and three Ethiopians. I think they attacked us because they expected that our herd would enter their project and damage the cultivation.[22]

One of the herders was left with an injury to his face, while the other managed to escape. In addition, one of their cows was seriously wounded. The herder who had escaped contacted the sheikh of the Beni Amer in Basunda locality council and told him about the attack. Immediately, the sheikh held a meeting with other local leaders of the Beni Amer in the area and contacted some of the tribe's influential members in Gedaref town. Instead of registering the case in the police centre of Basingga village, the tribal representatives of the herders' group registered it in the police centre of Basunda locality. Subsequently, the head of police sent some of his forces to arrest the attackers. The accused persons were detained and taken into the custody of the police in Basunda locality council.

The owner of the project was the first to contact the members of the Native Administration of the Beni Amer to settle the dispute. The Sudanese wage labourers were from outside Basunda locality council (and the state) and so had no tribal representatives who could represent them or contact the representatives of the herders' group to settle the dispute. They therefore agreed to be represented by the owner of the project, who negotiated with the herders on their behalf. He agreed with the herders' tribal representative to meet and negotiate the settlement of the dispute. The meeting was to take place in the police centre of Basunda locality council, whose head officer was chosen to be one of the mediators.

---

20 Makin Silihabi is one of the well-known merchants and owners of large-scale agricultural schemes in the Basunda area. He belongs to the Bargu tribe (a "non-Arab" western Sudanese group).

21 The term "sticks" (*asaya*) is used to indicate long dry branches cut from trees.

22 Muhammad Salih Adarub, a twenty-two-year-old pastoralist from the Beni Amer ethnic group, talking to the mediator during a negotiation meeting, held in Basunda locality on 27 July 2011. The reason he gives for the attack springs from the general knowledge that animal trespassing is among the key triggers of disputes between farmers (or owners of large-scale agricultural projects) and animal herders in Basunda area and south Gedaref State.

The Parties Involved in the Negotiation

On Wednesday, 27 July 2011, the disputing parties and their representatives gathered, in the presence of the mediators, at the police centre of Basunda locality to negotiate and settle their dispute. Three parties could be distinguished. First, were the two mediators (*ajawīd*): the head of the police centre of Basunda locality and one of the assistants of the *ṣulṭān* of the Fulbe group in south Gedaref State. Second was the herders' party: the two Beni Amer herders who had been attacked and four representatives. The representatives were all tribal leaders and members of the Native Administration in Basunda area and Gedaref town: the *ʿomda* of the Beni Amer in Basunda, two of his sheikhs and one of the geographical *ʿomda*s of the Beni Amer in Gedaref town. The geographical *ʿomda* was also the general secretary of the pastoralists' association in Gedaref state. The third party consisted of the four western Sudanese and the three Ethiopian wage labourers, with the project owner, who was representing them. Two of these four western Sudanese labourers were from Gedaref town, one was from Khartoum and one was from Gezira State in central Sudan. The Ethiopian wage labourers were from the Tigray and Amhara groups.

The Management of the Dispute and Its Final Agreement

All three parties were represented at the police centre of Basunda locality, but not all the individuals concerned were present; the Ethiopian wage labourers had been taken into custody and were not allowed to attend the meeting. After the mediators heard the story from the two disputing parties, the wage labourers were found guilty. The herders' negotiators forgave the Sudanese wage labourers, but not the Ethiopians; their status was left to be decided by the head of the police centre of Basunda locality. The difference in the treatment of the two groups was encouraged by the negotiators from the herders' group because the Sudanese were Muslims, whilst the Ethiopians were not. In particular, the geographical *ʿomda* of the Beni Amer strongly supported the forgiveness of the fellow Muslims as being in accord with the tenets of *sharīʿa* law. In his turn, the head of police decided to release the Ethiopians on condition that they sign a declaration that they would not take part in any dispute between two Sudanese parties in the future. Finally, the disputing parties agreed that the project owner should compensate the herders for the serious harm done to one cow.

Analysis and Discussion

The Role Played by Native Administration and Access to Political Power

Looking carefully at the case, one notices that the herders' negotiators had greater access to political power than the labourers' negotiators. This could be ascribed to two reasons. The first is that the wage labourers were from outside south Gedaref State and lacked any local tribal representation through Native Administration. In contrast, members of the Native Administration of the herders' group were present and active during all the stages of dispute management. Second, one of the herders' negotiators holds multiple political powers. The geographical *'omda* of the high council of Native Administration in Gedaref State is also an active member of the current ruling political party (the NCP), and is the general secretary of the pastoralists' association in Gedaref State. In contrast, the project owner was the only powerful figure representing the labourers. This remarkable inequality in access to political power between the two disputing parties is, I would argue, among the major factors that gave the herders' group the upper hand during the negotiation process.

In other words, the herders' negotiators led the proceedings. They saw to it that the Ethiopians were not allowed to attend the meeting, and that they were taken into custody. In this way, they succeeded in dividing the wage labourers into two groups, and shifted the discussion away from a mere dispute settlement. They brought into discussion the illegal entry of Ethiopians into Sudan, and the possible threat they posed to the safety of Sudanese people. The negotiation processes have shown that solving the dispute with the Ethiopians was not the main objective of the herders' negotiators. Their key objective was clearly to transmit a strong political message to Tigray and Amhara Ethiopian groups, whom they consider to be their enemies. The Beni Amer succeeded in sending that message because of their strong access to political power in Gedaref State.

The Nature of Social Relations and Its Impacts on the Disputing Process

During the negotiation meeting, the herders' representatives were extremely offensive and showed negative emotions whenever the Ethiopians were mentioned. For example, as the general secretary of the pastoralists' association was talking about the relationship between his group and the Ethiopians, he said: "The battle between us and the Ethiopians extends over a long period of time, and it has become bloody and complicated. But, we are able to stop them and they know us very well." There are at least three reasons for such sentiments. First, there is an antagonistic relationship between Beni Amer herders and the Ethiopian security forces along the Sudanese-Ethiopian border in south Gedaref State. My informants from various villages in Basunda locality told me that, since the 1980s, most herder groups (e.g. the Shukriyya, Lahawiyin and Fulbe) have maintained relatively stable relations with the Ethiopians, but the Beni Amer herders have been subject to constant harassment as they pass with their animals across the borders. Second, these negative relations are linked to the wider historical and protracted political conflicts between the Beni Amer (who are Muslims) and the politically dominant Tigray of Ethiopia and Eritrea who are predominantly Christians. These conflicts have been couched in ethnic and religious terms. Third, inside Eritrea a more recent conflict has developed between the Beni Amer and the ruling EPLF. According to my informants among the Beni Amer, that conflict has emerged because the Eritrean government wanted to impose a way of life that contradicts Islam as it is understood by the Beni Amer, who are mostly followers of Wahabi Salafism.[23]

Since Eritrean political organizations emerged as early as 1944, they have conflicted with the political elites of Ethiopia, who were against Eritrean Independence. Separatist parties such as the Muslim League of the Western Province of Eritrea have long attracted the antagonism of Ethiopian elites (Keller 1993). The Eritrean War of Independence (1961–1991), fought between the Ethiopian government and liberation movements, overshadowed other social relations at the grassroots level, resulting in mass ethnic polarization. The subsequent Ethio-Eritrean war of 1998–2000 has further antagonized relations between the ruling elites of the two countries, and between the peoples (i.e. Tigray and Tigrinya) from whom they are drawn (Reid 2003; Schlee 2003). Moreover, the antagonisms within and between these two states have negatively affected social relations in the Sudanese-Ethiopian border area.

Legal Pluralism

My observations and the narratives of my informants show that a variety of institutions are able to deal with the issue of dispute management in south Gedaref State. These institutions comprise: the damage assessment committees (*lajnat at-talāf*) at the village level; local councils of mediation (*jūdiya*) which are found at various levels; and the rural courts in Basunda, Doka and

23 Wahabi Salafisim is a branch of Sunni Islam, which is considered by many to be orthodox, fundamentalist, or puritanical because it calls for restoring "pure monotheistic worship" (*tawḥīd*) (Moussalli 2009).

FIGURE 6.2 *The gathering of the courts – civil, criminal and* sharīʿa *– in Gedaref town.* PHOTOGRAPH BY THE AUTHOR.

Kassāb.[24] In addition, members of the higher council of geographical *ʿomda*s and sheikhs are distributed among the areas in Gedaref state and take part in dispute settlements. Finally, village police centres also have a role. This participation of the police in the negotiation process, as shown by the above case, represents a remarkable transformation in the local system of conflict management. Before the mid-1990s, all customary negotiations of dispute settlement were supervised and administered by the *naẓāra* of Dār Bakur. The police have begun to intervene since the establishment of what is called the community police (*ash-shurṭa ash-shaʿbiyya wa-l-mujtamaʿiyya*) in the mid-1990s.

Understanding and Practising Sharīʿa *Law*

Almost all customary institutions of dispute settlement – including the newly established high council of *ʿomda*s and sheikhs – practise mediation and reconciliation rather than adjudication. In addition, *sharīʿa* law is considered a

24 Informants also indicated that some disputes were taken to formal courts in Gedaref town. These courts themselves are divided into civil, criminal and *sharīʿa* (see Figure 6.2).

main reference for the practices and decisions of these institutions. However, my observations confirm that local interpretations of Qur'anic texts and *sharīʿa* law are subject to the influence of socio-economic and political factors. In the above case, for example, the herders' negotiators interpreted the concept of forgiveness as an Islamic principle that should only be applied and allowed for the benefit of Muslims. Given that interpretation, they decided to forgive the Sudanese wage labourers but not the Ethiopians. The key sources of Islamic jurisprudence (*uṣūl al-fiqh*) the Qur'an, Sunna and Hadith, urge Muslims to forgive, describing such an act as evidence of true belief:

> The Quranic command is rooted in a vision of justice that requires reciprocity. However, in imitation of the Prophet, believers should forgive those who have not asked for forgiveness – even enemies. The Quran describes believers as "those who avoid major sins and acts of indecencies and when they are angry they forgive."[25] The same Surah later states, "The reward of the evil is the evil thereof, but whosoever forgives and makes amends, his reward is upon Allah."[26] Similarly, another Surah asserts, "If you punish, then punish with the like of that wherewith you were afflicted. But if you endure patiently, indeed it is better for the patient. Endure you patiently. Your patience is not except through the help of Allah".[27]
>
> POWELL 2012, P. 19

Many cases from the Sunna indicate that forgiveness should be granted even to non-believers. For this, two examples from the Prophetic tradition are cited:

> First, in the account of Muhammad's call to punish those who abused him in Ta'if, the Prophet forgave those who persecuted him without their request or contrition, and asked Allah to spare the city. Second, in his triumphant return to Mecca, Muhammad forgave his enemies. Both these examples of forgiveness calmed political tensions …
>
> *IBID.*, P. 21

Islamic criminal law (*qiṣāṣ*) does not compel the Muslim to forgive. In such a case, forgiveness "is to be preferred over retribution, but one must freely choose it" (*ibid.*, p. 28). As stated in the Qur'an:

---

25 The Qur'an 42:37.

26 The Qur'an 42:40.

27 The Qur'an 16:126–127.

> And we prescribed to them in it that life is for life, and eye for eye, and nose for nose, and ear for ear, and tooth for tooth, and (that there is) reprisal in wounds; but he who foregoes it, it shall be an expiation for him; and whoever did not judge by what Allah revealed, those are they that are the unjust.[28]

If there is support in Islamic legal traditions for the Ethiopians to be forgiven too, why were they not? What perspective does a processual approach in legal anthropology provide to the question of why the negotiators did not forgive the Ethiopian wage labourers? Here, one could argue that, because of the negative social relations between the Beni Amer and the Tigray and Amhara, the primary purpose of the representatives of the Beni Amer herders in taking this case for negotiation was not to solve it. As mentioned above, the purpose was to send a strong political message against wage labourers from the Tigray and Amhara groups. To do so, the Beni Amer strongly stressed the religious difference between them and the Ethiopians in the case, and consequently deciding not to forgive them by referring to what they claimed to be *sharīʿa*. This behaviour emphasizes the argument that "rational self-interest may explain selective enforcement of problematic norms" (*ibid.*, p. 29).

Forum Shopping Behaviour

Given the fact that this dispute took place in Basingga village, it was very likely from the outset that it would have been registered and managed at the village level through the village assessment committee (*lajnat at-talāf*). However, the herders' tribal representatives took it to the locality council level. This relocation of dispute settlement is an example of forum shopping behaviour. The representatives were able to choose between various institutions to manage their dispute. As their Native Administration had strong relations with the ruling political party in Sudan, they had more access to political power and an advantage in "shopping around".

Concluding Remarks

Negotiations are among the key tools of customary justice and dispute management in south Gedaref State, but they are not only defined by the techniques and strategies used by negotiators during the process of dispute management. Rather, factors that include Native Administration, access to political power,

28 The Qur'an 5:45.

and the nature of social relations among disputants in the pre-dispute period are crucial in the delineation of dispute management. In short, the customary justice system must be understood in connection with the surrounding socio-economic and political milieu within which the disputing parties exist and interact.

Local institutions of dispute management may be preferred because they are accessible, flexible, affordable and fast compared with formal justice institutions. However, they are not averse to supporting existing power hierarchies and social structures to the disadvantage of some groups. It could be strongly emphasized from our case that these institutions do not promote equity in the settlement of disputes between parties who occupy very different levels of power and authority.

References

Abdal-Kareem, ZM 2016, 'Group Identification and Resource Conflicts in Gedaref State, Eastern Sudan: Who allies with Whom? Why? And How?' PhD thesis. Halle (Saale), Martin Luther University of Halle-Wittenberg.

Abu-Manga, A & Miller, C 2005, 'The West African (Fallata) Communities in Gedaref State: Process of Settlement and Local Integration', in C Miller (ed.), *Land, Ethnicity and Political Legitimacy in Eastern Sudan*, CEDEJ/DSRC, Le Caire/Khartoum, pp. 375–423.

Assal, MAM 2005, 'Economy and politics in Gedaref: A Symbiotic Encounter', in C Miller (ed), *Land, Ethnicity and Political Legitimacy in Eastern Sudan*, CEDEJ/DSRC, Le Caire/Khartoum, pp. 173–201.

Bohannan, P 1969, 'Ethnography and Comparison in Legal Anthropology', in L Nader (ed.), *Law in Culture and Society*, University of California Press, Berkeley.

Delmet, C 2005, 'The Native Administration System in Eastern Sudan: From Its Liquidation to Its Revival', in C Miller (ed.), *Land, Ethnicity and Political Legitimacy in Eastern Sudan*, CEDEJ/DSRC, Le Caire/Khartoum, pp. 145–171.

Duffield, M 1983, 'Change among West African Settlers in Northern Sudan', *Review of African Political Economy*, vol. 26, pp. 45–59.

El Amin, KA 2004, 'Eastern Sudan Indigenous Conflict Prevention, Management and Resolution Mechanisms', *African Security Review*, vol. 13, no. 2, pp.7–22.

Forsyth, M 2009, *A Bird that Flies with Two Wings: The Kastom and State Justice Systems in Vanuatu*, Australian National University E-Press.

Gulliver, P 1977, 'On Mediators', in I Hamnett (ed.), *Social Anthropology and Law*, Academic Press, pp. 15–52.

Gulliver, P 1979, *Disputes & Negotiations: A Cross-Cultural Perspective*, Academic Press, London.

Harsanyi, JC 1977, *Rational behavior and bargaining equilibrium in games and social situations*, Cambridge University Press, Cambridge/New York.

Hoebel, EA 1954, *The Law of Primitive Man*, Harvard University Press, Cambridge, MA.

Holt, PM 1961, *A Modern History of the Sudan, from the Funj Sultanate to the Present Day*, Weidenfeld & Nicolson, London.

Holt, PM & Daly, MW 2000, *A History of the Sudan: From the Coming of Islam to the Present Day*, Longman, London.

Just, P 1992, 'History, Power, Ideology, and Culture: Current Directions in the Anthropology of Law', *Law & Society Review*, vol. 26, no. 2, pp. 373–411.

Keller, EJ 1993, 'The Eritrean National Question', in B Schechterman & MW Slann (eds), *The Ethnic Dimension in International Relations*, Praeger, Westport, CT, pp. 167–178.

Lombardi, CB 1998, 'Islamic Law as a Source of Constitutional Law in Egypt: The Constitutionalization of the Sharia in a Modern Arab State', *Columbia Journal of Transnational Law*, vol. 37, pp. 81–123.

Miller, C 2005, 'Power, Land and Ethnicity in the Kassala-Gedaref States: An Introduction', in C Miller (ed.), *Land, Ethnicity and Political Legitimacy in Eastern Sudan*, CEDEJ/DSRC, Le Caire/Khartoum, pp. 3–58.

Mohamed, AA & Badri, BY 2005, *Inter-communal Conflicts in Sudan: Causes, Resolution Mechanisms and Transformation: A Case Study of the Darfur region*, Ahfad University for Women, Omdurman.

Mohamed, MS 2000, *Al-Sudān: ḥurūb al-mawārid wa al-hawiyya* [in Arabic], translated as *Sudan: Wars Over Resources and Identity*, Cambridge Academic Press, Cambridge.

Moussalli, A 2009, *Wahhabism, Salafism and Islamism: Who Is the Enemy?*, Conflicts Forum, Beirut/London/Washington.

Mutisi, M & Sansculotte-Greenidge, K 2012, *Integrating Traditional and Modern Conflict Resolution: Experiences from Selected Cases in Eastern and the Horn of Africa*, African Centre for the Constructive Resolution of Disputes (ACCORD).

Nader, L & Todd, HF (eds) 1978, *The Disputing Process: Law in Ten Societies*, Columbia University Press, New York.

O'Fahey, RRS & Spaulding, JL 1974, *Kingdoms of the Sudan*, Taylor & Francis, Oxford.

Osman, EI 2008, 'The Pastoral Fulbe in the Funj region: A Study of the Interaction of State and Society', PhD Thesis, University of Khartoum, Khartoum.

Pantulliano, S 2014, 'Entangled Land and Identity: Beja History and Institutions', in J Gertel, R Rottenburg & S Calkins (eds), *Disrupting Territories: Land, Commodification and Conflict in Sudan*, James Currey, London, pp. 152–179.

Paul, A 1954, *A History of the Beja Tribes of the Sudan*, Cambridge University Press, Cambridge.

Pospisil, LJ 1971, *Anthropology of Law: A Comparative Theory*, Harper & Row, New York. http://archive.org/details/anthropologyoflaooposprich (accessed 17 May 2013).

Powell, R 2012, 'Forgiveness in Islamic Ethics and Jurisprudence', *Berkeley Journal of Middle Eastern & Islamic Law*, vol. 4, no. 1, pp. 17–34.

Reid, R 2003, 'Old Problems in New Conflicts: Some Observations on Eritrea and Its Relations with Tigray, from Liberation Struggle to Inter-State War', *Africa*, vol. 73, no. 3, pp. 369–401.

Schlee, G 2003, 'Identification in Violent Settings and Situations of Rapid Change', *Africa*, vol. 73, no. 3, pp. 333–342.

Schlee, G 2013, *Ruling over Ethnic and Religious Differences: A Comparative Essay on Empires*, Max Planck Institute for Social Anthropology, Halle/Salle.

Shepherd, A 1983, 'Capitalist Agriculture in the Sudan's Dura Prairies', *Development and Change*, vol. 14, no. 2, pp. 297–321.

Spaulding, J 1973, 'The Government of Sinnar', *The International Journal of African Historical Studies*, vol. 6, no. 1, pp. 19–35.

Tully, D 1988, *Culture and Context in Sudan: The Process of Market Incorporation in Dar Masalit*, State University of New York Press, New York.

Turner, VW 1972, *Schism and Continuity in an African Society: A Study of Ndembu Village Life*, Manchester University Press, Manchester.

van Velsen, J 1967, 'The Extended-case Method and Situational Analysis', in AL Epstein (ed.), *The Craft of Social Anthropology*, Tavistock Publications, London, pp. 129–149.

von Benda-Beckmann, K 1981, 'Forum Shopping and Shopping Forums: Dispute Processing in A Minangkabau Village in West Sumatra', *Journal of Legal Pluralism*, vol. 19, pp. 117–159.

von Benda-Beckmann, K 2003, 'The Environment of Dispute', in *The Dynamics of Power and the Rule of Law: Essays on Africa and Beyond, in Honour of Emile Adriaan B. van Rouveroy van Nieuwaal*, African Studies Centre / Lit Verlag, Leiden / Münster.

CHAPTER 7

Voluntary Dispute Resolution Forums in al-Ḥilla al-Jadīda Squatter Settlement, Omdurman

Musa A. Abdul-Jalil

Introduction

Order is a need that any community or society tries to achieve through various means. In the simplest of societies, the whole community may gather in one place in order to settle a dispute between some of its members (Roberts 1979). In societies that are more complex, the state intervenes in multiple ways to settle disputes and make justice possible among its citizens. The dichotomy between simple stateless societies and complex state-dominated societies has long been deserted by anthropologists and sociologists, because they became convinced that no pure type society exists. Most societies today exhibit features of both types, though in relative terms. Post-colonial societies, like those in Africa, Asia and Latin America, carry the features of what can be termed "transitional societies", in which traditional/customary institutions of order are found alongside a modern state apparatus. Nowhere is this considered clearer than in the domain of law and order.

Communities in post-colonial societies have kept their own customary ways of solving problems of law and order, whilst at the state level officials operate within institutions left behind by European colonial administrators, which were later reinforced by universal ideas of modernization and globalization. The situation whereby different legal orders operate in the same society is known as "legal pluralism". This applies not only to post-colonial societies but also to urban industrial societies, since it can always be argued that a multiplicity of legal ordering is present. It can therefore be claimed that in its broadest sense, legal pluralism exists in almost every society (Griffiths 1986; Merry 1988).

This chapter deals with a more typical case of legal pluralism: customary law operating in an urban milieu in Sudan. Rural-urban migration in post-colonial societies has typically produced a situation where customary institutions of order are resorted to by urban residents, despite their proximity to central government institutions of order. During the colonial period in Sudan, the remoteness of rural areas, the lack of infrastructure and adequate personnel, and financial restraints caused state authorities to leave rural people

 | DOI 10.1163/9789004362185_009

to manage certain levels and types of law and order according to their own customary practices. That tendency led to the promulgation of various Native Administration acts, in line with the philosophy of "indirect rule". The existence of three types of legal system that operated in rural Sudanese communities was all too obvious: the so-called modern law, *sharīʿa* law and the customary law of various tribal groups. Customary law courts (called "native courts") were established through acts of law from central judicial authorities and were operated by "native administrators". This situation continued during subsequent regimes of national governments with slight occasional alterations but no radical change (Abdul-Jalil 1985; Salman 1983).

The case with which this chapter is concerned goes beyond the above-described post-colonial legacy. It is the case of a multi-ethnic community occupying a squatter settlement outside the city of Omdurman that is called al-Ḥilla al-Jadīda (HJ). Because the settlement itself is not strictly legal, no proper institutions of law and order have been established in the neighbourhood. Instead, the residents have established their own voluntary dispute resolution forums, which try to emulate customary law courts from rural areas but operate without appropriate authorization from the judiciary. This case bears similarity to the case of the Shiva Sena organization, which is active in adjudication in urban neighbourhoods in Mumbai and mixes politics with law and social work in its functions (Eckert 2004). I shall try to look at the experience of voluntary dispute resolution forums in the HJ squatter settlement from different angles, including causes for its existence, types of cases handled, the type of law operated, and the procedures followed. Since court members are untrained, it will be interesting to know how they reach decisions. Questions regarding fees, documentation and appeals are all important to a sociological inquiry. It is also important to know how the official order institutions (i.e. police and formal courts) cooperate with this unofficial forum. Finally, the issue of how residents of the neighbourhood behave towards their court, as well as the general pattern of their justice-seeking behaviour will be looked at.

Squatting in Peri-Urban Land

The expansion of urban settlements into the surrounding rural areas is a worldwide phenomenon. Nevertheless, in each case, particular factors influence the rate, pattern, mode and results of such a process. In most developing countries, the capital city becomes the magnet to which the rural population is drawn in large numbers. The common reasons for such trends relate to poverty, uneven development and exclusion (or marginalization). However, in countries like

Sudan, where natural and man-made disasters have almost become a state of normality, additional factors such as drought and war become prime movers for large-scale rural urban migration. As a result, the city expands more rapidly than planners expect. More often, the race between city planners and newcomers to the city reaches a point where the latter take the lead by establishing new residential areas on land belonging to the surrounding rural areas. This leads to the formation of squatter settlements, which are a regular feature around most large cities in developing countries. This process has some important consequences from a sociological point of view. In the case of Sudan, a great number of rural migrants have moved into the urban conurbation of Greater Khartoum during the past two decades and half of them have come from areas where violent conflicts have affected human and geographical landscapes.

From the mid-1980s onwards, Sudan has witnessed two major events that have directly impacted the rate and direction of population movement across vast areas of the country: drought and the escalation of civil war. People who have become IDPs as a result of either environmental disasters or war have considered the urban conurbation of Greater Khartoum the best place for them to settle because of its provision of physical security and comparatively better opportunities to make a living. Newcomers to the city usually arrive at their new destination with very few possessions, so they prefer to stay at the peripheries of the city where the cost of renting housing is insignificant or non-existent (de Geoffroy 2015). Such a process usually ends in the formation of a new squatter settlement. The two most important characteristics of such settlements are the illegal occupation of land and the lack of appropriate services infrastructure.

The Context

Al-Ḥilla al-Jadīda lies at the westernmost outreaches of the city of Omdurman about 20 km from its centre. It is mostly occupied by people from western Sudan (Kordofan and Darfur), with considerable numbers from other states too. The leading tribes represented here are Nuba Mountains tribes (especially from the Alleri area), Fur, Tunjur, Masalit, Bargo, Dajo, Jawam'a, Hamar, Missiriya and Hawazma. There are no official population statistics for this neighbourhood, but unofficial estimates suggest 8,000 people, comprising about 1,600 families. Although the settlement was started earlier, there has been a fresh influx of newcomers after 2003 with many IDPs arriving from Darfur.

The neighbourhood is located on sandy desert land with scattered rocky outcrops and gravel in some places, on the traditional land boundaries between the Jamūʿiya and Giriyat tribal groups. The latter are transhumant pastoralists, who keep moving away whenever the city moves towards them. In fact, some Giriyat used to live in this location but deserted it when the nearby Jabarona IDP camp was established in the early 1990s. Jabarona lies just to the east of HJ and used to be solely occupied by IDPS from South Sudan; most of them left after the Independence of their country in July 2011.

The educational institutions include three government primary schools and eleven so-called parallel schools. These are schools established by civil society organizations to enrol youths too old to enrol in regular primary schools. Many such youths belong to war-affected families from the Nuba Mountains and Darfur. There are no secondary schools or kindergartens. There are four health centres, which are operated by para-medicals only, since there are no doctors in the neighbourhood. Environmental health is also bad as the streets are littered with household garbage as a result of irregular collection.

The water supply is relatively better. There are five boreholes that provide water for the population, who use donkey-drawn carts (*karro*) to distribute it. In fact, water distribution provides a livelihood for a portion of the population in the area. No mains electricity is available; instead, the place is filled with noisy privately owned small diesel-driven power generators. Again, they represent a form of investment for their owners, who offer services to neighbouring houses and shops. As most of the residents in this neighbourhood are labourers who seek work in the city, they need to leave the area early in the morning and return late in the evening. Privately run old buses operate rather efficiently to central Omdurman and sometimes directly to Khartoum and Khartoum North.

Religious institutions have a visible presence and popularity in HJ. There are nineteen Qura'n schools (*khalwa*), sixteen for males and three for females. Three of the male *khalwa*s have boarding facilities. In addition, there are eleven mosques and six *zawiyas* (non-Friday prayer mosques). They have mostly been built by the Islamic Daʿwa organization and the Committee for African Muslims. The area is also inhabited by many Christians, who have built five churches, mostly with the help of international NGOs.

The Making of a Squatter Settlement

Al-Ḥilla al-Jadīda is considered a new extension of the Dar as-Salam neighbourhood, which was established as a low-income area in the beginning of the 1990s after the evacuation of people from many illegal settlements around Greater Khartoum. By then, the newly established Ingaz regime that took power after a military coup in June 1989 had vowed to eradicate illegal settlements from the three towns of Khartoum, Omdurman and Khartoum North, which together constitute the national capital of Sudan. It managed to empty most of them successfully by giving each family a plot of 216 square metres in a planned residential area specially allocated for low-income segments of the population. Because people needed security of tenure, the policy became very popular at the time, even though the lack of infrastructure is a common feature of all of them.

Al-Ḥilla al-Jadīda started in the mid 1990s as a small squatter settlement west of Jabarona. It used to be called *rās al-shayṭān* (lit. "devil's head") because it was famous for its high crime rate and alcohol consumption. By 1997, conditions there started to change with the arrival of Abdalla Kafi, an ambitious leader from the Nuba Mountains. Before his arrival in the area, he had been a member of the Umma Party opposition contingent in Eritrea. When the Ingaz regime began its policy of "peace from inside" – according to which it signed unmediated agreements with opposition elements from South Sudan and the Nuba Mountains – Abdalla Kafi chose to come back. He asked the government to allow him to stay in this location with his people from the Alleri area in the Nuba Mountains. He renamed the place "al-Rahma" (mercy) neighbourhood, in order to attract new followers. Some people named it "Ḥillat al-Sultan Abdulla Kafi" after its new leader, but recently the name al-Ḥilla al-Jadīda has become better known.

By his own account, Abdalla Kafi had two ambitions when he established the new settlement: firstly, to unite his own people so that their voices could be heard, and second, to increase his followers. He knew that he would have no future in politics if he did not command a large following. For this reason, he was very concerned to promote security in the area by organizing the youth into vigilante groups based on tribal affiliation. To attract more followers, the leader of the new settlement announced that he was willing to accommodate residents from any tribe.

Acquiring a plot of land is a dream for most newcomers to the Greater Khartoum conurbation, where rents are relatively high and there is no security of tenure, since all available houses are owned by individuals who can evict tenants at any time. In addition, there are no laws to regulate rents in Sudan. When there is an opportunity to acquire a plot almost for free, it creates enough motivation for people to hurry and join in large numbers. In this way, squatter settlements keep springing up every now and then in the surrounding peri-urban land.

Newcomers were admitted through their representatives, who were later raised to the status of headmen (sheikhs). A tribal representative would approach Kafi asking for the allotment of a piece of land for him and his fellow tribesmen to settle on. Once Kafi's agents had demarcated the space, the representative would divide it into 200-square-metre plots and distribute them to his followers who were asked to pay 37 SDG for each plot. The money was used to issue a sponsorship certificate (*kafāla*), which is intended to be the basis for legitimatizing the plot later with official planning authorities whenever conditions permit. The fee continued to increase until it reached 150 SDG per plot in 2010.

Waiting for Planners: The Political Manipulation of Rights

Driven by peoples' desire to own a plot of land, the squatters soon became organized into smaller pseudo-native administration units with Abdalla Kafi at the top; he was now called "sultan". a title that does not exist among the Nuba ethnic group to which he belongs. It seems he got it from Southerners who lived in the nearby Jabarona IDP camp. Traditional leaders from the South were given this title and recognized by the government as representatives of their people. They were empowered to act as a native administration authority for their own followers living in IDP camps – a cheap substitute for establishing a modern administrative setup in an urban context. This is similar to the logic by which the British colonial authorities promoted Native Administration in Sudan as a form of indirect rule during the 1920s.

*ʿOmda*s (sectional tribal chiefs) started as agents for land allocation. Each group of 200 people could choose one of their members to be their *ʿomda* and Sultan Kafi would confirm his position. Each *ʿomda* operates through sheikhs (headmen), who represent families belonging to his tribe. Through this system, *ʿomda*s benefited from the sale of land to new followers. The price of a plot in 2008 reached up to 499 SDG (excluding sponsorship fees). To consolidate his authority, Sultan Kafi formed a council for his *ʿomda*s and a pseudo-native court where they would sit to settle dispute cases between residents, many of which happened to be about land issues. It is noticeable that until today the security services have no perceptible presence in the area apart from two ill-equipped police stations.

Before its abolition in 2012, there was a recognized pseudo-native administration system operating in Khartoum State, which was called the "Native System", to differentiate it from the famous system of administration that the British had established in Sudan and which is still operative in some parts of the country (mainly Darfur and Kordofan). There was a coordinating office in the locality and state headquarters responsible of promoting the system.

The office issued ID cards for *ʿomda*s showing their tribal affiliation. The Native System had been suggested after a conference held in 1995 reached the conclusion that "migrants from rural areas in Khartoum state can be best controlled through a system like what they were used to in their original homelands" (Ahmed 2003, p.3). So, they are treated basically as tribesmen who happen to be in town for a limited period of time. Their dealings with government bodies must be sanctioned by their sponsoring *ʿomda*. All *ʿomda*s are incidentally members of the NCP, so, when big rallies are mobilized in Khartoum, they are entrusted with the task of escorting several buses full of supporters to take part in the rally. They are provided with some cash facilities to enable them to fulfil their tasks. In short, HJ squatter settlement was partly allowed to continue because it provided the ruling party with supporters for rallies and voters in elections.

The native system operating in HJ is therefore part of a package or a mechanism for the social control of migrants coming from rural areas to Khartoum. It is also evident that the places they come from are the same parts of the country that are currently suffering from the ongoing civil war. While government authorities consider them as economic migrants, they in fact qualify as IDPs and, when Kafi first established his squatter settlement, he was in fact helped by some Islamic NGOs, which provided food and critical medical services for his followers on the basisi that they were IDPs. This fact later negatively affected the position of the settlement in terms of planning opportunities.

The *Rakūba* as a Voluntary Dispute Resolution Forum

Rakūba (lit., "windbreak") is a colloquial word that refers to a rectangular wooden frame whose walls and roof are thatched with grass or straw. The *rakūba* is a fixed feature of Sudanese homes not only in rural areas but also in urban settlements. In the latter case, some of them now have frames made of steel pipes or metal sheeting instead of wood. The main function of a *rakūba* is for people to sit with their neighbours and guests to discuss public issues and exchange information, but it has also become associated with voluntary dispute resolution practices. A mediatory style is used that aims at reconciling differences to restore social relations. For this reason, the *rakūba* gained symbolic value because people may use the word to refer to the dispute resolution process itself or to the meeting. Moreover, the *rakūba* of a traditional leader gains special recognition because of the dispute resolution processes that are performed in it.

From a practical point of view, the *rakūba* can be considered a lay tribunal or court that performs the function of promoting order by resorting to customary principles of adjudication and mediation. However, because they lack authorization from formal judicial authorities, I choose to call it a "voluntary dispute resolution forum". Today there are three main *rakūbas* operating as dispute resolution forums in HJ. The first and most important of them is the one founded by Sultan Abdalla Kafi. The second is known as the Sultan's council in Block 47. The third is known as *ʿomda* Husain's *rakūba* in Block 45. The popularity of these three *rakūbas* does not mean that other smaller forums are excluded from playing a role in dispute resolutions. Other *ʿomdas* and sheikhs can practise mediation within their own limited circles and amongst people they know, but more critical cases (especially those involving disputants from different tribes) are brought to one of the three famous *rakūbas*.

Although the self-appointed gathering of *ʿomdas* practising dispute resolution has been in existence for more than a decade now, there is no official recognition of these tribunals/courts at the headquarters of the Sudan Judiciary. This is the authority that sanctions the formation of customary law courts under the 1995 Town and Rural Courts Act. There are twenty-three such courts in Khartoum State, eight of which are in Omdurman. The one in HJ is not included in the list. The traditional leaders in the squatter settlement have formed it voluntarily but they call it a "court". Both police and local government authorities recognize its existence in the sense that it is real and it helps to settle disputes, thereby keeping the number of cases referred to the police station much lower than if the voluntary court did not exist. This certainly raises an interesting sociological question regarding the organization and administration of legal institutions: should they be recognized on the basis of their function and how people perceive them, or on the basis of being officially sanctioned?

Another important aspect of the voluntary forums for dispute resolution at the HJ squatter settlement regards the type of law that is being applied. Since the *ʿomdas* who run the court belong to more than one tribe, it is sociologically interesting to know how they adapt and make compromises between different tribal customs, especially when disputants belong to more than one tribe. It is generally known that Sudanese customary law courts combine tribal customs with Islamic jurisprudence in certain types of cases and often quote the Qur'an and Hadith texts when they pass judgements. They sometimes also apply parts of statutory law in these courts when they see fit. This practice is known in the legal anthropology literature as legal pluralism (Griffiths 1986; Merry 1988). However, as Dupret (2007) has shown, there is no single conceptualization of legal pluralism that is agreed upon by all scholars concerned with law – not even legal anthropologists for that matter. It is therefore quite interesting to consider the pattern of legal pluralism that the informal courts in HJ exemplify.

The *Rakūba* of Sultan Abdalla Kafi: Setting, Structure and Procedures

I will take Sultan Abdalla Kafi's *rakūba* as an example to show how the voluntary dispute resolution forum in HJ is structured and operates. To consolidate his authority, Sultan Abdallah Kafi, as he is known among his followers, formed a council and a tribunal where *ʿomdas* (sectional chiefs) representing different tribes would sit to settle dispute cases between residents under a *rakūba* next to his house in Block 48. It is a rectangular structure of 12 × 8 metres and about three metres high, with an open entrance on one side, without a door (see Figure 7.1). The roof is covered with straw but the sides are loosely covered with scrap steel bars and some branches, which one can see through. The floor is flattened earth covered with sand. People sit on old benches and chairs arranged next to the walls and the middle is kept empty. The Sultan or leader of the session sits near the entrance facing the people, as can be seen in the figure below.

Although the seating order looks very informal, one notes that the senior members of the forum sit near the leader to make consultations easier. At prayer times, the place is turned into a temporary mosque and is covered with

FIGURE 7.1 *Abdalla Kafi presiding over his "court".*
PHOTOGRAPH BY THE AUTHOR.

FIGURE 7.2 *Noon prayers in the* rakūba.
PHOTOGRAPH BY THE AUTHOR.

plastic sheets to enable those present to say their prayers collectively (see Figure 7.2).

The *rakūba* is erected at the side of the main road leading to the market and the bus-stop so that people pass by its wall as they walk. Curious passers-by can also stop and listen to the cases under deliberation. Initially, many of the cases they dealt with were about land rights. Later, the voluntary dispute resolution forum started handling other kinds of cases, such as petty crimes, civil transaction cases and familial disputes.

The procedures followed in the *rakūba* are quite informal. Those who want to complain can just come in, give greetings, sit down, and start talking about their case if there is nothing going on; otherwise they wait until an ongoing case is settled. There is no registration, no clerk, no fees are paid and the court does not impose fines or apply any physical punishment. More often, a culprit may be asked to pay compensation to the victim by way of a settlement, but the forum itself does not handle any money or take any fees. This is perhaps one of its advantages over conventional legal institutions. The Sultan has three principal aids. An *amīr* (tribal leader) from the Missiriya tribe acts as his first deputy when the Sultan is not available. Another deputy from the Nuba tribes also acts as the head of the popular committee in Block 48 and is a close adviser, especially on political matters. The Sultan's third aid is his personal secretary, who belongs to his own extended family. He is always around and takes care of the place and briefs the Sultan whenever he is away from the neighbourhood.

It seems that the *rakūba* has multiple functions. People exchange information and get advice on different practical matters of everyday life. They come there to meet someone or greet the Sultan to show respect. What is even more interesting is that people in need also pass by to ask for help. One day while I was there, a woman stood outside the *rakūba* and the Sultan directed one of his aids to see what she wanted. When it turned out that she needed some money to buy medicine for her sick child, the Sultan offered her 100 SDG and asked others attending the meeting to contribute too. I later learned that this kind of action is common in the *rakūba*. Taking all these things into consideration, it might qualify as a social centre or a club. To say the least, dispute resolution is only one function of the *rakūba*.

Members of the council arrive early to have breakfast paid for through collective contributions, but when the Sultan is present he usually pays for the meal. The usual business of considering cases starts at 10 am and ends at 1 pm with noon prayers. Although the Sultan may not attend every day, the place is never closed. However, the number of people present in the *rakūba* increases sharply when he is there and cases that are more serious are left until he comes. It should be noted here that Sultan Kafi is a member of parliament representing the constituency of Western Omdurman, which includes HJ. After winning a seat in parliament at the elections in 2010, he married a young woman who lives in Omdurman, so nowadays he does not spend much of his time in HJ, although his first wife and children still live in his old house next to the *rakūba*. He is all too aware of the importance of his continuous presence in this neighbourhood for his political career and he managed to retain his seat in parliament at the last elections in April 2015.

It is a general rule that, when someone is injured, the injured person must be taken to the police first and then to the hospital for treatment and assessment of the damage incurred. When the injured person recovers, the case is often brought back to the forum for a final settlement on a mediatory basis. If the two sides are satisfied by the solution offered, the victim will be asked to go to the police station (which is outside HJ) and declare that he is withdrawing the case. If the victim does not want to come to the *rakūba*, the case will then be referred to a proper court of law by the prosecutor. As a rule, criminal cases (including homicide) are always started at the police station but most of them are finally settled at the *rakūba*. Since 1983, Sudanese criminal law has followed the *sharīʿa* stipulation that blood money (*diya*) can be accepted by the victim or by his/her family in homicide cases. This gives ample space for mediatory style justice to prevail.

Cases of blasphemy and adultery are settled with a fine of 100 SDG to be paid to the victim. The forum may take a small amount from the paid fine to order tea for everyone attending the meeting. This is considered a good way to "wash hearts", as they say. Another general rule is that inheritance cases, when the parties disagree, are also taken first to a proper civil law court. Alternatively, inheritance can be settled at home according to the consensus of those involved with the help of a local imam or an expert in *sharīʿa* law. Although cases of marital disputes and divorce can be initiated either at the forum or at a matrimonial sitting at a civil court, divorce certificates for women must be obtained from a proper court of law, as women cannot remarry without such certificate. This is not required for men as they can have up to four wives at a time.

With regard to interaction with formal law institutions, it is noticeable that the only relationship between voluntary forums and official law and order institutions is through one "popular police" station and one "community police" station in the neighbourhood. These are semi-official bodies manned by youths from the same community who help to keep order and report any security breaches to the nearest proper police station, which will then take action. The popular police centre, which is part of the Sultans' council, is run by one trained policeman aided by local youths, while the community police centre is entirely manned by local youths. Although both centres are supposed to keep records of cases reported to them, only the popular police centre does in practice keep up-to-date records. They also participate in the procedures of the forums and keep records of agreements that emerge when cases are settled. It is interesting to note that some cases are settled by the perpetrator declaring that he or she will not repeat their bad behaviour (e.g. in cases of conjugal disputes).

Some Illustrative Cases

This section deals with summaries of selected dispute cases observed during fieldwork, with the aim of illustrating the various aspects of the processes followed within the *rakūba* or forums. All cases come from the *rakūba* of Sultan Abdalla Kafi because it is the most popular and most regular one, operating almost every day of the week, except for official holidays.

Case 1

A woman came to the *rakūba* and complained that another woman who worked for the locality (a municipal administrative unit) and was responsible for marking houses in preparation for planning, had cheated her by taking 200 SDG for numbering her house, although this service was free. She was asked if there were any witnesses, which she confirmed, so she was requested to summon them. The accused woman was also summoned to attend the forum on the same day. After a while, all were present in the *rakūba* and the meeting was chaired by the second deputy of the Sultan, who is also the head of the popular committee in Block 48. The meeting started with a recitation of verses from the holy Qur'an and then the chair asked the woman to state her complaint. The accused woman was then asked to respond to the allegation. The meeting then listened to three female witnesses who confirmed the complainant's story. The accused then confessed her wrongdoing. The *ʿomda*s and sheikhs who attended the meeting spoke and reprimanded the accused. The chair then asked her to return the money and apologize to the complainant and she immediately declared her acceptance to the ruling. She went to the other women and they hugged each other and left the *rakūba*. The case was over.

The above case illustrates the normative nature of *rakūba* dispute settlement, which emphasizes the restoration of social relationships as a priority. In a formal court, this case would have been considered as corrupt practice by a public official, and the criminal law would have been invoked. In this case, no fine was imposed and the culprit only returned the money owed to the victim. The apology was considered enough for the forum to pardon her since social relations had been amicably restored. A mixture of formal law and custom were used to settle the case.

Case 2

A young woman, aged 29, came to the *rakūba* and complained that her 45-year-old neighbour had made allegations that she had behaved inappropriately. This is usually a reference to promiscuity. She was asked by the Sultan's secretary to bring witnesses. After a few hours, the forum was considering the case in the presence of all parties. The accused denied what the complainant said about her and the witness confirmed her denial. The forum reprimanded the complainant but she insisted that she was in the right and announced that she would take the matter to the official court in Dar as-Salam. They told her she could go wherever she wanted to. It was clear that the meeting was angry with the woman as she disregarded their opinion. When she left, a lot of talk ensued about her bad manners, saying that she was not well brought up because she did not respect men.

This case shows the delicate nature of restoring social relations, especially when judgement on moral behaviour is involved. Such issues are usually handled within family circles, but when a woman does not have a male guardian, as in this case, it is not easy for the community to settle the dispute. As the forum has no power to enforce its decisions, it is possible for many to disregard it. The significance of the forum does not come from the law but from the social values and the communal solidarity that support it.

Case 3

An elderly man (aged over 60), a neighbour of Sultan Abdallah Kafi, complained at the forum that his new wife did not respect him and that she went out of their home without his consent. The man also alleged that his mother-in-law was behind the misunderstanding that he had with his wife because she wanted to keep his wife's daughter from a previous marriage. The protesting husband wanted his wife's daughter to stay in his house with her mother and said that he was willing to raise her because such an arrangement would make his wife happy to stay at home. Sultan Kafi asked for the wife's mother to be brought to the forum. When it became clear that the woman was away from the neighbourhood, he asked for her son's telephone number. He called the man and engaged him in a lengthy conversation with a loud voice, repeating what the man had said so that everyone present in the meeting could hear. He often referred to Qur'anic verses and texts from the Prophet. In the end, the problem was resolved by the wife's brother confirming that his family members would not interfere between the man and his wife. Sultan Kafi also advised the husband to be courteous and generous with his in-laws and to allow the woman to visit her mother from time to time. The man agreed but said he would accompany her as he felt that her mother might give her daughter bad advice if she visited her alone. He also asked the Sultan to tell his wife not to use the telephone in his absence.

This case illustrates the casual nature and relaxed procedures that are followed by the forum. The fact that the forum was able to settle the case in the absence of one party and without listening to any witnesses is quite telling. The use of the cell phone to interview the brother of the wife who was accused by her husband shows the flexibility and readiness of the forum members to adapt to new conditions. The husband felt relieved by the undertaking that his brother-in-law made to the forum leader. It is noticeable that both *sharīʿa* and custom law were invoked in settling the case.

Concluding Remarks

The voluntary dispute resolution forums or *rakūba*s operating in HJ were established by community leaders in a squatter neighbourhood to provide a viable alternative to formal legal institutions that are difficult to access, because they are either located far away or unaffordable. Furthermore, the mediatory style of justice they perform makes it easy for community members to reconcile differences in a more harmonious manner, without losing solidarity within the group, who interact daily. Although community members belong to different ethnic groups, the fact that they all come from rural areas means that they have similar experiences in terms of the nature of social relations and ordering institutions. Their common destiny on the margins of the urban milieu, with its opportunities and risks, has further united them behind their leaders, who are constantly struggling to secure tenure rights for the occupants through proper urban planning procedures. This has become a political game in which leaders of the squatter settlement have shown considerable skill. They have managed to achieve reasonable success by stabilizing the situation and getting recognition from government institutions, which have started to cooperate with them on a temporary basis. The voluntary dispute resolution forums they run are part of this success and this is one reason why they are multifunctional. The *rakūba* as a dispute resolution forum exhibits many features of legal pluralism. Although, generally speaking, they apply customary norms, they sometimes also draw on *sharīʿa* and statutory legal norms. They also follow mixed procedures, as when, in cases that involve injury, they require police and hospital reports, after which they can settle such cases through mediatory justice procedures. The forums also interact with formal legal institutions such as formal courts and police stations, which partially recognize their procedures by not objecting to their presence and sometimes referring people to them. Furthermore, in cases of family disputes and inheritance, the forums constantly refer to *sharīʿa* law by consulting religious experts such as local imams. The understanding of legal pluralism here fits well with the praxiological approach of Dupret who argues that "… what social sciences only can do is to observe and describe how actual people in actual settings orient to the production of a phenomenon which they call law" (Dupret 2007, p. 1).

On the other hand, the justice-seeking behaviour of the disputants points to the neighbourhood's residents' awareness of their options. Many of them adopt a forum shopping strategy to either make their claims in the *rakūba* or go to formal courts and police stations outside the neighbourhood. Such behaviour is not subject to fixed standards but rather to cost-benefit calculations by the individuals concerned and their expectations about where they might find the most favourable outcome for their case. During my fieldwork, I did not come across a single case where a disputant chose to resort to formal legal institutions as a first option. However, there are very few cases where unsatisfied disputants took their complaints to an ordinary law court located outside the neighbourhood.

Many researchers have previously pointed to the association between legal pluralism and forum shopping. In her study of Minangkabau village in West Sumatra Keebet von Benda-Beckmann (1981, p. 145) notes:

> On the one hand, villagers can always go to the state courts, which have the power to make and execute decisions. This has weakened the authority of village institutions. On the other hand, the state courts do not function as a real alternative. Besides being unpredictable and expensive, their procedural requirements tend to reinforce shopping activities and manipulation with disputes on the village level.

The disputants in HJ act in much the same way.

References

Abdul-Jalil, MA 1985, 'From Native Courts to Peoples Local Courts: The Politics of Judicial Administration in Sudan', *Verfassung und Recht in Ubersse* (*Law and Politics in Africa, Asia and Latin America*), vol. 18, no. 2, pp. 139–152.

Ahmed, ZA 2003, 'The Experience of the Native System in Khartoum State in the Period 1997–2000', Unpublished Report, Bureau of Federal Government, Khartoum (in Arabic).

de Geoffroy, A 2015, 'What Place in Khartoum for the Displaced? Between State Regulation and Individual Strategies', in B Casciarri, MA Assal & F Ireton (eds), *Multidimensional Change in Sudan 1989–2011: Reshaping Livelihoods, Conflicts and Identities*, Berghahn Books, New York/Oxford, pp. 201–225.

Dupret, B 2007, 'Legal Pluralism, Plurality of Laws and Legal Practices: Theories, Critiques, and Praxiological Re-specification', *European Journal of Legal Studies*, vol. 1, pp. 1–26.

Eckert, J 2004, 'Urban Governance and Emergent Forms of Legal Pluralism in Mumbai', *The Journal of Legal Pluralism and Unofficial Law*, vol. 36, no. 50, pp. 29–60.

Griffiths, J 1986, 'What is legal pluralism?', *Journal of Legal Pluralism and Unofficial Law*, vol. 24, pp. 1–55.

Merry, SE 1988, 'Legal Pluralism', *Law & Society Review*, vol. 22, no. 5, pp. 869–896.

Roberts, S 1979, *Order and Dispute: An Introduction to Legal Anthropology*, Penguin Books, London.

Salman, MAS 1983, 'Lay Tribunals in the Sudan: An Historical and Socio-legal Analysis', *Journal of Legal Pluralism and Unofficial Law*, vol. 21, pp. 61–128.

von Benda-Beckmann, K 1981, 'Forum Shopping and Shopping Forums: Dispute Processing in A Minangkabau Village in West Sumatra', *Journal of Legal Pluralism*, vol. 19, pp. 117–159.

CHAPTER 8

Conflict, Property, Mortgage and State Courts in Khartoum

Yazid Ben Hounet

Introduction

Anthropological approaches to law have been widely interested in conflict settlement practices. Fernanda Pirie (2013) argues that there has been a great interest on these practices because they address the question of social order and its eventual breaches. Indeed, in functionalist and structuralist anthropological perspectives, the maintenance of social order has long been the core focus of anthropologists interested in law, but also in a way to define law. To give law a universal definition, it should be defined, following these classical approaches, by its alleged objective – the maintenance of social order – and not necessarily by the existence of legal institutions, formal rules or identified legal actors. Such interest in conflict settlement practices is also due to the concomitant development and contributions by both the ethnographical and the legal realism approaches. We find in *The Cheyenne Way*, co-authored by the lawyer Karl N. Llewellyn and the anthropologist E. Adamson Hoebel, the inputs of ethnographic description and those of legal realism.[1] These authors consider three approaches to the understanding of law: the first, ideological, is that of the rule, the norm, the "right way"; the second is the description of practices; and the third is to look at conflict and dispute cases, to be able to identify the motivations and results of such cases. These three approaches are intertwined in the theoretical perspective of the authors (Llewellyn and Hoebel 1941, pp. 20–21).

In dealing with conflict settlement in present-day Sudan, I try neither to understand the logic of the maintenance of social order, nor to study the gap between the rules and the concrete practices. My aim is mainly to understand

1 The first, Karl N. Llewellyn, then a professor at Columbia Law School, is one of the figures of the American Legal Realist school, which emphasizes the political context applications of the rule of law. The second, E. Adamson Hoebel, is an anthropologist trained in the Anthropology Department at Columbia (founded by Franz Boas), and a specialist in American Indians (Cheyenne, Shoshone, Comanche and Pueblo).

© KONINKLIJKE BRILL NV, LEIDEN, 2018 | DOI 10.1163/9789004362185_010 the different perceptions of law and the different ways actors deal with it, and to also understand the different goals and roads that actors pragmatically follow. Studying conflict settlement is not only a way of understanding law in action; it is above all a way to analyse how people perceive law and justice, and the eventual gaps that exist between these two realms. I would also like to add that the different goals and roads that actors pragmatically follow constitute the reality of law. Law can thus be observed as a step-by-step construction that results from the contextual interactions between the people involved. Thus, the ethnographical approach I would like to pursue in this contribution is to look at the contextual practices and argumentations and how they interact, in order to understand how conflict is settled, or not. I do not try to evaluate the conformity of practices with legal norms, or to presuppose the main objective of conflict settlement.

Concerning blood money, *diya* in Arabic, Islamic rules are clear enough and in Sudan explicit penal rules exist, at least since 1991 (see below). But problematic cases sometimes occur, leading to an iterative, reciprocating process between the actors. In such cases, conflict settlements are often based upon negotiations over goods and properties, and are therefore about tangible elements.[2] This chapter will focus on the topics of property and mortgages through

2 In anthropological literature, blood money has been widely analysed as a regulated counterpart to revenge (blood feuds and vendettas). This practice was defined initially as the expression of private justice, found in what classical anthropologists called "primitive societies", which are societies without central authority. In this context, justice was often dispensed by the community and more specifically by the kinship group to whom the victim belonged (Lowie 1921, p. 383). In A.R. Radcliffe-Brown's structuralist considerations, for instance, the practice of blood money was worth attention when it was articulated with social organization, in particular with the logics of kinship, and more specifically with descent. Blood money is thus a practice that involves rights and duties for and towards a certain kind of people, the clan or an extended kinship group. Radcliffe-Brown referred to fifth cousins among ancient Anglo-Saxons (Radcliffe-Brown 1952). When discussing the Bedouin, Joseph Chelhod (1971) mentions that the relevant kin group includes members of the agnatic line up till the fifth degree, the *khamsa* (five). Edward Evans-Pritchard (1940) considered the obligation to pay blood money as one of the defining criteria of the Nuer clan and tribe. Rights and duties are viewed as inseparable from the status that individuals have in social organization, particularly vis-à-vis members of their clan. There has indeed been a clear link between material goods and blood money. Numerous anthropologists associate blood money with bride price, as transmissible capital between groups according to logics defined by the rules of descent and marriage. Blood money is also given to the groups with whom one exchanges (or with whom one can exchange) women. These logics of descent and marital exchange imply that compensation is sometimes excluded for certain categories of individuals, such as illegitimate children or slaves. While after the 1950's, some anthropologists such as Max

a case study of blood money from the Khartoum Penal Court (*maḥkama jinaniyyāt*) of the Traffic Administration (*shurṭat al-murūr*) – I will use the acronym KPCTA hereafter. This problematic case begins with a road traffic accident that occurred in June 2004. The case is quite complex because the guilty party (responsible for the accident) was not the owner of the car. The victim was injured by him and died soon after in hospital. The owner of the car (who was the guilty party's boss) was also made responsible of paying the blood money (*diya*) to the victim's family. First, his store was mortgaged, then to be replaced by three cars, and then by two cars. In March 2012, two cars were still mortgaged and the case was not yet solved because the victim's family had still not come to court. Meanwhile, the guilty party (the driver) died in an accident. The owner of the mortgaged cars was still engaged in negotiations with the family of the victim, who lived in the Jazira area.

This case thus brings together questions of property, conflict, conciliation (*ṣulḥ*) and blood money (*diya*). The empirical material I present in this chapter is based on the documents of the case, observations and interviews about the case, and some brief descriptions of the court. We are dealing with a case of homicide, city-land property, vehicle ownership and mortgages. I will explain the way this case was brought to court, the way actors tried to solve it, the reasoning behind the judgement, and the way the parties to the litigation tried to end the case. Some other topics are embedded within this case: questions of access to justice and the role of lawyers (advocates), the negotiations and conciliations that occurred inside and outside the court, and the temporality of law.

The aim of this chapter is – through an ethnographic approach to a specific case – to illustrate the contextual, and perhaps cultural, practices of people when they are confronted with state courts. It aims to understand the different rationalities and pragmatics of law and how people relate to state courts, and also to demonstrate that, even in an Islamic country that officially follows *sharīʿa*, the contextual and daily practices of law cannot be explained by religious or Islamic considerations. Rather, through ethnographic cases, it suggests the power of routine, pragmatic aspects, economic considerations, traditional and local practices, administrative rationalities, etc.

Gluckman (1965), Ian Cunnison (1972), Sally Falk Moore (1986), and more recently Gunther Schlee (2002) and Stephane Breton (1999a, 1999b, 2002) mention blood money practices and give some insights about this practice in different contexts, the subject has largely fallen into obscurity and is considered old fashioned. The exception, perhaps, is in research on Muslim societies, because of the inclusion of blood money (*diya*) within the Islamic normativity and within state criminal laws of countries following *sharīʿa*, like Sudan.

Discovering the Case from the State Courts

It is always useful, as Pierre Bourdieu (1980, p. 236) reminds us, to present the conditions of the production of knowledge. We can do this by starting with the explanation of the conditions in which the case was discovered and the perspectives that gives to the understanding of the case. I discovered the case in December 2011 at the KPCTA. I was there doing some research on blood money, following prior research done in Khartoum Penal Court in January 2009. Many of the cases about blood money in Khartoum were associated with homicide and injury caused by car accidents. I then moved from the Khartoum Penal Court to the KPCTA, as one of the judges I used to work with moved there too. Thus, during my work in Khartoum, I have mainly followed blood money cases through the way they were settled in court, offering me a comparative contrast with Algeria, where *diya* practices only take place outside court (Ben Hounet 2012a).

In contrast to Algeria, Sudan – an Islamic republic – has integrated *diya* and, logically, *qiṣāṣ* into its penal code. This important distinction between Algeria and Sudan allowed me to broaden the comparison and to provide some insights into the way blood money is applied in Muslim societies, both within and outside the courts. In Sudan, as in Algeria, the unintentionality of homicide was one of the main conditions for the application of *diya* as opposed to *qiṣāṣ* (see below). Indeed, *diya* is mostly recommended when the homicide is unintentioned: resulting from an accident, imprudence, self-defence and so forth. However, defining and determining intentionality is no simple matter, as it is directly connected to the idea of premeditation and can be influenced by several factors, such as the context, the actors involved, their standards, their background and the factual elements (Ben Hounet 2016). In court in Sudan, more formal legal aspects, along with the propensity of judges to judge according to the standards of their profession, strongly impact the results in *diya* cases (see Ben Hounet 2012b; Ben Hounet 2016). A tool, but also a symbol, *diya* is a practical and socially (traditionally) recognized (and in some legitimate way) as an instrument of reconciliation processes in Muslim contexts. Even so, it must be deliberately accepted, without which reconciliation can only be temporary and/or apparent, as can be the case when it is imposed at trial, with regard to Sudan, or by social pressure (in Algeria, Sudan or elsewhere).

Observing conflict settlements and the application of blood money within court implies that we only encounter one aspect of the totality: legal procedures, written legal documents, hearings and trials, abstract legal notions, etc. We observe case after case. For the judges and their colleagues, a case brought to their office and court is just one case amongst others. For those involved, i.e., the victims, culprits, their kin and friends, it can be a deeply traumatic experience that affects their whole lives. In a way, we are protected from all the emotions surrounding the cases, and also from the intimate perceptions of those who are most involved.

The KPCTA is in Khartoum North, just one block before the Blue Nile River and the bridge to Tuti Island, in front of the Khartoum *wilāya* (Khartoum State) directorate of traffic administration, and two blocks east from the Sudan Judiciary. We find there a vehicle pound, portacabins (prefabricated buildings) with police offices, and three courts of justice where judges hear cases in progress and adjudicate. Judge K.K.'s court, where I did my observations, is a small room divided into two parts: a slightly elevated part where the judge's desk stands, and the rest of the room where we find three chairs and a cupboard. There is also a small bench near the judge's desk, for the judge's visitors and friends. In this simple small room, around 20 square metres, only the elevated desk and the court robe hung on the wall behind it indicates the hierarchy that exists between the judge and the others.

Hearings take place during the morning, policemen bringing offenders with them for immediate arraignments and/or barristers with or without their clients bringing new elements or requests concerning their cases. Judge K.K., arraigns, hears and adjudicates alone, without juries or clerks. He has only one assistant, whose job is to bring folders and tea, and also works as a messenger. During the break, at around 11h30, other judges sometimes come for a short visit and chat. The overall impression is that the judges here, and also at the Penal Court where I did observations, are rather isolated and autonomous.

In case of immediate arraignments, as when the police present the offenders as driving over the speed limit or while intoxicated, adjudications are almost always expeditious. The judge often follows the police deposition by imposing a fine and/or a prison sentence. Things are different when barristers are involved, particularly barristers working for car insurance companies. These barristers are frequently in court and have a privileged relationship with the judges: they belong to the same professional body; they use the same language; and they know how to behave in front of and with the judge. Being there almost every week, and sometimes several times a week, they create a sense of proximity to the judge. In a way, the judge sometimes acts like a benevolent older brother. When barristers bring cases, adjudication is thus less expeditious: Judge K.K., takes more time to consider the case.

Judge K.K.'s speed in adjudicating cases is in a way linked to the large increase in the number of cars, car accidents and driving offences. Between 2005 and 2009, road traffic accidents were among the major causes of death in Sudan in the 21–60 years age group, accounting to 61% of deaths. The fatality rate of 35 per 10,000 vehicles was amongst the highest in the world, despite the low level of car ownership (one vehicle to 100 persons [Galal and Tayfour 2012]). The Directorate General of Traffic (2010) also reported a large increase in motor vehicle accident injuries, from 19 per day in 2005 to 26 in 2009 (Osman and Ahmed 2014).

The activities of the KPCTA are thus overloaded. People in and around the courts are numerous. In such a context, the work of the judges seems to be repetitive and restricted. The case I encountered in Judge K.K.'s court, in December 2011, was only one example of this tragic Sudanese reality. I discovered it while the new barrister in charge of the case was in negotiations to cut the number of properties mortgaged since 2004, after the accident. This case was interesting because of its complexity, evolving from homicide and *diya* matters to a property problem.

Describing the Case

Since I only discovered this case in December 2011, I was not able to follow it from the beginning (June 2004). Analyses of the case are thus based on documents and interviews with the judge, the barrister in charge of the case and the claimant (the owner of the mortgaged properties). I did not have the opportunity to meet the victim's family, who lived in Jazira region, south of Khartoum. Members of this family refused to meet me when I tried to get in touch through the contact given by the barrister. I thus have only one side of the case. I also attended hearings between the judges, the barrister and the claimant.

An overall description of the case and its development will allow us to understand the various sequences and goals reached by the actors involved.

On 28 June 2004, at 4 am, A.B., from Tuti Island, ran over F.H., who was lying on the ground (sleeping outside). He took the victim to hospital, but he died at 8.30 am. A.B. had his car registration number but the car was not insured. The same day, the police (general traffic administration) brought a claim against A.B., the driver and M.S., the owner of the car, for *diya* (compensation) payment (Annexe 8.1). The prosecuting attorney asked for an autopsy. The Khartoum teaching hospital proceeded to carry out the autopsy. The deceased, F.H., 38 years old, had a huge blood clot in the pelvis and a torn bladder. He died of a fractured pelvis and heavy bleeding. The autopsy was carried out but nobody came to collect the body. The driver was jailed.

On 29 June 2006, following the trial, the former judge who had dealt with the case from the beginning (not Judge K.K.), decided to register the land belonging to the car owner, in Omdurman, to be mortgaged for compensation (*diya*).

The victim's family still did not present themselves to the judge. He decided to register the land in Omdurman as compensation and to release the accused on condition that he has a mentor. The victim's family had to be questioned, but they still did not present themselves (they lived in Jazira, far from Khartoum).

In 2010, Judge K.K., formerly a judge at the Penal Court of Khartoum North, and newly appointed to the KPCTA, inherited the case. Between 2006 and 2010, the first accused, A.B., the driver, died. M.S., the owner of the car, hired a new barrister to resolve the case of the mortgage on the plot of land he owned in Omdurman.

Between 13 and 19 July 2010, three cars belonging to M.S. were evaluated at the request of Judge K.K., with the aim of replacing the mortgage on the land with a mortgage on the cars, as requested by the accused M.S. and his barrister (Annexe 8.2). They were given an estimated value of 36,000 SDG (around 6,000 euros). The cars were mortgaged and the mortgage on the land was cancelled.

On 4 December 2011, the mortgage on one car was cancelled, at the request of the barrister. The value of the two cars was estimated by the judge as sufficient.

On 6 December, the barrister asked for a replacement mortgage on only one of the cars, since the value of that car was sufficient for the compensation, estimated at 25,000 SDG (around 4,200 euros in 2012). When I left in March 2012, the judge was willing to accept the request of M.S. and his barrister, since no one from the victim's family had come to the court. He was still asking the accused to reconcile with the victim's family and to bring one of the family's representatives to the court, but with no result.

From the *Diya* Process to Property Mortgage Trouble

The first document in this case was written on the same day as the accident, by the police traffic administration. In the account of the accident, the police officer explained that the first accused, A.B., was driving a car (indicating the registration numberof the car) beside the Blue Nile when he injured the deceased, F.H., who was lying near a tree. The latter was taken to hospital but died. The second accused, M.S., was requested, by the police, to pay the *diya* but did not have enough money to do so. This first account shows the routine aspect of the process. After giving notification of the accident and the death that followed it, the police officer immediately requested the *diya* payment from the owner of the car, not from the driver, according to the registration number of the car and the responsibility that it carries.

Diya has been applied in Sudan for a long time within various rural tribes (Cunnison 1972).[3] In the countryside, the practice remains for the most part a tribal one. Indeed, the *nāẓir*, *ʿomda* and sheikh (i.e. the local leaders), still manage the application of *diya* within their tribes and between tribes. More broadly, legal practices in rural areas often rest upon the institution of the tribe (*gabīla*) – or upon the claim of the tribal paradigm – and local actors and leaders apply an "institutional bricolage", melding various legal sources and institutions together (customs, state law, Islamic law; oral/written; state courts and tribal leaderships), in order to resolve conflicts, as is the case with the Aḥāmda, a pastoral group in the rural area of Khartoum State (Casciarri 2009, 2015). Also, interestingly, in Sudan a national council of tribal leaders was created in January 2009, with the aim of bringing about reconciliations in Darfur and North Kordofan (interview with the *nāẓir* of the Shukriyya in Khartoum). This council promote collective blood money as a means of solving conflicts in these regions.[4]

Diya was incorporated into Sudan's penal code in 1983, but the current application follows the revised/new penal code of 1991. This law stipulates the conditions for *diya* and for evaluating its amount/nature. It distinguishes two types of *diya*: complete *diya* (for involuntary homicide) and aggravated *diya* (murder and forgiveness of the victim's family, instead of *qiṣāṣ*), but also stipulates the legal responsibility of the clan, *ʿāqila*. According to article 43 of the penal code, *diya* can be applied in the following cases: A. murder or deliberate injury, if the talion (*qiṣāṣ*) is foregone (by the victim or his legal claimant); B. semi intentional homicide or semi-intentional injury; C. homicide or injury caused by negligence; D. homicide or injury caused by a minor or an incapacitated person. Article 45 of the 1991 penal code mentions that those responsible for the payment of the *diya* are: A. the guilty person in case of deliberate homicide or injury; B. the guilty person and his clan (*ʿāqila*) in the case of semi-intentional homicide or injury or homicide caused by negligence.[5] In this article, the clan is defined as the agnatic kin of the guilty person, or his insurance company or agent, the persons legally responsible for the guilty person and his or

3 We can also find practices of blood money within the tribes of the current South Sudan, as the *cut* amongst the Nuer (Evans-Pritchard 1940).

4 On current dispute settlement in Sudan, see Zahir Musa Abdal-Kareem's chapter in this volume.

5 In schools of classical Islamic jurisprudence and as quoted by Rudolph Peters (2005, p. 43), "the basic distinction is between intentional (*ʿamd*) and accidental (*khata*) homicide or wounding. In addition, all schools but the Malikites recognize an intermediate category of semi-intentional homicide (*shibh ʿamd*)".

her employer if the offence takes place during working hours. The amount of *diya* for homicide was fixed in 2000 at a maximum of 3 million Sudanese dinars (SDD) (for aggravated *diya*) and a minimum of 2 million SDD (complete *diya*), equivalent to around 10,000 euros and around 6,600 euros, respectively, in 2010–2011.[6] These are the general stipulations. In practice, the modalities of judgement and settlement of compensation may vary (Ben Hounet 2012a).

So, the police (general traffic administration) asked the car owner to pay *diya* on the same day, after the accident was notified, following the routine practice in cases of accidental death. On 29 June 2006, after the trial and since the victim's family did not appear, the former judge, who had started to follow the case, decided to register the car owner's land in Omdurman to be mortgaged for compensation (*diya*). The explanation for this was that it was not possible to give the *diya* compensation to the victim's family and not fair to hold the car owner's money for *diya*, but it was still necessary to keep a means of ensuring *diya* compensation for the victim's family. At this point, the *diya* problem turned into a mortgage problem and the impossibility of conciliation became a problem of mortgage on property.

When I encountered the case, the issue was the negotiations about mortgaged properties. Conciliation and *diya*, even if they remained moral and legal obligations (see below), were not the main subjects of discussion. It was agreed that the fact that the victim's family did not appear in court, after being repeatedly asked to attend, led to a troublesome situation that the car owner, his barrister and the judge had to deal with, and in a way circumvent, in order to resolve the case, whilst remaining (at least with regard to the judge) within the law.

For the car owner, the goal – for which he hired a new barrister – was to reduce the number of properties mortgaged: from a mortgage on land to a mortgage on one car. When I discussed this with him, he explained to me that he had gone many times to Jazira to engage in conciliation. The victim's family, according to what he said, were willing, but they never came to court. Growing weary, he then decided to solve the problem of the mortgage on his properties, step by step, with his barrister. Judge K.K., with this impossibility of proceeding with the *diya* compensation, and tired of dealing with a case he had inherited from the previous judge, was willing to accept the repeated requests of the barrister, while remaining within the framework of the law. A favourite adage of his was *aṣ-ṣulḥ sayyid al-aḥkām* – "conciliation is the most honourable decision" – and he would have preferred the conciliation to take place

6 The average monthly wage was, in 2011, around 200 euros/month. The Sudanese Dinar (SDD) was changed by the Sudanese Pound (SDG) in 2007.

within the court. But this was not the feasible and he felt willing to accept the request of the car owner and his barrister.

Sharīʿa, Routine and the Law

As understood in *fiqh*, *ṣulḥ* is a form of contract (*ʿaqd*) consisting of an offer (*ījāb*) and an acceptance (*qubūl*). Its object may be material or non-material, but cannot be a prohibited commodity, as confirmed in the following Hadith: "Conciliation is permissible except when it makes forbidden that which is permitted and makes permitted that which is forbidden (*ḥarām*)." *Ṣulḥ* is both the process and the outcome to which it leads. Litigants may agree to compromise outside the scope of a judge's supervision, but such an agreement would be conditional upon its not being inequitable or contradictory to the principles of *sharīʿa*. But *ṣulḥ* can also be decided by a judge, as in family matters (Dupret and Ben Hounet 2014; Othman 2007). In its most restricted meaning, more common in law, *diya* only refers to compensation in the case of homicide: compensation for injuries is more accurately called *arsh* (Tyan 1965, p. 350). *Diya* existed in the pre-Islamic period. It is a customary practice which has its origins in both theology and law: in the Islamic tradition (Chelhod 1986, p. 141; Chelhod 1971). In the Qur'an, *diya* is defined as softening, a favour representing Allah's forgiveness and leniency regarding the rule of talion "an eye for an eye" (Qur'an 2: 178–179). *Diya* is expressly recommended in cases of the unintentional killing of one worshipper (i.e. Muslim) by another worshipper, in which case the conditions for setting compensation are stipulated (Qur'an 4: 92). In the Hadiths (reports of the deeds and sayings of the Prophet Muhammad), compensation was extended to cover deliberate homicide (*qatl ʿamdi*). Some Hadiths mention several forms of possible or permitted uses of *diya*, including in cases of deliberate homicide – that is, murder – that the Prophet Muhammad had to judge personally (Daaïf 2006). This possibility – *diya* for deliberate homicide – is accepted, but only if the victim's family (*awliyāʾ al-qatīl*) forgive the murderer and accept the compensation, which must be paid by the murderer himself and not by his clan *ʿāqila*). As stated in the Qur'an, the concept of *diya* is connected to forgiveness, mercy and tolerance.

Thus, conciliation (*ṣulḥ*) and blood money (*diya*) are two practices valorised in Islam. But, in the Sudanese example, and I would say in most of the cases we find in the KPCTA, it would be wrong to think that the people involved only follow Islamic recommendations, or are totally aware of these recommendations. The communications between the prosecutors, police officers and judges are basic and no explanation about the Islamic prescriptions for legal action is given. When the police (general traffic administration) registered a complaint for *diya* payment against A.B., the driver and M.S., the owner of the car, they did not explain that such compensation was in accordance with Islamic recommendations. The police must follow the law and, since Sudanese law is based on *sharīʿa*, it is implicitly agreed that it is in accordance with Islamic norms. But here, it appears that the request for *diya* compensation is much more a routine, something that is simply "procedure".[7]

At the initial stage, no conciliation is requested. It is up to the judge to try to settle the case in the best way. For Judge K.K., and the same seems to apply to the judge who had previously dealt with the case, conciliation was necessary to resolve the case. And conciliation was possible, because it was an accident and the stipulated amount of compensation (*diya*) was available. But still, no justification for conciliation and blood money was given. In each of his reports, Judge K.K. supported his arguments by referencing articles of the penal code, not Islamic recommendations. Here the judge is without doubt more concerned to demonstrate his ability to judge correctly according to the standards of his profession, the relevant formal constraints, the judicial sources on which it is based and the norms of the interpretative work that it implies, than to emphasize the Islamic legal notion that is in play (Dupret 2011).

Only Judge K.K.'s Arabic adage, *al-ṣulḥ sayyid al-aḥkām*, "conciliation is the most honourable decision" – suggests that, for him, conciliation was a kind of moral principle, a personal ethic that guided his decisions. When I talked to him about that case, he told me that it was important for him to see a victim's family and to hear that they did indeed forgive the car owner and accept the *diya* compensation. But the fact that no one attended, even though they had been asked to come to court, led the judge to think that they did not really

7 In one of his books, the Finnish ethnologist Hilma Grandqvist (1965) describes an extremely interesting case of reconciliation and blood money (*diya*) being replaced by adoption. A man of Hebron whose wives had given him only daughters, married again and, fortunately, had a son. Fifteen years later, some days before his wedding, the son was accidentally run over by a truck. The truck's driver was delivering goods to the son's house for preparations for the wedding party. The driver, who belonged to a small poor clan, and who was afraid of the dead man's powerful agnatic group's vengeance, sought safety with the police. Negotiations took place between the two parties and a *diya* of 330 Jordanian pounds was awarded. When the blood money ceremony had just finished, the dead man's elderly father said to the truck driver: "O my son! I did not have the chance to have a son in this world (to bear my name after me). I lost my only son by the way of fate and destiny. Now you are my son. My son's ransom is yours" (Granqvist 1965, pp. 128–129), and he handed him the blood-money. In this example, the judicial body plays a fundamental role in the reconciliation mechanism, since the police officers gave refuge to the culprit during the negotiations.

want to conciliate and accept the *diya*, or that the victim had been banished or exiled at the time when he had his accident. At this stage, he thought that the best option was to wait a little more. Conciliation and forgiveness sometimes need more time, but, according to the judge, it was the way things should be done.

Contract Security: From a Legal to a Technical Issue

Thinking about this case, I was particularly interested by the issue of property and mortgages. Why did property (land, then cars) have such a central place in this case? In other words, why did the court decide to proceed to the mortgage on properties and not ask for compensation in money that could be held by the KPCTA? I did not receive a satisfactory explanation of this choice from the judge. He just told me that it was the routine, the way that they proceed in the court.

I then thought about an anecdote related by the anthropologist Daniel de Coppet (1992): someone who came from a Pacific island ethnic group saw people in France bringing flowers to sick people in hospital, and to graveyards too, and therefore concluded that flowers were the real currency in France. Flowers were understood as possessing a kind of *mana*, the spiritual power of a social group (Malinowski 1922; Mauss 1925). We may also, in comparison, refer to the works of Stéphane Breton concerning shell money and compensation amongst the Wodani of New-Guinea (1999a, 1999b, 2002). He underlines the holistic dimension of the currency, which appears as part of the social body. This analysis is particularly interesting since it leads us to avoid the "countable" visions of compensation, which forget the symbolic and social dimensions carried by the goods and money circulating between social groups. More than a compensation, blood money is also mainly used to recreate or to weave the link between the groups involved, when considered as part of a larger social group (the same lineage or tribe).[8] But for that to happen, it must be embedded in something that symbolizes the identity of the persons or groups involved, or in a social process, such as ritual (Ben Hounet 2010).

Here, we must also remember that properties are not only goods. They are linked to the identity of the persons and groups to whom they belong. In their

8 On the extension of tribal ties and the changing political dynamics of tribes in Sudan, see Casciarri (2001, 2009).

introduction to *Changing Properties of Property*, Franz von Benda-Beckmann, Keebet von Benda-Beckmann and Melanie G. Wiber (2006, p. 2) emphasize that:

> Property is always multifunctional (…). It is a major factor in constituting the identity of individuals and groups. Through inheritance, it also structures the continuity of such groups. It can have important religious connotations. And it is a vital element in the political organization of society, the legitimate command over wealth being an important source of political power over people and their labour, no matter whether we think of domestic or kinship modes of production, capitalism or communism. Property regimes, in short, cannot easily be captured in one-dimensional political, economic or legal models.

Mortgage on property is thus not only an economic (monetary) or legal measure. It goes far beyond that and it has practical, symbolic and social implications. It binds the car owner to the court and beyond that to the victim's family. A part of his identity, of himself, of his history, is kept and mortgaged by the court. As such, a real contract – something that links people and creates obligations – between him and the victim's family remains possible. It is in a way a contract of security.

From July 2010, almost six years after the accident and the death of the victim, the case became mainly a technical issue. Exchanges and correspondence between the judge and the barrister were about the value of mortgaged goods (land then cars). At the barrister's request, the judge ordered several valuations by sworn experts. Three cars, then two cars were mortgaged. The estimated value of these cars was sufficient to guarantee compensation for the victim's family. As I wrote, on 6 December 2011, the barrister asked for a replacement mortgage on only one car, since the value of this car, estimated at 25,000 SDG (around 4,200 euros) was sufficient to cover the compensation. When I left the judge in March 2012, he was willing to accept the request of M.S. and his barrister.

The value of the mortgaged properties had to be enough to guarantee a possible conciliation between the car owner and the victim's family, but still no compensation in money was requested by the judge or even proposed by the barrister and his client. The main issue was thus to reduce the number of properties that were mortgaged. Unfortunately, I did not have an opportunity to follow the outcome of this thorny case, which had gone on for more than seven years.

Conclusion

The issues that anthropologists deal with when they try to understand the law, mainly concern its practical implementation, its uses and its effects in different social contexts: when, by whom and in what ways is the law mobilized as a reference, argument or justification for conduct? What are the reasons, means and resources used to implement, circumvent, reject or resist the law by the people we encounter in our fieldwork? Property and conflict over property are issues that may become a way to understand law in practice. Ethnographical and legal realism approaches to thorny cases give us the opportunity to study law in action, and above all to analyse how people perceive law and justice. In that sense, law can be observed as a step-by-step construction that results from contextual interactions between the people involved. The case of accidental homicide discussed in this chapter evolved, with time, from a matter of conciliation and compensation to an issue of property and mortgage on property. It led us to question the relationship between property and other aspects of law (criminal law) through the question of compensation (*diya*), to see how a case evolved over time, and to understand the reasoning processes and the interactions of the judges, police officers, the lawyer and his client. I have also discussed the ideas and representations of property: land property first and then car property.

We have also seen the minor role played by Islamic law in this example, even though it does refer to the practice of *diya*. *Diya* and the amount of *diya* is observed here as a routine method of dealing with the case. In all the arguments of the police officers, lawyers and judges, almost no reference to Islam is made except the canonical formulation *bismi Allah ar-Raḥmān ar-Raḥim*. As I have tried to show, the case – still not resolved in 2012, i.e., more than seven years after the accident and the death of the victim – must be understood in relation to the legal, moral, technical and pragmatic constraints that have evolved over time.

References

Ben Hounet, Y 2010, 'La *diya* (prix du sang): Gestion sociale de la violence et logiques sacrificielles en Algérie (Sud- Oranais)', *Annales de la Fondation Fyssen*, vol. 24, pp. 196–215.

Ben Hounet, Y 2012a, '"Cent dromadaires et quelques arrangements": Notes sur la *diya* (prix du sang) et son application actuelle au Soudan et en Algérie', *Revue des Mondes Musulmans et de la Méditerranée*, vol. 131, pp. 203–221.

Ben Hounet, Y 2012b, '"La réconciliation (*sulh*) c'est la base!": À propos des articulations entre cours de justice et instances non officielles de réconciliation (Algérie/Soudan)', *Diogène*, special issue 'Les frontières de la loi: Justice, pouvoirs et politique', vol. 239–240, pp. 210–224.

Ben Hounet, Y 2016, 'Crime, intentionnalité et conciliation en Algérie et au Soudan', *Cahiers d'Anthropologie Sociale*, vol. 13, pp. 78–93.

Bourdieu, P 1980, *Questions de sociologie*, Les Editions de Minuit, Paris.

Breton, S 1999a, 'Death and the Ideology of Compensation among the Wodani, Western Highlands of Irian Jaya', *Social Anthropology*, vol. 7, no. 3, pp. 297–326.

Breton, S 1999b, 'Social Body and Icon of the Person: A Symbolic Analysis of Shell Money among the Wodani, Western Highlands of Irian Jaya', *American Ethnologist*, vol. 26, no. 4, pp. 1–25.

Breton, S 2002, 'Tuer, manger, payer: L'alliance monétaire des Wodani de Papouasie occidentale', *L'Homme*, vol. 162, pp. 197–232.

Casciarri, B 2001, '"La *gabîla* est devenue plus grande": Permanences et évolutions du "modèle tribal" chez les pasteurs Aḥâmda du Soudan arabe', in P Bonte, E Conte & P Dresch (eds), *Emirs et presidents: Figures de la parenté et du politique dans le monde arabe*, CNRS Editions, Paris, pp. 273–299.

Casciarri, B 2009, 'Hommes, troupeaux et capitaux: Le phénomène tribal au Soudan à l'heure de la globalisation', *Etudes Rurales*, no. 184, pp. 47–64.

Casciarri, B 2015, 'Ethnographie des pratiques légales autour de la revendication des droits fonciers chez les groupes pastoraux de l'État de Khartoum', *L'Année du Maghreb*, no. 13, pp. 39–60.

Chelhod, J 1971, *Le droit dans la société bédouine: Recherches ethnologiques sur le 'orf ou droit coutumier des Bédouins*, Marcel Rivière, Paris.

Chelod, J 1986, *Les structures du sacré chez les Arabes*, Maisonneuve et Larose, Paris.

Cunnison, I 1972, 'Blood Money, Vengeance and Joint Responsibility: The Baggara Case', in I Cunnison & W James (eds), *Essays in Sudan Ethnography*, C Hurst, London, pp. 105–125.

Daaïf, L 2006, 'Le prix du sang (*diya*) au premier siècle de l'islam', *Hypothèses*, no. 1, pp. 329–342.

de Coppet, D 1992, 'Introduction', in D de Coppet (ed.), *Understanding Rituals*, Routledge, London/New York, pp. 1–10.

Directorate General of Traffic, 2010, *Annual Statistics Books 1991–2009*, Ministry of Interior, Khartoum.

Dupret, B 2011, 'Introduction: Pertinence et perspectives de la référence anthropologique à la catégorie "droit islamique"', in Y Ben Hounet & B Dupret (eds), *De l'anthropologie du droit musulman à l'anthropologie du droit dans les mondes musulmans*, Les rencontres du Centre Jacques Berque, Rabat, pp. 7–11. http://www.cjb.ma/images/stories/Rencontres_CJB_1.pdf (accessed 30 August 2017).

Dupret, B & Ben Hounet, Y 2014, 'Arbitration [Arbitration] (*ḥukm, taḥkīm, ṣulḥ*)', *The Encyclopaedia of Islam*, 3rd edition, Brill, Leiden, pp. 37–41.

Evans-Pritchard, EE 1940, *The Nuer*, Clarendon Press, Oxford.

Galal, AA & Tayfour, A 2012, 'Characteristics and Prediction of Traffic Accident Casualties in Sudan Using Statistical Modeling and Artificial Neural Networks', *International Journal of Transportation Science and Technology*, vol. 1, no. 4, pp. 305–317.

Gluckman, M 1965, *The Ideas in Barotse Jurisprudence*, Manchester University Press, Manchester.

Granqvist, H 1965, *Muslim Death and Burial*, Societas Scientiarum Fennica, Helsingfors.

Llewellyn, KN & Hoebel, EA 1941, *The Cheyenne Way*, University of Oklahoma Press, Norman OK

Lowie, RH 1921, *Primitive Society*, Routledge & Kegan Paul, London.

Malinowski, B 1922, *Argonauts of the Western Pacific*, Routledge & Kegan Paul, London.

Mauss, M 1925, 'Essai sur le don: Forme et raison de l'échange dans les sociétés archaïques', *Année Sociologique*, vol. 1 (series 2), pp. 30–186.

Moore, SF 1986, *Social Facts and Fabrications: 'Customary Law' on Kilimanjaro, 1880–1980*, Cambridge University Press, Cambridge.

Osman AAM & Ahmed GY, 2014, 'Traffic Injuries: Health Care Services and Clinical Outcome of Victims in Central Hospital, Sudan', *International Journal of Research in Health Sciences*, vol. 2, no. 1, pp. 9–19.

Othman, A 2007, '"And Amicable Settlment Is Best": Sulh and Dispute Resolution in Islamic Law', *Arab Law Quarterly*, no. 21, pp. 64–90.

Peters, R 2005, *Crime and Punishment in Islamic Law: Theory and Practice from the Sixteenth to the Twenty-first Century*, Cambridge University Press, Cambridge.

Pirie, F 2013, *The Anthropology of Law*, Oxford University Press, Oxford.

Radcliffe-Brown, AR 1952, *Structure and Function in Primitive Society*, Cohen & West, London.

Schlee, G 2002, 'Régularités dans le chaos: Traits récurrents dans l'organisation politico-religieuse et militaire des Somali', *L'Homme*, vol. 161, pp. 17–50.

Tyan, E 1965, 'Diya', *Encyclopédie de l'Islam* (Tome II), Brill/Maisonneuve & Larose, Leiden/Paris, pp. 350–352.

von Benda-Beckmann, F, von Benda-Beckmann, B & Wiber, WG 2006, 'Properties of Property', in *Changing Properties of Property*, Berghahn, New York/Oxford, pp. 1–39.

CHAPTER 9

Customary Courts: Between Accommodating and Countering the Hegemony of the Laws of the State: The Case of Mayo

Azza A. Abdel Aziz

Introduction

The focus of this chapter is driven by a concern with how the state instrumentalizes cultural templates, transforming them into artefacts. In this specific instance, based on an examination of ethnographic data, I take the continued presence of Southern Sudanese customary courts as an example that illustrates how consent is manufactured through the effective instatement of hegemony. Following Gramsci, in this context hegemony is to be taken as the form of the exercise of power that entails a "combination of force and consent" (Gramsci 2007, p. 1638). According to him the first step in establishing power lies in attaining moral and intellectual consent, which is then consolidated by later dominance through the state coercive apparatus (Gramsci 2007, pp. 2010–2011).

This chapter suggests that this reading of hegemony and its ordering[1] is recast by the circumstances that accompanied the advent of the National Salvation Revolution (Ingaz) at the juncture of its coming to power. There was no initial phase of cajoling citizens to accept the terms of the Islamist revolution, and concrete forceful measures were taken against all those who expressed their disdain (Simone 1994, pp. 65–70). Simultaneously, to attenuate the possible wrath of a city that was a crucible of discontent, and to placate

1 This vein is adopted by Musso (2015), when he elaborates the genesis of the Islamist movement in Sudan. He demonstrates how it was initially in the 1960s "an intellectual and student's movement" that, due to the efforts of its founder Hassan al-Turabi became a fully-fledged independent political party (p. 246) with wide appeal as a cross cutting movement transcending the traditional political dominance of northern riverine groups (p. 248). Through the stages of its development the Islamist movement (National Islamic Front) targeted a hegemonic vision of "moral leadership of society ... to be achieved through the spread of 'a high Islam' as opposed to the traditional 'popular Islam' of Sudan" (p. 250).

 | DOI 10.1163/9789004362185_011

many of its inhabitants, repressive measures were tempered with some concessions. Paradoxically, this instance of the "manufacture of consent", represented by allowing room for customary practices, existed in tandem with other avenues of political control based on coercion and force.

This constituted a strategy that consolidated itself by delving into and deploying a "Sudanese heritage or past" based on indigenous custom that would eventually become represented by the epistemological framework of Native Administration. In 2003, to anchor consent, the Sudanese state, embodied by the NCP, had reinstated a system or something akin to Native Administration[2] by allowing traditional modes of authority a presence in Khartoum. In doing so it deployed "strategies" that concur with the definition offered by de Certeau (1984, pp. 34–39) as the observable power relations that exist within institutional settings and which inform the manoeuvrings of the strong. They undercut another dimension of lesser power, that is not entirely ineffective in countering the afore-mentioned form of power, and which characterizes the behaviour of weaker members of society in the shape of what de Certeau classifies as "tactics".

In this chapter, I underscore the dialectic between strategic aspects and tactics, embodied in the existence of customary courts and their use, the attitudes they elicit, the social networks they expose and how they are deployed by the inhabitants of a specific zone of displacement, namely Mayo, within the capital city of Khartoum.

In attaining this objective through ethnographic analysis, I first introduce how the exercise of power in Khartoum serves as an essential backdrop to what occurs and exists in zones of displacement. I then proceed to give a snapshot of my area of fieldwork and situate it within the structures of power that are being used within it. In the second part, I elaborate the markings of Native Administration in Sudan and place it alongside its contemporary manifestation in order to finally explore the dynamics of the courts in Mayo, and link their presence to the temporal circumstances that accompany them.

2 According to Manfredi (2015, p. 288) the Native Administration system was reintroduced in the Nuba Mountains in 1995 in conjunction with a wide state policy. In Khartoum, the existence of a "native system" is addressed by Abdul-Jalil (2015). Assal (2011, p. 68) refers to the emergence of sultans and local courts with jurisdiction over communities of Southern Sudanese recognized by the authorities as "new forms of native administration".

Contextualization of IDPs Camps

A Controversial Demographic Manifestation

The massive influx of IDPs into Khartoum[3] gained momentum from the 1980s onwards and was characterized by two significant displacement patterns into the city. The first was due to the drought/famine that struck western Sudan during 1984–1985 (Bannaga 2002, p. 85; Eltigani 1995; African Rights 1995, p. 10), and the second, the subject of this chapter, involved the displacement of diverse groups from Southern Sudan fleeing the second civil war, which started in 1983 (Abdalla 2014; Assal 2002, 2006, 2008, 2011; Pérouse de Montclos 2001). This latter forced migration reached its height during the mid-1990s due to the increase in hostilities between the central government and the SPLA/M.

In response, the government took measures to regulate the uncontrolled expansion of Khartoum (Bannaga 2002; de Geoffroy 2009a, 2009b, 2014, 2015; Lavergne 1997). Part of this process involved the creation of four official camps starting from 1990: Mayo Farm, Wad al Beshir, Jebel Awlia and Omdurman as-Salam[4] (Bannaga 2002, p. 94), in addition to the squatter areas already inhabited by IDPs (Jacobsen 2008).

I specifically engaged with the area of Mayo, located approximately 18km south of the city centre of Khartoum. My first forays into this space date from the salient period of time between 2003 and 2005, when the historical peace deal, enshrined in the CPA, was signed between the government of Sudan and the SPLA/M. My engagement with this space was mainly through the eyes and experiences of diverse groups of southern IDPs who inhabited it. It exist to the present day and covers the ethnographic scope of a space that is in flux due to the status of the Southerners who inhabit it.

Within the space of eight years, Southerners had ceased to become citizens – albeit marginalized in the landscape of Khartoum – and since the separation of the South on 9 July 2011 they have had an ambiguous status (Abdel Aziz 2013, pp. 322–326). They were no longer southern Sudanese but South Sudanese,

3 According to Pérouse de Montclos (2001, p. 7), figures for the Khartoum displaced are debatable because of political expediency. De Geoffroy notes the difficulty of obtaining exact figures and places the number of Southerners at either 1.1 million (2009a, p. 517) or 1.5 million (2009b, p. 6). It has been highlighted that the numbers of Southerners had risen from 6% of the population in 1955 to 17 % in 1993 (Davies 1999, p. 44) and before the signing of the CPA in 2005 they were cited as forming a third of the population of Khartoum (Fouad 1991, p. 13; Motasim 2008, p. 13).

4 Mayo al Mazari (Mayo Farm/Mandela) was established on 30 June 1991 and Wad al Bashir was also established that year (Abdalla 2014, pp. 45–47); Omdurman as Salam was founded February 1992 (Assal 2011, p. 66).

not refugees but arrivals (*wāfidīn*), for those who had left and come back, and brothers and sisters, for those who never left and were stuck in new makeshift (camps) within the very marginal spaces of Khartoum that they had, for about 20 years, managed to appropriate and tame[5] to some extent.

Space in the Service of Power

The bulk of the ethnography in this chapter covers a temporal segment – 2003–2005 – within the life line of the Islamist regime that has held power in Sudan since 30 June 1989 following a military coup named the Revolution of National Salvation (*thawrat al-inqādh al-waṭanī*) masterminded by the National Islamic Front (later dissolved leaving room for the political domination of the NCP). The initial stages of this revolution saw power in the hands of the military under Brigadier Omar al-Bashir. However, this was eventually to lead to the appearance of Hassan al-Turabi, leader of the National Islamic Front in 1993. A split was to occur between Turabi and Bashir in 1999, with the former creating his own PCP. The focus of this chapter covers the period when Bashir held the upper hand as leader of the NCP.

In the early years of the Ingaz, repression was the order of the day and all political dissent was silenced (through "ghost houses" run by security forces, the "disappearance" of citizens, and the imprisonment of political opponents). These measures affected all political opponents, even those hailing from the north who exhibited more secular dispositions (Abusharaf 2009, p. 36). The combination of a revolutionary process modifying state institutions and social structures with great force (Marchal 1995, 2015, p. 321; Musso 2015, p. 252) and the implementation of an Islamic ethos (the Civilizational Project, *al-mashrūʿ al-ḥaḍarī*) on the fabric of the city was to modify its shape and the practices that were sanctified within it, framing it "as a city to be remade" (Simone 1994, p. 137). This process particularly impinged on the lifestyles of many Southerners, so that the dominant polarization of Muslim versus non-Muslim became irrelevant in the case of Southerners – who were increasingly present in the city[6] and who continued to hold cultural identifications that were

5 See Abusharaf (2009, p. 26) for a similar observation that IDPs, while confronted with difficulties in relation to their rights to freely inhabit certain parts of the city, still managed after years of displacement to finally feel at home in Khartoum.

6 Extensions of the Civilizational Project are represented by the introduction to the 1991 Sudan Penal Code, which later developed as the law of public order (*al-niẓām al-ʿāmm*) for Khartoum State in 1996. This law curtailed women's freedom to wear clothing considered un-Islamic, put an 11pm time limit on wedding parties, and prohibited the consumption and brewing of alcohol. It is characterized by a rigid gender policy that renders women

irreconciliable with the afore mentioned project close – since it is ethnographically important not to conflate Southerners' Islam with their trying to become Arabized or with their relinquishing all vestiges of their cultural mores.

However, the state was eventually, after the split within the movement in 1999 that set Turabi and Bashir in opposition to each other – to relent out of pragmatic concerns to ensure its longevity in the face of mounting pressure to maintain its power (Musso 2015, p. 258). The discourse and praxis of the Civilizational Project were relaxed to the advantage of a worldlier wider process of liberalization and enrichment tied to the advent of oil (Mann 2011, 2014), which was to affect the Khartoumian landscape. It impacted interest in land/space as a resource (Choplin and Franck 2010; Franck 2015) and ultimately fed into re-planning ventures related to investment potential (Denis 2006, p. 113).

These processes tie in with the observation that the Islamists were in any case only interested in standing against the occupation of certain spaces by populations (marginalized ethnicities through the course of history) perceived as threatening by controlling their rights to the city (de Geoffroy 2014, p. 259). From this perspective, such spaces were designated the "Black Belt of Khartoum", a term coined by the philosopher of the regime Hassan Makki (El-Tom 2009, p. 98), and worthy of pause (El-Bushra and Hijazi 1995, p. 508; Khalid 2003, p. 613) as a phrase that exacerbates identity problems in Sudan, contributing to their racist overtones and accounting for how they are transposed onto urban policy. Urban policy was guided by security concerns (de Geoffroy 2015, p. 202; Abdul-Jalil 2015, p. 228) and exploited valid public health issues (Abdalla 2008; Bannaga 1992, pp. 4, 41, 2002, pp. 40–41) to justify the removal of IDPs from the squatter settlements that they had appropriated. Spaces that were left undisturbed were not at that stage considered to have attractive investment potential (Simone 1994, quoted in Abusharaf 2009, ch.1 fn. 11).

At their inception, squatter areas and camps inhabited by IDPs were a new development in the cityscape of Khartoum. These peripheral areas and camps now constitute an integral feature of the city. Through their presence, Khartoum speaks loudly to the distinction between space and place. I highlight this crucial dialectic by drawing on the elaborations of de Certeau (1984, p. 117). According to him, the difference between place and space lies in the fact that the former is constituted by "elements that are distributed in relationships of coexistence". This suggests that no two things can be in the same place (they

---

particularly more vulnerable to the law (Abdalla 2008, p. 108) and is a bone of contention for those of minority religious status (Christians and followers of "noble spiritual beliefs" [*karīm al-muʿtaqadāt*]).

stand alongside each other) and each element becomes constitutive of a place and defines it: here there is an indication of stability. In contrast, space exists through the intersections of elements that are not fixed: it is determined by operations and acts situated within time and modified through it and through successive contexts. For the purposes of my analysis this theoretical framework is useful in establishing that space is less certain than place and hence, I suggest, more sensitively connected with actions including those of domination.

For example, the interaction with space is problematized in Lefebvre's formulation of the *domination* of space through private property, the state and forms of class and social power and the *appropriation* of space for individual and social purposes (Lefebvre 1974, p. 471) within focal points of the urban landscape. Neither option is applicable to spaces occupied by Southern IDPs, who, by occupying peripheral zones of the city (given their poverty), are confronted mainly with social relationships based on *distanciation*, framed by Giddens (1984, pp. 258–259) as the degree to which the friction of space has been overcome to accommodate social interaction: and which in human affairs involves the production and reproduction of the social order (labour, trade and social differentiation). From this perspective, the occupation of space does not involve IDPs, who are framed as superfluous to the smooth running of the city.[7]

The Case Study: Mayo

Mayo as a Subject of Power: Different Spaces, Different Places

According to my own findings between 2003 and 2005, the area of Mayo was widely populated by Southern IDPs, within Greater Khartoum. Various groups of Southerners predominantly resided in the blocks in Mayo quarter (*ḥilla*), near the Catholic Church (Ḥay al-Janūbiyyīn, "quarter of the Southerners") and within the camps (Mayo Farm and Mandela).[8] The area of Ḥay al-Janūbiyyīn

7 For Khartoum, Denis explains that the removal of squatters from the centre of the city was motivated by the desire to maintain property values in a metropolitan economy (2005, p. 23). Simone (1994, p. 40) justifies this removal as stemming from the potential of the urban poor to create an undesirable informal economy amid a devastated official economy.

8 To a lesser degree, they inhabited the area of Angola within Mayo quarter, which was predominantly inhabited by Ingessana and Nuba. This area was less planned than other areas in the vicinity and formed an isolated island of poverty within a wider circle of misery. I was warned of the danger of the place and told by Southerners that their fellow Southerners who frequented it were those who were prone to excessive drinking. It was clear from the number of young children roaming the extremely narrow streets and the adobes made of jute sacks that the services of the state and NGOs were remote.

hosted diverse ethnic groups from the South but the majority of those espousing one of the monotheistic religions were Christians: significantly, this only nominally reinforced the sense of unity/community[9] among the different ethnic groups from Southern Sudan in the area, since it was mainly constructed in the face of the onslaught by the state, rather than on the basis of any cleavage between them and Muslim Southerners.[10] In fact, I noted that most Southerners in Mayo predominantly self-identified as the "Black people of Sudan" (*nās as-sūd*), irrespective of religious affiliation, reinforcing the boundary between them and the "Arabs" of Sudan.[11]

In contrast to the afore-mentioned ethnic plurality, the population in the camps was predominantly Dinka. The area was notably occupied by Dinka Aweil (Northern Bahr El Ghazal), Dinka Malwal and Dinka Pariang. Dinka Bor were not numerous in the area although they were very famous and widely referred to within the location because adherence to Garang (the iconic leader of the SPLA/M) belonged to this clan. Other Nilotics (Nuer and Shilluk) were sparsely represented in the camp and the wider area of Mayo, while Equatorian Southerners were widely distributed outside the camp in the wider area of Mayo.

The wider area of Mayo was thus divided into two distinct segments: Mayo quarter and the camp(s). The area as a whole had a bad reputation, but the two camps Mandela and Mayo Farm were particularly singled out. I observed that Mandela was not subject to the same surveillance as Mayo quarter: it was quite usual to witness both men and women openly drunk on its narrow labyrinthine streets, and to see women ambling in the public eye scantily clad in their under garments, whereas Mayo quarter was increasingly subject to the terms

9 I use both terms in tandem to reflect how identity is situational and malleable in this site. Unity was evoked through alliances that were formed strategically between diverse social groups, but community was largely defined in ethnic terms, except when it was mobilized to distinguish Southerners from Northerners.

10 According to the research conducted by Abdalla (2014), the difference between Christians and Muslims is amplified by the state and its religious organizations in order to proselytize Christians (pp. 55–56). To demystify the existence of an essential cleavage or social distance between Southerners on the basis of religious affiliation, see Abdalla (2014, pp. 60–62).

11 The government was the embodiment of this "Arabness", which is the subject of much debate but remains a strong anthropological determinant as a self-identification that was accepted through time in everyday interaction between them and others. For this reason, Southerners who occupied positions of authority (chiefs and popular committee representatives) were skating on thin ice. Those who found themselves in such positions had to justify this convincingly, pledging that they remained faithful to their identities as Southerners and non-Arabs.

and values of wider Khartoum and its assimilative processes. The salience of this observation was underscored through conversations with two Southern informants who resided outside the camps but still within Mayo quarter, who agreed: "People move out of Mayo and into the camps in order to avoid the watchful eye of authority and to benefit from lower rents ... previously 90% of Mandela used to live in Mayo quarter".

The distinction between the two areas was also evident in variations in architecture. For instance, most of the blocks in Mayo district were composed of rectangular houses constructed with *jalūs* (dried mud mixed with dung). They housed courtyards within which rooms were dispersed as separate blocks. This kind of construction emulated that which is widespread in the arid central regions of Sudan, where there is a limited level of rainfall. In contrast, the camp had adopted an architectural style adapted to the heavy and frequent rainfall of southern Sudan, proving that populations there were still tethered to the "imagined" landscape of South Sudan. The difference between the two zones was stark, although inhabitants of the camps and those outside may be the same people, sharing the same concerns and daily struggles, and the areas are only separated by a road. The difference between the two zones is due to the fact that the camp was constructed on un-plotted land, allocated by the government to temporarily host IDPs who might be arbitrarily relocated at any time, whereas the area classified as non-camp (already divided into *muraba'āt* or "blocks") might potentially be allocated to its inhabitants, who were also more likely to get services and electricity delivered to them (the first blocks of Mayo had electricity poles in 2005 and water pipes, admittedly of inferior quality and liable to burst, were installed by 2006).

Perhaps the most poignant marker of the difference between the camp and the space outside it was the signification that certain structures came to convey. The numerical prevalence of churches over mosques was a significant feature of the camp: twenty churches representing various Christian denominations compared with only one mosque. This observation was made salient by the fact that the number of mosques outside the camp quickly redressed the balance. Conversely, the distribution of schools seemed to be more even between schools run by the church and those supported by Islamic organizations.[12]

The presence of these churches does not suggest heightened or more prolific religious observance within the camp than outside: on the contrary, the

12 Examples of schools: Rahma and Da'wa (Islamic) and Comboni, school of the Sudan Council of Churches and St. Philip (Christian). These schools follow the state curriculum but ideological undercurrents animate their pedagogies. Ironically, most children living in the camp cannot afford to go to any of these schools.

camp was a zone of rampant vice, as the state declared. Rather, the abundance of churches was indicative of the polarization of Southern Christian identity as opposed to Muslim state identity. The abundance of Christian edifices revealed that the state excluded the camp from its sphere of activity, thus condemning it to peripherality. In reality, these physical monuments testified to the deliberate isolation of IDPs living in the camps. These observable etchings on the landscape reiterate the salience of the creation of "places" to be easily assimilated and inhabited by certain types of citizens, and that of such "spaces" evoked above and subject to domination and inhabited by those who would be either ignored or manipulated at will.

Camps as Significant Spaces

The camp lying at the southern extremity of Mayo quarter was made up of five subdivisions and hosted a population of approximately 42,000 people.[13] The zone of the camp (or two camps) officially went by the name of Mayo al-Mazāriʿ (Mayo Farm) but was widely known as Mandela by the inhabitants of the area, since the two camps were virtually indistinguishable and formed a single space. Mayo Farm was designated at the administrative level but nobody at the local level recognized this distinction: thus, the delimitations of areas as camp and non-camp were purely administrative. This competing naming between the government authorities and the local population[14] shakes the conceptualization of the camp as a controlled space of containment that holds at bay those considered superfluous (Agier 2014). It undermines the notion of the camp as a place that is almost impenetrable to the outside world that extends beyond that of humanitarian actors and aid organizations

13 Information compiled courtesy of Michael Banja from local chiefs' lists prepared and written by themselves.

14 Mayo itself is, according to the name given by the Islamist government in 1992, Medīnat al-Nasr (Victory City), but this name has not been retained by the local population. For examples of renaming the camps as a form of resistance and the recreation of such space through the naming of sites (de Certeau 1984), it suffices to give some examples of squatter areas around Greater Khartoum: Zagalona ("They shoved us"), Ras al-Shayṭān ("Devil's head") in Omdurman West, Hillat Kusha ("Rubbish quarter") Hillat Shouk ("Thorn quarter") in Khartoum North. Motasim (2008, p. 18) cites a *temporary settlement* [my italics] in Mayo established in 2005 known as Hillat Silik ("Barricades quarter") hosting those who had been evicted from the nearby area of Al Salama; it was enclosed by wire fencing and known locally as Abu Ghreb in sardonic reference to a perceived similarity to the notorious Iraqi prison. De Geoffroy (2015, p. 211), Abu Sharaf (2009, p. 47) and Assal (2008, p. 148, 2011, p. 66) all allude to Al Salam camp being known by the name Jabarona ("We were forced") by displaced populations themselves.

(Kelly 2007). It equally highlights how, from an impersonal "non-place" devoid of historical significance (Augé 1995) it has become yet another form of "place" endowed with historical and relational attributes (*ibid.*, p. 69), informed by the lives of those who inhabit it and their interactions with a wider society, which informed the specificities of the world of Mayo as well as its own position within it.

The whole area of Mayo was the site of interesting interactions between IDPs and various stakeholders within Khartoum who were trying to make their lives in Khartoum more satisfactory. Many people in the area were obliged to rely on NGOs and the sluggish initiatives of the state to realize such ends. These structures included support by NGOs within the whole zone, and I was privy to the activities of FAR, which organized the construction of toilets within some households throughout Mayo. The toilets were pit latrines with a cement border constructed by individual house owners. The same endeavour existed within Mandela camp, where the government had restricted its infrastructural development to digging water wells. The inhabitants of the area were left with the responsibility of digging pit latrines (no sewage or pipes existed in Mayo) for communal use, as part of a project organized by CARE International.

The efforts by international NGOs ensured that participants received "food for work" and aimed at the local population taking sanitation and hygiene into its own hands. Such projects were primarily aimed at empowering the inhabitants and instilling a work ethic to help them transcend the status of vulnerable IDPs. Accordingly, they were considered a progression from the early days of displacement, when they were entirely dependent on relief (Duffield 2001, pp. 202–254).

In addition, these interventions were accompanied by the involvement of religious bodies on the landscape of Mayo. I was aware of *daʿwa* (proselytism) activity through my contact with Southerners active in the *mustashīriyyāt al-islām li-l-tanmiya wa al-wiḥda* (Islamic Council for Development and Unity) organization. The Peace Commission in Mayo exclusively employed Southerners working as part of Islamic *daʿwa*.

The religiosity of Southern Christians was supported by the efforts of Christian bodies. The Jesuit Seminary of Kober (Khartoum North), for example, maintained eight centres in Mayo.[15] The church also mediated in the proceedings of the peace and justice court located in the cited centres. The maternity hospital of Villa Jilda (run by Italian nuns in Shāriʿ al-Ḥurriyya, Central Khartoum) provided free maternity care for Southern women and the Mary

15 The main churches located in Farig Fur, Ingaz, Yarmuk, Mandela, Wihḍa and Dar El Naim held meetings once a week to discuss solidarity and fund raising.

Joseph Carpentry School run by Sabah Ponticipal (Industrial zone Khartoum 3) offered training schemes for young Southerners living in Khartoum.

Despite all this presence, it was noteworthy that, within the wider space of Mayo, the camps were clearly overwhelmingly ignored by the state. It was evident that the camp area, like the other three camps around Greater Khartoum, was subject to more prolific support offered by international NGOs, church organizations and Islamic relief groups (Bannaga 2002, p. 104; de Geoffroy 2014, p. 263).[16]

However, by the time I visited the area, the activities and efforts of organizations had become significantly reduced and remained so. This reduced presence of organizations working to aid IDPs is documented in the literature: Assal (2008, p. 144) notes that "since the start of the peace process in 2002, NGOs have scaled down their interventions in IDP camps in Khartoum".

The significance of this statement is amplified by the findings of de Geoffroy (2014, pp. 264–265), who affirms that, from 2002, organized returns were arranged for Southerners: she suggests that such potential returns were nonetheless connected with attachments to land in Khartoum as a security measure in the face of uncertain return. These factors would ultimately influence the presence of international organizations within these spaces.

My own observations, for instance, would indicate that, in 2003, MSF had been based in Mandela camp for slightly over ten years. Its initial involvement covered a wide scope of medical services.[17] However, I found that this health care facility, set up in 1993 and by 2003 renamed the TFC (Therapeutic Feeding Centre) was at the time largely specialized in child malnutrition (with a reduced focus on tuberculosis as an accompanying complication).[18]

Such closures might appear to imply that the IDP crisis in Khartoum was finally under control. They seemed to tally with the directives that stipulated that the nature of the aid that was available to Sudan from the international community should be emergency aid and could not be directed towards development goals (Loveless 1999, p. 10). The closures also seemed to correlate with the fact that, at that time, the peace process was well underway: international

16 For specifics on Islamic organizations in the camps in Khartoum, see Bellion-Jourdan (1997).

17 A few clinics had been established in Khartoum within zones of displacement by MSF, starting in 1993, but all but one of them, located in Mandela, had been closed by 1999.

18 When I approached the MSF headquarters in November 2003, I was informed that plans to close the clinic in early 2005 were already in motion. MSF was looking for a local NGO to take over the premises and continue the work. This eventually took place in January 2005. The clinic was handed over to a local NGO, Al-Manār.

NGOs, the UN and the European Commission all seemed to be concerned with a different discourse, and the transition of the sufferers of war from "internally displaced" to "returnees".

Native Courts as Pawns

Introducing Courts into the Dynamics of Life in Displacement

Between 2003 and 2005, the courts that existed in Mayo were within Mandela camp and therefore serve to embody the dynamic nature of interactions between IDPs and the structures of power that shroud their lives.

Delineating the structure of the camp is necessary for an understanding of the position of courts within them. The subdivision lying to the north-east was called South Kordofan and was largely populated by Nuba and Shilluk. The subdivision lying to the north-west was called Bahr El Ghazal and was mostly populated by Dinka from Bahr El Ghazal. The TFC lies on the border of these two subdivisions. West of Bahr El Ghazal subdivision lies the most dangerous area within Mandela camp, with prostitution, theft and friction with the police forces taking place in broad daylight. I personally saw brothels, directly behind the TFC, which were pointed out to me by members of the MSF staff. South of the TFC lay the main market, the principal Dinka court house and a mosque.

Towards the east and south of the South Kordofan subdivision, fell the Upper Nile subdivision, which was widely populated by Shilluk, Nuer and Dinka Panuru. In the west, south of Bahr El Ghazal subdivision, lived Equatorian ethnic groups: Nuba Nyemang, Muru, Pojulo, Latoka, Acholi, Azande and Madi. On the southern horizon lay the subdivision of Altabara, largely populated by Shilluk, Baggara, Nuba and Fellata. Within this area lay a big market known as Souk Alfain (established in 2000). There were ten locally recognized chiefs within the camp: Dinka Bentui, Dinka Aweil, Dinka Gogrial, Dinka Garr, Dinka Bahr El Ghazal, Nuer, Shilluk, Nuba, Equatoria. Each chief had sub-chiefs (Rahem 2003).

Notwithstanding this ethnic diversity, most inhabitants of the camp hailed from the Nilotic Dinka ethnic group. In addition, while a great ethnic diversity animated the camp, people were largely settled along ethnic lines within their spaces of habitation. Equatorian ethnic groups such as Muru, Latoka, Azande and Madi were represented by a single chief while the various Dinka clans each had a particular chief, each running his own court house. The number of Dinka court houses in Mandela amounted to 36.

Native Courts as Sites of Control

One needs to pause at the question of why, despite its control of space in Khartoum, the state allowed these courts to function in the camp. I suggest that, through the manipulation of power through the medium of space, it allowed leeway for the proliferation of certain modalities of practice that were more strictly curtailed in more visible parts of the urban landscape. For example, in Mayo I was to bear witness to the fact that the security forces were not always consistent in carrying out punitive measures against the production and consumption of alcohol. In addition, rituals (religious and curative) were allowed according to their classification as *ʿādāt wa taqālīd* (customs).[19]

This was not a validation of cultural rights, but rather spoke to the fact that some spaces were deliberately rendered invisible by the state: they signified places where northern cultural signifiers need not go and were well represented by stigmatized places in the popular consciousness, as in Mayo. Therefore, practices associated with them need not be disturbed unless they spread and moved to another place. In this way the government played its role in allowing a space to allay the resentments of its marginalized populations within the landscape of Khartoum.

The fact that the government allowed native courts was just another step in this direction. From this perspective, the existence of traditional courts presided over by local leaders (*sulṭān*, title in Khartoum for chiefs or sheikhs) decentralized power and allowed members of society an opportunity to self-rule and resolve local disputes (Bakhit 2013, p. 10). In the eyes of officials, this was considered an achievement. For example, Bannaga (2002), a well-known Islamist and at some stage minister of urban planning, writes about the state of affairs prevailing in the camps of Khartoum in the following terms:

19 The different treatment reserved for rituals is noteworthy. For instance, *zār* ceremonies which serve to placate a spirit (also known as *zār*; a distinct species of the invisible creatures known in the Islamic worldview as djinn) capable of possessing human beings and making them ill. Through the performance of such ceremonies, the afflicted accommodate these spirits so that they do not disturb them. *Zār* exists in two variants *zār boré* and *tumbura*. *Boré*, previously widespread in Khartoum and northern Sudan and associated with northern Sudanese women's practices (Boddy 1989; Constantinides 1972, 1979), was prohibited in the capital by the Islamist government from 1989, while *tumbura* – associated with populations of slave descent (Al Safi 1990; Al Safi and Makris 1990; Makris 2000), which I observed in Mayo, was ignored alongside existing engagements with ancestral spirits (*kujur*).

> To settle bickering among the displaced, it is deemed appropriate to organize the displaced communities into native administrative units, presided over by the chief of the native administrators, i.e. Sultans, Omdah and Sheikhs who have come with their tribes ... Consequently the HAC has established a specialized administration, which is "the camp and sultan affairs administration" to deal with the affairs of the displaced. The sultans who are entrusted with the administration are paid monthly salaries for fulfilling these tasks. The sultans are vested with judiciary powers and preside over native courts, which apply native and prevailing customary laws to settle disputes. These tribal communities have now acquired a basis for rules and social criteria, which is observed, resulting in the pervasion of peace and tranquillity throughout the camps of the displaced.
>
> BANNAGA 2002, P. 104

In typical fashion these laudatory terms were working to occlude the connection of this form of power (customary) with other forms that could be framed as either oppressive or exhibiting a superior balance of power. In reality, the existence of these court houses was imbricated with different manifestations of power operating within the landscape of Khartoum and within this specific zone of displacement. These were namely the NGO sector (elaborated above as needs-based rather than rights-based), an evocation of Native Administration that in fact, in the contemporary context, constitutes a form of urban governance and control (Abdul-Jalil 2015), and the presence of popular committees (*lajna sha'biyya*), which represented the state interaction with IDPs, among whom property rights were significant.

While this interconnection is admitted to by the official discourse of the state, it is idealized and its surveillance connotation neutered: once again this position is well illustrated by Bannaga (2000, p. 84), who says that, on the local level of controlling camps from the legal perspective, judiciary partnerships and civil judges serve as chair persons to release tension within local committees with support from local leaders and heads of tribes; according to him, this consolidates the creation of local governance in a decentralized manner. This, form of language, contained in Bannaga's writings represents the official line of the state and works to suggest a form of agency, available to IDPs, that needs to be tempered.

This has indeed been achieved by the efforts of multiple scholars who have highlighted the instrumentalization of the presence of indigenous structures. Based on his fieldwork observations in Mayo itself, Simone (1994, p. 121) asserts: "What indigenous institutions exist in Mayo are provisional arrangements designed to survey all those who enter or leave." Abdul-Jalil (2015, p. 230) discusses how Native Administration is applied, within al-Ḥilla al-Jadida (previously notorious in reputation and known as Ras al-Shayṭān located on the western outskirts of Omdurman, west of Dar as-Salam neighbourhood, west of Jabarona) as a "form of local governance based on tribes and ethnic groups as social units" (*ibid.*, pp. 223–224, 228). In this instance, the promotion of tribal leadership becomes "a component of political and security administration in Greater Khartoum", aiming to contribute to the Islamization of public life. This form of leadership in the shape of the "Native System" highlights the necessity for control of squatter areas and becomes "a mechanism for the social control of migrants coming from rural areas to Khartoum" (*ibid.*, p. 231).

Such measures are reminiscent of Native Administration (a Sudanese version of indirect rule) established by the British colonial system (Abusharaf 2009, p. 161 fn 3)[20] and abolished by President Nemeiri in 1970, only to be re-established in 1995 as the Native System in Khartoum (Abdul-Jalil 2015, p. 226), as well as within rural parts of the country (Casciarri 2009; Delmet 2005). Furthermore, the control of marginal spaces through the workings of popular committees, who as representatives of local communities manage local affairs, has been highlighted through field studies conducted by de Geoffroy (2015, p. 202). She says: "Political, security and social control relies on several means: the creation of popular committees (*lajna shaʿbīa*), which are the basic units of political representation …, and which often become a means of control for the party in power."[21]

Bakhit (2013, pp. 12–15) also highlights the tensions that he observed, in the shantytown of al-Baraka (previously Kartun Kassala) located in south-east Khartoum, between the popular committee (responsible for the planning of the area and service provision such as water and electricity) representing middle-class affiliations, and representatives of the native courts, whose leaders saw their contributions weakened and limited to intervening in personal matters, and even then only at the behest of the local community.

---

20 See Abusharaf (2009, pp. 48 and 161) on the existence of what she terms "informal tribunals/ tribal courts" in Khartoum, where sultans mediated conflicts. According to stories she was told, they were established by the Nuer military officer Paulino Mateep and approved by the government. They were perceived by many not as sites of redress and restoration, but rather as directed towards group revenge, and viewed with trepidation by many northerners. Thus, the setting up of these courts served to ostracize Southerners even further.

21 For more on the control of marginal spaces through popular committees, see de Geoffroy (2014, p. 264). Musso clarifies that such committees were inspired by the Libyan Jamahiriya model, serving as cells for grassroots political mobilization and providing some social services (2015, p. 253).

Beyond concerns with the control of marginal spaces, the absence of the state and its abandonment of its responsibilities towards vulnerable members of society (Bakhit 2013, p. 9) is another salient point, ethnographically illustrated by the research conducted by Nègre (2005). This research explores how the state – while implementing a policy that encourages local governance and the emergence of diverse actors such as civil society and NGOs in providing access to domestic water and its management – simultaneously appropriates and co-opts these efforts by holding back official recognition.

He cites the example of the collaboration, in Wad Al Bashir camp, Omdurman, between a French NGO (Action Contre la Faim) and popular committees in the area. Once the NGO has dug a well, it passes the responsibility of managing water for profit to the local committees, which in turn are subject to the structures of the state that choose the representatives within such committees. In this context, Nègre convincingly shows how the state opportunistically delegates its responsibilities to other stakeholders. He describes how this process is all the while informed by a concession to the local community to exercise its autonomy, which is paradoxically always subject to temporal adjustments (Nègre 2005, p. 39) and the state's intention to appropriate these efforts and hence to apply its hegemony.

I suggest that the same logic applies for the permissibility of the activities of customary courts in Mayo. Hence the existence of native courts in Khartoum needs to be problematized, since it constitutes a form of governmentality à la Foucault (1991), that is a salient marker of an "art of government" comprised of a range of control techniques that extend beyond top-down manifestations of the state, include forms of social control (in schools, hospitals, psychiatric institutions) and which encompasses the validation of certain forms of knowledge. I underscore the distinctiveness of courts as necessary to control to frame them as another bracketed domain of knowledge. I suggest that the permissibility of customary courts in Mayo was integral to this process, but that it was equally part of the efforts of the Islamist government in Khartoum to extend a tentacle of power throughout the urban landscape.

The Versatile Existence of Court Houses in Mandela/Mayo

The existence of customary courts in Mayo as embodying the tenets of customary law came about through the deployment of structures that had existed historically. The position of customary law in Sudan and the evolution of its status were the subject and fruit of the workings of Native Administration. This had gradually but significantly appeared on the route towards the creation of Sudan as a modern state: transitions from different states, Turko-Egyptian occupation (1821–1885), the reign of the Mahdiyya (1885–1898), to finally culminate in the modes of governance used by the Anglo-Egyptian Condominium (1898–1956, with Britain as the dominant partner), embodied in its use of Native Administration (Abdul-Jalil 2015, p. 223; Willis 2011, p. 54) and which we see revitalized and recycled by the NCP to great effect since 1995.

The spirit of allowing the deployment of cultural signifiers within the spirit of the law – without the negative connotations of the colonial manipulation of customs (Collins 2009, p. 63) – had remained enshrined in Sudan's permanent Constitution of 1973. The existence of structures that consolidated them was supported by Sudanese legislation, which was based on Islam, Christianity and the "noble spiritual beliefs" (referenced in Sudan's Constitution) (Badal 1999, p. 20). In the situation of diverse groups of Southerners living in Khartoum as IDPs, these spiritual beliefs were integral to their life worlds and were broadly essential components of measures they undertook to ensure their physical and psychological well-being within an environment informed by extreme duress, and they were central to healing practices used by various groups of Southerners (Abdel Aziz 2013).

For a protracted period during the rule of President Nimeiri, these laws had a privileged position within the Constitution. However, this conciliatory recognition was placed under duress with the introduction of Islamic *sharīʿa* law in Sudan in 1983. Although the territorial south did not fall under this jurisdiction, this development had serious detrimental effects on the relationship of the state to its Christian citizens living in the north. This tense state of affairs was exacerbated by the policies of the pro-Islamist regime of 1989 in its first years in power and with its aims at consolidating its power base. The terms of the 1973 Constitution remained in a state of quasi-ineffectiveness and were only to be reiterated by the terms of the CPA in 2005 according to the clause: Freedom of Thought, Conscience and Religion 1.6.2.7, Protocol between GoS and SPLM on Power Sharing: 8.

Yet while these constitutional rights remained suspended, the government allowed the working of native courts within specific segments of the city. In Mandela, native courts anchored the multiple life worlds of Southerners, and within Mayo forms of customary law continued to be deployed and problems of a communal (civil) nature (breaches of dowry payment, matrimonial difficulties, debt grievances, etc.) were resolved in special court houses. Disputes were resolved between different groups or within the same group in makeshift court houses (*rakūba*: wooden cabins) every Friday.[22] In cases where the

22 For a similar analogy see the contribution of Abdul-Jalil in this volume.

dispute was between individuals from different groups, a common court *rakūba* was used. In a non-negligible number of cases, Arabic served as a lingua-franca since all the Southern groups inhabiting the area retained the right to present within the local court.

In Mayo, a single court house existed for the following Equatorian groups: Baria, Kukua, Fujulu, Nyangbara, Made, Acholi, Lokoya, Mundare, Kaliko, Abokaya, Baka, Makaraka, Zande, Mudu, Moru, Latuka, Taposa, Buya, Didinga, Lofite, Loungu and Kuku. In contrast, the Dinka maintained their own main large court within Mandela camp.

The sense of community extended beyond Mayo to encompass all Southerners in Khartoum through the auspices of a bigger court house, located in Kalakla, representing the ten states of South Sudan. This court house served as a centre point for major cases and its decisions were more acceptable to the state judicial courts than those of other local courts when they did not contravene the spirit of the law more robustly sanctioned by the state. Court houses also existed in other areas of IDP habitation, such as Haj Youssif, Wad El Bashir, Jebel Awlia and Dikainat.

I was to bear witness to how essential these court houses were to the lives of many women and men in Mayo. They addressed notions of misfortune as they were presented by members of the community who presented to them. Such complaints ranged from accusations of foul play resulting in misfortune (illness, loss of employment, divorce) to breaches of dowry payments, all of which were redressed by the efforts of courts in Khartoum.

For the case of accusations of foul play mentioned above, I cite the example of a woman who addressed the misfortune that assailed her and deployed the courts to preserve the integrity of her life world as a Dinka. This social world was rendered meaningful through reproductive capacity where children largely constituted a valued possession and conferred social capital (Harragin and Chol 1998, p. 12). Her failure to bear a child therefore compromised her position as a viable social being. Because she was childless, this woman found herself rejected by her husband, but she was adamant that he was under the influence of his family. She believed that she had been bewitched by her husband's step-mother, who coveted him (and who by not treating him as her son was in breach of incest taboos and therefore a very reprehensible individual), and that her unborn baby was blocked inside her body unable to emerge.

This narrative of being the victim of her family-in-law, and the fact that her father-in-law was particularly becoming increasingly hostile towards her and claiming the return of his bride wealth, led an interesting engagement with the local Dinka court, explained in these terms:

> I have lodged a complaint against my husband at the local judicial court of the Dinka, specialized in customary law, and testified about how they (he and his family) have contravened the law by treating me so badly and trying to make him hate me and thus destroy my marriage. I have also lied about the measures that I have taken to reverse their evil; I told the judges that I had performed the ritual sacrifices, entailing the slaughter of a ewe and leaving it in the river (*sibr baḥr*) under orders from his father. I told this lie because the word of a man gives my initiative more legitimacy in the eyes of the court and the elders.

This ethnographic vignette elucidates the dynamic interactions of Southerners with institutions that embed them within a particular community, as a measure of existential safety, within the sea of ethnic groups that inhabit Khartoum; in this context, any subterfuge and toying with these institutions is part of a dynamic social game.

Unrealized dowry payments demonstrated the highly relevant issue of actively confronting the ravages displacement has played on shifting gender relationships (Grabska 2014, p. 43), such that Southern women were not as controllable as they once were. Southern women, coming from different walks of life, were increasingly the subject of controversy in Khartoum: they were more frequently being captured without the payment of dowries, which were difficult to obtain in Khartoum, either due of the shortage of cattle, so important for Nilotic Southerners, namely the Dinka and Nuer, and the lack of cash funds (acceptable to other groups) available to IDPs. This dilemma was represented in the fate of an educated Equatorian from Juba, who was enamoured of Rina, the daughter of one of the local sultans. Despite all his efforts, Albert could not provide the required dowry that would entitle him to take his love home with him and so had no option but to steal her. This ignited the wrath of the influential sultan and so he found himself obligated to attend the local court every Friday in an exercise of public shaming that quickly became widely known throughout Mayo and served as a warning to others that, despite its poverty, the area was still subject to rules and commitments.

These examples of court intervention reflect the specificity of Southern concerns and how they fare in the landscape of Khartoum. However, rather than being only a sign of success in preserving the cultural integrity of southern IDPs, I suggest that the presence of these courts was also the fruit of state machinations. The crux of the problem lies in how the existence of these courts brings to light a reification of culture and enlivens a trope that suggests a return to roots of some sort (creating an exoticization of Southerners and increasing their alterity in Khartoum). This reification supports reactive defensive identity politics that reassert primordial notions of identity that are, at times situationally, deployed by different groups of Southerners to face the onslaught of difficult lives in Khartoum, where their diverse cultural signifiers are largely universalized and treated with contempt.

Notwithstanding the continued use of native courts to contend with specific problems alien to the dominating world view advocated in Khartoum, the insistence on portraying Southerners as only invested in the perpetuation of exclusively Southern worlds that stand in contradiction to their valid concern to become well-established in Khartoum needs to be nuanced. This is achieved by ethnographically exposing the interface between accommodation of structures of power by IDPs as actors within the camp, and the interventions of the state. Structures of power that proliferated in the landscape of Mayo will be analysed according to what they portray about the lives of those engaging with them and with native courts. The following section will therefore elaborate on what the presence of these courts says in terms of contemporary concerns related to the context and processes of displacement in the specific locale of Mandela.

The distribution of authority within the camp and outside it is an important marker of where IDPs stand in relation to the wider power structures of Khartoum. Outside the camp in Ḥay al- Janūbiyyīn there was a maximum of five sultans. In the camp, they were numerous and were granted more autonomy by the authorities. This feature was a double bind for Southerners: it preserved the power of traditional leaders while simultaneously keeping them, as representatives of the inhabitants of the camp, at the periphery of the power structures, curtailing their wide-ranging participation at the local authority level. While this distance from the state was welcome – since it enhanced and preserved traditional Southern power structures – it deprived Southern IDPs of comprehensive citizenship rights by placing them outside the sphere of state intervention.

Each group within Mayo is represented by a sultan officially appointed by the *maḥalliyya* (local council governed and dominated by the representatives of the state). Theoretically, these sultans represent the interests of the population at the local council level. In reality, the situation was more complex and this form of local politics did not go unremarked by the inhabitants of the area. Several people stated that some of these sultans had been appointed by the government and were therefore not real sultans[23] and would be unable to

23 This dynamic is not exclusive to Southern marginal people. Similar patterns of conflict between government appointed sheikhs and those chosen by local people have been

preserve the prestige of this role once back in the South. Some of them were selected because they had previously been employed as policemen in Khartoum and because they manifested allegiance to the regime.

Two informants explained that, in Khartoum, sultans collaborated with the police before they undertook their functions. They had to be trained by the national police force for forty-five days, upon which they were given khaki or white uniforms. In lieu of salaries they received bonuses and were therefore not on any official payroll. This automatically excluded them from the right to an end of service pension, indicating that these positions of authority did not necessarily ensure employment rights or long term financial security.

It was widely agreed that the title of sultan recognized by the authorities was a tool of political expediency and was necessary, since it was stipulated and legally binding in the hierarchy of functions of the *maḥalliyya*. The popular committee was an integral part of this hierarchy and had to recruit from within the population of the area. The role of sultan, which had been hereditary in the South, had been modified in Khartoum and was seen by most as making a mockery of the real power that the title had once wielded.

With regard to the control exercised by local committees in Mandela, I noted that a parallel needs to be drawn between them and indigenous institutions such as native courts. It is pertinent to interrogate what they said about the legitimacy of certain leaders and how, as institutions, they were not in this situation removed from the tensions that existed between various Southern actors, depending on where these individuals stood in the hierarchies of power that existed within the camp. Some sultans within the area commanded more respect from the local population: these had been nominated for the role by the community, in the present circumstances, and not based on the assumption of a hereditary title as would have been the case back in the South. One such individual was Sultan Augustino, originally from Meridi (Equatoria) and living in Ḥay al-Junūbiyyīn. His recognition as a sultan was based on the deference he inspired, since he was one of the first Southerners to settle in Mayo during the 1970s before mass displacement, and therefore considered a guide to IDPs arriving in Khartoum in more adverse circumstances.

Ironically, those who had previously been *authentic* leaders but who had fled the conflicts in the South would have no authority once they went back. This was explained through the disruption caused by war, in which the state machinery and security forces exerted their military muscle and disrupted customary power structures. While it was recognized that this arguably weakened

underscored by Casciarri (2009) in the context of Native Administration revival among Arab groups.

the chiefs' authority, they were still expected to support their communities and remain with them in the midst of armed conflict. Those who failed to do so were designated as fleers who had abandoned their people and subsequently accused either of becoming collaborators with the government or of being too cowardly and individualistic to retain the prestigious role of sultan.

The prolific presence of courts in Mayo and their importance within a network of power structures that affected the lives of its inhabitants as described above, contrasts with the findings of Abdalla (2014, pp. 47–48), who states that, although in Mandela she found a grand sultan court and native courts based on ethnic affiliations, these were less cared for and respected during her fieldwork in 2007. It is pertinent to address this variation in findings through the prism of elements that started to appear to me during the last phases of my first stretch of fieldwork.

While courts were visible in the camp, their impact was being challenged by the circumstances that Southerners were being exposed to. Alternative structures of power that were more in touch with aspirations conveyed by Khartoum were to affect the status of these courts. Examples of this state of affairs were demonstrated by a female Muslim Southerner, resident in Mandela, originally from Wau in western Bahr al-Ghazal from the Bai ethnic group, and by the experiences of a young Christian Dinka male, who was a member of the local committee in Mandela.

This female was active in Islamic *daʿwa,* which metaphorically stood for the tight rope that she had to walk between a past life and identity and a new one that was still being formed. According to her, before embracing Islam she had been a merely nominal Christian, only interested in sex and *merīsa* (sorghum beer): "I had no thought for education or country".

At the time of our meeting Salima had a distinctly strict interpretation of Islam and she constantly volunteered to give me lists of all the "houses of immorality" where alcohol was brewed, as well as lists of the churches in Mayo suspected of subverting the spread of Islam among Southerners. She was running a *daʿwa* centre in Mandela but perpetually complained that within her work for the GHT (Islamic Council for Development and Unity) her salary was a meagre 75,000 Ls (28 USD) and only amounted to 116,000 Ls (44 USD) after she joined the *shurṭa al-shaʿbiyya* (the police force recruited from within the community with lesser power than the national police).

Despite her complaints and the fact that her strong connections with Islamic based sources of authority placed her under suspicion within the wider community of Mayo, Salima was committed to her choice to become a Muslim, which she affirmed did not constitute an abandonment of her Southern identity, since she genuinely held Islam to be an answer to the needs of all Southerners. From this perspective, this instance of conversion was negotiated on terms that limited engagement with customs that lay outside the fold of Islamic parameters, but which seemed to befit new personal needs and aspirations within Khartoum. This also resonates with the experiences shared by many other Muslim Southerners in Mayo.

Another example of how Southerners were obligated to make a choice between a life based on customary modes of cultural life and being more included within the structures of power within Khartoum is illustrated by the experiences of Dominic. His negotiation implicated the instrumentality of Khartoum in the creation of identity and knowledge. This ponderous dilemma is resolved by the fact that Southern IDPs observe, comment on and sometimes participate in alternative newer sources of action available within Khartoum. This is evident in the observation of Dominic, a young Dinka representative of the popular committee in Mandela:

> The older generation of Dinka living in Mayo still continue to invest part of their money in cattle and this reflects their hope of return, while the younger generation that is settled in Khartoum is less concerned with this and do not have such close attachments.

In being involved in the local politics of Mayo, Dominic believes that he reflects the attitudes of the younger generation. His ambitions led him to become an intermediary between the government and (all) Southern IDPs. He is part of the organized structured life in Mayo, which shows his concern with integration. Dominic disparages all traditions based on metaphysical ancestral understandings, while he notes how his fellow Southerners in the camp have to contend with reconciling two vastly distant and contradictory worlds:

> 50% of the displaced population is still involved in therapeutic redressive activities outside the domain of the church, yet the camp is a flourishing site of multiple activities; look at the church procession that has just crossed the market commemorating the day Jesus Christ rode into Jerusalem.

The reflections offered by Dominic facilitate the observation of the dynamic encompassing involvement and "distanciation" (Giddens 1984, pp. 258–259) that underscores the stretching of social systems across time-space. This dynamic is crystallized in activities relating to a sphere beyond Khartoum, reflected in the workings of native courts.

Conclusion

The macro structures of power that exist in Khartoum that have been cursorily presented in this chapter affect diverse squatter areas and IDP camps. The presence of native courts highlights the complexity of these interactions through the prism of the prominent difference between "camps", as more autonomous and turbulent spaces of negotiation, and "non-camp" as more in line with the wider social landscape of the city. The nature of the interactions that take place in the camps underscore how important it is to see the transformation of the former – framed as worlds apart through a facile interpretation of it – into a place that speaks to these elements.

Accordingly, in this context, place is acted on, lived and experienced with more agency. The camps that were created on the landscape of Khartoum following the influx of IDPs, counter-intuitively, became places where one could witness alternatives to the hegemonic narrative of Khartoum. They were in fact an arena of confrontations that exposed how the state manipulated the behaviour of the inhabitants of Khartoum through the practice of space.

The discussion introduced here clarifies how Mayo becomes a microcosm or offers a reading of other zones of displacement around the city, while simultaneously showing how it is distinct from these other areas of marginalization within the metropolis. The paradox of Mayo is contained in its simultaneous isolation from the symbols of power and its more positive remoteness from their constraints. While Mayo is an enclosure, it is characterized by its potential to offer a glimpse of the world outside it, and then to offer the protection and containment necessary to combat the uncertainties of the sphere represented by Greater Khartoum.

In the present day, this continues to be the case and the current situation of local courts within Mandela speaks to this continued and fraught dialogue with the wider landscape of Khartoum. At the time of my fieldwork, the courts were less numerous than they had been in the past, from 2003 until the Independence of South Sudan in 2011, and I quickly came to learn that the morphological changes that had affected the area since the separation of the South had cut deep. As the Southerners I met in July 2015 told me, what I was seeing did not exist in 2012 because it was not needed, since most Southerners had gone, and it was only in the past year that they had re-emerged. This reduced presence of courts reflected the precarious situation that Southern inhabitants were living in after separation.

Nonetheless, I did find active engagement of one court as recently as February 2016 in Souk Alfain Mandela. It was a large cabin (*rakūba*) that was teeming with Dinka men from a range of age groups. This overwhelming presence was perhaps explained by the fact that I arrived on a Friday morning, when the inhabitants of Mayo did not have to leave the vicinity in search of work. I was told to await the arrival of the sultan, who was the only person authorized to give information about the current state of the court. This tallied with the remarks of younger members of the crowd, who told me that, as youngsters, they relied on the sultan to guide them and explain the workings of customary law.

Sultan Deng eventually arrived but since he did not speak fluent Arabic the task of interpreting was undertaken by a young Dinka man who seemed to bridge the Dinka world and that of Khartoum with greater ease than his slightly older counterpart. I learnt that this court represented North Bahr al-Ghazal and that this was in line with my observations dating from 2005 that confirmed the regional organization of different clans of Dinka. However, the courts now functioned in the form of committees representing each Dinka clan. Any interchange or consultation within the courts took place based on regions, regardless of where the event to be discussed had taken place in the landscape of Khartoum. I was told that if, for instance, an incident occurred in Haj Youssif (Khartoum North approximately 30 km from Mandela) the consultation pertaining to it could be transferred and take place in this court house, provided those implicated were from the region in proximity to Aweil. To corroborate this claim, I was informed that the court representing the people of Rumbek had been transferred to Kalakla (south east of Mandela).

In contradiction to this explanation, a caveat was introduced related to identifying those who could benefit from an intervention by this court. The interpreter stated that the court did not discriminate by passing judgements on the basis of ethnicity. He said: “We resolve issues for those who consult us even if they are Northerners.”

This comment shows that, in the context of displacement, for the majority of Southerners, northerners continued to be framed as the ultimate “Other”. However, more importantly, it underscores that the stress on ethnic divides was not rooted in social customs and did not manifest the deep echoes of social division that one might anticipate: rather it was the fruit of political manipulation. I suggest that the continued presence of Native Courts was a double-edged sword: for while they gave recognition to Southern cultural values, they simultaneously served to create an “imagined community” of Southerners in Khartoum, and this was not without its problems, since it camouflaged the differentiations between them as groups and as individuals with different vested interests in Khartoum.

This was clarified in the words of a Southern young man who denounced the settlement of Southerners in ethnic peripheries, which he thought distanced them from the promise of affluence associated with settlement in parts of the city conducive to individual attainment and entrance into the individuated sphere of monetary success.

From this perspective, one might claim that the presence of Native Courts militated to undermine the full inclusion of Southerners in the ethos of city life, which was in any case a perpetual subject of debate within Khartoum perhaps best crystallized in the idiom of negative ruralization (Ahmad 2000). Khartoum had always been prey to a warring dualism of ethnic affiliation and appropriate city dwelling,[24] which saw to it that over determination of the former contravened the latter. Displacement was constantly viewed as contributing to this friction. I suggest that the segmentation of courts in Mandela as ethnic enclaves would reinforce these analytical frameworks.

Notwithstanding these challenges to appropriate Khartoum beyond ethnic parameters, the courts continued to exist. However, despite their continued presence, I was told that they did not enjoy the same position as they had had in the past *vis-à-vis* the state authorities. Although the police continued to respect the court, it did not wield the same legal status as before the referendum and it was no longer constitutional (the committee of chiefs/sultans that had a place in the judicial courts of Khartoum had been dissolved). Nonetheless, all those present agreed with the sultan when he explained that the judgement of a customary sultan was framed as his legitimate position as a primary witness within the federal courts even up to the present day.

The Dinka North Bahr al-Ghazal elders who were the representatives of the court in Souk Alfain explained that, while they were responsible for overseeing any disputes that came to them, they increasingly enjoined the participation of youth. They explained that in normal circumstances youth would not be privy to portentous matters that were integral to preserving social harmony and well-being, since they did not have the knowledge to ensure either. However, in the context of life in Khartoum, an exception had been made and they were now allowed to attend court consultations and proceedings as part of a devised pedagogy.

This concession was marked by a significant caveat: while the local courts allowed young people to be present, they mobilized them to represent their communities who were once again in a liminal situation – which they had transcended by 2011 as citizens having potential if unrealized rights – living

24 See El Hassan (2015) on how older inhabitants of Omdurman create the exclusionary Sudanese urban identity par excellence. See El-Sadaty (2015, p.79) for the mistake of classifying modifications to the urban scene as "ruralization".

in examples of "open areas"[25] and within three self-designated camps they set up themselves. These were Yarmuk located in Galb al-Asad, Gumbullah in Mandela near Souk Alfain, and Juba camp or Mandela camp Block 7, established in 2011 in Andalous block 7, and named after the old camp.

Within the "open areas", I observed structures of power established through the initiatives of the inhabitants themselves. These took the form of organizing committees representing Southerners by region rather than courts (although the inhabitants still tried to preserve a modicum of continuity with tradition by continuing to call the two representatives of each region "sultans"). This suggests that, whatever their limitations, the proliferation of courts in the past correlated with the status of citizenship, however compromised it was. The fact that these new camps did not have courts highlights their possibly temporary and uncertain status and underscores the legal position of Southerners as non-citizens, but yet almost just that (i.e. citizens): it seemed that the ethnic differentiation that was a feature of native courts was no longer a viable option when Southerners were vying to establish themselves as worthy "returnees".

Within these camps, a minority had kept their houses in Mandela while simultaneously registering in the camps. The majority of the inhabitants of these new camps could only look at their old houses, which had by this stage been appropriated by different people. In light of this lack of rights (Grabska and Mehta 2008) young people, who were more versed in the signifiers of Khartoum than their older counter parts, through their mobility in the city (Abdel Aziz 2013, ch. 1, fn. 4 and 8),[26] through education, and through more

---

25 These were established as departure points around different parts of Khartoum in October 2010 for the voluntary repatriation scheme to the South. Returns were suspended by early 2011 but these spaces, devoid of infrastructure and functioning services, continue to host diverse groups of Southerners who have either relinquished their previous abodes or maintained a presence in multiple areas out of pragmatic concerns not to lose all access to habitation. According to de Geoffroy (2014, p. 266), who cites data provided by the International Organization for Migration, these locations amounted to 40 and gathered 40,000 individuals.

26 My own fieldwork observations unambiguously confirm generational bias in terms of visible presence of Southerners within the swathe of the urban landscape. Young Southerners (girls and boys) were more likely to frequent social, recreational and educational spaces within central Khartoum. Examples include Comboni ground, Kwoto cultural centre (presenting aspects of southern folklore), and English language centres (Selti). Southern female students frequented Ahfad University for women more than other institutions, and so on. Young Southern men could often be seen offering cigarettes for sale in affluent areas of Khartoum (Amarat) and trading Italian goods (clothes

frenzied social mobility aspirations, exhibited more familiarly with bureaucracy. They were therefore in a more robust position to represent the more remote community of Mayo within different sectors of civil society (willing to help them surmount their ambiguous fate in Khartoum) and reach out to governmental and non-governmental actors at the opportune moment.

The fact that the courts were instrumental in driving this initiative illustrates that they are pragmatic institutions inscribed in the everyday concerns of Southerners. This highlights the point made by Bureau (2011, pp. 148–152), at the time of the fateful referendum, that the inscription of Southerners in the landscape of Khartoum remained unfinished business that interrogates the notions of home, being embedded in a specific city habitation and concepts of constrained return.

These interrogations appear almost prophetic since they were posed before the outbreak of the conflict in South Sudan in December 2013. In light of these developments, the appearance of Southerners in Khartoum is once again increasingly perceptible and this perhaps indicates that the continued presence of Southern native courts still has a tale to tell about the destiny of South Sudanese within the landscape of Khartoum.

References

Abdalla, MA 2008, *Poverty and Inequality in Urban Sudan: Policies, Institutions and Governance*, University of Leiden, African Studies Centre, Leiden.

Abdalla, SM 2014, 'Contradicting State Ideology in Sudan: Christian-Muslim Relations among the Internally Displaced Persons in Khartoum. The Case of Mandela and Wad-al Bashīr camps', in JA Chesworth & F Kogelmann (eds), *Shari'a in Africa Today: Reactions and Responses* (Islam in Africa, 15), Brill, Leiden.

Abdel Aziz, AA 2013, 'Confronting Marginality and Otherness: Knowledge Production and the Recasting of Identity through Therapeutic and Embodied Encounters among Internally Displaced People from Southern Sudan', PhD thesis, SOAS, University of London.

Abdul-Jalil, MA 2015, 'From Native Administration to Native System: The Reproduction of a Colonial Model of Governance in Post-Independence Sudan', in AM Assal & MA Abdul-Jalil (eds), *Fifty Years of Anthropology in Sudan: Past, Present and Future*, Chr. Michelsen Institute, Bergen.

Abusharaf, RM 2009, *Transforming Displaced Women in Sudan: Politics and the Body in a Squatter Settlement*, University of Chicago Press, Chicago IL.

and shoes) in Naivasha market, located on one of the verandas of the Souk al-Afranji (European market) downtown.

African Rights 1995, *Sudan's Invisible Citizens: The Policy of Abuse against Displaced people in the North*, African Rights, London.

Agier, M 2014, 'Introduction: L'encampement du monde', in M Agier (ed.), *Un monde de camps*, Editions la Découverte, Paris, pp. 11–28.

Ahmad, AM 2000, 'Khartoum Blues: The "Deplaning" and Decline of a Capital City', *Habitat International*, no. 24, pp. 309–325.

Al Safi, A 1990, 'Tumbura Revisited (the Story of Abuya Sambu)', unpublished paper, Traditional Medicine Research Institute and WHO Collaborating Centre for Traditional Medicine.

Al Safi, A & Makris GP 1990, 'Tumbura in Sudan: A Reappraisal', unpublished paper, Traditional Medicine Research Institute, National Research Centre, Khartoum.

Assal, AM 2002, 'A Discipline Asserting Its Identity and Place Displacement: Aid and Anthropology in Sudan', in AM Ahmed (ed.), *Anthropology in the Sudan: Reflections by a Sudanese Anthropologist*, International Books, OSSREA, Addis Ababa.

Assal, AM 2006, *Whose Rights Count? National and International Responses to the Rights of IDPs in the Sudan*, UK Development Research Centre on Migration, Globalization and Poverty, University of Sussex, Brighton.

Assal, AM 2008, 'Rights and Decisions to Return: Internally Displaced Persons in Post-war Sudan', in K Grabska & L Mehta (eds), *Forced Displacement: Why Rights Matter*, Palgrave Macmillan, London.

Assal, AM 2011, 'From the Country to the Town', in J Ryle, J Willis, S Baldo & JM Jok (eds), *The Sudan Handbook*, James Currey, London, pp. 63–69.

Augé, M 1995, *Non-lieux: Introduction à une anthropologie de la surmodernité*, Editions du Seuil, Paris.

Badal, RK 1999, 'Tensions in the Core Periphery: Cultural Relations in Sudan', *Mahawir*, no. 2.

Bakhit, MAG 2013, 'From Illegal Squatter Settlements towards Legal Shantytowns: Negotiations of Power and Responsibilities in Khartoum Shantytowns', *BIGSASWorks* 11, pp. 7–21.

Bannaga, SEI 1992, 'Unauthorised and Squatter Settlements in Khartoum: History, Magnitude and Treatment', Ministry of Engineering Affairs. Khartoum State.

Bannaga, SEI 2000, *Al -shorouk: The Organization of Villages in the State of Khartoum*, Ministry of Engineering Affairs, State of Khartoum in collaboration with The Habitat group at the Swiss Federal Institute of technology, Zurich.

Bannaga, SEI 2002, *Peace and the Displaced in Sudan: The Khartoum Experience*, Habitat Group, School of Architecture, Zurich.

Bellion-Jourdan, J 1997, 'L'humanitaire et l'islamisme soudanais: Les organisations Da'wa Islamiya et Islamic African Relief Agency', *Politique Africaine*, special issue 'Le Soudan, l'échec d'une expérience islamiste?', no. 66, pp. 61–73.

Boddy, J 1989, *Wombs and Alien Spirits: Women, Men, and the Zar Cult in Northern Sudan*, University of Wisconsin Press, Madison WI.

Bureau, L 2011, 'Sudistes au Nord, Sudistes du Nord? Les déplacés du Sud à Khartoum (Soudan) entre marginalisation et citadinisation', Master thesis, Paris 1 Panthéon- Sorbonne.

Casciarri, B 2009, 'Hommes, troupeaux et capitaux: Le phénomène tribal au Soudan à l'heure de la globalization', *Etudes Rurales*, no. 184, pp. 47–64.

Choplin A & Franck A 2010, 'A Glimpse of Dubai in Khartoum and Nouakchott: Prestige Urban Projects on the Margins of the Arab World', *Built Environment*, vol. 36, no. 2, pp. 64–77.

Collins, RO 2009, *The Southern Sudan in Historical Perspective*, Transaction Publishers, New Brunswick/London.

Constantinides, P 1972, 'Sickness and the Spirits: A Study of the Zar Spirit Possession Cult in the Northern Sudan', Unpublished PhD dissertation, University of London.

Constantinides, P 1979, 'Women's Spirit Possession and Urban Adaptation in the Muslim Northern Sudan', in AP Caplan and J Bujra (eds), *Women United, Women Divided*, Indiana University Press, Bloomington IN, pp. 185–205.

Davies, HRJ 1999, 'Migration in the Sudan during the Anglo-Egyptian Condominium (1898–1955)', *The Arab World Geographer*, Vol.2, No.1, pp. 41–55.

de Certeau, M 1984, *The Practice of Everyday Life*, University of California Press, Berkeley.

de Geoffroy, A 2009a, 'Fleeing War and Relocating to the Urban Fringe: Issues and Actors. The Cases of Khartoum and Bogotá', *International Review of the Red Cross*, vol. 91, no 875, pp. 509–526.

de Geoffroy, A 2009b, 'Political Authorities, Humanitarian Agencies and Southern Sudanese IDPs in Greater Khartoum', paper presented at the World Conference of Humanitarian Studies, University of Groningen, Wageningen University, 4–7 February.

de Geoffroy, A 2014, 'Khartoum (Soudan) : Le sort des deplacés et la transformation des camps apres l'indépendence du Soudan du Sud', in M Agier (ed.), *Un monde de camps*, Editions la Découverte, Paris, pp. 255–267.

de Geoffroy, A 2015, 'What Place in Khartoum for the Displaced? Between State Regulation and Individual Strategies', in B Casciarri, M Assal & F Ireton (eds), *Multidimensional Change in Sudan (1989–2011): Reshaping Livelihoods, Conflicts and Identities*, Berghahn Books, Oxford/New York.

Delmet, C 2005, 'The Native Administration System in Eastern Sudan: From Its Liquidation to Its Revival', in C Miller (ed.), *Land, Ethnicity and Political Legitimacy in Eastern Sudan*, CEDEJ/DSCR, Cairo/Khartoum, pp. 145–172.

Denis, E 2005, 'De quelques dimensions de Khartoum et de l'urbanisation au Soudan', *La Lettre de* L'OUCC, no. 6/7, pp. 21–31.

Denis, E 2006, 'Khartoum ville refuge et métropole rentière', *Cahiers du Grémamo* no. 18, pp. 87–127.

Duffield, M 2001, *Global Governance and the New Wars: The Merging of Development and Security*, Zed Books, London.

El Bushra, ES & Hijazi NB 1995, 'Two Million Squatters in Khartoum Urban Complex: The Dilemma of Sudan's National Capital', *Geojournal*, vol. 35, no. 4, pp. 505–514.

El Hassan, IS 2015, 'Old Omdurman and National Integration: The Socio-historical Roots of Social Exclusion', in M Assal & MA Abdul-Jalil (eds), *Fifty Years of Anthropology in Sudan: Past, Present and Future,* Chr. Michelsen Institute, Bergen, pp. 81–94.

El-Sadaty, FZ 2015, 'Urbanisation and Social Change in the Sudan', in M Assal & MA Abdul-Jalil (eds), *Fifty Years of Anthropology in Sudan: Past, Present and Future,* Chr. Michelsen Institute, Bergen, pp. 69–80.

Eltigani, EE (ed.) 1995, *War and Drought in Sudan: Essays on Population Displacement,* University Press of Florida, Gainsville FL.

El Tom, AO 2009, 'Darfur People: Too Black for the Arab-Islamic Project of Sudan', in HM Salah & CE Ray (eds), *Darfur and the Crisis of Governance in Sudan: A Critical Reader*, Cornell University Press, Ithaca NY.

Fouad, IN 1991, 'The Southern Sudanese Migration to Khartoum and the Resultant Conflicts', *Geojournal*, vol. 25, no. 1, pp. 13–18.

Foucault, M 1991, 'Governmentality', in G Burchell, C Gordon and P Miller (eds), *The Foucault Effect: Studies in Governmentality*, University of Chicago Press, Chicago IL, pp. 87–104.

Franck, A 2015, 'Urban Agriculture Facing Land Pressure in Greater Khartoum: The Case of New Real Estate Projects in Tuti and Abu Se'id', in B Casciarri, M Assal & F Ireton (eds), *Multidimensional Change in Sudan (1989–2011): Reshaping Livelihoods, Conflicts and Identities*, Berghahn Books, Oxford/New York, pp. 33–51.

Giddens, A 1984, *The Constitution of Society: Outline of the Theory of Structuration*, Polity Press, Cambridge.

Grabska, K 2014, *Gender, Home and Identity: Nuer Repatriation to Southern Sudan*, James Currey, London.

Grabska, K & Mehta, L (eds) 2008, *Forced Displacement: Why Rights Matter*, Palgrave Macmillan, London.

Gramsci, A 1971, *Selections from the Prison Notebooks of Antonio Gramsci*, edited and translated by Quintin Hoare and Geoffrey Nowell Smith, London: Lawrence and Wishart, (translation of *Quaderni dal carcere*, Torino: Einaudi, 2007).

Harragin S & Chol CC 1998, *The Southern Sudan Vulnerability Study*, Save the Children Fund, UK.

Jacobsen, K 2008, 'Internal Displacement to Urban Areas: The Tufts-IDMC Profiling Study. Case 1: Khartoum, Sudan', Feinstein International Centre, Tufts University (in collaboration with the Internal Displacement Monitoring Centre, Geneva).

Kelly, M 2007, 'The Experiences of Refugee Youth from the conflicts in the Sudan: A Collective Case Study', PhD Dissertation, Louisiana State University and Agricultural and Mechanical College, Baton Rouge, Louisiana.

Khalid, M 2003, *War and Peace in Sudan: A Tale of Two Countries*, Kegan Paul, London.

Lavergne, M 1997, 'La violence d'Etat comme mode de régulation de la croissance urbaine : le cas de Khartoum (Soudan)', *Espaces, Populations et sociétés*, 1, pp. 49–64.

Lefebvre, H 1974, *La production de l'espace*, Anthropos, Paris.

Loveless, J 1999, *Displaced Populations in Khartoum: A Study of Social and Economic Conditions*, Report for Save the Children Denmark, Channel Research, Ohain, Belgium.

Makris, GP 2000, *Changing Masters: Spirit Possession and Identity Construction among Slave Descendants and Other Subordinates in the Sudan*, North Western University Press, Evanston IL.

Manfredi, S 2015, 'One Tribe, One Language. Ethnolinguistic Identity and Language Revitalization among the Laggori in the Nuba Mountains', in B Casciarri, M Assal & F Ireton (eds), *Multidimensional Change in Sudan (1989–2011): Reshaping Livelihoods, Conflicts and Identities*, Berghahn Books, Oxford/New York, pp. 281–301.

Mann, L 2014, 'Wasta! The Long-term Implications of Education Expansion and Economic Liberalisation on Politics in Sudan', *Review of African Political Economy*, vol. 41, no. 142, pp. 561–578.

Mann, L 2011, 'The Retreat of the State and the Market: Liberalisation and Education Expansion in Sudan under the NCP', Unpublished PhD thesis, University of Edinburgh.

Marchal, R 1995, 'Eléments d'une sociologie du Front National Islamique soudanais', *Les Etudes du CERI* 5, Paris. http://www.ceri-sciences-po.org/publica/etude/etude5.pdf (accessed 2 March 2016).

Marchal, R 2015, 'Epilogue: A New Sudan?', in B Casciarri, M Assal & F Ireton (eds), *Multidimensional Change in Sudan (1989–2011): Reshaping Livelihoods, Conflicts and Identities*, Berghahn Books, Oxford/New York, pp. 320–331.

Motasim, H 2008, 'Deeply Divided Societies: Charting Strategies of Resistance', *Respect: Sudanese Journal for Human Rights Culture and Issues of Cultural Diversity*, no. 8.

Musso, G 2015, 'The Islamic Movement and Power in Sudan: From Revolution to Absorption into the State', in B Casciarri, M Assal & F Ireton (eds), *Multidimensional Change in Sudan (1989–2011): Reshaping Livelihoods, Conflicts and Identities*, Berghahn Books, Oxford/New York, pp. 245–262.

Nègre, M 2005, 'Développement local, ONG internationales et autoritarisme dans le Soudan réformé d'Al-Bashir: Prisme de la question du contrôle des ressources hydrauliques à Khartoum et études de cas', *La lettre de* L'OUCC, no. 6–7, pp. 36–39.

Pérouse de Montclos, MA 2001, *Migrations forcées et urbanisation: Le cas de Khartoum* (Les Dossiers du CEPED, 63), CEPED Paris.

Rahem, K 2003, 'Sous le sceau de l'invisible, malnutrition et centres de santé au Soudan : Le cas de Mayo Farm', unpublished Report for MSF.

Simone, TAM 1994, *In Whose Image? Political Islam and Urban Practices in Sudan*, University of Chicago Press, Chicago IL.

Willis, J 2011, 'The Ambitions of the State', in J Ryle, J Willis, S Baldo & JM Jok (eds), *The Sudan Handbook*, James Currey, London, pp. 54–62.

CHAPTER 10

Customary Law and Courts in the Context of Sudan's Legal Pluralism: Marginalized or Empowered under English Common Law and Islamic Law?

Mohamed A. Babiker

Introduction

This chapter focuses on the status of customary courts in Sudan and how they interrelate with formal statutory courts in cases of disputes of a communal nature. It examines customary laws and institutions operating at the local level and explores areas of actual or potential conflict between formal statutory laws (including *sharīʿa* law) and international human rights law. The coexistence of this legal pluralism in Sudan is marked with some degree of competition and dominance. Customary law and the operation of its institutions, this author argues, is limited by statutory laws, which not only undermine powers of traditional leaders but also strip such powers from them (whether judicial or executive), despite the fact that customary law as a normative legal system satisfies the aspirations of wide communities in Sudan. Similarly, modern or contemporary legal norms such as statutory laws, *sharīʿa* law and international human rights norms limit the operation of customary norms and institutions, particularly regarding issues related to communal land rights, equality before the law, administration of justice, access to justice, non-discrimination and women's rights. Despite these limitations on customary courts and traditional institutions, I argue that traditional justice institutions should remain an integral part of Sudan's pluralistic justice system and not be marginalized or undermined. This is simply because traditional judicial structures and the Native Administration system in Sudan are more accessible to the poor and marginalized groups, and play a critical role in ensuring the peaceful settlement of disputes through the application of traditional justice norms. Thus, there is a need to analyse the role and position of traditional systems. Concerted measures should then be taken to strengthen the traditional justice system while at the same time creating harmonization and viable linkages between the formal

 | DOI 10.1163/9789004362185_012

and informal justice systems. Traditional structures were historically recognized in Sudan as legitimate institutional mechanisms for conflict resolution and transformation, based on the indigenous mediation (i.e., *jūdiya*) system.

Accordingly, this chapter seeks to examine in depth both customary norms and their traditional structures, and potential tensions between them and contemporary statutory laws. The chapter first looks at the legal status of customary courts in terms of their substantive applicable norms, their operation as customary institutions, and their mandate and powers to adjudicate cases on various aspects of law including criminal law (such as murder cases) and family affairs. Whilst examining these norms, the chapter does not claim to cover all customs in Sudan but rather examples of certain regions in Sudan where customary law is applied by both formal and informal courts.

The chapter also provides a historical review of customary institutions since colonial times and explores their relationship with the statutory and Islamic legal system. It examines the impact of customary courts on individual human rights, particularly when applying customary law to women (such as inheritance rights including land, custody, divorce), and in murder crimes. In this respect, the chapter looks at the possible conflict that may arise between customary norms and international human rights norms and treaties.

The chapter also examines other layers of conflict between Sudan's statutory laws, individual human rights and communal customary rights and assesses the extent to which the first two dominate the last. It also focuses on the tripartite dynamic relationships between customary courts and the formal justice system, and how these justice institutions operate in terms of applicable substantive customary laws (i.e., *ʿurf* principles), powers, and the appointment of personnel (native leaders such as sheikhs, *ʿomdas*, *nāẓir*s – and *ṣulṭān*s).

The chapter concludes by proposing possible linkages that could be put in place between formal and informal justice institutions, to ensure that such institutions operate in harmony without one dominating or marginalizing the other, for the purpose of protecting community aspirations and individual rights.

Legal Recognition of Customs in Colonial and Post-colonial Sudan (1902–1983)

Recognition of Custom as One of the Sources of Law

Historically, customary law was recognized as one of the important sources of law in Sudan, among other sources such as the principles of justice, equity and good conscience (applied as part of the English common law during the colonial era) and *sharīʿa* law. In this respect, it is pertinent to note that sources of law in Sudan passed through various stages of development. The sources of law during the Funj Kingdom, for example, were a blend of Islamic law and custom (Thompson 1965, p. 468; Mustafa 1971). In the period of Turkish rule (1821–1884), Islamic law and local customs were also acted upon. During the Mahdist State (1884–1898), the basic philosophy was that justice was to be administered upon the dual basis of the Qur'an and Sunna (Mustafa 1971). In the Condominium period (1898–1956), legislation, custom, judicial precedents and justice, equity and good conscience, were all recognized as sources of law. Legal sources in Sudan are thus a blend of legislation, custom, Islamic Law and judicial precedents.[1] Although legislation has been regarded as the primary and most important source of law, various Sudanese constitutions have recognized the aforementioned sources, including custom. For example, in May 1973, the Permanent Constitution of the Sudan was adopted and Islamic Law and custom were recognized as the main sources of legislation (Sallawi 1983). Article 9 of this Constitution not only recognizes customs but also emphasizes legal pluralism. It states: "[...] the Islamic Law and custom shall be the main source of legislation – personal matters of non-Muslims shall be governed by their personal laws." However, legislation has assumed higher status and courts must apply its express provisions (Zakaria 1991). The courts were also given a residual power to fill in the gaps in legislation by reference to the formula "justice, equity and good conscience".[2] Legislation has also assumed great importance over the past decades and there is a consistent resort to legislation by various regimes, apparently as a means of implementing social change or governmental policies.[3]

Although legislation (as the primary source of law in Sudan) minimizes the role of other sources such as custom, it is pertinent to note that customary law is also recognized as an important source of law, to the extent that a Sudanese common law could develop upon it (Abu Rannat 1960). As a legal source, custom has been recognized by the state and given formal validity by various laws.

1 The doctrine of binding precedents had been followed. Initially, judges referred to cases decided in England, India and other places. Later, Sudanese precedents were accumulated and eventually followed (Zakaria 1991).

2 During the Colonial era, this formula was interpreted to mean English law. However, the formula later was interpreted in the context of a Sudanese common law system and after 1983 was limited by the application of *sharīʿa* law (Zakaria, 1991).

3 For example, the statutes enacted during the period between 1970 and 1985 are about two-thirds the number of all those promulgated in the period between 1956 and 1970 (Zakaria, 1991).

As a result, customary law has been applied as part of various branches of law such as personal matters (e.g., Section 3 (a) of the Civil Justice Ordinance, 1900, Section 5 (a) of the Civil Justice Ordinance, 1929) and in land disputes (e.g., Section 13 (iii) of the Land Settlement and Registration Ordinance, 1925). In other areas, criminal law was also dealt with in accordance with custom.[4] *Sharīʿa* law was referred to in personal matters of Muslims.[5] If the parties were non-Muslims, custom was resorted to as a source of law.[6]

In the period from Independence to 1983, all legal sources in Sudan were approached with the same philosophy: namely legislation is the primary source of law while other sources such as custom, judicial precedents, *sharīʿa* and justice, equity and good conscience were regarded as secondary or subsidiary sources which were only applied in the absence of legislation (Zakaria 1991, p. 161).

Although customary law has been recognized as a source of legal rights, those who rely on its norms must establish the existence of the custom by evidence, which must show that, *inter alia*: (a) it is prevalent in the locality in question and; (b) it is applied to a specified class or relationship of persons (El Mahdi 1971, p. 42). However, the criticism that can be levelled against the application of customary laws is that they are silent as to the definition or content of customary norms (El-Hada 1976, p. 150). It is submitted that the definition of custom is necessary because judges need to have a satisfactory criterion by to which they can distinguish customary legal norms from merely moral, religious, and traditional and social practices.[7] The other problem accompanying the interpretation of the term "custom" is whether local custom originating from usage in Sudan refers to the laws of the religious community to which the parties belong (El-Hada 1976, p. 154).

Custom originating from usage was recognized in *Bamboulis v. Bamboulis*.[8] In this case, the plaintiff, a Greek national domiciled in Sudan, petitioned for divorce on the ground of his wife's adultery. He succeeded in the High Court, which applied Greek Orthodox law. C.J. Lindsay explained that custom in S. 5 (a) of the Civil Justice Ordinance 1929, refers to custom originating

---

4 See Section 7 of the Chiefs Courts Ordinance, 1932.

5 See Section 3 (b) of the Civil Justice Ordinance, 1900, and Section 5 (b) of the Civil Justice Ordinance 1929.

6 Section 5 (a) of the Civil Justice Ordinance 1939.

7 In Ghana, Section 2 of the Native Courts Ordinance 1944 defined the term "customary law" as follows: "Native customary law means a rule or body of rules regulating rights and imposing correlative duties, being a rule or body of rules which obtains and is fortified by established native usage and which is appropriate and applicable to any particular cause, action, suit, matter, dispute, issue or question" (§150).

8 AC/REV/58/53; cases in the Court of Appeal and the High Court 1/153–306/54, p. 40.

from usage in Sudan and does not refer to the religious customary law of the community to which the parties belong.[9] However, it is argued that Lindsay overlooked the previous decision laid down in *Abdulla Charcheflie v. Merie Bekyarellis*. In this case J. Gorman held that "… where the parties are domiciled in Sudan it has been held it is the customs of the religious community to which they belong which are looked to, and comprise their personal law".[10] In two other cases, *George Helal v. Gamila Helal*[11] and *Munira Zaki Awad v. Nargis Rezeig*,[12] it was decided that custom within the meaning of Section 5 (a) of the Civil Justice Ordinance 1929 meant the custom of the religious community to which the parties belong. Thus, custom stood as a source of law in personal matters of non-Muslims, in so far as it was not contrary to justice, equity and good conscience. For Muslims, however, Islamic law remains the source of law.

Statutory Recognition of Custom

Various statutory laws have recognized customary law in Sudan and the legislature has retained custom in various ordinances and enactments. This was first seen in Section 3 of the Civil Justice Ordinance 1900. Section 3 provides:

> Where in any suit or other proceedings in a Civil Court any question arises regarding succession, inheritance, will, legacies, gifts, marriage, divorce, family relations, or the constitution of wakfs, the rule of decision shall be:
>
> (a) Any custom applicable to the parties concerned, which is not contrary to justice, equity and good conscience, and has not been by this or any other enactment altered or abolished, and has not been declared void by competent authority.
> (b) The Mohammedan law, in cases where the parties are Mohammedans, except in so far as that law has been modified by any such custom as is above referred.

Section 3 of the Civil Justice Ordinance 1900 was then re-enacted in Section 5 of the Civil Justice Ordinance 1929 (*Laws of the Sudan*, vol. 10, p.12).[13] Although

---

9 2 SLR. 129 (1932–1940).
10 2 SLR. 131 (1932–1940).
11 2 SLR. 274 (1932–1940).
12 AC/REV/53/1948, p. 290.
13 *Laws of the Sudan*, vol. 10, p. 12.

the Civil Justice Ordinance 1929 was repealed by the Civil Procedure Act 1974,[14] Section 5 is re-enacted in Section 5 of the Civil Procedure Act 1974. Section 3 and 4 of the Civil Justice Ordinance 1900, which laid down the law to be applied in the administration of civil justice, instructed the courts to apply "the custom applicable to the parties concerned", and Islamic law in cases where the parties were Muslims, to settle suits in personal matters. If there was no custom or law applicable to the parties to a suit involving personal matters, the courts were to act in accordance with "justice, equity and good conscience". For practical reasons, the Anglo-Egyptian Regime decided in 1900 to exclude the administration of Islamic personal Law (*sharīʿa*) to Muslims from the jurisdiction of the courts established under the Civil Justice Ordinance 1900, and entrusted it to *sharīʿa* courts, which were formally organized in 1902 by the Sudan Mohammeddan Law Courts Ordinance 1902 (Akolawin 1973, pp. 149–150). Also, under the Civil Justice Ordinance 1929, Section 5 (b) (later Section 5 of the Civil Procedure Act 1974) the Civil Court is required to apply *sharīʿa* in cases involving the personal affairs of Muslims, as long as that law is not modified by custom. This means that the legislature had not only allowed a local custom to triumph over the Islamic law, but also intended that Islamic law shall be applicable only if it is not contrary to justice, equity and good conscience (El Hada 1976, p. 184).

Other provisions providing for the statutory application of customary law can be found in various ordinances, namely Section 7 of the Chiefs Courts Ordinance 1931[15] and Section 9 of the Native Courts Ordinance 1932.[16] The position under the latter Ordinance is also similar to that of the Civil Justice Ordinance 1929 outlined above. Section 9 (1) of the former Act provides that a Native Court administers the native law and customs prevailing in the locality over which the jurisdiction of the court is established, provided that such native law and custom is not contrary to justice, morality or order. The section is silent, however, on the question of what effect shall be given to such custom if it conflicts with *sharīʿa* (El Hada 1976, p. 186). As Native Courts are manned by tribal and traditional leaders, such courts normally apply customs that diametrically differ from the relevant rules in *sharīʿa* (*ibid.*, p. 187). In Kordofan Province in western Sudan, for example, in the Missiriya tribe, custom dictates that a girl's property devolves absolutely to her brothers when she marries, but according to Islamic law the doctrine of the estate of a married woman is

14 Legislature Supplement to Sudan Gazette, no 1162 (July 1974), p. 1016.

15 *Laws of the Sudan*, vol. 10, p. 166.

16 *Laws of the Sudan*, vol. 10 Title XXVI, p. 172.

recognized.[17] A conflict arose over this before the Native Court. It was resolved by sending the case to the Province Council, which held that the custom in question was contrary to justice, morality and order. In this case, it is evident that the Province Council adopted Islamic standards as being synonymous with justice and morality (El Hada 1976, p. 187). A similar case in which a conflict may arise between custom and *sharīʿa* can be found among the Bisharin tribe in eastern Sudan. This tribe has a custom called *taʿatlig*. In this case, one of the Bisharin *ʿomda*s divorced his wife and stipulated that she could not remarry unless she paid him two camels of a type that could never be found in his locality (Clark 1938, p. 11). This custom is derived from a practice according to which a husband in the event of divorcing his wife, may stipulate that his ex-wife shall not remarry unless she comply with certain conditions. Failure to adhere to such conditions will render the divorce invalid, in the sense that the woman will not be regarded as an ex-wife and will not be free from matrimonial relations, i.e., she cannot seek a new husband. Such types of cases can also be found among the Beja and Rashida tribes in eastern Sudan.

The above survey of statute reveals that, in instances where custom conflicts with *sharīʿa*, and as has been seen in the application of Section 5 (b) of the Civil Justice Ordinance 1929 and Section 9 (1) of the Native Courts Ordinance 1932, custom may modify *sharīʿa* whenever any conflict exists. Again, this can be explored in relation to the Civil Procedure Act 1974. Section 5 (b) of this Act indicates that courts shall apply Islamic law except in so far as that law is modified by custom. On the other hand, Section 16 of Schedule 11 provides that the courts shall administer Islamic law in accordance with the authoritative doctrines of the Hanafi jurists, except in matters in which the Panel for Personal Matters of the Supreme Court otherwise directs them in judicial circulars to act in accordance with such other doctrines of Hanafi, or other Muslim jurists as are set forth in such circulars. The pertinent question here is: should the court apply Section 5 (b) of the Civil Procedure Act 1974, according to which Islamic law shall be modified by custom whenever any conflict exists, or should it follow Section 16 of Schedule 11 of the same Act, according to which Islamic law shall be administered in accordance with the Hanafi Islamic school? (El Hada 1976, p. 190). It is submitted that, although the Act does not contemplate this uncertainty, it is nevertheless evident from the preamble of the Act that the legislature intended that personal matters for Muslims shall be governed by Section 16 of Schedule 11, according to which Islamic law is to be administered in accordance with the Hanafi Islamic School, even though a conflict of norms may arise between custom and Islamic law (*ibid.*).

---

17 For this case, see Abu Rannat (1961, esp. p. 11).

Limitation of Customary Law by the English Common Law Principles of Justice, Equity and Good Conscience

Although Sudanese statutory laws outlined above recognize customary law, such laws impose certain limitations on the application of customary law. First, customary law shall be compatible with legislation. For instance, Section 5 (a) of the Civil Justice Ordinance 1929 specifically stipulates that customary law will be excluded where it is incompatible with legislation and where it is repugnant to the principles of justice, equity and good conscience. The limitation that customary law must be compatible with legislation and shall not be "repugnant to justice and morality or order" is also mentioned in the Civil Procedure Act 1974, the Chiefs Courts Ordinance 1931 and the Native Courts Ordinance 1932.[18]

Second, customary law shall be compatible with the principles of justice, equity and good conscience, which had been considered as a residual source of law in the absence of statutory provisions. As indicated earlier, the philosophy behind the introduction of this formula was to fill gaps in the law. It is pertinent to note here that it was first introduced in Section 4 of the Civil Justice Ordinance 1900, which states: "in cases not provided for by Section 3 (dealing with personal matters) or by any other law for the time being in force, the Court shall act according to justice, equity and good conscience". Similarly, Section 9 of the Civil Justice Ordinance 1929 was based on Section 4 of the Civil Justice Ordinance 1900, although there are slight differences.[19] Accordingly, statutory laws emphasize that any custom applicable to the parties concerned shall not be contrary to justice, equity and good conscience, and has not been by this or any other enactment altered or abolished, and has not been declared void by competent authority. This means that customs, as a source of law, are subject to the aforementioned principles derived from English common law, although the delimitation of the exact meaning of these principles has proved to be very vague and problematic in a variety of ways. First, the principles of justice, equity and good conscience are derived from English common law and hence conditioned by time, place, cultural contexts and circumstances of different communities, having their own traditions and customs, which are completely

18 The Chiefs Courts Ordinance 1931 and the Native Courts Ordinance 1932 have clauses that are worded slightly differently: custom shall not be "repugnant to justice and morality or order".

19 This section applied not only to cases not provided for by the Civil Justice Ordinance, but also to all cases not provided for in the Ordinance and any other enactment in force at the time. It reads: "in cases not provided for by this or any other enactment for the time being in force, the Court shall act according to justice, equity and good conscience".

different from those principles belonging to the English legal system. Second, as El Hada has shown at length, the decision in each case on the interpretation or application of justice, equity and good conscience may depend on the whim and subjective views of the judge. For example, an inter-community marriage dispute cannot be resolved according to justice, equity and good conscience without imposing the standards of justice of one community on the other. As a matter of law, in applying the principles of justice, equity and good conscience, Sudanese courts in various areas of law have resorted to English law. This approach is evident in case law and decisions of British judges during the Anglo-Egyptian regime in Sudan. At the time, judges felt free to resort to or consult several systems of jurisprudence and apply these principles, considering the justice of the case under review and the social and economic conditions of the country. However, it seems that British judges had followed this approach only in matrimonial matters, but in areas other than family law they were biased in favour of English law. In fact, they adopted a rigid attitude that led to a narrow outlook in the administration of justice in cases not covered by legislation: their attitude was later followed by Sudanese judges, who have judicially equated the term "justice, equity and good conscience" with the principles of English law (El-Hada 1976, p. 161.).

However, custom has occupied a distinct place as a legal source, particularly in personal matters of non-Muslims, as well as being a basis for legal rights over land (Zakaria 1991, p. 73). It is pertinent here to refer to some Sudanese court cases related to personal matters. In *Anis Ibrahim v Maria Gindi*, according to the personal laws of the parties, the Coptic law, the husband had a customary right to chastise his wife, but this was unknown to English law. In Islamic law, such a customary right to chastise is recognized and the relevant Qura'nic provision states: "And those you fear may be rebellious admonish; banish them to their coushes and beat them".[20] Although both Islamic and Coptic personal laws recognize the husband's customary right to chastise his wife, Judge Abdel Mageed Imam regarded this customary right as an archaic law that pertained to the Middle and Dark Ages. He held it invalid on the grounds that it was contrary to the standards of justice in English law (El Hada 1976, p. 196).

However, other Sudanese cases reflect a different view from that adopted in *Anis Ibrahim v Maria Gindi*, submitting that it is wrong to judge the validity of African customary law according to the standards of justice in England. In *S.G. v. Rainado Legge*, the Resident Magistrate, when examining the compatibility of a Bari tribal custom with morality and justice, followed the approach that the only standard of justice and morality is that which dictates justice and

20 *Ayat al-Nisa* 4:34.

morality "within the community in question"; otherwise the terms justice and morality are abstract conceptions and their standards are not the same everywhere.[21] The adoption of other standards outside the community may strike down the customary law prevailing in the community and defeat its purpose (El Hada 1976, p. 200). However, it is submitted that if a custom is "outrageous and barbarous" in view of the modern conditions in the world at large, it must be altered irrespective of its recognition in the community in question (*ibid.*). Thus, legislature is given full control over custom and courts may declare a custom void if it is contrary to justice, equity and good conscience, or justice, morality and order. Sudanese courts, as outlined above, have also been given powers to scrutinize custom to the extent of declaring it void. So, state recognition of custom was accompanied by complete control over it: it may be altered or abolished by legislation (Zakaria 1991, p. 73).

However, it must be emphasized here that, although the Anglo-Egyptian regime imposed English law in preference to Islamic and Egyptian laws as the territorial law of Sudan, it recognized legal pluralism as a practical necessity in the field of personal law (Sallawi 1983, p. 50). Accordingly, a major characteristic of the existing legal structure is legal pluralism, the co-existence of several legal systems in each area (Thompson 1965, p. 497). This means that English law has never been applied in Sudan either rigidly or exclusively. For instance, Sections 3 and 4 of the Civil Justice Ordinance 1900, which laid down the law to be applied in the administration of civil justice, instructed Sudanese courts to apply "the custom applicable to the parties concerned", and Islamic law in cases where the parties were Muslims, for settling suits in personal matters. If the parties to a suit involving personal matters had no custom or law applicable to them, the courts were to act in accordance with "justice, equity and good conscience". For practical reasons, the Anglo-Egyptian regime decided in 1900 to exclude the administration of Islamic (*sharīʿa*) personal law to Muslims from the jurisdiction of the courts established under the Civil Justice Ordinance 1900, and entrusted it to *sharīʿa* courts, which were formally organized in 1902 by the Sudan Mohammeddan Law Courts Ordinance 1902 (Akolawin 1973, pp. 149–150). Thus, custom stood as a source of law in personal matters of non-Muslims, in so far as it was not contrary to justice, equity and good conscience. For Muslims, therefore, Islamic law remains the source of law. Nevertheless, a question here arises: do Muslims have customs in personal matters that may conflict with *sharīʿa* law. Judge Abu Rannat believes that it is wrong to believe that there is no customary law that concerns Muslims in Sudan (Abu Rannat 1960, p. 11). He asks: what happens where the

21 SLJR (1963) at p. 54.

custom prevailing in the area conflicts with *sharīʿa*?[22] Thus, as a matter of fact, Muslims do have customs in personal matters. As a matter of law and until 1983, when the parties were Muslims, it was Section 5 (b) and not Section 5 (a) of the Civil Justice Ordinance that was applied to the parties. Also, in cases of conflict between *sharīʿa* and custom, the Native Courts normally apply custom in matters of personal status, even when it conflicts with *sharīʿa*. It is therefore clear that Islamic law was subject to modification in Civil, Chiefs and Native Courts. But the problem (up to 1983) remained that, since Islamic law could be modified by custom, logically there could be a possibility of applying Section 5 (a), i.e., custom as between Muslims, in so far as the Islamic law governing their case was modified by custom.[23]

Limitation of Customary Law by Sharīʿa *after the Islamization of Laws since 1983*

Before 1983, Islamic law was one of the sources of law in Sudan in personal matters of Muslims or non-Muslims if they submitted to the jurisdiction of *sharīʿa* courts (Zakaria 1991, p. 73). However, since 1983 a new trend has emerged. The enactment of the Judgment (Basic Rule) Act 1983 paved the way for a new trend in ideas about the sources of law. Section 3 of this Act provides that, in cases where there is no legislation governing the incident in question, a judge shall apply an established legal rule in accordance with the Qur'an and Sunna. If he cannot find a relevant law therein, he shall use his independent reasoning and seek guidance in the following Islamic principles, which shall be considered complementarily and to be prioritized as follows: first, the observation of

22 He illustrated that a problem arose in Kordofan regarding the property of a married woman. The Missiriya, who inhabit Western Kordofan did not recognize the doctrine of estate of a married woman by making it impossible for the husband to acquire it for his own benefit. According to their custom, if the woman committed a tort, her blood relations and not her husband were responsible for the payment of damages to the aggrieved party. Also, in cases of inheritance, conflict arises between Native Courts and Sharia Courts. If a married woman went before a Sharia court she would be given any property she might be entitled to under Islamic Law of inheritance. If the question arose in a Native Court it would decree that she could get a separate property. The case was resolved by referring the case to the Province Council who agreed to declare the custom contrary to justice, morality and order. It is pertinent to evoke here that if the case was held after the Islamization of laws in Sudan in 1983, the outcome of the case would be different. Another example is given among the Humur (a Muslim Baggara tribe of Western Kordofan, where most of their practices fall outside the scope of *shari'a*) (Abu Rannat 1960, pp. 11–12).

23 However, no decision has been found involving a case where custom modified Islamic law (Zakaria 1991, p. 68).

ijmāʿ (consensus) and the fundamentals of *sharīʿa*, its general principles and guidance regarding the detailed rule for the case in question; second, the application of *qiyās* (analogy), according to *sharīʿa* law, in order to discern its causes (*ʿilal*); third, the consideration of whatever serves the public interest in accordance with the ends of *sharīʿa* and its valid purposes; fourth, seeking guidance from recognized Sudanese judicial precedents that do not contradict *sharīʿa*, and the views adopted by Islamic scholars such as legal *fatwā* or opinion and established principles; fifth, the taking into account of recognized custom in all transactions in a manner that does not contradict *sharīʿa* law or the principles of natural justice; finally, observe the sense of justice recognized by noble religions and humanistic laws and the rule of equity enshrined in the dictates of good conscience.

Section 3 of the above Judgments (Basic Rules Act) 1983 can then be regarded as the new common law of Sudan, against which all laws are measured. It is very novel in the sense that it applies to various branches of law, including penal, civil and personal law.[24] The enactment of this section relegates customary law to a minor status and the application of custom is confined to specific areas of law such as land rights and usage and personal law. Hence, *sharīʿa* does not only stand as the main source of law but also governs the validity of other sources. The admissibility of both custom and precedents is made subject to *sharīʿa* rules (Zakaria 1991, p. 93). Legislation is also governed by *sharīʿa* in two aspects: one is that legislation is presumed not to contradict *sharīʿa* and the other is that legislative enactments shall be interpreted in accordance with the rules, principles and the general spirit of *sharīʿa*. Moreover, Islamic law has become the source of legislation for enactments such as the Penal Code, the Code of Criminal Procedure, the Civil Procedure Act 1983, the Zakat and Taxation Act 1984. The Civil Procedure Act 1983, for example, (although similar to that of 1974 in various aspects) provided for remarkable differences under Section 5 (a). It provides that courts shall apply *sharīʿa* law to both Muslims and non-Muslims in cases where the parties are Muslims or when a marriage is concluded in accordance with *sharīʿa* law.[25] Also, *sharīʿa* may not be modified by custom and thus Muslims could not, as a matter of law, have their personal matters governed by custom, though they may as a matter of fact, have their

24 However, this law was amended on 24 April 1986 by Law No. 55, 1986. Section (3) is now applicable to civil matters.

25 It is pertinent to note here the same powers given by section 5 (a) of the Civil Procedure Act 1983, were once exercised under Section 6 (a) by the *sharīʿa* Courts under the Mohammedan Law Courts Ordinance 1902. The latter section reads that the *sharīʿa* Courts had jurisdiction in family matters if "the marriage to which the question related concluded in accordance with *sharīʿa* Law".

own customs (Zakaria 1991, p. 88). Furthermore, *sharīʿa* law is placed above custom, which formally means that reference should be made first to *sharīʿa* law unless the requirements of the section are not satisfied (*ibid.*). This is apparent in Section 6 (a) of the Civil Procedure Act 1983, which is made subject to the Judgments (Basic Rules) Act 1983. Reference to *sharīʿa* in Section 6 (a) means reference to the Qur'an, Sunna, *ijmāʿ*, *ijtihād*, etc. These are the sources of law in Islamic jurisprudence (Zakaria 1991, p. 93). Thus (as in the case of colonial and post-colonial times when custom was controlled by legislation and English common law principles) in the post-1983 era, customary law is controlled by *sharīʿa* law, in the sense that any application of custom by the courts should not contradict legislation and *sharīʿa*. These structural changes in Sudan's legal system brought about by the adoption of the Judgments (Basic Rules) Act 1983, particularly Section 3, completely changed the fundamental set-up of the sources of law in Sudan and relegated customary law to a minor status. Legislation, as the primary and overriding source of law, is based on the principles of *sharīʿa* and should be interpreted in accordance with its rules and spirit, and there is also a presumption that the legislature intends that *sharīʿa* should not be contradicted (*ibid.*, p. 95). Thus, any enacted laws that contradict *sharīʿa* rules should be regarded as null and void (*ibid.*, p. 96). Thus, the Sudanese legal system has become gradually dependent upon Islamic jurisprudence (i.e., the Qur'an, Sunna, *ijmāʿ* [consensus] and *qiyās* [analogy]), which represents the ultimate or eventual source of law.

In terms of court practice, the Judgment (Basic Rules) Act 1983 makes it possible for judges, in the absence of express provisions, to resort to the Qur'an, Sunna, *ijtiḥād* (independent reasoning), the consensus of the community of Muslim jurists, analogical deduction, the consideration of whatever serves the public interest in accordance with the ends of the *sharīʿa* and its valid purposes, and judges' preferences (*istiḥsān*) (*ibid.*, p. 97).

Critics argue that what is novel about Section 3 of the Act is its generality and scope of application, as it applies to all matters whether civil or criminal, a fact that has caused many controversies regarding the constitutionality of this Act (Zakaria 1991, p. 97). For example, under Section 3 of the Act, the court might, in the absence of a provision, fill in the gap in the Penal Code and find persons guilty of crimes unknown to the Penal Code. This violates the basic rights of the defendant, as nobody should be subjected to retroactive laws. This has certainly raised serious issues in controversial cases in which Section 3 was invoked.[26] Nevertheless, Sudanese courts still believe in the

26 See 'Laliet, the Indian Merchant's Case', *Al-Ṣaḥāfa*, 9 November 1984, pp. 2–7. Laliet, a merchant and Indian national was reported to have been running a currency exchange

principle of legality and non-retroactivity of penal laws,[27] following the celebrated maxim: *nullum crimen sine lege, nulla poena sine lege* or "there must be no crime or punishment except in accordance with fixed predetermined law". However, in all circumstances post-1983, customary law has been limited by statutory laws based on *sharīʿa* law. Any application of custom by the courts should not contradict legislations or *sharīʿa* law.

Customary Courts Regulated by Statutory Laws

Having highlighted in the previous part the status of customary norms in Sudan vis-à-vis other sources of law, this part examines customary law institutions and looks at two types of customary or traditional institutions: (a) customary institutions that are not formally part of the justice system but still play an essential and effective role in resolving communal disputes ranging from those related to murder to family issues, and (b) formal customary institutions, namely Town and Rural Courts. The latter are regulated by statutory laws, manned by traditional leaders and mandated to apply customary law. The purpose of this part is also to examine the relationship between the formal and informal justice systems, and to see whether traditional institutions enjoy real powers or are undermined by the hegemony of the formal justice system.

Town and Rural Courts

The Criminal Procedure Act 1991 in Article 6 (g) identifies certain types of customary courts. This Article refers to the People's Criminal Courts (Town or Rural Court). These courts apply local customs and are recognized as part of the formal structure of Sudan's courts or judiciary. Jurisdiction and powers of these

---

and banking business without a licence, giving loans to many merchants and businessmen at high rates of interest up to 105% per annum, and to have been smuggling hard currency abroad. Laliet was charged under the provisions of Section 3 of the Act. The court stated that "the dealing in usury is punishable [in Islamic law] by way of *taʿzir* [punishment inflicted for transgression where no punishment is prescribed as *ḥadd*], by the confiscation of the means by which the prohibited act was done according to the Judgments (Basic Rule Act) 1983, which gives the Judge the right to refer to a rule in the Quran or the Sunna where there is no provision in the law. The accused will be liable under section 3 of the Judgements (Basic Rule Act), 1983. The view taken by the Counsel of the Defence is that this section is against Article 70 of the Constitution which states that 'No person shall be punished for an act which was not an offence at the time he committed the crime'."

27 See the case of *Asma Mahmoud Mohamed Taha and Another v. Sudan Government*, SLJR (1986) p. 163; *Sudan Government v. Osman Mohamed Suliman*, SLJR 1983, p. 147.

courts, including the appointment of their members, are defined under the law. They are statutorily mandated to apply customary law and are an integral part of the formal courts structure. These courts, because they are manned by prominent influential tribal figures (who normally tend to resolve serious disputes at the tribal council), play similar roles to those assumed by the formal judiciary in most situations.

Rules of Procedure and Regulation of Town and Rural Courts, 2004

Rural and Town Courts were given jurisdiction to "apply the predominant custom in their geographic jurisdiction and other laws".[28] However, the establishing order of these courts provides that the "customs shall not contravene the law, the principles of justice and *sharīʿa* law".[29] The Rules of Regulations of 2004 establish three categories of courts having specific competences to apply customary law: (a) Town Courts, (b) Middle Rural Courts, (c) Rural Courts. These courts can be constituted or established by the Chief Justice in any geographical area in Sudan, if he determines that there is a need to establish such types of courts.[30] The Chief Justice also has the power to dissolve, amend or repeal any order establishing such courts if he considers this to be appropriate. Under the Rules of Regulations 2004, any order establishing such courts shall determine, in its constitutive act, the following: (a) the name and type of the court; (b) the geographic jurisdiction; (c) the Head, Deputy Head and members of the court; (d) the number of court sessions; (e) the powers or competences of the court.[31]

Selection Criteria, Membership and Candidacy of the Courts

Members of the Town Courts, Rural Courts and Middle Town Courts are to be selected in accordance with specific criteria: members must enjoy good health, be above the age of thirty, of good conduct and able to read and write (particularly for members of the Town Courts). However, one of the most important criteria for our purpose is that a member of one of these courts "must enjoy high respect and appreciation among his local community and be an eminent figure of weight and influence in his area". Furthermore, he must be a resident of the geographic area of the court's jurisdiction and be living the same

---

28 See Article 10 (h) of the Judiciary Act 1406 and the Rules of Regulations of the Town and Rural Courts 2004.

29 Article 22 (2) (author's translation) of the Rules of Regulations of the Town and Rural Courts 2004.

30 Article 3 (Establishment and Dissolution of the Courts).

31 Article 4.

life style as the dominant population in the area.[32] The Rules of Regulations requires from candidates for the positions of Head and Deputy Head of the Middle Rural Courts or Rural Courts to be knowledgeable about the customs and traditions of the inhabitants of the area.[33]

The selection procedures for members of the courts are also stipulated in the Rules of Procedures 2004. The District Judge, after consultation and seeking opinion of the inhabitants of the area and government employees, nominates qualified members to be Heads, Deputy Heads and members of the Town Courts, Middle Rural Courts and Town Courts.[34] The law is silent, however, on how the opinion of the inhabitants can be sought regarding such nominations. Once the names of the nominees are identified, a “memorandum of recommendation” shall be attached and submitted by the District Judge to the General Court Judge. This Judge shall then submit his recommendation to the Chief Justice of the relevant State. After consultation with the Governor of the State, that Chief Justice will submit his recommendations through the Department of the Town and Rural Courts, with a memorandum justifying the selection of the nominees. All supporting documentation for the nominees must be attached. The Chief Justice, on his part, appoints the nominees in accordance with the aforementioned recommendations.[35] If a candidate is not considered suitable for the nominated position, the Chief Justice may issue a directive to nominate another person, provided that the same procedure is followed.[36] It is pertinent to note here that the Chief Justice has sweeping and unfettered powers: he can establish these courts and cancel the appointment of the Heads or Deputy Heads or members of any court for any reason he sees fit.[37]

Civil and Criminal Jurisdiction of Town Courts, Middle Rural Courts and Rural Courts

The Town and Rural Courts have limited civil and criminal jurisdiction, as such courts are only mandated to look at limited categories of cases. Such courts exercise geographic jurisdiction in accordance with the rules provided for in their establishment, and accordingly can be barred from hearing disputes

32 Article 5.
33 Article 6.
34 Article 7.
35 Article 8.
36 Article 9.
37 Article 10.

falling outside their competence.[38] For example, the Town and Rural Courts have no criminal jurisdiction in cases of murder, retribution (not involving murder), *ḥudūd* cases (with the exception of the punishment for drinking alcohol), juvenile cases, civil claims related to land ownership and any claims against the government or any public corporation.[39] It is pertinent to note here that the criminal jurisdiction of the Rural and Town Courts is very limited, particularly with regard to murder cases.

The Town and Rural Courts can be established in any town in Sudan in accordance with the provisions of the Rules of Regulation or Procedures.[40] They have civil jurisdiction over minor cases involving small sums.[41] The Town Courts also have criminal jurisdiction and can impose the following punishments and measures: (a) imprisonment for a period not exceeding three years; (b) fines not exceeding 100,000 dinars; (c) lashing not exceeding 25 lashes (40 lashes in the case of drunkenness); (d) releasing of a convicted prisoner on the basis of good conduct up to two years before the end of his sentence; (e) measures decided by sheikhs (tribal chiefs).

The Middle Rural Courts have civil jurisdiction over the following cases: (a) claims related to pasture and farm damage or trespassing or injury to cattle, without specifying the amount of damages; (b) cases related to land and boundary disputes; (c) appellate powers over decisions and orders issued by the Rural Courts related to civil cases.

The Middle Rural Courts have criminal jurisdiction and the power to impose the following punishments and measures: (a) imprisonment not exceeding seven years; (b) fines not exceeding 400,000 dinars; (c) lashing not exceeding 25 lashes (40 lashes in the case of drunkenness); (d) releasing of a convicted prisoner on the basis of good conduct up to two years before the end of his sentence; (e) measures decided by sheikhs.[42]

The Rural Courts have the following civil jurisdiction: (a) claims related to pasture and farm damages or injury to cattle, without specifying the amount of damages; (b) cases related to land and boundary disputes. The Rural Courts have also criminal jurisdiction including (a) imprisonment for a period not exceeding five years; (b) fines not exceeding 200,000 dinars; (c) lashing not exceeding 25 lashes (40 lashes in the case of drunkenness); (d) releasing of a convicted prisoner on the basis of good conduct up to two years before the end

38 Article 11.

39 Article 12.

40 Article 2 (a) Preliminary Rulings.

41 Article 14.

42 Article 17(1).

of his sentence; (e) measures decided by sheikhs; (g) confiscation of property; (h) destruction or demolition of property.

Native Administration and Tribal Customary Courts

Having highlighted the customary courts administering customary law, this part seeks to examine the relationship between the formal and informal justice systems, and assesses the role of customary native institutions. Like most parts of Sudan, traditional institutions form an integral part of the informal justice system, and play a critical role in resolving disputes ranging from criminal, civil and personal matters, to social order and maintaining social equilibrium between various groups. Tribal and customary institutions do not generally resort to formal courts to settle their disputes. Rather, certain tribes resort to tribal councils and apply their own customs in disputes. In most cases, tribal councils resolve disputes in a satisfactory manner (Ohaj 1971). This ability to resolve disputes, no doubt, gives them great legitimacy among the people.

However, the relationship between the traditional justice system and the state is normally marked by domination and hegemony on the part of the state. In recent years, there has been a tendency by the government or the executive organs of the state to enact laws that interfere in the appointment of traditional leaders, even though such leaders were historically appointed in accordance with their recognized tribal customs and traditions. Under such laws, the government has been accorded massive executive powers and this largely undermines the autonomy of the Native Administration.[43] In eastern Sudan, for example, one of the controversial powers recently accorded to the Wali, or Commissioner, under Native Administration laws, is that a member can be removed if there is a security lapse or a breakdown in law and order in their areas or locality caused by their mismanagement.[44] Accordingly, administrative and judicial powers accorded to the members of the Native Administration will automatically be lost upon their removal or being released from office. These powers clearly undermine the role of traditional institutions in applying certain customary laws, particularly in criminal cases such as homicide, grievous bodily harm and wounding. Customary law in such situations is normally applied by Tribal Councils (*majlis*), as informal institutions operate in parallel with the formal justice system. When any of the aforementioned crimes, including murder, are committed by a member of a tribe, the police

43 See for example, Article 13 of the Native Administration Act of Kassala State.

44 Article13 (b) and 15 of the Native Administration Act of Kassala State 2007.

will immediately be involved and enforce the law by applying the relevant criminal laws and procedures (the Criminal Act 1991, the Criminal Procedure Act 1991), including the investigation of the crime and the arrest of the accused person or persons. However, in such situations, what matters is the mediation conducted by tribal customary institutions to reach an amicable settlement between the parties, irrespective of what is achieved by the formal criminal justice system. In such cases, the tribal dignitaries intervene and appeal for the suspension of the criminal case pending a positive outcome of the mediation efforts or *ṣulḥ*. Efforts towards *ṣulḥ* exert further pressure on the aggrieved party, particularly in murder cases, to accept the *dīya* rather than retribution. Thus, matters such as murder, that are regarded as serious crimes in Western jurisprudence and call for punishment by the state, are treated from a tribal point of view as private wrongs calling for compensation. The payment of *dīya* or blood money for murder is common, and often no additional punishment is to be imposed. This is because, in most cases, tribes are simply anxious to settle their own disputes out of court, and to achieve what was known as a *ṣulḥ* or "reconciliation" (Sallawi 1983, p. 40). In such cases, courts or the central authority do not exercise power. This has been confirmed in court practices.[45]

Also, in some situations, tribal leaders may ask the court, albeit informally, to delay issuing a verdict to allow more time for tribal mediation. In this approach, the traditional conception of law extended only to restitution rather than retribution. This approach is natural in the traditional tribal societies of Africa, as the killing of a member of a tribal group or clan by a member of another clan had the effect of disturbing the peace between the two groups. Unless appropriate satisfactory settlement is obtained, the injured clan would take retaliatory action against the killer's clan (Sallawi, 1983). The ultimate purpose is to maintain communal and social peace. Nevertheless, such customary criminal laws and practices may not be in harmony with international human rights standards related to the administration of justice in situations where the accused person is denied the right to have a lawyer, to call witnesses or to have legal assistance for the sake of communal settlement.[46]

---

45 In *Sudan Government v. El Deig Adam Abbas* (SLJR (1968) p. 104, the Court ruled that: "The amount of *Dīya* is left for local customs and the agreement of the parties, i.e., the relatives of the accused. Payment of *dīya* is recommended not ordered.... if *dīya* is agreed to between the parties and is duly paid the court recommends that sentence passed against the accused be reduced in the number of years". *Dīya* in this sense operates as diminished sentence for the defendant. However, in certain cases the rate for homicide is fixed by the deceased's relatives.

46 See Article 14 (3); Article 14 (3) (d) Article 14 (3) (e).

In addition to criminal matters, we find that personal matters are also settled by the informal justice system by customary law rather than in formal courts or the justice system. In matters of personal law, people do not resort to courts to resolve family law disputes including divorce and inheritance, as these issues are sensitive and associated with stigma, which is degrading and humiliating for the whole tribe. Such disputes are normally settled by customary institutions through religious judges according to *sharīʿa* law, without resorting to the formal justice system.[47] Judges invite the parties to the dispute to appear before the traditional courts and can also call witnesses. However, it is customary in certain tribes in eastern Sudan for women not to be allowed to appear before the judge, and their fathers or brothers represent them, particularly in cases related to divorce or inheritance. According to Rashaida customs in eastern Sudan, consent to marriage is not required from the woman: she has to accept the husband chosen by her family. If she refuses, she will be compelled to marry him. However, in the case of a woman who has been married before, she must be consulted. With regard to the permitted age for marriage, women normally marry at the age of thirteen while men marry between the ages of fifteen and twenty (Abdella 1974). In divorce cases, if a woman is granted a divorce by the court for whatever reason, it will not be recognized by the clan or the tribe unless the husband consents to it. The husband has also the prerogative right of *ḥajr*, or barring her from re-marrying, even if the court grants her divorce. In this case, she has two choices: her ex-husband can re-marry her if she accepts him. If she continues to refuse to re-marry him, she must pay what is called *nahawa* money to release herself or buy her freedom. These customs are clearly not in harmony with either Sudanese personal law or international human rights standards (Babiker 2009). Therefore, divorce by formal courts may not be recognized among the Rashaida under Sudanese personal laws as such laws are not considered as binding on the husband. Furthermore, the divorced woman cannot get married again unless the concerned families or parties consented to it; the husband must also be present to approve it. Any divorce unless consented to by all parties will not be recognized even if granted by courts.

47 However, in certain situations they resort to the courts for formal approval or registering of marriages in official records. This is merely procedural and pragmatic because certificates authenticated by the authorise are required in certain circumstances.

Incompatibility between Customary Law, Statutory Laws and Human Rights Law

This part identifies actual or potential conflicts between substantive customary norms, statutory laws and *sharīʿa* law. It also highlights the incompatibility between customary law and international human rights, particularly those standards dealing with women's rights and the administration of justice.

Customary Law and Statutory Criminal Law

As indicated elsewhere in this chapter, the concept of punishment or retribution barely exists in customary criminal law, where it is reconciliation that takes priority with the aim of achieving social harmony rather than requiring retribution. Where a loss or damage has been caused, the law will require reparations of such loss or damage (Macek 1993). These penalties are normally merged with compensation in civil law. When loss or damage is incurred, whether by a criminal act or because of a civil wrong, the result is the same: the wrongdoer will be required to pay compensation to the aggrieved person, or to his relatives if the victim has died. No imprisonment or other physical penalty is imposed by customary law. It seems that this tendency is manifested in the fundamental principles of the Criminal Procedure Act 1991, which seek to settle *ḥudūd* punishments through pardon and reconciliation. In this respect, one may argue that there is some harmony between statutory criminal law and customary law, at least in their philosophical orientations. Article 4 (h) of the Criminal Procedure Act 1991 stipulates: "Conciliation or pardon may be made in every offence involving a private right, to the extent of such right, subject to the provisions of *ḥudūd* offences."

However, a structural conflict still exists in certain areas between customary law and statutory law. In some tribal communities, in order to prevent the escalation of hostilities between tribes in homicide cases, the accused person is normally denied under tribal custom (such as the *galad* custom of the Beja tribes in eastern Sudan) his or her natural rights. For example, he may be denied the right to his own lawyer or to call defence witnesses; he may be exiled from the area of his habitual residence and his family may not be allowed to visit (Babiker, 2009). Furthermore, in certain extreme cases where the court does not have enough evidence to convict the accused, tribal dignitaries may interfere and appeal to the trial judge to keep him in custody and postpone issuing a verdict, pending amicable settlement of the case by the traditional councils or *majlis*. The rationale behind this request is that any acquittal may jeopardize tribal negotiations and trigger violence or encourage the aggrieved tribe to target members of the defendant's tribe. Although the accused is not legally bound to pay *diya* after being acquitted, the outcome of the criminal trial is irrelevant as it will not be recognized by the aggrieved tribe. What matters is that the tribe of the accused (whether guilty or innocent) is urged to reach a final settlement through informal justice mechanisms, for the sake of realizing stability and communal peace, rather than settling the case through the formal justice system. Although these customary norms are widely respected and play a vital role in the maintenance of social equilibrium, such norms conflict with statutory law as well as international human rights standards, particularly those standards related to the administration of justice (such as the right to a fair trial). One of the fundamental principles of any criminal justice system is that no punishment shall be imposed on the accused person until he is proven guilty by a competent and impartial court or tribunal. Article (4) (c) of the Criminal Procedure Act 1991, for example, provides that "an accused is presumed innocent until his conviction is proved, and he is entitled to be subject to fair and prompt enquiry and trial". Proving whether the accused is innocent or guilty matters very little for many tribal communities: what matters is that the aggrieved tribe must be compensated for the wrongful criminal act, irrespective of the trial outcome and whether the accused person is guilty or innocent. Customary norms also entail that *diya* must be paid, irrespective of the court judgement and even if the accused is innocent. This violates the Criminal Procedures Act 1991. Article 141 (Dismissal of Criminal Suit During Trial) provides that "where it transpires to the court after hearing the prosecution evidence and examination of the accused, that evidence does not lead to his conviction, it shall pass an order dismissing the criminal suit and release the accused".[48] Accordingly, the accused is not legally bound to pay *diya* if not convicted.

Furthermore, under Sudanese criminal law, the accused normally has the fundamental right to a fair trial. The Criminal Procedures Act 1991 provides that "the accused shall have the right to be defended by a lawyer and the right to receive legal aid in criminal cases, in particular those cases which involve punishments with imprisonment for the term of ten years or more, amputation or death is insolvent".[49] Although the Criminal Procedure Act secures the right of the accused to have a lawyer, as well as his right to request legal assistance as a matter of statutory law, assistance under the Act cannot automatically be guaranteed unless requested by the accused. In traditional tribal contexts, the accused does not normally ask for assistance as he well understands that he should not request such assistance to guarantee a prospective

48 English official translation.

49 Article 34 (1) and (3) of English official translation.

positive settlement, entrusted to the tribal customary councils as a parallel informal justice mechanism. The pertinent question here is: is it legitimate for the accused not to ask for a lawyer in such circumstances? Or does the interest of justice dictate that the court should nevertheless urge the accused to have a lawyer for the sake of achieving justice?

Customary Law and Statutory Personal Law

In personal matters or disputes, most tribes do not resort to courts or the formal justice system, as this would be considered to attract stigma to the whole tribe, particularly women. However, this is generally contested as many women now tend to resort to official courts as customary institutions are weakened and gradually in decline. When women resort to customary law institutions, they are not allowed to appear before the religious or traditional judges, and their fathers or brothers represent them, particularly in cases related to divorce or inheritance. As explained above, divorce granted by courts is sometimes not recognized by the husband under customary norms, even if granted or validated by a *sharīʿa* Islamic court.[50] This is a clear example of how customary law conflicts with statutory law. Thus, it seems that there is an institutional conflict between the informal customary justice system and the formal justice system represented by courts; however, the latter do not enjoy recognition among tribes particularly when it comes to decisions made under Sudanese personal law. The fact that women cannot access the formal legal system denies them their basic right to access justice, and also contradicts various provisions of the Personal Affairs Act 1991, as well as the constitutional guarantees related to equality before the law.[51]

Incompatibility between Customary Law and Human Rights Law

One of the contentious areas to be examined here relates to the incompatibility between the customary justice system and international human rights standards, including the Bill of Rights of the INC 2005. In this respect, it is pertinent to refer to the Human Rights Committee's recent Commentary on Article 14 of the ICCPR, with regard to customary institutions. The Committee states that Article 14 is relevant where a state, in its legal order, recognizes courts

---

50 For example, in Eastern Sudan men have the prerogative right of *ḥajr* (barring the woman from getting married even if granted divorce by the court). In order to get her freedom, she has to pay what is called *nahawa*.

51 For example, Article 31 of INC 2005 provides that "all persons are equal before the law and are entitled without discrimination, as to race, color, sex, language, religious creed, political opinion, or ethnic origin, to the equal protection of the law".

based on customary law, or religious courts, to carry out, or entrusts them with, judicial tasks. It must be ensured that such courts cannot hand down binding judgments recognized by the state, unless certain requirements are met: (a) proceedings before such courts are limited to minor civil and criminal matters; (b) they meet the basic requirements of fair trial and other relevant guarantees of the ICCPR, and; (c) their judgements are validated by state courts in light of the guarantees set out in the ICCPR and can be challenged by the parties concerned in a procedure meeting the requirements of Article 14 of the ICCPR. These principles are in addition to the general obligation on the state to protect the rights under the ICCPR of any persons affected by the operation of customary and religious courts. This means that any process of harmonization or integration (of customary law, statutory law and human rights) in Sudan's pluralistic legal system shall not negatively affect individual rights. Maintaining this legal pluralism in a balanced way may be difficult to achieve.

References

Abdella, A 1974, *The Cultural Heritage of the Rashaida Tribe*, Institute of African and Asian Studies, University of Khartoum, Khartoum.

Abu Rannat, CJ 1960, 'The Relationship between Islamic Law and Customary law in the Sudan', *Journal of African Law*, vol. 4, no. 12, pp. 9–16.

Akolawin, NO 1971, 'Islamic and Customary Law in the Sudan: Problems of Today and Tomorrow', in Y Fadl Hassan (ed.), *Sudan in Africa*, University of Khartoum, Khartoum, pp. 279–301.

Akolawin, NO 1973, 'Personal Law in the Sudan: Trends and Developments', *Journal of African Law*, vol. 17, no. 2, pp. 149–195.

Babiker, M 2009, *Customary Law in the Kassala State*, UNDP, Khartoum.

Clark, WT 1938, 'Manners, Customs and Beliefs of the Northern Beja', *Sudan Notes & Records*, vol. 21, pp. 1–30.

El Hada, H 1976, 'Aspects of Choice of Jurisdiction and Choice of Law in Matrimonial Matters in English and Sudanese Law', LLM Thesis, University of Khartoum, Faculty of Law.

El Mahdi, S 1971, *A Guide to Land Settlement and Registration*, Khartoum University Press, Khartoum.

Macek, J 1993, 'The Essentials for the Role of Customary Law in Southern Sudan', *Sudan Journal of Law and Reports*, pp. 1–23.

Mustafa, Z 1971, *The Common Law of the Sudan: An Account of Justice, Equity, and Good Conscience Provision*, Clarendon Press, Oxford.

Ohaj, A 1971, *The Beja Cultural Heritage*, Institute of African and Asian Studies, University of Khartoum, Khartoum.

Sallawi, I 1983, 'Local Superstition as a Cause of Crime in the Democratic Republic of the Sudan', LLM Thesis submitted to the Faculty of Law, George Washington University, Washington DC.

Thompson, C 1965, 'The Formative Era of the Law of the Sudan', *Sudan Law Journal and Reports*.

Zakaria, I 1991, 'An Analytical Study of Some Legal Theories and Their Relevance to the Sudan', LLM Thesis, University of Khartoum, Faculty of Law.

Case Law

- Laliet, The Indian Merchant's case. Published in *Al-Sahafa* 9th November 1984.
- Asma Mahmoud Mohamed Taha and Another v. Sudan Government, SLJR (1986) p. 163.
- Sudan Government v. Osman Mohamed Suliman, SLJR 1983.
- Heirs of Eltoma Bint Ali v Ali Mohammed El Sayed (D.C.C.S-472-5, 519, 805-1942 (Khat).
- Taha El Egeil v. Suliman Dawood Mandil (A.C. rev-35-8-1953).
- Atta El Manan Ahmed Falag v. Owners of Sagia No 6 El Damer, H.C.S-401946.
- Mahmoud Elnur Omer v. Ibrahim Mohamed, H.C.-REV-65-1955.
- Omer Ali Omer v. Fadl El Mula El Hussein and others, SLJR (1962).
- Heirs of Abdel Aziz Khames v. Heirs of Habib Habram SLJR (1967).
- Abdulla El Hassan Hamza v. Safiya Ali Abu Ali and another SLJR (1962).
- Mohamed Abdel Gabbar v. Suliman Salib Tambal, HC.-REV-28-1951.
- Ahmed Abdel Hadi v. Sudan Government, H.C.-REV-6-1946.
- Magboul Abdel Aal v. Zeinab Bint Mohammed, H.C.-C.S.-138-1937.
- Heirs of Abdel Gabbar Mohamed v. Fatma Mohamed (1964) SLJR 156.
- Heirs of Fadlalalla Oklah v. Hussein Ali Brar (1964) SLJR (1964) 96.
- Osman Omar v. Mohamed Idrsi (1958) SLJR (1958) 62.
- Heirs of Abdel Aziz Khamees v. Heirs of Habib Habram (1967) SLJR 64.
- The Sudan Government v. El Deig Adam Abbas (1968), SLJR

Annexes

Fieldwork Legal Documents

1.1 *Map of the 42 registered* sagiyya *land plots of Kerma Balad in 1929 (photographed in the land office in Argo, 15 November 2016).*

 | DOI 10.1163/9789004362185_013

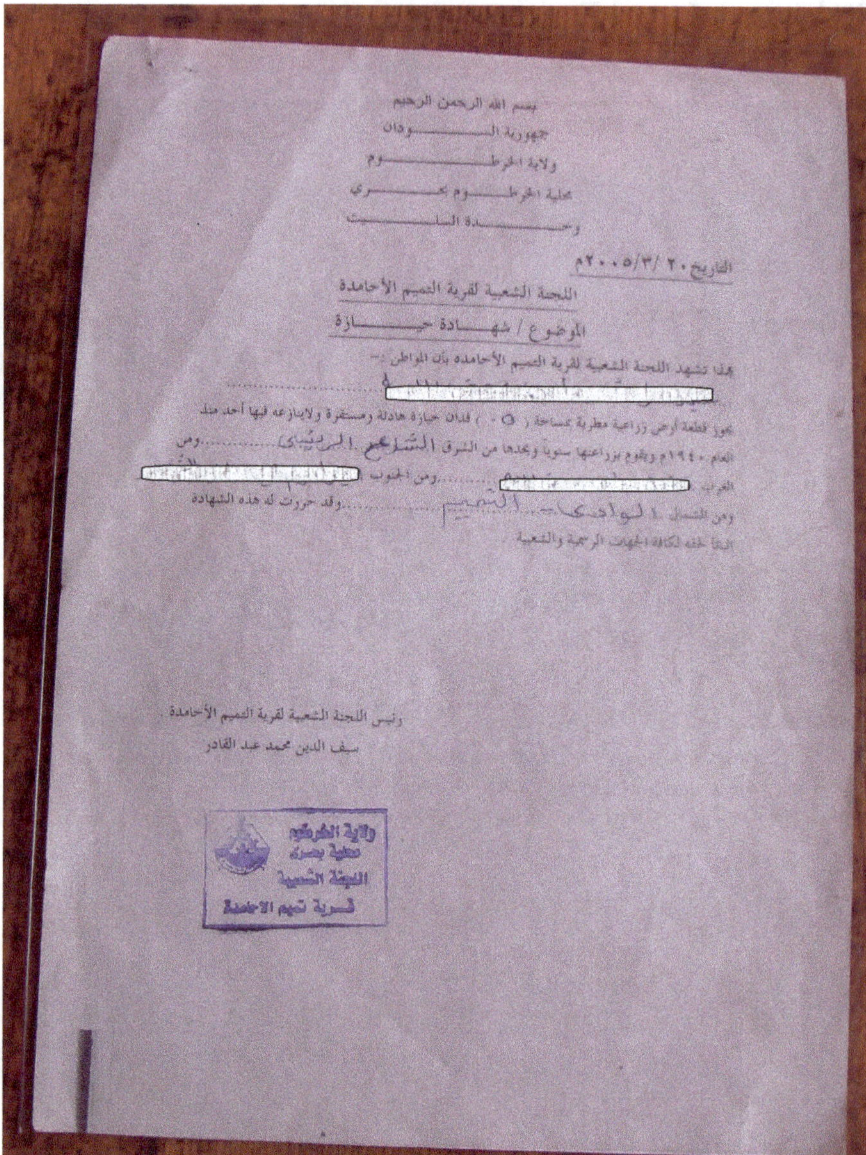

بسم الله الرحمن الرحيم
جمهورية السودان
ولاية الخرطوم
محلية الخرطوم بحري
وحدة السليت

التاريخ ٢٠ /٣/٢٠٠٥م

اللجنة الشعبية لقرية التميم الأحامدة

الموضوع / شهادة حيازة

هذا تشهد اللجنة الشعبية لقرية التميم الأحامده بأن المواطن :-
[illegible]
يحوز قطعة أرض زراعية مطرية بمساحة (٥٠) فدان حيازة هادئة ومستقرة ولاينازعه فيها أحد منذ
العام ١٩٤٠م ويقوم بزراعتها سنويا ويحدها من الشرق الشارع الرئيسي..........ومن
الغرب [illegible]..........ومن الجنوب [illegible]
ومن الشمال الوادي التميم..........وقد حررت له هذه الشهادة
بناءً على طلبه لكافة الجهات الرسمية والشعبية

رئيس اللجنة الشعبية لقرية التميم الأحامدة.
سيف الدين محمد عبد القادر

ولاية الخرطوم
محلية بحري
اللجنة الشعبية
قرية تميم الاحامدة

2.1 *Land possession certificate* (shihādat ḥiyāza) *for a rain-fed agricultural plot issued by the village Popular Committee, Timaim, 20 March 2005.*

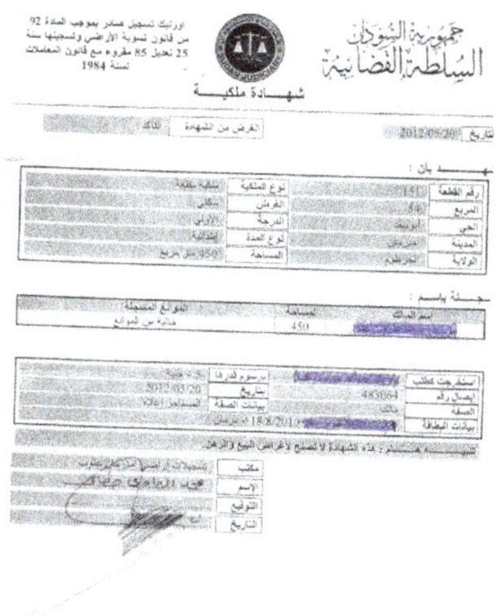

جمهورية السودان
السلطة القضائية

اورنيك تسجيل صادر بموجب المادة 92 من قانون تسوية الأراضي وتسجيلها سنة 25 تعديل 85 مقروء مع قانون المعاملات لسنة 1984

شهادة ملكية

التاريخ 2012/05/20 — الغرض من الشهادة: للتأكد

نشهد بأن :

رقم القطعة	151	نوع الملكية	
المربع	64	الغرض	سكني
الحي	أبو سعيد	الدرجة	الأولى
المدينة	أم درمان	نوع العدة	إبتدائية
الولاية	الخرطوم	المساحة	450 متر مربع

مسجلة باسم :

اسم المالك	المساحة	الموانع المسجلة
	450	خالية من الموانع

استخرجت كطلب		برسوم قدرها	
إيصال رقم	483064	بتاريخ	2012/05/20
الصفة	مالك	بيانات الصفقة	
بيانات البطاقة	18/8/2010		

هذه الشهادة لا تصلح لأغراض البيع والرهن.

مكتب	
الإسم	
التوقيع	
التاريخ	

3.1 *Land property certificate* (shihādat milkiyya) *issued by the Sudan Judiciary, Abu Seʿid, 2 May 2012.*

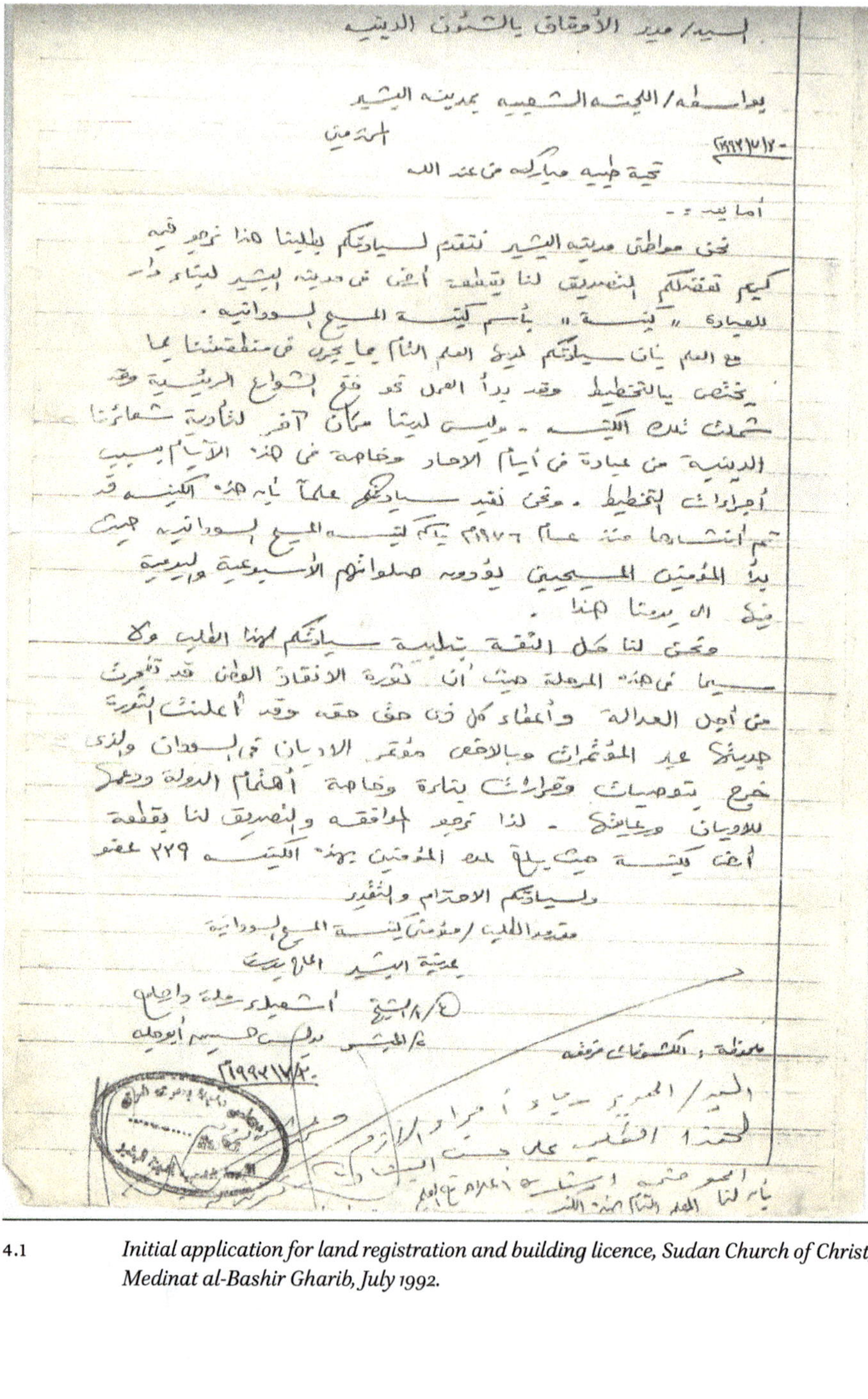

السيد/ مدير الأوقاف بالشئون الدينيه

بواسطة/ اللجنه الشعبيه بمدينه البشير

المحترمين

١٩٩٢/٧/٢-

تحية طيبه مباركه من عند الله

أما بعد :-

نحن مواطني مدينه البشير نتقدم لسيادتكم بطلبنا هذا نرجو فيه كريم تفضلكم بالتصديق لنا بقطعة أرض في مدينة البشير لبناء دار للعبادة " كنيسة " بأسم كنيسة المسيح السودانيه .

مع العلم بأن سيادتكم لديكم العلم التام بما يجري في منطقتنا بما يختص بالتخطيط وقد بدأ العمل في فتح الشوارع الرئيسية وقد شملت تلك الكنيسه . وليس لدينا مكان آخر لتأدية شعائرنا الدينيه من عبادة في أيام الاحاد وخاصة في هذه الأيام بسبب أجراءات التخطيط . ونحن نفيد سيادتكم علماً بأن هذه الكنيسه قد تم أنشاءها منذ عام ١٩٧٦م باسم كنيسه المسيح السودانيه حيث بدأ المؤمنين المسيحيين يؤدون صلواتهم الأسبوعية واليومية فيها الى يومنا هذا .

ونحن لنا كل الثقة بتلبية سيادتكم لهذا الطلب ولا سيما في هذه المرحلة حيث أن ثورة الانقاذ الوطني قد تفجرت من أجل العدالة وأعطاء كل ذي حق حقه وقد أعلنت الثورة حديثاً عن المؤتمرات وبالاخص مؤتمر الاديان في السودان والذى خرج بتوصيات وقرارات بناءة وخاصة أهتمام الدولة ودعمها للاديان وعبادتها . لذا نرجو الموافقه والتصديق لنا بقطعة أرض كنيسة حيث يبلغ عدد المؤمنين بهذه الكنيسه ٢٢٩ عضو

ولسيادتكم الاحترام والتقدير

مقدمو الطلب/ مؤمني كنيسة المسيح السودانيه

مدينة البشير [illegible]

ع/ الشيخ [illegible]

ع/ المبشر [illegible]

١٩٩٢/٧/٣

[illegible]

4.1 *Initial application for land registration and building licence, Sudan Church of Christ, Medinat al-Bashir Gharib, July 1992.*

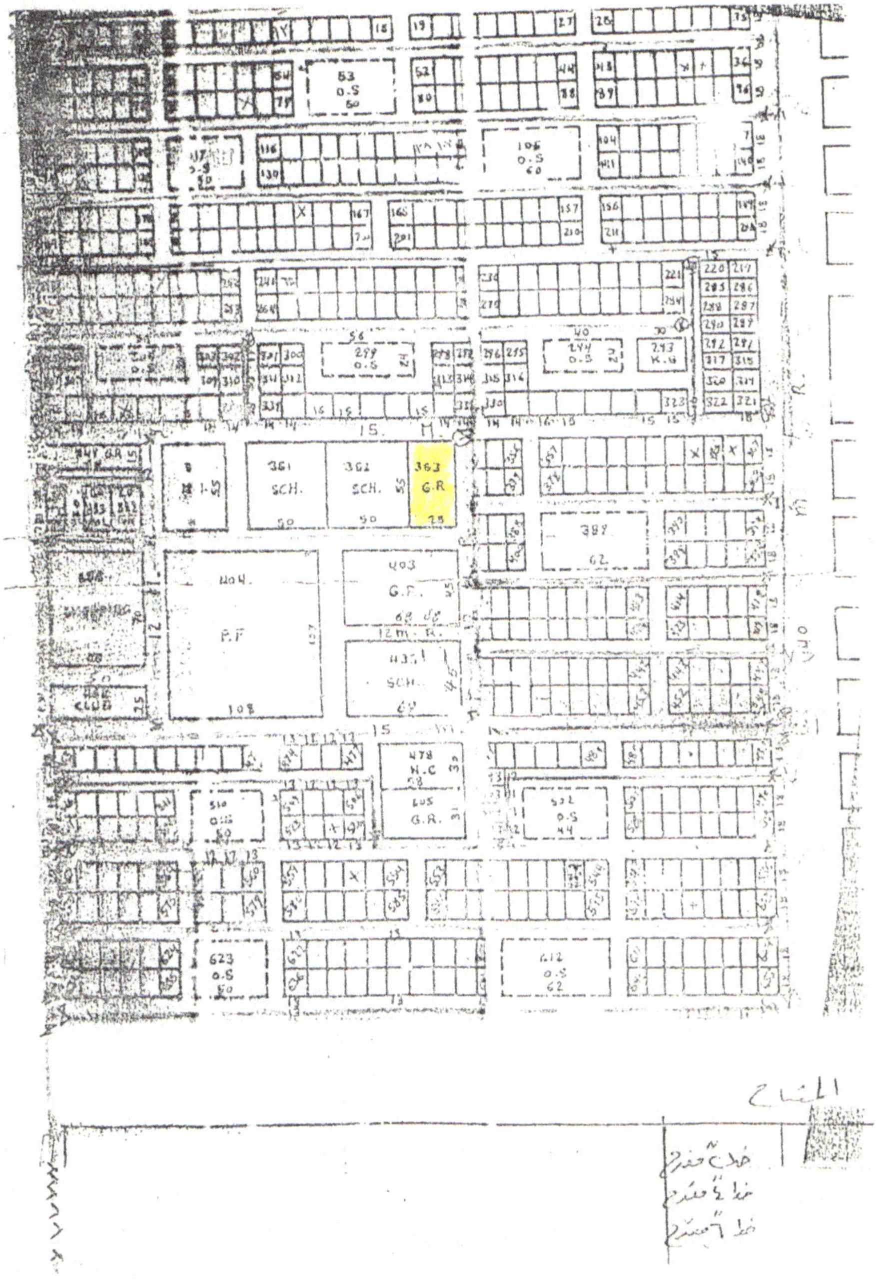

4.2 *Cadastral plan of Medinat al-Bashir Gharib, Local Planning Office, 1992.*

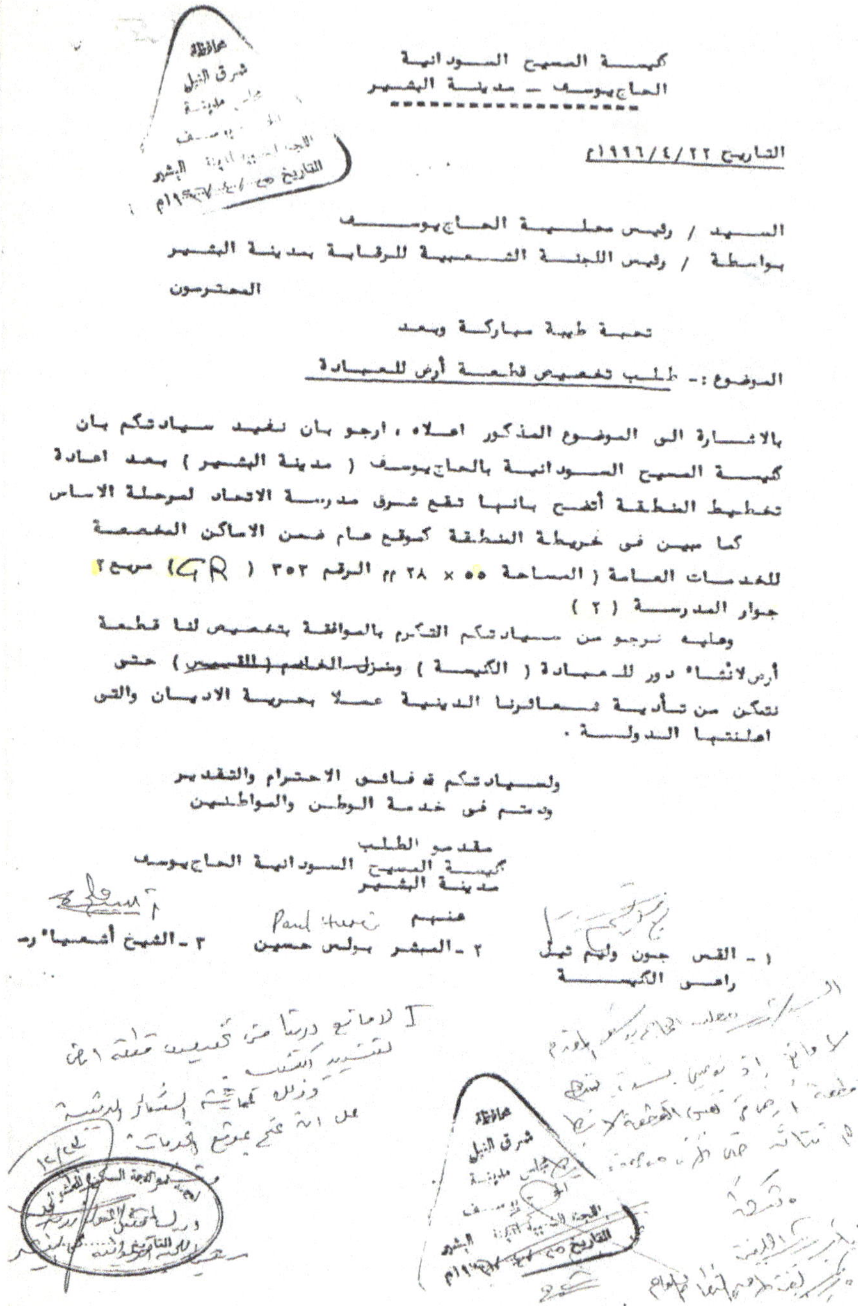

كنيسة المسيح السودانية
الحاج يوسف – مدينة البشير

التاريخ ٢٢/٤/١٩٩٦م

السيد / رئيس محلية الحاج يوسف
بواسطة / رئيس اللجنة الشعبية للرقابة بمدينة البشير
المحترمون

تحية طيبة مباركة وبعد

الموضوع :- طلب تخصيص قطعة أرض للعبادة

بالاشارة الى الموضوع المذكور اعلاه ، ارجو بان نفيد سيادتكم بان كنيسة المسيح السودانية بالحاج يوسف (مدينة البشير) بعد اعادة تخطيط المنطقة أتضح بانها تقع شرق مدرسة الاتحاد لمرحلة الاساس كما مبين فى خريطة المنطقة كموقع عام ضمن الاماكن المخصصة للخدمات العامة (المساحة ٥٥ × ٢٨ م م الرقم ٣٥٢ (GR مربع ٢ جوار المدرسة (٢)
وعليه نرجو من سيادتكم التكرم بالموافقة بتخصيص لنا قطعة أرض لانشاء دور للعبادة (الكنيسة) ومنزل الخادم (القسيس) حتى نتمكن من تأدية شعائرنا الدينية عملا بحرية الاديان والتى اعلنتها الدولة .

ولسيادتكم فائق الاحترام والتقدير
ودمتم فى خدمة الوطن والمواطنين

مقدمو الطلب
كنيسة المسيح السودانية الحاج يوسف
مدينة البشير
عنهم

١ - القس جون وليم تيك
راعى الكنيسة
٢ - المبشر بولس حسين
٣ - الشيخ أشعيا ر

4.3 *Complaint to Haj Yusif Locality* (Maḥalliyya)*, Sudan Church of Christ, Medinat al-Bashir Gharib, 22 April 1996 & hand-written reply from the Director of the Mahalliya.*

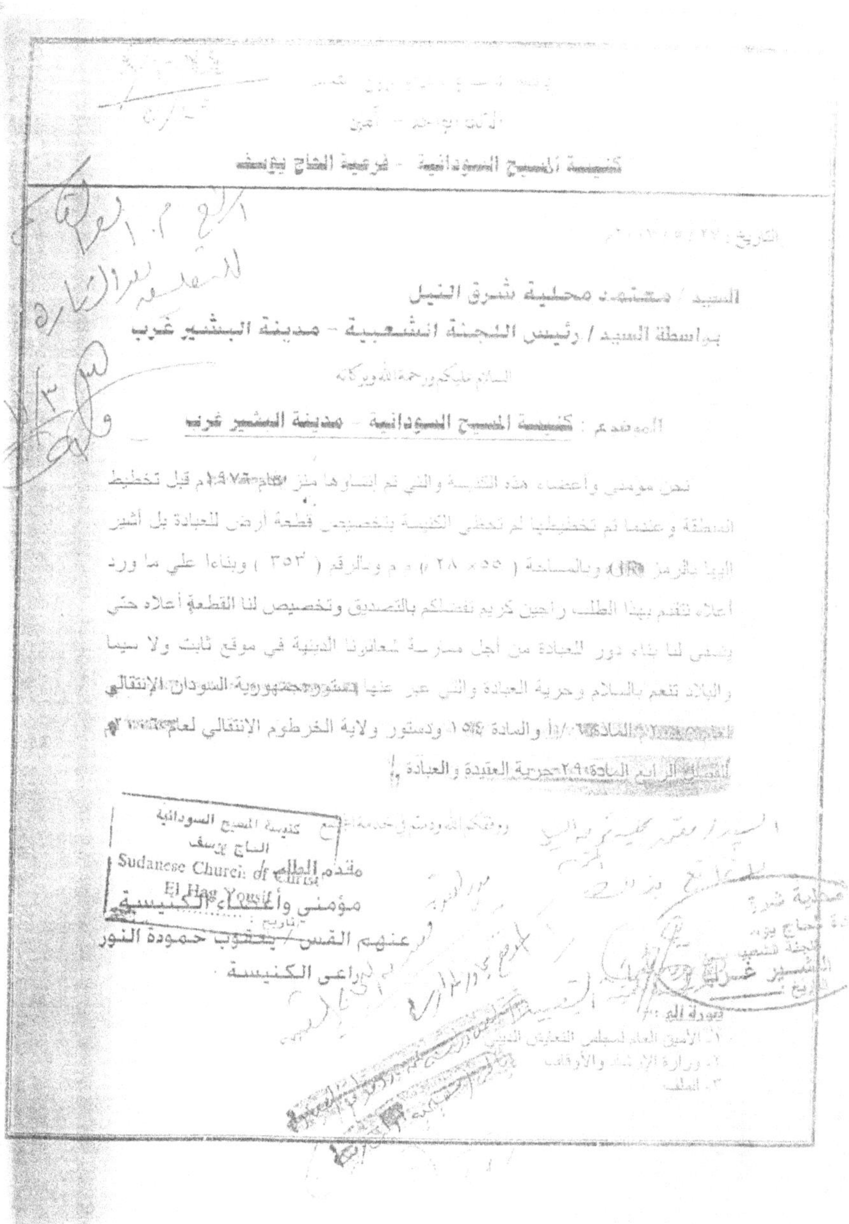

كنيسة المسيح السودانية - فرعية الحاج يوسف

السيد / معتمد محلية شرق النيل

بواسطة السيد / رئيس اللجنة الشعبية - مدينة البشير غرب

السلام عليكم ورحمة الله وبركاته

الموضوع : كنيسة المسيح السودانية - مدينة البشير غرب

نحن مؤمني وأعضاء هذه الكنيسة والتي تم إنشاؤها منذ عام ١٩٧٨م قبل تخطيط المنطقة وعندما تم تخطيطها لم تحظى الكنيسة بتخصيص قطعة أرض للعبادة بل أشير إليها بالرمز (ك) وبالمساحة (٥٥ × ٢٨) م م وبالرقم (٣٥٣) وبناءاً على ما ورد أعلاه نتقدم بهذا الطلب راجين كريم تفضلكم بالتصديق وتخصيص لنا القطعة أعلاه حتى يتسنى لنا بناء دور للعبادة من أجل ممارسة شعائرنا الدينية في موقع ثابت ولا سيما والبلاد تنعم بالسلام وحرية العبادة والتي عبر عنها دستور جمهورية السودان الإنتقالي لعام ٢٠٠٥م المادة ٦/أ والمادة ١٥٤ ودستور ولاية الخرطوم الانتقالي لعام ٢٠٠٥م الفصل الرابع المادة ٢٩ حرية العقيدة والعبادة.

وفقكم الله وسدد خطاكم

مقدم الطلب

مؤمني وأعضاء الكنيسة

عنهم القس / يعقوب حمودة النور

راعي الكنيسة

كنيسة المسيح السودانية الحاج يوسف

Sudanese Church of Christ El Hag Yousif

صورة إلى :

١- الأمين العام لمجلس التعايش الديني

٢- وزارة الإرشاد والأوقاف

٣- الملف

4.4 *Application for land registration and building licence before the Head of the Popular Committee for Medinat al-Bashir Gharib, Sudan Church of Christ, Medinat al-Bashir Gharib, 27 May 2007.*

بسم الله الرحمن الرحيم

ولاية الخرطوم

وزارة التوجيه والأوقاف

مكتب المدير العام

التاريخ : ٣١/ ٨/ ٢٠١٠م النمرة : و خ / و ت ق / م م ع /

الأخ الكريم / مدير التخطيط العمراني محلية شرق النيل

حفظه الله

السلام عليكم ورحمة الله وبركاته

الموضوع :ــ قطعة أرض كنيسة المسيح السودانية الحاج يوسف

مشيرا للموضوع أعلاهـ ..... نفيدكم بموافقتنا المبدئية بخصوص الموضوع أعلاهـ على ترك أمر الموافقة النهائية لتقديرات السلطات المحلية

والله الموفق

المطيع محمد أحمد السيد

4.5 *Initial approval from the State Ministry of Guidance and Endowments & decision of non-objection from the Council of Appeals of the State Ministry of Social and Cultural Affairs, Khartoum, 31 August 2010.*

ولاية الخرطوم
وزارة الشئون الاجتماعية و الثقافية
مجلس الدعوة
ادارة الشؤون المالية و الإدارية

الأخ الكريم المدير العام
السلام عليكم ورحمة الله
الموضوع: قطعة أرض كنيسة المسيح السودانية الحاج يوسف

أفيدكم بأن الكنيسة المذكورة كان لديها مبنى يتبع للكنيسة مبني بالطين والقش.
تم تخطيط المنطقة ولم يصدق لهم القطعة كنيسة.
بل أشير إلى القطعة بأنها تتبع للحكومة (G.R).
تمت العديد من المخاطبات دون نجاح للموضوع.
أخيراً طلب منهم التخطيط العمراني بالمحلية بإحضار خطاب من طرفنا بعدم الممانعة.
عليه أرى أنه يتم مخاطبة التخطيط العمراني بمحلية شرق النيل عن موافقتنا المبدئية من حيث الخصوص ونترك الأمر للسلطات المحلية.
وجزاكم الله خيراً

حاكم إسكندر يوسف
مدير إدارة الكنائس
٢٢/٨/٢٠١٣م

مرفقات
الخطابات المعنية.

أوافق

السودان – الخرطوم – ...
شارع اللواء محمد نجيب – شمال جهاز المغتربين
هاتف ٨٣٤٣٨٤٠٢١ – فاكس: ٨٣٤٣١١٩٩

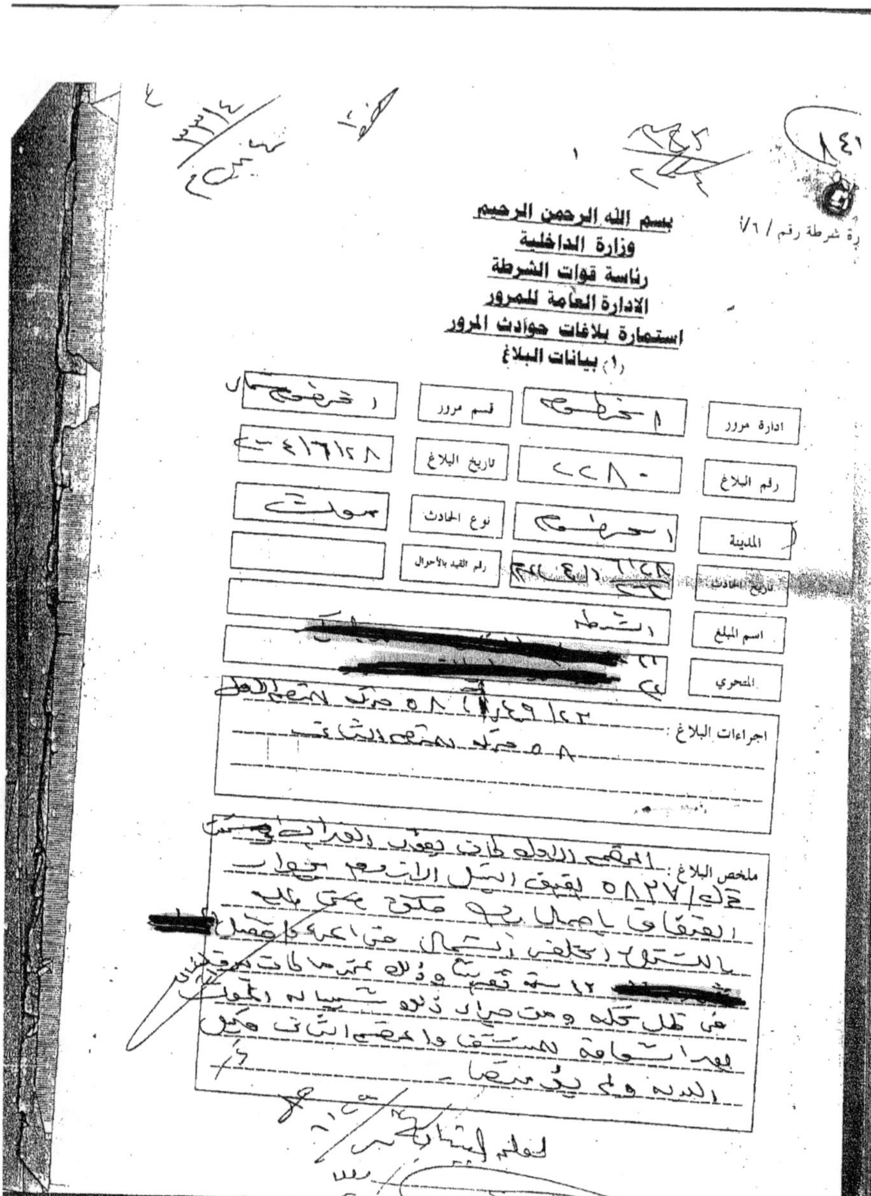

رة شرطة رقم / ٦/١

بسم الله الرحمن الرحيم

وزارة الداخلية

رئاسة قوات الشرطة

الادارة العامة للمرور

استمارة بلاغات حوادث المرور

(١) بيانات البلاغ

ادارة مرور — قسم مرور

رقم البلاغ — تاريخ البلاغ

المدينة — نوع الحادث

تاريخ الحادث — رقم القيد بالأحوال

اسم المبلغ

المتحري

اجراءات البلاغ :

ملخص البلاغ :

8.1 *Road traffic accident complaint form, General Administration of Traffic, Khartoum, 28 June 2004.*

بسم الله الرحمن الرحيم

محكمة الحركة الخرطوم شمال

البلاغ 2280 / 2004

19/ يوليو / 2010

السيد / رئيس مكتب تسجيلات – ام درمان وسط

الموضوع : فك الحجز عن القطعة 3/220

مربع 22 سوق ام درمان

بالإشارة الي خطابكم بالنمرة ملف القطعة رقم 3/220/مربع 22 سوق ام درمان

بتاريخ 2004/6/29 والذي بموجبه تم الحجز علي القطعة اعلاه .

عليه تأمر بفك الحجز عن القطعة رقم 3/220/مربع 22 سوق ام درمان وافادتنا بذلك .

١٩/٧/٢٠١٠م

[illegible]

قاضي المحكمة العامة

الحركة الخرطوم شمال

8.2 *Withdrawal of mortgage on land, Khartoum Penal Court of the Circulation Administration, 19 July 2010.*

Excerpts from Sudan's Statutory Land Laws 1900–2015

Selected and Compiled by Mohamed Abdelsalam Babiker

The excerpts of the Sudan's statutory land laws below were revised and updated until the 28th of February 2010 according to the provisions of the revised edition of laws 1974. Some of these excerpts have been prepared, revised and translated by the translation section affiliated to Legislation Department in the Sudan Ministry of Justice. In particular, the texts of the laws since 1900 to 1970 represent the official translated versions which were published in the Gazette. However, the laws from 1983 to 2015 were only published in Arabic language in the Gazette and no official translations were made since then from Arabic into English. Some of these laws were partially translated and edited by the editor of this book and largely represent accurate translations from Arabic into English.

No	Title	Volumes, dates
1	Civil Justice Ordinance, 1900	1900
2	The Land Demarcation and Survey Act, 1905	*Laws of the Sudan*, Vol. I, 1901–1925, Fifth Edition, pp.19–23
3	Land Acquisition Act, 1930	*Laws of the Sudan*, Vol. II, 1926–1938, Fifth Edition, pp. 239–255
4	The Unregistered Land Act, 1970	*Laws of the Sudan*, Vol. V, 1962–1970, pp. 226–229
5	The Civil Procedure Act, 1983	*Laws of the Sudan*, Vol. III, 1984–1981, Eighth Edition
6	The Civil Transaction Act, 1984	*Laws of the Sudan*, Vol. III, 1984–1981, Eighth Edition
7	The Physical Planning and Disposition of Land Act, 1994	16th April 1994
8	The Investment (Encouragement) Act, 1999	1999
9	The Investment (Encouragement) Act, 2013	2013
10	Towns and Rural Courts Regulations, 2004	2004
11	The National Land Commission Act, 2009	28th June 2009
12	Interim National Constitution, 2005	2005, Amendments 2015
13	Interim Constitution of Blue Nile State, 2005	November 2005

 | DOI 10.1163/9789004362185_014

No	Title	Volumes, dates
14	Interim Constitution of North Darfur State, 2005	24th November 2005
15	Interim Constitution of West Darfur State, 2005	13th December 2005

1 Civil Justice Ordinance, 1900

Section 3:

Where in any suit or other proceedings in a Civil Court any question arises regarding succession, inheritance, will, legacies, gifts, marriage, divorce, family relations, or the constitution of wakfs, the rule of decision shall be:

(a) Any custom applicable to the parties concerned, which is not contrary to justice, equity and good conscience, and has not been by this or any other enactment altered or abolished, and has not been declared void by competent authority.

(b) The Mohammedan law, in cases where the parties are Mohammedans, except in so far as that law has been modified by any such custom as is above referred.

2 The Land Demarcation and Survey Act, 1905

An Act for facilitating the demarcation of boundaries and the making of surveys.

Title

1. This Act may be cited as the "Land Demarcation and Survey Act, 1905".

Authority to demarcate or survey lands

2. It shall be lawful for the Governor of the State concerned and the Director of Surveys Department or any other officer empowered by any law, or instrument in writing signed by him to authorize the Government official to demarcate or survey any lands described in such instrument.[1]

1 1974 Acts No. 40, 1983 Act No. 26.

General Powers of Survey Officers

3. (1) Any officers authorized to demarcate or survey any lands may at any reasonable time enter upon any lands which he is required to demarcate or survey and upon lands contiguous thereto, and may make any inquiries and may fix any stone, post, pillar or other boundary or survey mark in or upon the land and may dig up any ground for the purpose of fixing the same and he may cut down and remove any timber or other plant which may obstruct any survey line; provided always that as little damage as possible shall be done to the land or to any property thereon.

Power of survey Officers to summon persons to give information

4. Any officers authorized to demarcate or survey any land may order any person or persons occupying or interested in such land or any land abutting thereon or any person employed or in connection therewith or any person who can give information relating to the boundaries of the same or in whose possession or power any instrument relating to such boundaries is alleged to be:[2]

(a) to attend before him at a fixed time and place;
(b) to point out the boundaries of the land;
(c) to give any information required for the purpose of the demarcation or survey;
(d) to produce any instrument in his power or possession relating to such boundaries.

Owners and occupiers may be ordered to demarcate their lands

5. (1) Any officer authorized to demarcate or survey any land may order the owner or occupier of such land within a reasonable time to be fixed by such officer, to:-

(a) demarcate his land and for the purpose of such demarcation to erect such stones, pillars, posts or boundary or landmarks as the such officers may direct;
(b) clear any boundary or other line which it may be necessary to clear for the purpose of the demarcation of his land;
(c) provide labour or otherwise assist in the demarcation of his land.

Such order may be in the form set forth in Schedule (B).

2 1974 Act No. 40.

Liability of the Public to obey orders

6. (1) Every person called upon to do any of the matters mentioned in sections 4 and 5 shall be legally liable so far as he may be able to do any of such matters which he may be so called on to do.

(2) A notice calling upon any person to do any of the matters mentioned in sections 4and 5 may be addressed to him individually or to him and other persons jointly and such calling shall unless the contrary appears, be deemed to have been communicated to him where delivered to the people's administration of the village in which such land situated.[3]

Duties of sheikhs as regards landmarks

10. Every people's administrator may to prevent the injury, destruction or removal of any official landmark, boundary mark or survey mark within the local limits of his jurisdiction and to report immediately to the competent locality whenever he becomes a ware that any such mark has been so interfered with.[4]

Penalties for defacing, removal of etc. landmarks

11. Whoever defaces, removes, injures or otherwise impairs any landmark, boundary mark or survey mark unless duly authorized to do so shall be punishable upon conviction with imprisonment, for a term which may extend to one year, or with fine or with both.

Schedule A

(See section 4)

Summons to attend and furnish information

To the owners and occupiers of the (*sagia*) land numbered .... In the village of .... or to A B owner of .... Take notice that by virtue of section 4 of the Demarcation and survey Act, 1905, you are hereby required (either personally or by your authorized agent)

(a) To meet .... at .... on the .... day of .... and not to depart without his permission;

(b) To point out to him the boundaries of the land owned or occupied by you;

(c) To furnish him with any information which he may require for the purpose of the survey;

(d) To produce to him any document in your power or possession relating to the boundaries of such land.

3 The same.

4 *Ibid.*

Schedule B

(See section 5)

Notice to assist in demarcation

To the owners and occupiers of the .... Lands in the village of ...., or to AB of ....

Take notice that by virtue of the power given by the provisions of section 5 of the Demarcation and Survey Act, 1905, you are hereby (respectively) required:-

(a) to fix or repair the marks of the lands so owned or occupied by you before the .... Day of ....

(b) to clear the boundary lines of such lands;

(c) to meet the said .... on the .... day of .... On the land so owned or occupied by you and to assist him in the demarcation of the said land.

Schedule C

(See section 8)

Notice to maintain boundary marks

To .... Take notice that by virtue of the powers given by section 8 of the Demarcation and Survey Act, 1905, I hereby order that the boundary and landmarks erected on your land and specified on the back hereof are placed under your charge and you are hereby required to keep and maintain the same in good repair.

3 Land Acquisition Act, 1930

(20.8.1930)

Title

1. This Act may be cited as the "Land Acquisition Act, 1930"

Interpretation

2. In this Act the following words and expressions have the following meanings, unless a different intention appears from the subject or context:

"Land subject to village or tribal rights", means land which is owned by the Government subject to rights of watering, grazing, cultivating, wood cutting and the like, enjoyed by the members of any tribe or section of a tribe, or of any town, village or part thereof;

"Registered Land", means the land settled and registered under the provisions of this Act, and it includes houses, premises and date trees not settled or registered before, arise out or grew in the land that its right or ownership had been settled and registered as aforesaid;

"Register", means a register of title to land, established under the land Settlement and Registration Act, 1925 or any statutory re-enactment;

Powers before acquisition has been determined upon

4. (1) Where it appears to the Governor that land in any locality is likely to be required permanently or temporarily for any public purpose a notification to this effect shall be published in the Gazette, and the Governor shall publish the substance of such notification at convenient places in such locality, and thereupon it shall be lawful for any person, either generally or specially authorized by the Governor and for its servants or workmen, to do all or any of the following things.[5]

(a) to enter upon and survey and take levels of any land in such locality;
(b) to dig or bore into the sub-soil;
(c) to do all other acts necessary to ascertain whether the land is adapted for such purpose;
(d) to set out the boundaries of the land proposed to be taken and the intended line of the work proposed to be made thereon;
(e) to make such levels, boundaries and line by placing marks and cutting trenches;
(f) where otherwise the survey cannot be completed, the levels taken or the boundaries or line of the work marked, to cut down and clear away any crop, fence trees or undergrowth; provided that no person shall under this section enter into any building or any enclosed court or garden attached to a dwelling house (unless with the consent of the occupier thereof) without previously giving such occupier at least seven days' notice in writing of his intention to do so.

(2) The Government shall pay compensation for the damage (if any) caused by any acts carried out under the provisions of sub-section (1) and the Government shall at the time of entry the land pay or tender payment of such amount (if any) as it thinks sufficient to cover the damage likely to be caused as aforesaid.[6]

---

5 1924 Act No. 40, 1983 Ac No. 26, 1985 Act, No. 12.
6 1961 Act, No. 10, 1973 Act No 43.

Declaration of intended acquisition

5. (1) Where the President of the Republic has determined to make use of the powers conferred by this Act for the acquisition of land for a public purpose a declaration signed by him shall be made to that effect.[7]

(2) Such declaration shall be published in the Gazette and shall contain

(a) a description of the land and its approximate area, and a statement of the place where the plan of the land may be seen, and

(b) a statement that the President of the Republic has decided to acquire the land for a public purpose.[8]

Declaration to be conclusive evidence that land is required for public purpose

6. The declaration of intended acquisition mentioned in section 5 shall be conclusive evidence that the land specified in such declaration is required for a public purpose cancellation and modification of notice or declaration and assessment and payment of compensation in respect thereof.

6A. (1) Where following the publication of a notice or declaration under section 4, 5 or 31 it is found that the lands or any part thereof included in such declaration are not required for the purpose in respect of which the notice was published, the President of the Republic may by notice published in the Gazette cancel or modify such notice or declaration accordingly.

(2) Where following the publication of a notice or declaration under section 4,5 or 31 and the subsequent cancellation or modification thereof under the provisions of sub-section (1) any person being the owner of any land included in such notice or declaration claims that he has suffered damage in consequence thereof the Governor shall appoint a compensation officer to assess the same and the provisions of this Act relating to the assessment and payment of compensation shall, so far as may be, apply to the assessment and payment of such compensation.

Procedure where land is not registered

9. (1) Where the land is not registered land, it shall be settled and registered in accordance with the provisions of the Land Settlement and Registration Act, Land Settlement 1925 before the acquisition is carried out.

---

7 1985 Act No. 12.

8 1955, 1973.

(2) The notice required by section 4 of the land settlement and Registration Act. 1925 may be published at the same time or after the publication of the declaration made under section 5.

(3) The expropriation officer may be appointed as settlement officer.

Expropriation officer to publish notices

10. (1) After his appointment, the expropriation officer shall cause notices to be published at the office of the competent locality within which the land to be acquired lies and at the land Registry offices (if any) in which the land is registered and at convenient places in the neighbourhood of the land and shall cause such notices to be served upon the occupiers and persons interested and upon the popular administrators sheiks) within whose administrative jurisdiction the land lies;[9]

(2) Such notices shall contain the substance of the declaration made under the Provisions of section 5, and shall call upon all persons claiming compensation under the provisions of this Act to appear personally or by agent or by representative before the expropriation officer at a time and place mentioned in the notice (such time not being earlier than fourteen days after publication of the notice) and to state the particulars of their claims for compensation.

Representatives to be appointed in the case of land subject to village or tribal rights

11. (1) Where the land is registered or has been adjudged to Government subject to village, or tribal rights and no trustees for such rights have been registered or appointed, there shall be appointed from among the persons entitled to share in such rights one, or five representatives who shall represent for the purpose of all proceedings under this Act all the persons entitled to share in such rights.

(2) The persons entitled to share in such rights shall be called upon the nomination of the representatives, and if they agree upon the nomination of any person the expropriation officer shall appoint such person a representative for the purpose of this section.

(3) In default of agreement the representative or representatives shall be appointed by the Governor and there shall be no appeal against the appointment made by the Governor under this section

(4) An agreement made under the provisions of section 14 and signed by all such representatives Shall be binding upon all those entitled to share in such rights.

---

9 1974 Act No. 40.

(5) A receipt signed by the majority of such representatives for any compensation paid by the Government under this Act shall be a good discharge of the Government's liability to pay such compensation.

(6) The persons entitled to share in such rights shall in such rights shall have no right to appear before the expropriation officer or take part in proceedings under this Act but the expropriation officer shall hold a meeting, at which all such persons shall be entitled to attend before the appointment of the representatives and before the conclusion of an agreement the provisions of under section 14 and before a reference is made to a board of arbitrators under section 15.

Assessment and Payment of Compensation
Who may take part in proceedings under this Act[10]

13. (1) Save as hereinafter provided in this section, no person other than a person interested shall have the right to appear before the expropriation officer or to take part in any proceedings under the provisions of this Act.

Agreement as to compensation

14. The expropriation officer shall attempt to come to an agreement as to the amount of compensation with those persons interested who appear in person or by agent or who are represented as provided in sections 11 and 12.

Constitution of board of arbitration

16. (1) The board of arbitration shall consist of the expropriation officer as president and tow members.

(2) One member shall be appointed by the Governor; the other member shall be appointed by the persons interested, the compensation due to whom is to be assessed.

(3) Where such persons interested are unable to agree upon the appointment the expropriation officer shall appoint the second member.

Procedure before the board

17. (3) In proceedings before the board the procedure laid down in the Civil Procedure Act, 1983 with regard to the examination of claimants and witnesses and the recording of statements shall be followed so far as it can be made applicable.[11]

---

10 1974 Act No 40.

11 1974 Act No 40.

Duties of the board

18. The board after hearing the statements of any persons interested who appear before it and after making such inquiry as is necessary shall assess the amount of compensation to be paid in respect of the interests of every person interested.

Rules for the assessment of compensation

19. In assessing compensation the board of arbitration shall give due regard to the following rules:

(1) There shall be taken into consideration the following matters:-

(2) (h) where the land is agricultural land registered or adjudged to Government subject to village, tribal or individual rights and under the customary methods in use with regard to it is cultivable at irregular intervals, any increase in its value due to the installation of pumping machinery to irrigate it; provided that such machinery has not been set up or development works carried out by or at the expense of the persons interested.

Payment of compensation

25. (1) Subject to the provisions of sub-section (2) payment of the compensation shall be made by the Government or award.[12]

(2) Where any person entitled to compensation cannot be found or does not come forward to receive compensation or cannot be found or does not come forward to receive it or refuses to receive it, the Government shall publish in the Gazette notice of its readiness to pay all compensation due in respect of the acquisition which has been made.[13]

Temporary Occupation of Land

Power to Occupy Land Temporarily

26. (1) Where it appears to the Governor that the temporary occupation and use of any land is needed for a public purpose or for the development of such land either solely or in conjunction with any neighbouring land or lands in such a way as to promise material benefit to the public generally or to the persons residing or owning land in the neighbourhood, the Governor may be directed to the competent locality to procure the occupation of such land either by the Government or by such other person, persons or body of persons as the Governor may direct, for a period not exceeding thirty years.

12 1974 Act, No 40.

13 1974 Act, No 40.

(2) The Governor shall appoint an expropriation officer who shall settle the amount of rent to be paid for such use and occupation by agreement or in the manner hereinbefore the provisions of this Act relating to the acquisition of land and the assessment and payment of compensation thereof shall, so far may be, apply to the obtaining of the land for temporary occupation and the assessment and payment of rent therefor.

(3) At any time during the period of such occupation the Governor shall have power by notice in writing to terminate the period of occupation on any date not less than one year after the service of such notice upon the owner of the land. Upon the date of such termination the rent due to that date shall become payable as well as the compensation, if any which may be due under the provisions of section 27.

Power to take Immediate Possession

28. (1) Where the Governor has decided that any waste or agricultural lands are needed for a public purpose either permanently or temporarily he may, in cases of urgency, direct the Competent locality to take possession of such lands at any time after the expiration of seven days from the publication of the declaration mentioned in section 5 notwithstanding that the amount of compensation or rent has not been settled by agreement or award.

(2) Where such declaration has stated that the Government has determined to acquire such lands, such lands shall vest absolutely in the Government free of encumbrances upon the Government taking possession of them under subsection (1).

(3) The Governor may on taking possession offer to pay compensation for the growing crops, if any on the land, and where such offer is not made, or is made and not accepted, the value of such crops shall be allowed for in awarding compensation for the land.

Acquisition of Land for Use by Private Persons

31. Where the President of the Republic is satisfied that any person, who is desirous of obtaining the use of land, propose to make use of such land for a public purpose or to develop such land in such a way as to promise material benefit to the public generally or to the persons residing or owning land in the neighbourhood, the President of the Republic may acquire such land in like manner as if the land was being acquired for a public purpose and as a condition of such acquisition may impose such terms as to the use of such land and otherwise on such person as he thinks proper or may direct that such land be registered to such person in full ownership.

4 The Unregistered Land Act, 1970

Title

1. This Act may be cited as the Unregistered Land Act 1970,

All Unregistered Land to be Government Land

4 (1) Notwithstanding anything contained in the Land settlement and Registration Act, 1925 or any other law in force, all land of any kind, whether waste, forest, occupied or unoccupied, which is not registered before the commencement of this Act, on such commencement, be the property of the Government and shall be deemed to have been registered as such, as if the provisions of the Land settlement and Registration Act, 1925, have been duly complied with.

5 The Civil Procedure Act, 1983

Jurisdiction of Towns and Suburbs Benches

20. (1) Towns and Suburbs Benches shall have jurisdiction to consider suits of a simple nature, and the jurisdiction of which as to value shall be specified by the warrant of establishment of every one thereof.

(2) Towns and Suburbs Benches shall not consider the suits which:–

(a) thereto any government department or unit, institution or other association, having corporate personality is a party;

(b) relate to ownership of any registered land, or ownership of estates;

(3) Where there is submitted to the Town and Suburbs Benches, during considering the jurisdiction, the same shall refer that matter to the competent Court, and the court, to which such matter is referred shall determine the same, as if it arises in a suit instituted before it.[14]

Procedure of instituting suits before Towns and Suburbs Benches

21. (1) A suit shall initially be instituted before the competent Towns and Suburbs Benches; and where a complaint is presented to the District Court Judge of any Grade, he may transfer it to such courts.

14 Act No. 36, 1986.

(2) Where it transpires to Towns and Suburbs Benches that they have no jurisdiction, they shall transfer the suit to the competent District Court Judge.[15]

Decree for amendment of the land register

107. Where the judgement ordains amendment of the register of an estate property registered, under the Land Settlement and Registration Act, 1925, or any other law, the decree shall contain specific direction to the Registrar of Lands to carry out such amendment.

6 The Civil Transactions Act, 1984

Title

1. (1) This Act may be cited as the, "Civil Transactions Act, 1984".*

Repeal and exceptions

2. As of the date of commencement of this Act, the following laws shall be repealed; provided that all the regulations, proceedings and orders, made under any of them shall remain in force, until revoked, or amended, under the provisions of this Act:-

(a) the Sudanese Disposition of Land (Restriction) Act. 1918;
(b) the Disposal of Unoccupied Towns and Villages Lands Act, 1922;
(c) the Recovery of Lost and Stolen Property Act, 1924;
(d) the Pre-emption Act, 1928;
(e) the Prescription and Limitation Act, 1928;
(f) the Unregistered Lands Act, 1970;
(g) the Rent (Restriction) Act, 1982;
(h) the Sales Act, 1974;
(i) the Agency Act, 1974;
(j) the Contract Act, 1974;
(k) the Land Settlement and Registration Act, 1925, Part IV.

15 *Ibid.*

* Made as Provisional Order No.(6) 1984; became Act No.8, 1984.

Interpretation

3. In applying the provisions of this Act, interpreting the words and phrases, set out therein; and also in cases not provided for by any law, the courts shall be guided by the principles of Sharia, and follow the rules provided for in the Judicature (Origins of Judgments) Act, 1983.

Types of real estate ownership

559. (1) Land is to Allah; and the State is successor thereof and responsible therefor and owner of the corpus thereof. All lands of any type, which are not registered prior to the coming into force of this Act, shall be deemed as if they have been registered in the name of the State, and the provisions of the Land Settlement and Registration Act, 1925 have been given due regard, with respect to the same.[16]

(2) Notwithstanding the provisions of sub-section (1), there shall be deemed corporeal property every real estate ownership, which have been registered in the name of its proprietor as freehold, at a date prior to 6/4/1970, and shall remain as such even though it has been transferred to others*.

(3) There shall be deemed usufruct ownership every real estate ownership, every ownership registered as freehold in the name of its owner, or owners, on, or after 6/4/1970.

(4) There shall be deemed usufruct ownership, every ownership registered as leasehold, at any date.

(5) There shall be deemed usufruct ownership, every ownership, which has been acquired, under the provisions of this Act.

(6) The old register shall be rectified in accordance with the provisions of the above sub-sections.

(2) Where the State is the owner of the corpus, it shall have an interest in and be a party to any dispute with respect to usufruct.

(3) No court shall be competent to consider any claim, suit or proceedings against the Government, or the registered owner of any investment land, allotted by law with respect to any subject relating to ownership.[17]

---

16 Act No. 131, 1990.

* This sub-section has not been amended since the promulgation of the Act, and there has been set out therein in the previous revised edition the phrase "before the promulgation of this Act" on place of the phrase "in a date prior to 6/4/1970", and the above corrigendum has been made the Special Legislative Supplement of the Republic of the Sudan Gazette No. 1340, dated 16th February, 1984.

17 Act No. 131, 1990; Act No. 7, 1993.

(4) There shall be void, of the coming into force of this Act, all the proceedings prior to this date pending before any court and relating to the right of ownership in accordance with the provisions of sub-section (6).[18]

Ownership of the usufruct of land and real estates and cultivation of waste land

560. (1) Whoever cultivates waste land far from construction, by cultivation, building or irrigation shall be entitled thereto to the exclusion of others, and whoever drills a well in waste land far from construction shall be entitled to its water, to the exclusion of others.

(2) Whoever cultivates waste land for the purposes of essential building shall be entitled to the usufruct to the exclusion of others; provided that in areas of planned and organized construction, no building shall be made in an area demarcated by a competent authority, and unorganized building is prohibited thereon, without the permission of such authorities; and demarcation shall be made conclusively and clearly, and due regard shall be given to the right of citizens to essential residence and the duty of the State to create organized construction, in accordance with a studied plan.

(3) Registered usufruct is like registered ownership, and shall not be acquisited, save for public interest and for just compensation according to the type and degree of the real investment of the usufruct.

(4) Lawful usufruct under the provisions of this Act, even though not registered, is protected by law, within the limits of real usufruct, and shall not be acquisited save for public interest, and for just compensation.

(5) Nominal cultivation, or cultivation intended to be trade, or brokerage in land shall not be considered, and mere possession shall not be considered, and cultivation customarily given regard shall be considered.

(6) For the sake of organizing utilizing land uses, the national, or state's authorities, as the case may be, shall take the such measures, as may secure the demarcations, survey, settlement and registration of land, and may divide the same into equal shares, or of variable areas, and organize use operations, in such way, as may be sufficient for the good investment of land, and arrange honorable livelihood of the inhabitants of every area, or owners of lawful uses of land.[19]

18 *Ibid.*

19 Act No. 40, 1974.

Grant of the Usufruct of Lands

Usufruct of agricultural land granted

561. In granting the usufruct to agricultural land regard shall be given to the following:

(a) preservation of the entities of the areas, villages, rural areas, natural and environmental resources, animals health and natural pastures;
(b) non-prejudice to small agricultural entities and encouraging settlement of families of limited capabilities for utilizing land for the benefit of the family, or the public interest;
(c) non-grant of extensive areas, save after taking sufficient guarantees for investment of all the granted area in the best and favorable means;
(d) due regard shall be given to water flow and easements for all the area affected by, or adjacent to the land granted;
(e) sufficient areas may be granted to more than one person, a family or families, societies or companies with intent to utilize the same by modern means in agriculture, or agricultural production;
(f) agriculture is entitled to uses, to the exclusion of others, where the return thereof is beneficial to the group of people and the need for its return is greater than any other need.

Agricultural roads

562. (1) Upon granting usufructs of agricultural lands there shall be agricultural roads leading to all the neighbouring lands, for use by owners of adjacent lands, villages and livestock instead of the highways and their width shall not at all be less than seven cubits.
(2) Every person having interest in using the roads provided for in subsection (1) shall have the right to claim opening them for public use.

Granting lands usufruct and residential estates

563. In granting the usufructs of lands and residential real estates, the following shall be given due regard:-
(a) the usufruct shall be allotted to the family whenever it is possible and practical;
(b) no usufruct of land for residence shall be granted, which is less than two hundred square metres in towns, and four hundred square metres in villages and rural areas;
(c) no permanent construction shall be allowed, without opening roads leading to the main streets, the width of which is not less than seven cubits;

and any buildings which do not comply with such restriction may be demolished without consideration;

(d) in every residential planning, due regard shall be given to leave areas and squares for public use and provide fresh air in every town, village or permanent residential camp; and also adequate areas for graveyards and public benefits and activities;

(e) due regard shall be given to leave spaces for planting trees in the facades of houses, roads and streets in every town, village or permanent camp, without prejudice to the right of owners of the used benefit, or users of the roads;

(f) residence is preferred in areas of clearness, fresh air and natural environment suitable for human life.

Organizing the procedure of granting usufructs and cheating in granting or obtaining them

566. (1) The National, or State's Authorities, as the case may be, shall organize the procedure of granting the usufructs of land and real estates.[20]

(2) Where a committee is entrusted with granting, the number of its members shall not be less than three and not more than five.

(3) Every person, who is granted by cheating the usufruct of land, or real estate, for himself or any other person, shall be deemed to have contravened the provisions, provided for in this Act with respect to personal, occupational, and professional prejudice.

(4) Every person, who obtains the usufruct of land, or real estate, by way of cheating shall have been unjustly enriched; and the provisions provided therefor in this Act shall apply thereto in this respect.

Contest permissible

567. Every person having interest may institute a suit to contest any contravention of sections 565, 564, 563, 562, 561 and 566, to the competent court, in accordance with the Constitutional Court Act, 2005.[21]

Protection of the rights of usufruct of land

568. The proprietor of the usufruct of agricultural, residential, commercial, industrial, and pastural land and wood-cutting usufruct shall enjoy all the immunities

20 Act No. 40, 1974.

21 Act No. 9, 1998; Act No. 40, 1974.

and protection against the acts of others, in such way, as may enable him to harvest, construct or use the same in the best form; and the court shall prevent the occurrence of any aggression, or trespass thereon, remove the effects thereof, and compensate for the aggression, or trespass.

Acquiring Ownership by Accession and Confrontation

Land displaced by act of God

603. (1) The owner of land displaced by an act of God may claim ownership thereof, where its identification is ascertained; and the owner of the land of more value shall indemnify the owner of the land of less value, its value, and shall acquire it, where the same cannot be separated, without considerable injury.

(2) No suit or claim of land displaced by an act of God shall be heard, after the expiry of one year, of the date of the incident.

Gusad right

605. (1) Usufruct of lands, from which the river recedes shall be owned by the owners of the exposed land, which lies opposite to their lands; and they shall be entitled to own it, up to a presumed line in the middle of the river course, unless there is custom, which rules otherwise.

(2) Where the river takes a new course, the owners of the lands adjacent to the old course shall be entitled to the usufruct of such course, each in the part, which lies opposite to his land, at the like value, up to a presumed line in the middle of the river; and the owners of the land submerged by the new course shall be indemnified each proportionate to such land, as he may have lost.

(3) The provisions provided for in sub-sections (1) and (2) shall apply in case the river reverts to its first, or any other course.

Acquiring Ownership by Possession (hiaza)

Definition of possession

631. (1) Possession is actual power over a material object exercised by the person in possession either by himself, or through others in such way, as in its external appearance and in the intent of the person in possession the exercise of ownership, or other corporeal right.

(2) Possession shall not be established by work carried out by a person, as being from permissible, or by work borne by others, as being of tolerance.

Possession through others

632. Possession shall be through others, whenever the intermediary exercises control over the object on account of the possessor.

Possession of persons lacking or of deficient capacity

633. A person lacking capacity, or of deficient capacity, may acquire possession through whoever may legally deputize therefor

Possession for the account of others

634. (1) Whoever may be in possession for the account of others shall not by himself own act change the character of his possession for himself.
(2) The character may be changed either by an act of others, or act of the person in possession, and considered adverse to the owner's title, and the possession in its new character shall not commence, expect from the date of such a change.

Proof of possession

636. (1) Where establishment of possession is proved, at a particular prior time, and it has been established forthwith, the same shall be presumption of its establishment between the two periods, unless the contrary is proved.
(2) Where several persons dispute on possession, whoever may exercise the material control shall be presumed to be in possession, until the contrary is proved.
(3) Possession shall remain keeping the character it has begun with, at the time of its being acquired, unless the contrary is proved.

Possession in good faith

637. (1) A person in possession shall be deemed to be in good faith, where he is ignorant that he trespasses on the right of others, unless such ignorance arises out of a grave mistake.
(2) Where the person in possession is a corporate person the intention of his representative shall count.
(3) Good faith shall be presumed unless the contrary is proved, or the law otherwise provides.

Possession in bad faith

638. (1) The person in possession shall become a possessor in bad faith, from the time he knows that his possession is trespass on the right of others.
(2) The person in possession shall be deemed a possessor in bad faith from the time of his service in the plaint of suit, to the effect that his possession is

trespass on the rights of others, and shall be deemed of bad faith where he extorts dispossession by coercion from others.

7 The Physical Planning and Disposition of Land Act, 1994

(16.04.1994)

Title

1. This Act may be titled as "the Physical Planning and Disposition of Land Act, 1994".

Repeal and savings

2. (1) There shall be repealed:
   (a) the Physical Planning Act, 1406 A. H,
   (b) the Disposition of Land, 1406 A. H,
   (c) the Town Re-planning Act, 1950.

Interpretation

3. In this Act, unless otherwise understood from the context:[22]

"Government land" means every land registered in the name of the Government of the Sudan, or any other land not registered in the name of any person, in any of the states of the Sudan

The Council

Establishment, supervision and seat of the Council

4. (1) There shall be established a national council to be named as "the Physical Planning and Disposition of Land National Council ", and it shall have corporate personality.[23]
   (2) The Council shall be subject to the supervision of the Prime Minister.

Constitution of the Council

5. The Council shall be constituted by a decree of the Council of Ministers as follows:[24]

22 Act No. (40), 1974.
23 Act No. (40), 1974.
24 Act No. (40), 1974.

Functions and powers of the Minister

9. (1) For the purpose of this Chapter, the Minister shall have the following functions and powers; namely to:

(c) lay down, upon approval of the state Council of Ministers, the housing plans projects of the state, in accordance with the national physical plans, in integration with the National Social and Economic Plan;

(e) demarcate the boundaries of any town or village and modify such boundaries from time to time, upon recommendation of the Committee;

(f) recommend change of the use of public spaces and squares to any purpose, whenever necessary to do so;

Acquisition of land for public interest

13 Ownership of land may be acquisitioned for public interest under the Land Acquisition Act, 1930, upon exercising by the Minister of his powers under the provisions of section 9 (c), (e) and (f).

Power of the Government in respect of unconstructed land

14. (1) In this section, "unconstructed land" means any land not materially constructed in such manner and for such purposes, as for which its class has been specified, regardless of whether inability to carry out such material construction is not due to the negligence or neglect of the owner, or the owner being prevented from carrying out such construction for causes beyond his control.

(2) Where any land the class of which has been specified, whether such specification is before or after coming into force of this Act, remains under the possession of owners as unconstructed land, the Committee may require the acquisition of such land in accordance with the provisions of the Land Acquisition Act, 1930 as if the acquisition is required for a public interest; provided that the owner shall be given one-year notice before the commencement of the acquisition procedure where the same has not been constructed or to pay the amount of the increment in its value to the Government.

(3) Notwithstanding the provisions of section 19 of the Land Acquisition Act, 1930, the compensation due for payment in case of acquisition shall be as follows:

(a) there shall be no compensation in respect of the areas intended to be used for the purposes of roads, including road-sides thereof, and public squares and utilities needed in the area in pursuance of the planning condition endorsed by the competent planning authority; or

(b) compensation in respect of all the other remaining areas shall be at the rate of 25% of the area or the market value of the land at the date of acquisition.

Pre-disposal procedures

45. No disposition in any Government land shall be carried save after being subjected to the following procedures:

(a) that it shall be free from any encumbrances, whether registered or unregistered, in the case of lands that have not yet been registered, or any possession establishing any right *in rem* or usufruct right; and

(b) that:

(i) its planning has been approved by the planning authorities,

(ii) it has been surveyed and demarcated in situs;

Disposition in Government Agricultural Lands Committee

54. (1) There shall be established in every state a committee for the agricultural schemes to be known as the " Disposition in Government Agricultural Lands Committee" the number of its members shall not be less than five and not exceed seven members, to be constituted and the functions and powers thereof shall be specified by the Minister of Agriculture, Natural Resources and Animal Wealth of the state; provided that the members shall be selected from amongst the directors of the departments having competence.

Change of class of the agricultural land

58. (1) The Council of Ministers of the state shall be competent to change the class of any agricultural land to residential land, and in this case the enhancement difference shall be assessed in accordance with the provisions of section 16.

(2) Where the land concerned is leased Government land, the change of the class thereof may be postponed until the end of the lease period, unless the change is within the framework of a general project by reason of which the lease shall be terminated pursuant to a legal notice; provided that the lessee shall be compensated in accordance with the Land Acquisition Act, 1930.

Aliens not to acquire land

59. Without prejudice to the provisions of section 41 (c) or the provisions of any other law, no alien person shall acquire any plot of land in the Sudan by any of the ways of ownership, unless he obtains the consent of the Council of Ministers.

8 The Investment (Encouragement) Act, 1999

Title

1. This Act may be cited as the, "Investment (Encouragement) Act, 1999".

Repeal and saving

2. The Investment (Encouragement) Act, 1996 shall be repealed; provided that the regulations and orders made, and measures taken thereunder, shall remain in force, as if they have been made, under the provisions of this Act, until revoked, or amended.

Provisions of the Act to prevail

3. The provisions of this Act shall, in case of inconsistency with the provisions of any other law, prevail to the extent of removing the inconsistency between them.

Objects of encouragement of investment

6. This Act targets encouragement of investment into such projects, as may achieve the objects of the development policy, and the investment initiatives, on the part of the Sudanese and non-Sudanese private sector, the co-operative, mixed and public sector. Without prejudice to the generality of the foregoing, it aims at encouragement of investment into the projects of any of the fields set out in section 7 and the rehabilitation projects.

Fields of investment

7. This Act encourages investment, into the fields of agricultural, animal and industrial activities, energy and mining, transport, communication, tourism and environment, storage, housing, contracting, infrastructure, economic, administrative and consultative services, information technology, education, health, water and culture and information services and any such other field, as the Council of Ministers may specify.

Privileges and Guarantees

Strategic projects

9. (1) Investment, in the following fields, shall be deemed strategic investment, namely:-
   - (a) relating to infrastructure, roads, ports, electricity, dams, communications, energy, transport, contracting business, education, health and tourism and information technology services and water projects;

(b) relating to extraction of subterranean and deep seas wealth;
(c) agricultural, animal and industrial production;
(d) crossing more than one state;
(e) any such other fields, as the Council of Ministers may prescribe.

Privileges

Exceptional provisions

10. (1) Strategic and non-strategic projects exercising their activities or production shall continue to enjoy tax exemption granted therefor, until the end of the specified period of such an exemption.

Exemption from custom fees

11. (1) Subject to provisions of section 19, each strategic and non-strategic projects specified in the regulations, after registration thereof in accordance with laws organizing the same, shall enjoy customs privileges prescribed by the Council of Ministers.
(2) Notwithstanding provisions of sub-section (1), custom privileges for cars, salons, boxes cars and station cars shall be granted in accordance with what specified by regulations.
(3) The Council of Ministers, upon a recommendation of the Minister may amend customs privilege as he may think appropriate.

Project granted the privileges of allocation of land and depreciation account

12. The Minister may grant such strategic and non-strategic projects, as may be specified in the regulations:-

(a) the land necessary for the strategic project free of charge, and at the encouragement price for the non-strategic project, in co-ordination with the bodies concerned, from such lands, as may have been planned by the competent bodies;

State's projects granted privileges

13. The state's minister may grant such state's project, as may be specified in the regulations, the following privileges:-

(a) total, or partial exemption, from such taxes and fees, as may be levied by a state's, or local law, for a period not exceeding five years; provided that he may, upon the approval of the State's Council of Ministers, extend such exemption for another similar period;

(b) any such other state's taxes, or fees, as may subsequently be levied on the project;

(c) allocation of the land necessary for the state's project, at the encouragement price, in co-ordination with the bodies concerned, from the lands allocated by the competent bodies.

No taxes or fees levied on national projects

15. No state, or locality shall levy any state's, or local taxes, fees or returns, on any investment project federally licensed, during the period of the tax exemption, provided for in sections 10 and 11, save in consideration of such services, as may be of public nature, performed by the state, or the locality.

Investment guarantees

17. (1) An Investor shall enjoy the following guarantees:-

(a) the non-nationalization, or non-confiscation of his project, non-acquisition of all, or part of the estates of the project thereof, or his investments, for public interest, save by law and in consideration of just compensation;

(b) the non-attachment, non-confiscation, non-custody or non-sequestration of the property of his project;

Privileges and guarantees of the project protected

18. Notwithstanding the provisions of any other law, no administrative body shall refrain from implementing the privileges and guarantees, granted under the provisions of this Act.

Grant of license and privileges requested

21. An application, for the grant of license, for any project, or of any of the privileges provided for in this Act, shall be presented, on the prescribed form as follows:-

(a) strategic and non-strategic national projects, to the Ministry;

(b) strategic and non-strategic state's projects, to the state's minister.

Land allocated for the project delivered

23. The federal, or state's competent authority, shall deliver the land allocated for the project, within a maximum period of one month, of the date of granting the license.

9 The Investment (Encouragement) Act, 2013

Pursuant to the Interim Constitution of the Republic of the Sudan 2005, the National Assembly has promulgated and the President of the Republic has executed this Act the provisions of which are as follows:

Title of the Act and the Commencement date

1- This Act shall be called a "The Investment Encouragement Act 2013" and shall come into force from the date of its execution.

Repeal and Exception

2 (1) Investment Encouragement Act 1999 shall be repealed.

Aims of the Act

6- This Act aims to encourage investment in projects that achieve the national strategy, development plans and investment initiatives of Sudanese and non-Sudanese private sector, cooperative, mixed and public sector, rehabilitation and expansion in investment projects.

Strategic National Investment Projects and Exemptions and Concessions Exemption and Concessions

20- (1) The Council of Ministers may, upon recommendation of the Minister, grant exemption of business profit tax to strategic investment project.

Exemption of Customs Duty

21- (1) The Authority may grant the project exemption of:

a. Customs duty on capital expenditures which are not enrolled in custom tariff, in coordination with the concerned ministry, provided that exemption for state investment project shall be made upon recommendation of the state minister to the Chairman of the Authority.

Survey and Demarcation of Lands allotted for National Projects

22 (1) Notwithstanding the provisions of any other law, the Authority may allot the land required for establishing national or strategic investment project at encouraging rate in coordination with the states' authorities.

(2) The Authority, in coordination with states' authorities, may renew the term of the leasehold of the land where the project established thereon.

(3) The concerned authorities at states shall register lands for industrial and services projects; and shall carryout the detailed technical planning as well as preparation of the required maps and deposit them with the Authority for allotment.

(4) The concerned authorities at the states shall register agricultural lands and carryout technical survey and detailed planning and deposit the same with the Authority for allotment.

Handing over the Land Allotted for the Project

23- The land allotted for the project shall be handed over within maximum period of one month from the date of project registration, and shall be registered forthwith project completion.

Granting License

25- (1) The Authority upon receipt of license application for any project, shall within maximum period of one week, grant initial approval for the establishment of the project, if the project satisfied all prescribed conditions.

(2) The Authority shall grant the license within a period not exceeding one week of the date of receiving the business name.

Conditions for Continuity of Enjoying the License

27- (1) The investor, with the consent of the Authority and recommendation of the concerned ministry, within validity period of the license take any of the following actions:

c. Change of utilization object of the land allotted for the project, its sale, mortgage or wholly or partial lease.

d. Mortgage of the project, equipment, machines or conveyances against which concessions have been granted.

(2) The land allotted for the project should not be sold or mortgaged unless it has been invested wholly or partially in accordance with the regulations.

Guarantees and Facilities of the Investment

29- The project existing according to the provisions of this Act shall enjoy the following facilities:

a. The Assets and properties of the project shall not be subject to nationalization, seizure, confiscation or appropriation either wholly or partially, except for public interest against fair and immediate compensation.

b. The Funds of the project shall not be subject to seizure, confiscation, appropriation, freezing, attachment or receivership, except with judicial decree or order from the competent Prosecution.

Protection of the Project

32- Notwithstanding the provisions of any other law, the concerned authority shall implement exemptions, concessions and guarantees granted pursuant to the provisions of this Act

Final Provisions

Resolving of Investment Disputes

39- (1) With exceptions to the disputes governed by the terms of the agreements stipulated for in item (2), if any legal dispute ensues in respect of the investment, shall be initially presented to the competent court unless the parties agree to refer it to arbitration or reconciliation.

(2) The terms of the Unified Agreement for the Investment of Arabic Capital in Arab States 1980, Agreement for Settlements of Investment Disputes among Arab States 1974, Agreement for Settlement of Investment Disputes Among States and Nationals of other Countries 1965, General Agreement for Economical, Technical and Commercial Co-operation among Members Sates of Islamic Conference 1977 or any other agreement in this respect where Sudan is a party thereof, shall be applicable on any legal dispute arises directly from any of the said agreements.

Establishment of Specialized Court

40- The Chief Justices shall constitute specialized courts to consider suits related to investment.

Establishment of Specialized Prosecution Offices

41- The Minister of Justice shall constitute specialized Prosecution offices for breaches related to the investment.

10 Towns and Rural Courts Regulations, 2004

Pursuant to Article 10(e) of the Judiciary Act, 1406H, I hereby issue the following regulation:

Preliminary Provisions

1. These regulations may be cited as "Town and Rural Courts Regulations, 2004", and shall enter into force the date it is signed, provided that all procedures and

orders, duly made by virtue of Establishment Orders shall remain in force until repealed or amended in accordance with the provisions herein.

Interpretation

2. In these Regulations, unless the context otherwise requires, the following words and phrases shall have the meanings set opposed to each of them:

(a) Town Court: means a court established in any town in accordance with these Regulations or by virtue of an Establishment Order.
(b) Central Rural Court: means any court established in any rural area our countryside with primary and appeal competences in accordance with the provisions herein or the Establishment Order.
(c) Rural Court: means the court established in any rural or nomadic area in accordance with these Regulations or the Establishment Order.
(d) Establishment Order: means the order issued by the Chief Justice on the establishment of town, central rural or rural court.
(e) Judge of the General Court: means the judge of the general court assuming supervision over a geographical area of jurisdiction.
(f) District Judge: means the first instance district judge assuming supervision over a geographical area of jurisdiction.
(g) Wali: means the state's governor.

Establishment and Dissolution of Courts

3. The Chief Justice may establish, pursuant to an establishment order, any town, central rural or rural court to operate in any region of the Sudan wherein they deem appropriate to establish such court. Chief Justice may, at their discretion, amend or repeal establishment order of any court.

Establishment Order Contents:

4. The Establishment Order may contain the following details:

(a) Name and type of the court.
(b) The geographical area of jurisdiction and in case of courts established in nomadic area, persons whom the court has a jurisdiction to decide on their disputes shall be specified.
(c) Name of the President, deputy and members of the courts.
(d) Number of the courts' sessions.
(e) The court's competences.

Eligibility of Candidate

5. Any member, to be eligible for the membership of towns, central rural or rural court, shall be:

(a) be in good health.
(b) be over thirty years of age.
(c) have a record of good conduct and behavior.
(d) be respectable, of dignity and influence in the area.
(e) be resident in the geographical area of the court's jurisdiction and is leading the same life style as the residents of the area.
(f) In case of candidates for town courts, candidate shall be able to read and write.

6. In addition to the conditions set forth in Article 5, the candidate to occupy the position of President or Deputy President of the central rural or rural court shall be acquainted with the customs and traditions of the residents of the area.

Selection Method

7. (1) Following consultation with the dignitaries of the area and personnel of government agencies in the area and other persons, the District Judge shall nominate persons qualified to fill the position of the President, Deputy President and members of the town, central rural and rural courts.

Appointment and Cancellation thereof:

8. The Chief Justice shall appoint Presidents, Deputy Presidents and members of the town, central rural and rural courts upon recommendation submitted thereto pursuant to Article 7 herein.

Powers and Jurisdictions

Area and Nature of Jurisdictions

9. The town, central rural and rural court shall exercise their jurisdictions within their geographical area as specified in their respective Establishment Orders and they shall not hear any suit or dispute if it is barred by these Regulations, the Establishment Order, any Act or a decree issued by the Chief Justice.

10. No town, central rural or rural court may hear criminal case with regard to killing, *qasas* below killing or *hidoud* (save drinking alcohol), suits involving children, suits pertaining to land ownership or any suit against the State, public authority or corporation.

11. (1) Town court, central rural and rural courts shall have jurisdictions to hear crime offenses provided for in the Criminal Act, save the crimes excluded by this Regulation or by virtue of the court's Establishment Order, a decree issued by the Chief Justice or an Act.

Competences of the town court regarding civil suits:

14. The town court is competent to hear simple cases of such values as may be specified by their establishment order.

Competences of the town court regarding criminal cases

15. The town court may order the following penalties and measures:

a. Imprisonment for a period not exceeding three years.
b. Fine not exceeding one hundred thousand dinnars.
c. Whippings not exceeding twenty-five lashes, forty lashes in case of drinking alcohol.
d. Releasing a convict whose remaining term does not exceed two years, for good conduct and behaviour under such terms and conditions as the court may deem convenient.
e. Measures that may be taken by the *sheikhs*.

Competence of the Central Rural Court regarding civil suits

16. 1. The Central Rural Court is preliminarily competent of hearing the following suits:

a. If the suit is related to damage of farms or pastures or damages to cattle without evaluating the damage.
b. If the subject of the suit is other than what is mentioned in Para (a) above, the value of the suit shall not exceed five hundred thousand dinnars.
c. Suits related to conflict on land boundaries.

2. The central rural court is competent to hear appeals against judgments and orders issued by the rural court regarding civil suits.

Competence of the Central Rural Court regarding criminal cases

17. (2) When preliminarily considering a criminal suit, the Central Rural Court may inflict the following penalties and measures:

a. Imprisonment for a period not exceeding seven years.
b. Fine not exceeding Four hundred thousand dinnars.
c. Whippings not exceeding twenty-five lashes, forty lashes in case of drinking alcohol.
d. Releasing a convict whose remaining term does not exceed two years, for good conduct and behaviour under such terms and conditions as the court may deem convenient.
e. The measures that may be taken by *shiekhs*.

(2) The central rural court is competent to hear appeals against judgments and orders issued by the rural court regarding criminal suits.

Competences of the Rural Court regarding civil suits

18. The Rural Court is competent to hear the following suits:

a. If the suit is related to damage on farms or pastures or damages to cattle without determining the amount of damage.
b. If the subject of the suit is other than what is mentioned in Para (a) above, the value of the suit shall not exceed two hundred thousand dinnars.
c. Suits related to conflict on land boundaries.

Competence of the Rural Court regarding criminal cases

19. The Rural Court may inflict the following penalties and measures:

a. Imprisonment for a period not exceeding five years.
b. Fine not exceeding Two hundred thousand dinnars.
c. Flogging not exceeding twenty-five lashes, forty lashes in case of drinking alcohol.
d. Releasing a convict whose remaining term does not exceed two years, for good conduct and behaviour under such terms and conditions as the court may deem convenient.
e. The measures that may be taken by *sheikhs*.
f. Confiscation.
g. Condemnation.

The Applicable Law

22. (1) The Town Court shall apply the law and the principles of justice without prejudice to Islamic Sharia'a.

(2) The Central Rural Courts and the Rural Courts shall apply the common tradition within its area competence and the other laws stated in these regulations or the establishment order provided that this tradition shall not contradict with the law, principles of justice and Islamic Sharia'a.

26 *Power to Summons and Arrest*

1. The town court shall, as far as summons of accused persons, defendants, and witnesses provided for, have the competencies and powers in relation to notice and arrest stipulated in the Criminal Procedures Act, 1991 and the Civil Procedures Act, 1983.
2. The chair of the central rural court, his deputy, chair of the Rural Court, or his deputy shall exercise the same powers contained in (1) here above.

Issued under my hand this 17th day of May 2004.

Jalal el-Din Mohamed Osman
Chief Justice

11 The National Land Commission Act, 2009

(28.6.2009)

Title

1. This Act may be cited as the, "National Land Commission Act 2009".

Interpretation

2. In this Act, unless the context otherwise requires:-

"Land", means all lands of the Republic of the Sudan, on which the State exercises sovereignty, and the possession, exploitation and exercise of rights over which are a joint competence, to be exercised at the National level, the Government of Southern Sudan level and the state's level;

"Commission", means the National Land, Commission established under the provisions of section 4(1);

"Custom", means group of customs, traditions and stable local or general principles having connection with land and rights thereon;

Establishment, quarters and responsibility of the Commission

4. (1) There shall be established an independent commission, to be known as "National Land Commission", having corporate personality, a common seal and the right to litigate in its own name.

(3) The Commission shall be responsible to the Presidency.

Tasks of the Commission

7. (1) Without affecting jurisdiction of the courts the Commission shall have the following tasks, to:-

(a) arbitrate between disputant parties desirous of resorting for arbitration thereby with respect to lands disputes; and the arbitration parties shall be bound by the Commission award on bases of mutual consent, and upon registering the arbitration award before the court;

(b) consider allegations on land against the competent government body, or against otherwise of parties having interest in land, and it may in its discretion treat such allegations;

(c) apply the law in force in the area, in which the land lies, or any other law, as may be accepted by parties of the arbitration including principles of equity;

(d) admit such as may be referred thereto by the competent government organs, or as may be perused thereby during consideration of suits, and recommend with respect thereto to the competent governmental level, relating to land reform policies, and admit customary rights, or customary law of land;

(e) assess the appropriate compensation for land including monetary compensation;

(f) tender advice to the various levels of government with respect to co-ordination of its policies towards the national projects affecting land or rights thereon;

(g) conduct studies and register aspects of land use in the areas where investment of national resources is made;

(h) hold hearing sittings, and make the procedure regulations thereof;

(j) any other tasks, as may be entrusted thereto by the Presidency.

Provisions of this Act to prevail

16. The provisions of this Act in case of inconsistency with the provisions of any other law, shall prevail to the extent of removal of such inconsistency.

12 Interim National Constitution, 2005

Bill of Rights

Right to Own Property

43 (1) Every citizen shall have the right to acquire or own property as regulated by law.

(2) No private property may be expropriated save by law in the public interest and in consideration for prompt and fair compensation. No private property shall be confiscated save by an order of a court of law.

Land Regulation[25]

186 (1) The regulation of land tenure, usage and exercise of rights thereon shall be a concurrent competence, exercised at the appropriate level of government.

(2) Rights in land owned by the Government of the Sudan shall be exercised through the appropriate or designated level of Government.

(3) All levels of government shall institute a process to progressively develop and amend the relevant laws to incorporate customary laws, practices, local heritage and international trends and practices.

National Land Commission

187 (1) Without prejudice to the jurisdiction of the courts, there shall be established a National Land Commission that shall have the following functions:-

(a) arbitrate between willing contending parties on claims over land,

(b) entertain claims, at its discretion, in respect of land, be they against the relevant government or other parties interested in the land. The parties to the arbitration shall be bound by the decision of the Commission on the basis of mutual consent and upon registration of the award in a court of law,

(c) enforce the law applicable to the locality where the land is situated or such other law as the parties to the arbitration agree, including principles of equity,

(d) accept references on request from the relevant government or in the process of resolving claims, make recommendations to the appropriate level of government concerning land reform policies and recognition of customary rights or customary land law,

(e) assess appropriate land compensation including but not limited to monetary compensation, for applicants in the course of arbitration or in the course of a reference from a court,

(f) advise different levels of government on how to co-ordinate policies on national projects affecting land or land rights,

(g) study and record land use practices in areas where natural resource development occurs,

(h) conduct hearings and formulate its own rules of procedure,

25 See amendments of Article 186 Interim constitution, 2005, amendments, 2015, *infra*.

(2) The National Land Commission shall be independent and representative of all levels of government.
(3) The Chairperson of the National Land Commission shall be appointed by the President of the Republic with the consent of the First Vice President.
(4) The National Land Commission shall be accountable to the Presidency which shall approve the budget of the Commission.

The Interim National Constitution, 2005, Amendments, 2015

Land Regulation

Article 186
(1) Acquisition and exploitation of land and enjoyment of rights over it is concurrent jurisdiction to be exercised across the relevant level of government according to the provisions of the law.
(2) The President of the Republic may, from time to time, issue Presidential Decrees to define the lands to be exploited for investment purposes, how the investment returns shall be used, and determine the competent level of government to administer it.
(3) The National Legislature shall approve the National Investment Plan.

Schedules of the Interim Constitution of the Republic of the Sudan 2005

Schedule (C)
Powers of States

The exclusive executive and legislative powers of state of the Sudan shall be as follows:-

3. Local Government;
7. The State Judiciary and administration of justice at state level including maintenance and organization of state Courts, and subject to national norms and standards, civil and criminal procedure;
8. State Land and state Natural Resources;
13. The management, lease and utilization of lands belonging to thestate;
19. Enforcement of state laws
23. Laws in relation to agriculture within the state;
32. Town and rural planning;
34. Traditional and customary law;

13 Interim Constitution of the Blue Nile State, November 2005

Land organization

94- (1) the law shall organize the possession of the land in the state, and its occupation, and the exercise the rights there on.

(2) The state shall assume the exercise of the rights which own by the Sudan government according of the provisions of the article 186(2) from the national transitional constitution to the year 2005.

(3) The state shall start gradual procedures and measures, to promote the relevant laws to the lands to include the conventional practices, and the local folk, and the international orientations and practices.

Land Commission

95- (1) it shall be established under the law of state land commission, and include qualified expert persons in the state. And exercise all the powers of the national land commission on the level of the state.

(2) The state land commission shall review the use and the contracts of the land, and check the current standards, and recommend with necessary changes to the state authority including the confirmation of the rights of possessing land, or to compensate it.

14 Interim Constitution of North Darfur State, 24th November 2005

Land Organization

84 (1) The land tenure in the state, land usage and the exercise of rights on it shall be regulated by the law.

(2) The State shall exercise the government land rights in accordance with article 186 (2) provision in the Interim National Constitution.

(3) The State shall start gradual proceedings and measures for developing laws concerning land that include the traditional practices, local heritage and the international guidance.

15 Interim constitution of West Darfur State, 13 December 2005

Land Regulation

94-1 The law shall regulate tenure, usage and exercise of rights over land.

94-2 The State shall exercise rights owned by the Government pursuant to Article 186 (2) of the Interim National Constitution.

94-3 The State shall institute a process of measures to progressively develop land relevant laws to incorporate customary laws and practices, local heritage and international trends and practices.

Land Commission of West Darfur State

95-1 Without prejudice to the jurisdiction of the courts, there shall be established a Land Commission of the State of West Darfur that shall, *inter alia*, have the following functions:

(a) Arbitrate between willing and contending parties. The Parties to the arbitration shall be bound by the decision of the Commission upon registration in a court of law.
(b) Entertain, without prejudice to the jurisdiction of the courts, claims on the States' land, at its discretion, in respect of land be they against the relevant parties interested in the land.
(c) Enforce the law in view of the principles of equity and justice.
(e) The State's Land Commission shall be accountable to the *Wali*.

Index

Abdalla Kafi 14, 175–179, 182
Abu Si'id [place] 82
agriculture
  commercial 55, 57, 59, 137–138
  irrigated 29, 41, 81, 153–154
  mechanized 59, 136–138, 151n8, 153–154, 289
  rain-fed 56–58, 63, 70, 81, 264
Aḥāmda [group] 53–73, 194
al-Ḥilla al-Jadīda [place] 171–175, 217
al-Ṣalḥa [place] 76–84
amīr, See also: Native Administration 156–156, 180
ANDROMAQUE 1–3, 10
ʿāqila 194, 196
ʿarab 5, 56
Arab groups 4–9, 223n23
Arabic 7, 10n10, 28n5, 69n21, 134, 227
  and Arabicization 6–7
  as lingua franca 220
Arabization 4–5, 9
Arabness 5, 8, 209n11
ʿarrifiyyīn 65–67
awlād ʿamm 57, 60, 63

Basunda [place] 148–164
Beja [group] 9n9, 126, 153–154, 242, 256
Beni Amer [group] 148, 153–156, 160–167
Bill of Rights 56n5, 102–104, 142, 258, 307
Black Belt of Khartoum 207

camps
  for IDPS 14, 42, 98–99, 120, 176, 205
  nomad 6n8
car accident 14, 190–191
cattle herders 13, 148, 153
Christians 12, 164, 174, 207n6, 209–212
  Nuba 96–98, 110–115, 119
  Southerners 7, 114, 206, 209
churches 12, 100, 113–119, 174, 210, 224
civil war 6, 9, 11–12, 15, 95, 173, 177, 205
Civilizational Project 9, 14, 206–207
Civil Justice Ordinance 239–246, 274–275
Civil Transaction Act 27, 131–132, 134, 274
compensation
  and *diya* 14, 188n2, 192–193, 195–200, 254–256
  and resettlement 37, 42, 180
  for land 32, 37–38, 45–47, 77, 86, 111, 121, 138, 159, 278
Comprehensive Peace Agreement (CPA) 13, 15, 102, 111, 120, 126, 139, 141–142, 205, 219
conciliation 158, 165, 190, 195–197, 254, 256, 301
conflict negotiation 13
culturalism XIV
Customary Courts 13–15, 203, 236, 249, 253
  Southern Sudanese 203

Dam Implementation Unit (DIU) 37
Darfur 6, 25, 121, 127, 159, 173–174, 176, 194, 310–311
De Certeau, Michel 204, 207
dhimma 12, 96–98, 104, 106, 108, 114
displacement 25, 55n2, 204–205, 213n17, 214–216, 221
  and civil wars 12, 205–206, 212, 223, 226–228
  and dam projects 48, 138
dispute
  management 147
  resolution 14, 148n1, 158, 171
diya, See also: blood money 14, 181, 188–200, 254, 257
Dongola 9, 25, 27, 29n6n7, 38
Dupret, Baudoin 1
Durkheim, Émile XIV

English Common Law 130, 236, 237, 243, 248
English Law 126, 129, 134, 238, 244, 245
Ethiopians 154, 161–163, 165–167
ethnography 4, 54, 206

farmers 41, 56, 59, 130, 137–138, 158, 160n20
fiqh 70, 111n27, 196
forgiveness 14, 162, 165–166, 194, 196, 198
forum shopping 14, 148, 167, 185–186
Foucault, Michel 218
Fourth Nile Cataract 25, 36–37, 48

gabīla 10n10, 12, 53, 56, 60
game theorists 147
Gedaref State 147
Geertz, Clifford XIV

Gramsci, Antonio 203
Greater Khartoum 3, 94
 christian communities 95–96, 105, 114
 peripheral quarters of 174, 211–213
 urbanization of 12, 14, 53, 121
guadab 127

Hadandowa [group] 127
Haj Yusif [place] 12, 40, 94–95, 98, 101
ḥaqq al-aṣl 29–36, 129n9
ḥarām al-ḥilla 138
ḥiyāza 78, 80–81, 84, 85, 89–92, 131, 134
homicide 14, 158n17, 159, 181, 189–192, 194, 253–254, 256
human rights 12, 97, 138, 139
 international 15, 98, 103, 119, 142, 236–237, 254–255, 256, 258
 violation of 37, 111, 135

identity
 Afro-Arab 6
 Arab and Islamic 6
 ethnic 4–9, 81, 83, 95–96, 105, 113–122, 148, 153n10, 164, 176, 207, 209, 214, 217, 227–228
 national 6, 8
 tribal 9, 11
ijmāʿ 247, 248
ijtiḥād 248
Ingaz 95, 107, 157, 174–175, 203, 206
inheritance 8n8, 28, 30–32, 35, 40, 44–45, 59, 61, 64, 69, 109, 134, 182, 185, 199, 237, 240, 246n22, 255, 258
institutional bricolage 53, 54, 73, 194
Internal Displaced People (IDPs) 12, 85, 98–100, 110, 113–114, 118–121, 173–174, 177, 205, 208, 210–214, 216, 229, 221–223, 225–226
Islamic government 11–13, 15, 45, 63
Islamic law, *See also: sharīʿa* 2, 8–11, 17, 53, 64, 68, 71–73, 94–96, 107, 110, 125, 149n6, 194, 200, 236
Islamization 2, 4–7, 9, 95, 217, 246

Jamūʿiya [group] 82, 84–85, 174
jūdiya 84, 92, 148, 159, 164, 237
justice
 administration of 236, 244, 254, 256–257, 309
 and equity 140, 311
 criminal 254, 257
 formal 13, 167, 237, 249, 253, 255, 257–258
 informal 13, 57, 158, 236–237, 249, 253, 255, 257–258
 principles of 129–130, 237, 243–244, 250, 305
 traditional 236, 253

Kerma [place] 25, 28, 32–34, 263
Khartoum Penal Court 14, 189, 190, 273
Khartoum State 11, 53, 100, 102, 105, 114, 120–121, 176–178, 191, 194, 206n6

lajnat al-arḍ 60
lajna shaʿbiyya 12, 59–61, 70–71, 73, 78, 82, 89, 100, 158, 216
land
 alienation 12, 23
 commercialization of 76
 communal 125, 130, 156
 dispossession 54, 72
 grabbing 11, 13, 24, 53, 55–56, 73, 76, 125, 131, 133, 135
 legislation 12–13, 29, 37, 48, 125–126, 132, 142
 ownership 11, 27, 28, 40, 42–43, 76, 125–127, 130, 132–134, 252, 303
 property 24–27, 30–33, 36–37, 121, 189, 200, 265
 registration 26–30, 32, 39, 48, 84, 86, 88–89, 91, 94, 98, 100–102, 104, 116, 131, 134, 266, 269
 sale 31–32, 34, 43, 48
 survey 27, 33–34, 48
 tenure 76, 132, 139–141, 308, 310
 transaction 76, 79, 81, 87, 89, 91
 unregistered 29, 55, 76–77, 80, 85–86
land rights
 communal 40, 87, 125, 236
 customary 125
 for non Muslim 94
 tribal 53
laws
 customary 10, 12, 30, 61, 65, 67–68, 71–72, 125, 130, 132, 139–141, 216, 236–237, 239, 253, 308, 311
 investment 37, 125, 130, 135, 137, 142
 state 12, 64n13, 65, 309
 statutory 125–126, 128, 131, 236–237, 240, 243, 249, 256

lease 30, 41, 76, 79, 132, 136, 295, 300, 309
Lefebvre, Henry 208
legal
insecurity 54, 71, 73
pluralism XII, 2, 10, 13, 26, 34, 68, 73, 96–97, 108–110, 164, 171, 178, 185–186, 236
practices 1–2, 4, 6, 10–11, 26, 28, 48, 53, 57, 68, 71–73, 194
liberalization 53, 207

Manāṣīr [group] 25, 31, 33–34, 36–39, 44–46
Mayo [place] 15, 121, 203, 208, 218
Merowe Dam 11, 25, 37, 47–48
migration
forced 47, 205
labour 95
of Arab groups 4
rural-urban 91, 171, 173
minorities *See also: dhimma*
discrimination of 96, 98, 108, 118–119
Muslim XIV
religious and non-Muslim 71, 105–106, 110–11, 113–115
Mohammedan Law 240, 247n25, 275
mortgage 34, 132, 187, 193, 273, 300
Muslim
Arabs 6, 7n7
Southerners 209, 225

National Congress Party (NCP) 37, 70, 163, 177, 204, 206, 219
Native Administration 7–9, 14, 35, 55, 63, 67, 150, 153, 155–159, 161–163, 167, 172, 176, 204, 216–219, 223, 236, 253
Native Courts 8, 13, 30, 131, 172, 214–219, 222–230, 241–243, 246
Native System 176–177, 204n2, 217
naẓāra 127, 154–159, 165
nāẓir, See also: Native Administration 67, 127, 151–152, 155–157, 159, 194, 237
Nile Valley 23
non-Arab groups 6–7, 9
Nuba Mountains 7, 25, 95, 115, 117, 121, 127n2, 173–175, 204n2

ʿomda, See also: Native Administration 63, 67, 82, 127, 155, 157, 159, 162–165, 176–179, 183, 194, 237, 242

Omdurman [place] 76, 171, 192–193, 195, 205, 211n14, 217–218, 228n24

pastoralists 53, 127, 130, 137–138, 162–163, 174
political elites 7, 29, 164
Polanyi, Karl 72
Popular Committees, *See also: lajna shaʿbiyya* 59n7, 62n11, 70–71, 82, 89, 92, 216–218
property
concepts of 33
family 58
full 30, 64n12
government 29, 92
individual 116
land 24–27, 30–33, 36–37, 121, 189, 200, 265
private 29, 64n13n14, 68–69, 111, 208, 307
rights 30, 36–37, 64, 120, 216
state 23–24, 286
tribal 56

qiṣāṣ 166, 190, 194
Qur'an 9, 165–166, 178, 183–184, 196, 238, 246, 248

rakūba 121, 177–185, 219–220, 226
Rashaida [group] 42, 127, 255
resettlement 37, 39, 41–49, 138, 144
returnees 27, 214, 229

sāqiyya 28n4, 29, 32–35, 40–41
sharecropping 40, 42–43
sharīʿa 2, 8, 12, 31, 64, 68–71, 95, 97, 103, 109, 130, 148–149, 162, 165, 167, 172, 181–182, 184–185, 189, 196–197, 212, 219, 236, 238–239, 241–242, 245–250, 255–256, 258
sheikh, *See also*: Native Administration 28, 63, 65n15, 66n18, 67, 69–71, 82, 111, 127, 154–155, 157–158, 161–162, 164–165, 176, 178, 183, 194, 215–216, 222, 237, 252–253, 277, 304, 305
Shukriyya [group] 127, 153, 156, 194
South Sudan 115, 121, 174–175, 210, 220
separation of 2, 6, 15, 87n22, 94, 99, 114, 226, 230
Southerners 7, 114, 117, 120–121, 148, 176, 205–209, 212–213, 217n20, 219–230

South Kordofan 6, 95, 99, 214
squatter (areas or settlement) 14, 80n7, 171, 174, 205, 207–208, 211, 217, 226
Sufi Islam 69, 70
ṣulḥ 189, 195–197, 254
ṣulṭān, See also: Native Administration 156, 162, 175–176, 178–179, 215–217, 221–224, 227–229

Town and Rural Courts 130, 178, 249–252, 301
tribal
  land 53, 54, 126
  leadership 9, 62n11, 63, 194, 217
  paradigm 54, 57, 61, 63–64, 194
  rights 12, 278, 281

urbanization 47, 53, 61n10
ʿurf 12, 53–54, 61, 68, 71, 237

Von Benda Beckmannn, Franz 199
Von Benda Beckmannn, Keebet 148, 199

waḍʿ al-yad 40, 58
wage labourers 13, 14, 148, 154, 160–163, 165, 167

zār 215n19

www.ingramcontent.com/pod-product-compliance
Lightning Source LLC
Chambersburg PA
CBHW071423230926
51846CB00001B/115
* 9 7 8 9 0 0 4 3 5 9 1 1 6 *